English Skills with Readings

First Canadian Edition

English Skills with Readings

First Canadian Edition

John Langan
Atlantic Community College

Sharon Winstanley
Seneca College

McGraw-Hill Ryerson Limited
Toronto Montreal New York Auckland Bogotá Caracas
Lisbon London Madrid Mexico Milan New Delhi
San Juan Singapore Sydney Tokyo

McGraw-Hill Ryerson Limited

A Subsidiary of The McGraw·Hill Companies

ENGLISH SKILLS WITH READINGS
First Canadian Edition

Copyright © 1997 McGraw-Hill Ryerson Limited, a Subsidiary of The McGraw-Hill Companies. Copyright © 1995, 1991, 1988 by McGraw-Hill Inc. All rights reserved. No part of this publication may be reproduced or transmitted in any form or by any means, or stored in a data base or retrieval system, without the prior written permission of McGraw-Hill Ryerson Limited, or in the case of photocopying or other reprographic copying, a licence from CANCOPY (the Canadian Copyright Licensing Agency), 6 Adelaide Street East, Suite 900, Toronto, Ontario, M5C 1H6.

Any request for photocopying, recording, or taping of any part of this publication shall be directed in writing to CANCOPY.

ISBN: 0-07-552632-8

3 4 5 6 7 8 9 10   BG   6 5 4 3 2 1 0 9

Printed and bound in Canada

Care has been taken to trace ownership of copyright material contained in this text. The publisher will gladly take any information that will enable them to rectify any reference or credit in subsequent editions.

Editor-in-Chief: Dave Ward
Supervising Editor: Margaret Henderson
Production Editor: Kate Forster
Developmental Editor: Laurie Graham
Production Co-ordinator: Nicla Dattolico
Designer: Rafael Hernandez
Cover Designer: Dianna Little
Typesetter: Bookman Typesetting Co.
Typeface(s): Times Roman
Printer: Best Gagné

Canadian Cataloguing in Publication Data
Langan, John, 1942–
   English skills with readings

1st Canadian ed.
Includes bibliographical references and index.
ISBN 0-07-552632-8

1. English language - Rhetoric.   2. College readers.
I. Winstanley, Sharon.   II. Title.
PE1408.L28 1997   808'.0427   C96-932045-0

TO MY WIFE,
JUDITH NADELL
  John Langan

TO MY DAUGHTER,
CLAIRE
  Sharon Winstanley

CONTENTS

READINGS LISTED BY RHETORICAL MODE

Note: Some selections are listed more than once because they illustrate more than one rhetorical* mode of development.

EXAMPLES

PROCESS

COMPARISON–CONTRAST

* The word "rhetorical" refers to a particular structuring method or format chosen by a writer for its effectiveness in communicating the selection's message to an audience. Many of these selections, and most writers, make use of more than one rhetorical mode or format in any one piece of writing; for example, an essay may be *narrative* in basic style, but may also *contrast* two different ideas.

PERSUASION

TO THE INSTRUCTOR

English Skills with Readings, First Canadian Edition, will help students learn and apply the basic principles of effective composition. It will also help them master essential reading skills. This nuts-and-bolts book is based on a number of assumptions about the writing and reading process:

■ First of all, *English Skills with Readings* assumes that four principles in particular are keys to and goals for effective writing: unity, support, coherence, and sentence skills. These four principles are highlighted on the inside front cover and reinforced throughout the book. Part One focuses on the first three principles; Part Four treats sentence skills fully. The rest of the book shows how the four principles apply in different types of paragraph development (Part Two), in traditional five-paragraph essays (Part Three), and in both paragraphs and essays (Part Five).

■ The book reflects the belief that, in addition to the four principles, there are other important factors in writing effectively. After a brief introductory chapter, the second chapter of the book discusses prewriting, rewriting, and editing. Besides encouraging students to see writing as a process, the chapter also asks students to examine their attitude about writing, to write on what they know about or can learn about, to consider keeping a writing journal, and to include outlining as part of the writing process.

■ *English Skills with Readings* assumes that the best way to begin writing is with personal experience. After students have learned to support a point by providing material from their own experience, they are ready to develop an idea by drawing on their own reasoning abilities and on information in notes, articles, and books. Students are asked to write on both experiential and objective topics in Parts Two and Three. And the reading selections in Part Five generate a variety of first- and third-person assignments.

■ The book also assumes that beginning writers are more likely to learn composing skills through lively, engaging, and realistic models than through materials remote from the common experiences that are part of everyday life. For example, when a writer argues that formal dances should be banned, or catalogues ways to harass an instructor, or talks about a daily drive to college, students are more apt to remember and follow the writing principles that may be involved. After reading vigorous papers composed by other students and some of the stimulating selections by professionals in Part Five, students will understand better the power that good writing can have. They will then be more likely to aim for similar honesty, realism, and detail in their own work.

- Another premise of *English Skills with Readings* is that mastery of the paragraph should precede work on the several-paragraph essay. Thus Part One illustrates the basic principles of composition using paragraph models, and the assignments in Part Two aim at developing the ability to support ideas within a variety of paragraph forms. The essential principles of paragraph writing are then applied to the traditional five-paragraph essays in Part Three. Finally, in Part Five, each reading selection is followed by two paragraph assignments and one essay assignment.

- Another assumption is that, since no two people will use an English text in exactly the same way, the material should be organized in a highly accessible manner. Because each of the five parts of the book deals with a distinct area, instructors can turn quickly and easily to the skills they want to present. At the same time, ideas for sequencing material are provided by three boxes titled "Some Suggestions on What to Do Next"; these boxes appear in the opening chapters of the book. And a detailed syllabus is provided in the Instructor's Manual.

- An assumption central to this book is that reading and writing are closely connected skills—so that practising one helps the other, and neglecting one hurts the other. Part Five enables students to work on becoming better readers as well as better writers. An introductory section to Part Five offers a series of tips on effective reading, and ten questions after each of the selections provide practice in key reading comprehension skills. A set of discussion questions also follows each selection, serving to deepen students' understanding of the content and to make them aware of basic matters having to do with structure, style, and tone. Last, there are three writing assignments for each selection, along with guidelines to help students think about and get started with the assignments.

- Finally, this first Canadian edition includes certain cultural modifications to practice exercises, example sentences, and media references. New student essay and paragraph examples are Canadian in context and origin, and reflective of Canada's diverse geography and cultures.

   The spelling used throughout is a hybrid of *The Oxford Advanced Learner's Dictionary* and various Canadian style guides. Certain relatively British spellings such as "emphasised" and "programme" have been avoided, while many Canadian doubled *l*'s, as in "travelled," have been retained, so that the result reflects a decent model of Canadian spelling for the 1990s. A note concerning Canadian spelling variants appears at the end of the chapter on spelling (see page 391).

DIFFERENCES BETWEEN THIS BOOK AND *ENGLISH SKILLS*

- Parts One to Three are essentially the same as the three rhetoric sections of *English Skills*. There are three omissions: the research assignment (typically "Writing Assignment 4") has been omitted from the sequence of writing assignments that follow each type of paragraph development in Part Two; the "Additional Paragraph Assignments" have been removed from the end of Part Two; and an article titled "A Suicide at Twelve—Why, Steve?" has been taken out of Part Three.

- There is also an addition: an extra writing assignment appears at the end of each chapter in Part Three. Titled "Writing about a Reading Selection," this assignment asks students to read one of the professional essays in Part Five illustrating a certain rhetorical mode, often a selection which illustrates a certain rhetorical mode. They are then asked to write a paragraph using the mode of development in question.

- Part Four of *English Skills*, "Special Skills," has been omitted to help create space for the fifteen readings. Note, however, that some of the content of "Key Study Skills" can be found in the selection "Power Learning"; and much of the information that originally appeared in "Writing a Resume and Job Application Letter" now appears (in a somewhat different form) in the selection "Why Should We Hire You?"

- Part Five of *English Skills*, "Sentence Skills"—which becomes Part Four in *English Skills with Readings*—has been reduced somewhat, again to create space for the readings. Material omitted includes the diagnostic and achievement tests, "Sentence Sense," and five of the ten editing tests.

- As the title indicates, what is most different in this book is the inclusion of fifteen reading selections by professional writers, along with detailed reading and writing apparatus following each selection.

THE READINGS

- The fifteen selections have been chosen for their content as much as for rhetorical mode. They are organized thematically into three groups: "Goals and Values," "Education and Self-Improvement," and "Human Groups and Society." Some reflect contemporary Canadian and global concerns; for instance, "What to Do with a Severance," "Decoys and Denial," "Spiritual Storyteller," and "The True Meaning of Literacy." Some provide information students may find helpful; examples are "Power Learning," "How to Write a Test," and "Why Should We Hire You?" Still other selections discuss basic human experiences and dilemmas: "Adolescent Confusion," "Truth or Consequences," and "What Good Families Are Doing Right." Finally, some selections which provoke thought, yet are light and amusing, appear in this first Canadian edition: "Have You Seen My Missing Math Gene?" and "The Importance of Cooking Dinner." All the selections should capture the interest of a wide range of students. (A list on pages xii–xiv presents the readings by rhetorical mode.)

■ Each reading begins with a preview that supplies background information where needed and stimulates interest in the piece.

■ The ten reading comprehension questions that follow each selection give students practice in five key skills: summarizing (by choosing an alternative title), determining the main idea, recognizing key supporting details, making inferences, and understanding vocabulary in context. Reading educators agree that these are among the most crucial comprehension skills. A special chart at the back of the book enables students to track their progress as they practise these skills.

■ Discussion questions following the reading comprehension questions deal with matters of content as well as aspects of structure, style, and tone. Through the questions on structure in particular, students will see that professional authors practise some of the same basic composing techniques (such as the use of transitions and emphatic order to achieve coherence) that they have been asked to practise in their own writing.

When assigning a selection, instructors may find it helpful to ask students to read the preview as well as to answer the reading comprehension and discussion questions that follow the selection. Answers can then be gone over quickly in class. Through these activities, a writing instructor can contribute to the improvement of his or her students' reading skills.

NOTES ON THIS EDITION

The audience for *English Skills with Readings* has expanded each year. Instructors continue to say that the four bases really do help students learn to write effectively. And they continue to comment that students find the model passages, activities, assignments, and readings in the book especially interesting and worthwhile.

At the same time, more and more instructors have said that the book would benefit from an earlier emphasis on the writing process. In this edition, therefore, the treatment of prewriting and other important factors in writing has been expanded; those materials now comprise the second chapter of the book. Instructors who are more comfortable with the previous format of the text can easily skip the second chapter and move directly to the next chapter and its treatment of the first two steps in effective writing. The material skipped can then be worked into a course a bit at a time.

Here is an overview of what is in this new edition:

- The first chapter, "Getting Started," now offers students a more detailed introduction to the basic principles of effective writing. After reading and discussing an initial model paragraph, students immediately write one of their own, thus engaging in the process and pattern which are reiterated throughout the text. The benchmark model supplies the student and the instructor with a standard of comparison for measuring writing progress during the semester.

- The second chapter, "Important Factors in Writing," includes material from Part Two of earlier editions of the book. Some material has been revised. New sections appear on writing's initial stages as process: originating in the private and subjective, as in journal-keeping, or in various less formal prewriting activities such as diagramming and idea-mapping.

- "Introduction to Paragraph Development"—the chapter that begins Part Two—now includes rhetorical considerations basic to all effective business, technical, or personal writing: those of purpose and audience. Also included are in-class peer review techniques and a personal checklist to encourage students in areas in which they need improvement.

- Part Four, "Sentence Skills," has been enlarged to include two new chapters: "Pronoun Types" and "Adjectives and Adverbs." The first chapter of Part Four, "Subjects, Verbs, and Objects," has been expanded to include additional explanations of the names and uses of nouns, pronouns, objects, and predicate nominatives. New exercises have been added to reinforce students' grasp of these aspects of basic grammar.

- Many small changes appear throughout. For example, there is a new introduction to "Transitions" in Part One; and the chapter on run-ons in Part Four now covers subordination in some detail. Two rhetorical modes, "Explaining a Process" and "Examining Cause and Effect," and three sentence-skills chapters in Part Four ("Misplaced Modifiers," "Dangling Modifiers," and "Faulty Parallelism") have been resequenced.

- Generic instructions for the use of the word processor to facilitate most stages of the writing and editing processes have been added to this edition, for students who make increasing use of their computers and for instructors who teach writing classes in processor labs.

■ Finally, twelve new Canadian selections covering a wide range of subject matter and tone appear in Part Five, including "Shots on Goal" by Brian Preston, "Have You Seen My Missing Math Gene?" by Tony Wong, and "Memoirs of a Book-Molesting Childhood" by Adele Wiseman. The new selections deal with themes that should engage the interest of Canadian community college students from a variety of backgrounds and make for rewarding writing assignments.

SUPPLEMENTS

A newly designed Instructor's Manual includes, whenever possible, separate answer sheets for each skill. Instructors can easily copy the appropriate sheets and pass them out to students for self-teaching. The manual and a computer disk of mastery tests (in both IBM and Macintosh formats) are both available from your local McGraw-Hill Ryerson representative or by writing to the College English Editor, 300 Water Street, Whitby, Ontario, L1N 9B6.

ACKNOWLEDGMENTS

Reviewers who have provided assistance, offered helpful suggestions, and broadened my view of the Canadian postsecondary student include Esther Chassé, Yukon College; Jim Howard, Selkirk College; Judy Mendelsohn, Dawson College; and Cecilia Vasiloff, Humber College. I wish to offer special thanks to Fred Joblin, Georgian College, whose careful and common-sense attention to the text has resulted in some distinct improvements and additions which should prove helpful to students and to their instructors.

Again, and as always, my gratitude to Dave Ward at McGraw-Hill Ryerson for having initiated and pursued this project; to Laurie Graham, Developmental Editor in the College Division at McGraw-Hill Ryerson, for having nipped at my heels so graciously when necessary; and to Kate Forster for her consistency and care in handling the final editing. McGraw-Hill Ryerson is to be commended for their approach to production, scheduling, and editing of Canadian texts; they are professional, intelligent, and humane.

SHARON WINSTANLEY

English Skills with Readings

First Canadian Edition

PART ONE

BASIC PRINCIPLES OF EFFECTIVE WRITING

PREVIEW

Part One begins by introducing you to this book and to paragraph form. As you work through the brief activities in the first chapter, "Getting Started," you will gain a quick understanding of the book's purpose, the way it is organized, and how it will help you develop your writing skills. After presenting a series of important general factors that will help you create good papers, Part One then describes four basic steps that can make you an effective writer. The four steps are:

1 Make a point.

2 Support the point with specific evidence.

3 Organize and connect the specific evidence.

4 Write clear, error-free sentences.

Explanations, examples, and activities are provided to help you master the first three steps. (You will be referred to Part Four of the book for a detailed treatment of the fourth step.) After seeing how these steps can help you write a competent paper, you will learn how they lead to four standards, "bases," or goals of effective writing: unity, support, coherence, and sentence skills. You will then practise evaluating a number of papers in terms of these four bases.

GETTING
STARTED

This chapter will

- **Introduce you to the American and Canadian authors of this book**
- **Introduce you to the basic principles of effective writing**
- **Ask you to write a simple paragraph**
- **Explain how the book is organized**
- **Suggest a sequence for using the book**

INTRODUCTION TO THE AUTHORS

John Langan: *English Skills* grows out of experiences I had when learning how to write. My early memories of writing in school are not pleasant. In the middle grades I remember getting back paper after paper on which the only comment was "Handwriting very poor." In high school, the night before a book report was due, I recall working anxiously at a card table in my bedroom. I was nervous and sweaty because I felt so out of my element, like a person who knows only how to open a can of soup being asked to cook a five-course meal. The act of writing was hard enough, and my feeling that I wasn't any good at it made me hate the process all the more.

Luckily, in college I had an instructor who changed my negative attitude about writing. During my first semester in composition, I realized that my instructor repeatedly asked two questions of any paper I wrote: "What is your point?" and "What is your support for that point?" I learned that sound writing consists basically of making a point and then providing evidence to support or develop that point. As I understood, practised, and mastered these and other principles, I began to write effective papers. By the end of the semester, much of my uneasiness and bad feelings about writing had disappeared. I knew that competent writing is a skill that I or anyone can learn with practice. It is a nuts-and-bolts process consisting of a number of principles and skills that can be studied and mastered. Further, I learned that while there is no alternative to the work required for competent writing, there is satisfaction to be gained through such work. I no longer feared or hated writing, for I knew I could work at it and be good at it.

Sharon Winstanley: Typical of my generation of Canadians, I enjoyed several career changes. The last of these shifts taught me John Langan's invaluable lesson that writing is a learnable skill, with clear, practical rules for effective delivery of a message. As both an undergraduate and graduate student, I wrote essays and theses in excruciating "one-shot" night-shift sessions. My basic theory suggested that writing was a form of magic or alchemy, wherein I had to "recreate the world in 25 pages," based on the "please the professor" principle. My province's high schools had not mentioned thesis statements, deductive structure, or even transitions.

During fifteen years in business, writing tasks fell to me because I had English degrees, but agony and imitation remained my basic approaches to writing. Advertisements, brochures, training manuals, speeches, and proposals all emerged torturously from my keyboard, without my ever realizing there were basic general principles I might have followed.

Release from this torture came with my final career change. Teaching is the great joy of my life. As I prepared my first lessons, I finally read writing texts, among them John Langan's. For the first time, I realized there were *formats* and *logical structures* behind most good writing: rational approaches to the agonizing mystery of organizing words. For this epiphany, I, and numerous students, owe John Langan a great debt. The writing process may never be streamlined ecstasy, but the road to clear communication is well marked with clear signposts and is accessible to all of us.

English Skills explains in a clear and direct way the basic principles and skills you must learn to write effectively. And it provides a number of practice materials so that you can work on these skills enough to make them habits. This chapter will introduce you to the most basic principles of effective writing. The chapter will also show you how the rest of the book is organized and how it can help you become an effective writer.

THE FIRST TWO BASES OF EFFECTIVE WRITING: UNITY (MAKING A SINGLE POINT) AND SUPPORT

Point and Support: An Important Difference between Writing and Talking

In everyday conversation, you make all kinds of points, or assertions. You say, for example, "I hate my job"; "Cara's a really generous person"; or "That exam was unfair." The points that you make concern such personal matters as well as, at times, larger issues: "A lot of doctors are arrogant"; "The death penalty should exist for certain crimes"; "Tobacco and marijuana are equally dangerous."

The people you are talking with do not always challenge you to give reasons for your statements. They may know why you feel as you do, or they may already agree with you, or they simply may not want to put you on the spot; and so they do not always ask "Why?" But the people who *read* what you write may not know you, agree with you, or feel in any way obliged to you. If you want to communicate effectively with readers, you must provide solid evidence for any point you make. An important difference, then, between writing and talking is this: *In writing, any idea that you advance must be supported with specific reasons or details.*

Think of your readers as reasonable people. They will not take your views on faith, but they *are* willing to accept what you say as long as you support it. Therefore, remember to support any statement that you make with specific evidence.

Point and Support in a Paragraph

A *paragraph* is a short paper of 150 words or more. It usually consists of an opening point called a *topic sentence* followed by a series of specifics, in the form of sentences, that support the point. Most of the writing featured in this book will be paragraphs.

A Sample Paragraph: Below is a student's paragraph on why the writer plans not to go out with Tony any more.

Good-Bye, Tony

I have decided not to go out with Tony any more. First of all, he was late for our first date. He said that he would be at my house by 8:30, but he did not arrive until 9:20. Second, he was bossy. He told me that it would be too late to go to the new Steve Martin movie I wanted to see, and that we would go to a horror classic, The Night of the Living Dead, instead. I told him that I didn't like gruesome movies, but he said that I could shut my eyes during the gory parts. Only because it was a first date did I let him have his way. Finally, he was abrupt. After the movie, rather than suggesting a hamburger or a drink, he drove right out to a back road near Oakcrest High School and started necking with me. What he did a half hour later angered me most of all. He cut his finger on a pin I was wearing and immediately said we had to go right home. He was afraid the scratch would get infected if he didn't put disinfectant and a bandage on it. When he dropped me off, I said, "Good-bye, Tony," in a friendly enough way, but in my head I thought, "Good-bye forever, Tony."

Notice what the details in this paragraph have done. They have provided you, the reader, with a basis for understanding why the writer made the decision she did. Through specific evidence, the writer has explained and communicated her point successfully. The evidence that supports the point in a paragraph often consists of a series of reasons introduced by signal words (*First of all*, *Second*, and the like) and followed by examples and details that support the reasons. That is true of the sample paragraph above: three reasons are provided, followed by examples and details that back up those reasons.

Activity 1: Creating a Skeleton or X-Ray Outline

Complete the following outline of the sample paragraph. Summarize in a few words the details that develop each reason, rather than writing the details out in full.

Point: _____

_____

Reason 1: _____

   Details that develop reason 1: _____

_____

_____

Reason 2: _____

   Details that develop reason 2: _____

_____

_____

Reason 3: _____

   Details that develop reason 3: _____

_____

_____

Activity 2

Complete the statements below.

1. An important difference between writing and talking is that in writing we absolutely must _____ any statement we make.

2. A _____ is a collection of specifics that support a point.

Writing a Paragraph: An excellent way to get a feel for the paragraph is to write one. Your instructor may ask you to do that now. The only guidelines you need to follow are those described here. There is an advantage to writing a paragraph right away, at a point where you have had almost no instruction. This first paragraph will give a quick sense of your needs as a writer and will provide a baseline — a standard of comparison that you and your instructor can use to measure your writing progress during the semester.

Activity 3

Here, then, is your topic: write a paragraph on the best or worst job you have ever had. Provide three reasons why your job was the best or the worst, and give plenty of details to develop each of your three reasons. Note that the sample paragraph, "Good-Bye, Tony," has the same format your paragraph should have: the author (1) states a point in her first sentence, (2) gives three reasons to support the point, (3) clearly introduces each reason with signal words (*First of all*, *Second*, and *Finally*), and then (4) provides details that develop each of the three reasons. Write your paragraph on a separate sheet of paper.

When you are pleased with your paragraph, and have gone over it with your instructor, think about this writing experience. Was it easy for you? Was it a struggle? Why, in either case? Did this assignment remind you of previous writing experiences in school? What importance does writing have in your life right now? What purposes can you think of for writing in your future career? What skills will you need to work on? Be prepared to discuss your responses to these questions with your instructor and class-mates as the semester progresses. Try to keep track of possible changes to your attitudes, and of areas of real improvement, in your journals.

AN INTRODUCTION TO THIS BOOK

How the Book Is Organized

English Skills with Readings is divided into five parts. Each part will be discussed briefly below. Brief questions appear as well, not to test you but simply to introduce you to the central ideas in the text and the organization of the book. Your instructor may ask you to write in the answers or just to note the answers in your head.

Part One (Pages 1–116): A good way to get a quick sense of any part of a book is to look at the table of contents. Turn back to the contents at the start of this book (pages vii–xi) and answer the following questions:

■ What is the title of Part One? _____

■ "Getting Started" is the opening chapter of Part One. What is the title of the *next* chapter in Part One, and what are the first seven subheadings after the title?

Title _____

Subheading _____

Subheading _____

Subheading _____

Subheading _____

Subheading _____

Subheading _____

Subheading _____

These seven headings refer to important general factors that will help you become an effective writer.

■ The title of the third chapter in Part One is "The First and Second Steps in Writing." According to the subheadings, what are the first and second steps in writing?

_____

_____

■ The title of the fourth chapter in Part One is "The Third and Fourth Steps in Writing." According to the subheadings, what are the third and fourth steps in writing?

_____

_____

Part One describes three of the four steps in writing. The fourth step, which includes all the skills involved in writing clear, error-free sentences, has been placed in a later part of the book, where these sentence skills can be treated in detail and can be easily referred to as needed. Use the table of contents (pages vii–xi) to answer the following questions:

■ In what part of the book are sentence skills treated?

_____

_____

■ The title of the final chapter in Part One is "Four Bases for Evaluating Writing." Look at the table of contents (pages vii–xi) again. What are the first four subheadings following the title?

Subheading _____

Subheading _____

Subheading _____

Subheading _____

Inside Front Cover: Turn now to the inside front cover. You will see there a *(fill in the missing word)* _____ of the four bases of effective writing. These four standards or goals can be used as a guide for every paper that you write. They are summarized on the inside front cover for easy reference. If you aim for and follow them, you are almost sure to write effective papers.

Part Two (Pages 117–206): The title of Part Two is _____.

Part Two, as the title explains, is concerned with different ways to develop paragraphs. Read the preview on page 118 and record here how many types of paragraph development are presented: _____.

Turn to the first method of paragraph development, "Providing Examples," on page 125. You will see that the chapter opens with a brief introduction followed by several paragraphs written by students. Then you will see a series of six *(fill in the missing word)* _____ to help you evaluate the example paragraphs in terms of unity, support, and coherence. Finally, some writing topics that can be developed by means of examples are presented. The same format is used for each of the other methods of paragraph development in Part Two.

Part Three (Pages 207–228): The title of Part Three is _____

_____.

As the preview on page 208 notes, in Part Two you were asked to write single paragraphs; in Part Three, you are asked to write papers of more than one *(fill in the missing word)* _____.

Part Four (Pages 229–432): The title of Part Four is _____

_____.

Part Four is the largest part of the book. It gives you practice in skills needed to write clear and effective sentences. You will note from the table of contents (pages vii–xi) that it contains the skills themselves and editing activities.

The skills are grouped into four sections: "Grammar," "Mechanics," (*fill in the missing word*) "_____," and "Word Use."

Part Five (Pages 433–547):   The title of Part Five is _____
_____.

Part Five contains a series of fifteen reading selections, along with activities that will help you improve both reading and writing skills. Turn to the first selection, "Shots on Goal," on page 440. You will see that the selection begins with a short preview that gives you background information on the piece. Following the selection there are ten comprehension (*fill in the missing word*)
_____ to help you practise important reading skills. Then, after a series of discussion questions that have to do with both reading and writing, there are several writing assignments.

Inside Back Cover: On the inside back cover is an alphabetical list of (*fill in the missing words*) _____.
Your instructor may use these symbols in marking your papers. In addition, you can use the page numbers in the list for quick reference to a specific sentence skill.

Charts in the Book: In addition to the guides on the inside front and back covers, several charts have been provided in the book to help you take responsibility for your own learning.

■   What are the names of the charts on pages 554–559?

_____

_____

_____

_____

_____

_____

How to Use the Book

Here is a suggested sequence for using this book if you are working on your own.

1   After completing this introduction, read the next four chapters in Part One and work through as many of the activities as you need to master the ideas in these chapters. Your instructor may give you answer sheets so that you can check your answers. At that point, you will have covered all the basic theory needed to write effective papers.

2 Turn to Part Four and do the introductory projects. These projects will help you identify the sentence skills you need to review. Study those skills one or two at a time while you continue to work on other parts of the book.

3 What you do next depends on course requirements, individual needs, or both. You will want to practise at least several different kinds of paragraph development in Part Two. If your time is limited, be sure to include "Providing Examples," "Explaining a Process," "Comparing or Contrasting," and "Arguing a Position." After that, you could logically go on to write one or more of the several-paragraph essays described in Part Three.

4 Read at least one of the fifteen selections in Part Five every week, always being sure to work through the two sets of questions that follow each reading.

AS YOU BEGIN ...

English Skills with Readings will help you learn, practise, and apply the writing skills you need to communicate clearly and effectively. But the starting point must be your determination to do the work needed to become an independent writer. If you decide — *and only you can decide* — that you want to learn to write effectively, this book will help you reach that goal.

IMPORTANT FACTORS IN WRITING: AN OVERVIEW OF THE WRITING PROCESS

This chapter will discuss the importance of

- **Your attitude about writing**
- **Writing for a specific purpose and audience**
- **Knowing or discovering your subject**
- **Keeping a journal**
- **Prewriting**
- **Outlining**
- **Revising, editing, and proofreading**

The preceding chapter introduced you to the paragraph form, and the chapters that follow in Part One will explain the basic steps in writing a paragraph and basic standards for evaluating a paragraph. The purpose of this chapter is to describe a number of important general factors that will help you create good papers. These factors are (1) having the right attitude about writing, (2) writing for a specific purpose and audience, (3) knowing or discovering your subject, (4) keeping a journal, (5) prewriting, (6) outlining, and (7) revising, editing, and proofreading.

Your Attitude about Writing

Do you think that writing is a natural gift, rather like throwing a great fastball? Well, such opinions can only make you less confident about your own very real ability to write competently. When you feel that writing is an innate gift, and a source of misery and mystery, you may be worsening your own chances of becoming as good a writer as you can be. Do you feel that only you find writing as difficult as you perhaps do? Relax. Writing is work for everyone. Writing is also an invaluable source of joy, and a unique way for you to express yourself. You have a "writing voice," as much your own as your speaking voice. Students who say "English was always my worst subject" or "I'm just no good at writing" imply that their experiences and feelings have led them to believe they have no talent for writing, while other people do. So perhaps these students do not try their best, or they allow self-defeat and low self-esteem to keep them from trying. Psychiatrists sometimes call this thinking "playing old tapes." Writing *is* work for everyone, from Stephen King to your favourite sportswriter. But everyone must start somewhere. A good beginning point is to learn that writing, like throwing a ball or learning to drive well, is a *skill*. A tiny percentage of people are "natural writers," but even they must learn and polish their writing skills constantly.

A realistic attitude about writing, rather than the mistaken notion that writing is a "natural gift," should build on two crucial ideas.

1   ***Writing is hard work for almost everyone.*** It is difficult to do the intense and active thinking that clear writing demands. (We learn from graphics, movies, and video screens, but it is a different form of learning and requires different concentration.) It can be frightening to sit down before a blank sheet of paper and know that an hour later, nothing on it may be worth keeping. It is frustrating to discover how much of a challenge it is to transfer thoughts and feelings from one's head onto a sheet of paper. It is upsetting to find that an apparently simple writing subject often turns out to be complicated. But writing is not an automatic process, we will not get something for nothing, and we cannot expect something for nothing. Competent writing results only from plain hard work — determination, sweat, and head-on battle.

2   ***Writing is a skill.*** Writing is a skill, like driving, typing, or cooking. Like any skill, it can be learned — if you decide that you are going to learn it, and if you then really work at it. This book will give you the extensive practice needed to develop your writing skills.

Activity

Answering these questions will help you evaluate your attitude about writing.

1. How much practice were you given in writing compositions in high school?

    _____ Much   _____ Some   _____ Little

2. How much feedback on your compositions (positive or negative comments) did your teachers give you?

    _____ Much   _____ Some   _____ Little

3. How did your teachers seem to regard your writing?

_____ Good   _____ Fair   _____ Poor

4. Do you feel that some people simply have a gift for writing and others do not?

_____ Yes   _____ Sometimes _____ No

5. When do you start writing a paper?

_____ Several days before it is due

_____ About a day before it is due

_____ At the last possible minute

Many people who answer *Little* to questions 1 and 2 also answer *Poor* to question 3, *Yes* to question 4, and *At the last possible minute* to question 5. On the other hand, people who answer *Much* or *Some* to questions 1 and 2 also tend to give more favourable responses to the other questions. The point is that people with little practice in writing often have understandably negative feelings about their ability to write. They need not have such feelings, however, because writing is a skill that they can learn with practice.

Writing for a Specific Purpose and Audience

The three most common purposes of writing are *to inform*, *to entertain*, and *to persuade*. Most of the writing you will do in this book will involve some form of persuasion. You will advance a point or topic sentence and then support it in a variety of ways. To some extent, also, you will write papers to inform — to provide readers with information about a particular subject.

Your audience will be primarily your instructor, and sometimes other students as well. Your instructor is really a symbol of the larger audience you should see yourself as writing for — an educated, adult audience that expects you to present your ideas in a clear, direct, organized way. If you can learn to write to persuade or inform such a general audience, you will have accomplished a great deal.

It will also be helpful for you to write some papers for a more specific audience. By so doing, you will develop an ability to choose words and adopt a tone of voice that is just right for a given purpose and a given group of people. For example, Part Two of this book includes assignments asking you to write with a very specific purpose in mind, and for a very specific audience.

Knowing or Discovering Your Subject

KNOWING YOUR SUBJECT

Whenever possible, try to write on a subject that interests you. You will then find it easier to put more time into your work. Even more important, try to write on a subject that you already know something about. If you do not have direct experience with the subject, you should at least have indirect experience — knowledge gained through thinking, prewriting (to be explained on pages 18–26), or talking about the subject.

If you are asked to write on a topic about which you have no experience or knowledge, you should do whatever research (in the library or in interviews, for example) is required to gain the information you need. Without direct or indirect experience, or the information you gain through research, you will not be able to provide the specific evidence needed to develop whatever point you are trying to make. Your writing will be starved for specifics.

DISCOVERING YOUR SUBJECT

At times you will not know your subject when you begin to write. Instead, you will discover it in the actual process of writing. For example, when a student named Gene sat down to write a paper about a memorable job (see page 32), he thought for a while that his topic was going to be an especially depressing moment on that job. As he began to accumulate details, however, he realized that his topic was really the job itself and all the drawbacks it entailed. When he began to write, Gene only *thought* he knew the focus of his paper. In fact, he *discovered his subject in the course of writing*.

Another student, Rhonda, after writing a paper, explained that at first her topic was how she relaxed with her children. But as she accumulated details, she realized after a page of writing that the words *relax* and *children* simply did not go together. Her details were really examples of how she *enjoyed* her children, not how she *relaxed* with them. She sensed that the real focus of her writing should be what she did by herself to relax, and then she thought suddenly that the best time of her week was Thursdays after school. "A light clicked on in my head," she explained. "I knew I had my paper." Then it was a matter of detailing exactly what she did to relax on Thursday evenings. Her paper, "How I Relax," is on page 72.

The moral of these examples is that sometimes you must write a bit in order to find out just what you want to write. Writing can help you think about and explore your topic and decide just what direction your paper will finally take. The techniques presented in "Prewriting" — the section starting on page 18 — will suggest specific ways to discover and develop a subject.

One related feature of the writing process bears mention. Do not feel that you must proceed in a linear fashion when you write. That is, do not assume that the writing process is a railroad track going straight from your central point to supporting detail 1 to supporting detail 2 to supporting detail 3 to your concluding paragraph. Instead, as you draft the paper, proceed in whatever way seems most comfortable. You may want to start by writing the closing section or by developing your third supporting detail.

Do whatever is easiest; as you get material down on the page, it will make what you have left to do a bit easier. And sometimes, of course, as you work on one section, it may happen that a new focal point for your paper will emerge. That's fine: if your writing tells you that it wants to be something else, then revise or start over as needed to take advantage of that discovery. Your *goal* is to wind up with *a paper that solidly makes and supports a point.* This goal helps you achieve the first and second bases of effective writing: *unity* and *support.* Be ready and open to change direction and to make whatever adjustments are needed to reach your goal.

Activity 1: Approaching the Writing Process

Answer the following questions.

1. What are three ways of gaining the knowledge you need to write about a subject?   a. _____   b. _____   c. _____

2. A student begins to write a paper about her favourite vacation. After writing for a half hour, she realizes that the most vivid details coming to her are of her worst vacation. What has happened in the process of writing?

   _____

   _____

   _____

3. Suppose you want to write a paper on different kinds of drivers. You think you can discuss slowpoke drivers, high-speed drivers, and sensible-speed drivers. You feel you have the most details about high-speed drivers. Should you start with that type of driver, or should you start with one of the other two types?

   _____

   _____

   _____

Activity 2: Freewriting and Finding a Point

Write for five minutes about the house, dormitory, or apartment where you live. Simply write down whatever details come to you. Don't worry about being neat; just pile up as many details as you can.

Afterward, go through the material. Try to find a potential focus within all those details. Do the details suggest a simple point that you could make about the place where you live? If so, you've seen a small example of how writing about a topic can be an excellent way of discovering a point about that topic.

Keeping a Journal

Because writing is a skill, it makes sense that the more you practise writing, the better you will write. One excellent way to get practice in writing is to keep a daily or almost daily journal.

At some point during the day — perhaps in a study period after your last class, perhaps before dinner, or perhaps before going to bed — spend fifteen minutes or so writing in your journal. Keep in mind that you do not have to prepare what to write or be in the mood or worry about making mistakes; just write down whatever words come out. As a minimum, try to complete at least one page in each writing session.

You may want to use a notebook that you can easily carry with you for on-the-spot writing. Or you may decide to write on loose-leaf paper that can be transferred later to a journal folder or binder on your desk. No matter how you proceed, be sure to date all your entries.

The content of your journal should be some of the specific happenings, thoughts, and feelings of the day. Your starting point may be a comment by an instructor, a class-mate, or a family member; a gesture or action that has amused, angered, confused, or depressed you; something you have read or seen on television — anything, really, that has caught your attention and that you have decided to explore a bit in writing. Some journal entries may focus on a single subject; others may wander from one topic to another.

Your instructor may ask you to make journal entries a set number of times a week, for a set number of weeks. He or she may ask you to turn in your journal every so often for review and feedback. If you are keeping the journal on your own, try to make entries three to five times a week, every week of the semester.

Your journal can serve as a sourcebook of ideas for possible papers. More important, keeping a journal will help you develop the habit of thinking on paper, and it can help you make writing a familiar and enjoyable part of your life.

Following is an excerpt from one student's journal. (Sentence-skills mistakes have been corrected to improve readability.) As you read, look for a general point and supporting material that could be the basis for an interesting paper.

October 6

Today a woman came into our department at the store and wanted to know if we had any scrap lumber three metres long. Three metres! "Lady," I said, "anything we have that's three metres long sure as heck isn't scrap." When the boss heard me say that, he almost canned me. My boss is a company man, down to his toe tips. He wants to make a big impression on his bosses, and he'll run us around like mad all night to make himself look good. He's the most ambitious man I've ever met. If I don't transfer out of Hardware soon, I'm going to go crazy on this job. I'm not ready to quit, though. The time is not right. I want to be here for a year and have another job lined up and have other things right before I quit. It's good the boss wasn't around tonight when another customer wanted me to carry a bookcase he had bought out to his car. He didn't ask me to help him — he <u>expected</u> me to help him. I hate that kind of "You're my servant" attitude, and I told him that carrying stuff out to cars wasn't my job. Ordinarily I go out of my way to give people a hand, but not guys like him....

■ If the writer of this journal was looking for an idea for an essay, he could probably find several in this single entry. For example, he might write a narrative supporting the point that "In my sales job I have to deal with some irritating customers." Can you find another idea in this entry that might be the basis for an interesting paragraph? Write your idea in the space below.

_____

■ Take fifteen minutes to prepare a journal entry right now on this day in your life. On a separate sheet of paper, just start writing about anything that you have seen, said, heard, thought, or felt, and let your thoughts take you where they may.

Prewriting

If you are like many people, you may sometimes have trouble getting started writing. A mental block may develop when you sit down before a blank sheet of paper. You may not be able to think of a topic or an interesting slant on a topic. Or you may have trouble coming up with interesting and relevant details to support your topic. Even after starting a paper, you may hit snags — moments when you wonder "Where do I go next?"

The following pages describe five techniques that will help you think about and develop a topic and get words down on paper: (1) brainstorming, (2) freewriting, (3) making a list, (4) diagramming, and (5) making a scratch outline. These techniques, which are often called *prewriting techniques*, are a central part of the writing process.

TECHNIQUE 1: BRAINSTORMING

In *brainstorming*, you generate ideas and details by asking as many questions as you can think of about your subject. Such questions include *What? When? Why? How? Where?* and *Who?*

Following is an example of how one student, Sal, used brainstorming to generate material for a paper. Sal felt that he could write about a painful moment he had experienced, but he was having trouble getting started. So he asked himself a series of brainstorming questions about the experience. As a result, he accumulated a series of details that provided the basis for the paper he finally wrote.

Here are the questions Sal asked and the answers he wrote:

Questions	Answers
Where did the experience happen?	In my girlfriend's dorm room at Carleton University
When did it happen?	A week before Thanksgiving.
Who was involved?	My girlfriend, her room-mate (briefly), and I.
What happened?	I discovered my girlfriend was dating someone else.
Why was the experience so painful?	Bonnie and I were engaged. She had never mentioned Blake. My surprise visit turned into a terrible surprise for me.
How did Bonnie react?	She was nervous and tried to avoid answering my questions.
How did I react?	I felt sick and angry. I wanted to tear up the poster with Blake's name on it. I wanted to slam the door, but I walked out quietly. My knees were shaking.

After brainstorming, Sal's next step was to prepare a scratch outline. He then prepared several drafts of the paper. The effective paragraph that eventually resulted from Sal's prewriting techniques appears on pages 190–191.

Activity: Brainstorming

To get a sense of brainstorming, use a sheet of paper to ask yourself a series of questions about a pleasant restaurant you have visited. See how many details you can accumulate about that restaurant in ten minutes.

TECHNIQUE 2: FREEWRITING

When you do not know what to write about a subject, or when you are blocked in writing, freewriting sometimes helps. In *freewriting*, you write on your topic for some limited length of time. Do not worry about spelling, punctuation, erasing mistakes, or finding exact words. You just write without stopping. If you get stuck for words, you write "I am looking for something to say" or repeat words until something comes. There is no need to feel inhibited, since mistakes do not count and you do not have to hand in your paper.

Freewriting will limber up your writing muscles and make you familiar with the act of writing. It is a way to break through mental blocks about writing and the fear of making errors. As you do not have to worry about making mistakes, you can concentrate on discovering what you want to say about a subject. Your initial ideas and impressions will often become clearer after you have gotten them down on paper. Through continued practice in freewriting, you will develop the habit of thinking as you write. And you will learn a technique that is a helpful way to get started on almost any paper that you write.

Here is the freewriting that one student did to accumulate details for a paper on why he stopped smoking:

> I was way overdue to stop smoking cigarettes and I finally did. I had a friend who went to the hospital with lung cancer. No one can say that he's going to recover. He's in Victoria Hospital. When I heard about him, it was the last straw for me. Smoking is a life-and-death matter. My friend is the one who brought this message home to me. Smoking is a life-and-death matter just like the ads say. When I think about it, I hated the fact that I was helping corporations make a lot of money all the while that I smoked. The corporations produced all this slick advertising and I felt I was one of the puppets who listened to it. I marched to their tune. I didn't want to make wealthy corporations even richer, and I hated it every time I gave over hard-earned dollars for a carton of cigarettes. Cigarettes were a very expensive habit. I can hardly say how much a year I had to put out for them. You could see I smoked as you walked through my house. There were ashtrays in the living room, dining room, bathroom, and kitchen. My wife said there was a smell of smoke in the house. I couldn't tell. I had a nose so clogged that I couldn't smell much at all. Cigarettes were a bum trip that I am not going to take any longer.

The writer's next step was to use the freewriting as the basis for a scratch outline. The effective paper that eventually resulted from the author's freewriting, a scratch outline, and a good deal of rewriting appears on pages 143–144.

Activity: Freewriting

To get a sense of freewriting, use a sheet of paper to freewrite about your everyday worries. See how many ideas and details you can accumulate in about ten minutes.

TECHNIQUE 3: MAKING A LIST

Another way to get started is to make a list of as many different items as you can think of concerning your topic. Do not worry about repeating yourself, about sorting out major details from minor ones, or about spelling or punctuating correctly. Simply make a list of everything about your subject that occurs to you. Your aim is to generate details and to accumulate as much raw material for writing as possible.

Following is a list prepared by one student, Erika, who was gathering details for a paper on abuse of public parks. Her first stage in doing the paper was simply to make a list of thoughts and details that occurred to her about the topic. Here is her list:

    Messy picnickers (most common)
    Noisy radios
    Graffiti on buildings and fences
    Games that disturb others
    Dumping car ashtrays
    Stealing park property
    Nude sunbathing
    Destroying flowers
    Damaging fountains and statues
    Litter

Notice that Erika puts in parentheses a note to herself that messy picnickers are the most common type of park abusers. Very often as you make a list, ideas about how to develop a paper will occur to you. Jot them down.

Making a list is an excellent way to get started. Often you can then go on to make a scratch outline and write the first draft of your paper. A scratch outline for Erika's list is shown on page 23.

Activity: Making a List

To get a sense of making a list, use a sheet of paper to list specific problems you will face this semester. See how many ideas and details you can accumulate in about ten minutes.

TECHNIQUE 4: DIAGRAMMING

Diagramming, also known as *mapping* or *clustering*, is another prewriting activity that can help you generate ideas and details about a topic. In diagramming, you use lines, boxes, arrows, and circles to show relationships among the ideas and details that come to you.

Diagramming is helpful to people who like to do their thinking in a visual way. Whether you use a diagram, and just how you proceed with it, is up to you.

Here is the diagram that one student, Devon, prepared for a paper on differences between his job as he imagined it and as it turned out to be. The diagram, with its clear picture of relationships, was especially helpful for the comparison–contrast paper that Devon was doing. His final essay appears on pages 157–158.

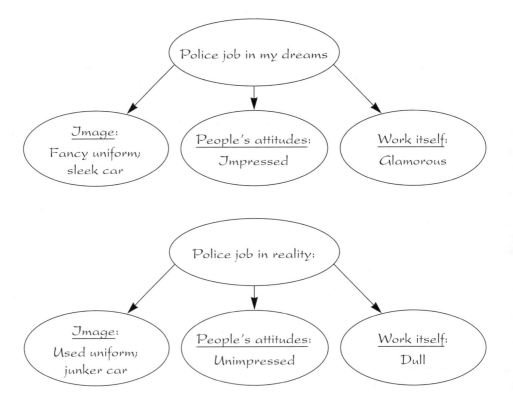

Activity: Diagramming

To get a sense of diagramming, use a sheet of paper to make a diagram of differences between two instructors or two jobs. See how many ideas and details you can accumulate in about ten minutes.

TECHNIQUE 5: PREPARING A SCRATCH OUTLINE

A scratch outline is usually the *single most helpful technique* for writing a good paper. It is an excellent complement to the prewriting techniques already mentioned: brainstorming, freewriting, making a list, and diagramming. In a scratch outline, you think carefully about *the exact point* you are making, about *the exact items* you will use to *support* that point, and about *the exact order* in which you will *arrange* those items. The scratch outline is a plan or blueprint that will help you achieve a unified, supported, and organized composition.

Here is the scratch outline that Erika prepared from her general list about abuse of parks:

Some people abuse public parks.
1. Cleaning out cars
   a. Ashtrays
   b. Litter bags
2. Defacing park property
3. Stealing park property
   a. Flowers, trees, shrubs
   b. Park sod
4. Not cleaning up after picnics
   a. Paper garbage
   b. Bottles and cans

This scratch outline enabled Erika to think about her paper — to decide exactly which items to include and in what order. Without writing more than one sentence, she has taken a giant step toward a paper that is *unified* (she has left out items that are not related); *supported* (she has added items that develop her point); and *organized* (she has arranged the items in a logical way — here, in emphatic order). The effective paragraph that eventually resulted from Erika's list and scratch outline is on page 51.

Activity: Making a Scratch Outline

To get a sense of preparing a scratch outline, make an outline of reasons why you did well or did not do well in high school. See how many ideas and details you can accumulate in about ten minutes.

USING ALL FIVE TECHNIQUES

Very often a scratch outline follows brainstorming, freewriting, diagramming, and making a list. At other times, the scratch outline may be substituted for the other four techniques. Also, you may use several techniques almost simultaneously when writing a paper. You may, for example, ask questions while making a list; you may diagram and outline the list as you write it; you may ask yourself questions and then freewrite answers to them. The five techniques are all ways to help you go about the process of writing a paper.

Activity 1: Reviewing Prewriting Techniques

Answer the following questions.

1. Which of the prewriting techniques do you already practise?

    _____ Brainstorming

    _____ Making a list

    _____ Freewriting

    _____ Making a scratch outline

    _____ Diagramming

2. Which prewriting technique involves asking questions about your topic?

    _____

3. Which prewriting technique shows in a visual way the relationship between ideas and details?

    _____

4. Which prewriting technique involves writing quickly about your topic without being concerned about grammar or spelling?

    _____

5. Which prewriting technique should always be part of doing an essay?

    _____

6. Which techniques do you think will work best for you?

    _____

Activity 2: Identifying Prewriting Techniques

Following are examples of how the five prewriting techniques could be used to develop the topic "Inconsiderate Drivers." Identify each technique by writing *B* (for *brainstorming*), *F* (for *freewriting*), *L* (for *making a list*), *D* (for *diagramming*), or *SO* (for making a *scratch outline*) in the answer space.

_____

High beams on
Weave in and out at high speeds
Treat street like a garbage can
Open car door onto street without looking
Stop on street looking for an address
Don't use turn signals
High speeds in low-speed zones
Don't take turns merging
Use horn when they don't need to
Don't give walkers the right of way

_____

What is one example of an inconsiderate driver?

A person who suddenly turns without using a signal to let the drivers behind know in advance.

When does this happen?

At city intersections or on smaller country roads.

Why is this dangerous?

You have to be alert to slow down yourself to avoid rear-ending the car in front.

What is another example of inconsideration on the road?

Drivers who come toward you at night with their high beams on.

_____

Some people are inconsiderate drivers.
1. In city:
   a. Stop in middle of street
   b. Turn without signalling
2. On highway:
   a. Leave high beams on
   b. Stay in passing lane
   c. Cheat during a merge
3. Both in city and on highway: Throw garbage out the windows

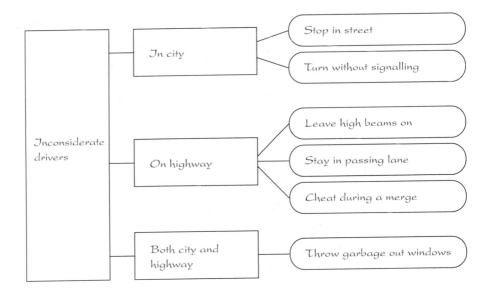

I was driving home last night after class and had three people try to blind me by coming at me with their high beams on. I had to zap them all with my high beams. Rude drivers make me crazy. The worst are the ones who use the road as a dumpster. People who throw butts and cups and hamburger wrappings and other stuff out the car windows should be tossed into a dumpster. If word got around that this was the punishment maybe they would wise up. Other people do dumb things as well. I hate the person who will just stop in the middle of the street and try to figure out directions or look for a house address. Why don't they pull over to the side of the street? That hardly seems like too much to ask. Instead, they stop all traffic while doing their own thing. Then there are the people who keep what they want to do a secret. They're not going to tell you they plan to make a right- or left-hand turn. Instead, you've got to figure it out yourself when they suddenly slow down in front of you.

Outlining

As already mentioned, often the best way to write an effective paragraph is to outline it first. (At times, you may have to do a fair amount of writing first to discover your topic, but a stage will come when outlining, or re-outlining, will help.) Outlining is an organizational skill that will develop your ability to think clearly and logically. An outline lets you work on, and see, the bare bones of a paper, without the distraction of a clutter of words and sentences. Outlining provides a quick check on whether your paper is *unified*. It suggests right at the start whether your paper will be adequately *supported*. And it shows you how to plan a paper that is *well organized*.

The following series of exercises will help develop the outlining skills that are so important to writing an effective paper.

Activity 1: Finding a Subject or Topic Heading

One key to effective outlining is the ability to distinguish between major ideas and the details that fit under those ideas. This exercise will develop your ability to generalize from a list of details and to determine a major thought. In each case on the opposite page, write in the heading that accurately describes the list provided. Note the two examples below.

Examples   Signs of a cold   Fuels

Headache   Wood
Runny nose   Oil
Fever   Gas
Chills   Kerosene

1. _____   5. _____
Vanilla fudge   Robbery
Strawberry   Murder
Chocolate   Assault
Butter almond   Kidnapping

2. _____   6. _____
Laurier   Loafers
Trudeau   Moccasins
Chrétien   Sneakers
Mulroney   Sandals

3. _____   7. _____
Birthday   Caesar
Get well   Oil and vinegar
Anniversary   Blue cheese
Graduation   French

4. _____   8. _____
Anacin   Washing dishes
Bufferin   Taking out garbage
Aspirin   Preparing meals
Tylenol   Dusting

9. _____   10. _____

Cash	Writing
Cheque	Speaking
Money order	Listening
Credit card	Reading

Activity 2: Finding Major Ideas and Supporting Details

Major and minor ideas are mixed together in the two paragraphs outlined below. Put the ideas in logical order by filling in the outlines.

1. **Topic sentence:** People can be classified by how they treat their cars.

Seldom wax or vacuum car	a. _____
Keep every mechanical item in top shape	(1) _____
	(2) _____
Protective owners	
Deliberately ignore needed maintenance	b. _____
	(1) _____
Indifferent owners	(2) _____
Wash and polish car every week	
Accelerate too quickly and brake too hard	c. _____
	(1) _____
Abusive owners	(2) _____
Inspect and service car only when required by provincial law	

2. **Topic sentence:** Living with an elderly parent has many benefits.

Advantages for elderly person	a. _____
Live-in baby-sitter	(1) _____
Learn about the past	(2) _____
Advantages for adult children	
Serve useful role in family	b. _____
Help with household tasks	(1) _____
Advantages for grandchildren	(2) _____
Stay active and interested in young people	c. _____
	(1) _____
More attention from adults	(2) _____

Activity 3: Ordering and Discovering Major Ideas and Supporting Details

Again, major and minor ideas are mixed together. In addition, in each outline one of the three major ideas is missing and must be added. Put the ideas in logical order by filling in the outlines that follow and adding a third major idea.

1. ***Topic sentence:*** Extending the school day would have several advantages.

   Help children academically

   Parents know children are safe at the school

   More time to spend on basics

   Less pressure to cover subjects quickly

   More time for extras like art, music, and sports

   Help working parents

   More convenient to pick up children at 4 or 5 p.m.

   Teachers' salaries would be raised

   a. _____

   (1) _____

   (2) _____

   b. _____

   (1) _____

   (2) _____

   c. _____

   (1) _____

   (2) _____

2. ***Topic sentence:*** Living in a mobile home has many disadvantages.

   Cost of site rental can go up every year

   Tiny baths and bedrooms

   Few closets or storage areas

   Crowded conditions in park

   Lack of space

   Noise from neighbours

   Resale value low compared with houses

   No privacy outside in tiny yards

   a. _____

   (1) _____

   (2) _____

   b. _____

   (1) _____

   (2) _____

   c. _____

   (1) _____

   (2) _____

Activity 4: Creating "X-Ray" Outlines

Read the following two student paragraphs. Then outline each one in the space provided. Write out the topic sentence in each case and summarize in a few words the primary and secondary supporting material that fits under the topic sentence.

1.
Why I Hate the Drive to Work

I hate my drive to work so much that some days I'd rather move than sit in my car for two or three hours a day. I live in the east end of Toronto, and work in a western suburb, so I have to drive forty-five kilometres each way. The speed limit on Highway 401 is one hundred kilometres per hour, so a trip across the top of the city *should* take me less than an hour. Road crew vehicles, salt-truck drivers, and snow ploughs result from Toronto's two seasons: winter and construction. Winter means icy surfaces, salt trucks, and ploughs slowing down traffic. Every summer, out come the road crews to repave the sections of the 401 they repaved last year, which causes lane closings and bumper-to-bumper traffic. Then there are two kinds of terrible drivers of ordinary cars. Some days I think the province just gives away drivers' licences. The "speed demon" drivers think that suddenly speeding up and irrationally switching lanes over and over again will get them to their destination that much more quickly. These are the drivers you see half an hour later, their cars smashed into the back of the car in front, a situation which worsens traffic flow, as everyone slows down to take a look at the damage. Most stupidly dangerous of all are the cell-phone addicts, the drivers who concentrate more on their conversations than on actually driving well. Can anyone dial, talk, and drive, all at the same time? The answer is no; cell-phone drivers never seem to look in their rear-view mirrors, they change speeds for no apparent reason, and they weave slowly out of their lanes without signalling. Ordering a pizza, selling a house, or calling home make these drivers the most hazardous to traffic. I guess, instead of complaining about my drive to work, I could always move closer to work, but I don't think I'll change my life that drastically. I'll just put a new tape in the deck, and try to hate the daily drive a bit less.

Topic sentence: _____

_____

a. _____

    (1) _____

    (2) _____

b. _____

    (1) _____

    (2) _____

c. _____

    (1) _____

    (2) _____

2.

Why I Dislike English

I dislike English because I have struggled with it all my life. First of all, I grew up in an environment where writing English was not considered important. I was born in a Canadian steel town. Growing up there exposed me to the life of blue-collar workers who put no priority on English. Dinner-time conversations centred around the basics of how a large steel mill operated and how machines worked. This environment continued into elementary school, where a concentration on math emphasized skills needed by the blue-collar tradesperson. I cannot remember writing a paragraph, or even a sentence, in class. Later, teenage boys were assumed not to have any aptitude for English. I attended a technical high school, which reinforced my attitudes about boys and proper written English. In fact, my English teacher began each year by stating that he must do his duty and try to pass as many boys as possible. This teacher was short, thin, and disliked sports. English spelled sissy, or not manly. <u>We</u> were to graduate with technical diplomas to prepare us for trades: carpentry, plumbing, and electrical repair work. Girls, on the other hand, supposedly better at English, would graduate with commerce diplomas, to prepare them for secretarial jobs. My most dramatic encounter with English was in my first year of college, where I received a mark of 15 per cent on my first essay. This was a shock to me. I realized that I was in a new league, one that demanded a reasonable command of the English language to graduate. I did not have to decide what course of action to take. I was recruited, along with a number of other male students, by the English professor. I was advised that we were all enrolled in evening remedial English class. We were at his mercy for eight torturous weeks, writing paragraphs while our fellow class-mates got a head start on the three hours of nightly homework. My parents never did understand why their son had to attend school during the day and the evening as well for that first semester.

Topic sentence: _____

_____

a. _____

    (1) _____

    (2) _____

b. _____

    (1) _____

    (2) _____

c. _____

    (1) _____

    (2) _____

Revising, Editing, and Proofreading

Writing an effective paper is almost never done all at once. Rather, it is a step-by-step process in which you take your paper through a series of stages — from prewriting to final draft.

In the first stage, you get your initial ideas and impressions about the subject down on paper; *you accumulate raw material.* You do this through brainstorming, making lists, freewriting, making scratch outlines, and diagramming.

In the second stage, *you shape, add to, and perhaps subtract from your raw material* as you take your paper through a series of two or three or four rough drafts. You should begin with a "formal," revised version of your scratch outline. You work to make clear the single point of your paper, to develop fully the specific evidence needed to support that point, and to organize and connect the specific evidence. For example, perhaps in the second draft you will concentrate on adding details that will further support the main idea of your paper. At the same time you also may eliminate details that, you realize, do not truly back up your main point. And perhaps in the next draft, you will work on reorganizing the details and adding connections between sentences so that your material will hold together.

In the last stage, you *edit* and *proofread.* You *edit* the next-to-final draft — that is, you check it carefully for sentence skills — grammar, mechanics, punctuation, and usage. Then you *proofread* the final copy of the paper for any mistakes in keyboarding or handwriting. Editing and proofreading are important steps that some people neglect, often because they have worked so hard (or so little) on the previous stages.

Ideally, you should have enough time to set your paper aside for a while, so that you can check it later from a fresh point of view. Remember that locating and correcting sentence-skills mistakes can turn an average paper into a better one and a good paper into an excellent one. A later section of this book will give you practice in editing and proofreading in the form of a series of editing tests (pages 427–432).

Practice in Seeing the Entire Writing Process

This section will show you the stages that can be involved in writing an effective paper. You will see what one student, Gene, does in preparing a paper about his worst job.

There is no single sequence that all people follow in writing a composition. However, the different stages in composing that Gene goes through in writing his paper should give you some idea of what to expect. As you'll see, Gene does not just sit down and proceed neatly from start to middle to finish. Writing seldom works like that.

STAGE 1: THINKING AND PREWRITING ABOUT YOUR TOPIC

In retrospect, here is what Gene says about his initial writing topic and his reaction to it:

> "The assignment was to write about a memorable job. I rejected several ideas; I wanted something I had strong feelings about. Then I thought of a job that I had really hated, working in an apple plant. I remembered a moment when I thought I was at the end of the world. It was a cold winter morning about 5 a.m. I had just loaded apple juice all night and was now cleaning one of the apple vats. The vat was an old gasoline truck body. I was inside it, slipping on its rounded stainless steel floor. It was dark in there, the only light coming from a porthole entrance that I had used to crawl in. Apple juice residue was dripping onto my head, and I was using Ajax and a scrub brush to clean off the residue. I felt incredibly depressed. I didn't have a girlfriend then, and my parents were always fighting, and I was incredibly lonely. I felt I was at the bottom of the barrel in my life, and I was never going to get out.
>
> "All this is what I wanted to write about, I thought, and I scribbled down a lot of the details I just mentioned. After I had over two pages of material, I began to think, 'This is too large a topic. It involves a whole terrible phase in my life. I need to narrow my topic down.' Then I decided to focus on the job itself and what I didn't like about it. I felt I was on my way."

STAGE 2: MAKING A LIST

At this point Gene makes up an initial list of details about the job. The list is shown below:

Apple factory job—worst one I ever had
Boss was a madman
Working conditions were poor
Went to work at 5 p.m., got back at 7 a.m.
Lifted cartons of apple juice for ten hours
Slept, ate, and worked—no social life
Gas money to and from work
Loaded onto wooden skids in a truck
Short breaks but breakneck pace
No real companions at work
Cold outside
Floors of trucks cold metal
Had to clean apple vats

■ Comments and Activity

Fill in the missing words: Gene is fortunate enough to know almost from the start what the _____ in his paper will be. Most of his work can thus go into developing details to support the point. Details seldom come automatically; they must be dug for, and Gene's sketchy list of unpleasant aspects of the job is an early stage in the development of his subject. Making a _____ is an excellent way to get started.

Note that, in his list, Gene is not concerned about ordering the details in any way, or about deciding whether any detail really fits, or even about repeating himself. He is just doing first things first: getting raw material down on paper. In the second stage, Gene will also concentrate on accumulating raw material and will start to give attention to shaping that material.

STAGE 3: ADDITIONAL PREWRITING

After making a list, Gene continues on to a partial draft of the paper.

Note: To keep Gene's drafts as readable as possible, his spelling and sentence-skills mistakes have been corrected. Ordinarily, a number of such mistakes might be present, and editing a paper for them would be a part of the writing process.

> I hated my job in the apple factory. I hated it because the work was hard. I loaded cartons of apple juice onto wooden skids in tractor trailers. Two parts to job: ten hours on line; two hours cleaning. I hated the job because the working conditions were bad and the pay was poor.

Why were working conditions bad?	Why was pay poor?
Outside weather cold	Two dollars an hour (minimum wage at the time)
Usually zero degrees	
Floor of tractor trailer was cold steel	Quarter more for working the second shift
Breaks were limited—10 minutes every $2\frac{1}{2}$ hours	Only money was in overtime—when you got time-and-a-half
$\frac{1}{2}$ hour for lunch	No double time
	I would work twenty hours Friday through Saturday to get as much overtime as possible

1 Work hard
3 Working conditions were poor (temperature outside, cleaning of the vats)
2 Money poor

■ Comments and Activity

Fill in the missing words: The second stage of Gene's paper combines freewriting, brainstorming, and a scratch _____. Gene uses all these techniques as he continues to draw out and accumulate _____. At the same time, he has also realized how to organize his details. He decides to focus *not* on his unpleasant boss but on the job itself. In a rough scratch outline, he lists his three reasons (hard work, bad working conditions, poor wages) for hating the job. He then tentatively decides on working conditions as the worst part of the job and numbers the reasons 1, 2, 3—the order in which he might develop them. Keep in mind that as you accumulate and develop details, you should, like Gene, be thinking of a way to _____ them.

STAGE 4: WRITING A DRAFT

Gene puts his work aside for the day and then continues writing the next morning. He now moves to a fuller draft:

> Working in an apple plant was the worst job I ever had. The work was physically hard. For ~~a long time~~ ten hours a night, I stacked cartons in a tractor trailer. The cartons rolled down a metal track. ~~Each carton was very heavy Each carton was heavy with with cans or bottles of apple juice.~~ Each carton contained twelve litre-sized bottles of apple juice, and they were heavy. ~~At the same time, I had to keep a mental count of all the cartons I had loaded.~~ The pay for the job was another bad feature. I was getting the minimum wage at that time plus a quarter extra for night shift. I worked ~~long hours~~ over sixty hours a week. I still did not take home much ~~money~~ more than $100. Working conditions were poor at the plant. During work we were limited to ~~short breaks~~ two ten-minute breaks and unpaid lunch.... The truck-loading dock had zero temperatures.... Lonely on the job ... no interests with other loaders ... worked by myself at the end of the shift ... cleaned up the apple vats.

■ Comments and Activity

Fill in the missing words: At this stage, Gene has enough details to write the initial draft of his paper. Notice that he continues to accumulate specific supporting details as he writes the draft. For example, he crosses out and replaces "long hours" with the more specific _____; he crosses out and replaces "short breaks" with the more specific _____. He also works to improve some of his sentences (for instance, he writes three different versions of the sentence beginning with the words _____). In addition, he crosses out and eliminates a sentence about a _____ because he realizes it does not develop his first supporting point, that the work was physically hard.

Toward the end of the paper, Gene either can't find the right words to say what he wants to say or he doesn't quite know yet what he wants to say. So he freewrites (shown by the ellipses ...), putting down on paper all the impressions that come into his head. He knows that the technique of _____ may help him move closer to the right thought and the right words.

In a second and a third draft, Gene continues to work on and improve his paper. He then edits his next-to-final draft carefully, and the result is the final draft that follows.

STAGE 5: WRITING THE FINAL VERSION

Thanks to the work done during the earlier stages, Gene can now progress to a final draft of the paper:

My Job in an Apple Plant

Working in an apple plant was the worst job I ever had. First of all, the work was physically hard. For ten hours a night, I took cartons that rolled down a metal track and stacked them onto wooden skids in a tractor trailer. Each carton contained twelve litre-sized bottles of apple juice, and they were heavy. The second bad feature of the job was the pay. I was getting the minimum wage at that time, two dollars an hour, plus the minimum of a quarter extra for working the night shift. Even after working over sixty hours a week, I still did not take home much more than $100. The worst feature of the apple plant job was the working conditions. During work we were limited to two ten-minute breaks and an unpaid half hour for lunch. Most of my time was spent outside on the truck-loading dock in near-zero-degree temperatures. And I was very lonely on the job, since I had no interests in common with the other truck loaders. I felt this isolation especially when the production line shut down for the night, and I worked by myself for two hours cleaning the apple vats. The vats were an ugly place to be on a cold morning, and the job was a bitter one to have.

■ Comments and Activity

Fill in the missing words: Notice the many improvements that Gene has made as a result of his second and third drafts. He has added *transitional words* that mark clearly the three supporting points of his paper. The transitional words are "first of all," "_____," and "_____." He has *sharpened his details*, *improved the phrasing of his sentences*, and found the words needed to complete the last section of his paper. He has also edited and proofread his paper carefully, checking the spelling of words he was unsure about and correcting several sentence-skills mistakes.

Almost every effective writer, like Gene, is engaged in a continuing process of moving toward a completely realized paper. The final version is seldom, almost never, attained all at once. Instead, it is the end result of a series of _____. All too often, people stop writing when they are only partway through the writing process; they turn in a paper that is really only an early draft. They have the mistaken notion that a paper is something you should be able to do "all at once." But for almost everyone, writing means hard work and lots of _____. Be sure, then, to take your paper through the entire series of drafts that you probably will need to write an effective composition.

STAGES IN THE WRITING PROCESS

Activity 1: Evaluating Your Attitude toward Writing

Answering the questions below will help you evaluate your attitude about writing, revising, editing, and proofreading.

Timing/Prewriting

1. When do you typically start to work on a paper?

    _____ Several nights before it's due

    _____ Night before it's due

    _____ Day it's due

Drafting

2. How many drafts do you typically write when doing a paper?

    _____ One _____ Two _____ Three _____ Four or more

Editing and Revising

3. How would you describe your editing (checking the next-to-final draft for sentence-skills mistakes)?

    _____ Do little or no editing

_____ Look quickly for and correct obvious errors

_____ Consult a sentence-skills handbook and a dictionary about all possible errors

Proofreading

4. How would you describe your proofreading (checking the final draft for typing or handwriting errors)?

    _____ Do not look at paper again after the last word is written

    _____ May glance quickly through the paper

    _____ Read paper over carefully to find mistakes

5. Do you ever get back papers marked for obvious errors?

    _____ Frequently _____ Sometimes _____ Almost never _____ Never

Activity 2: Identifying Stages in the Writing Process

Listed in the box below are five different stages in the process of composing a paragraph titled "Dangerous Places":

> 1. Prewriting (list)
> 2. Prewriting (list, brainstorming, and outline)
> 3. First draft
> 4. Second draft
> 5. Final draft

The five stages appear in scrambled order below and on the next page. Write the number *1* in the blank space in front of the first stage of development and number the remaining stages in sequence.

_____

There are some places where I never feel safe. For example, subway stations. The people there ~~look strange~~ look tired and angry. The absence of security people there makes me feel ~~something bad could happen~~ a fight could start. I'm also afraid in parking lots. ~~Late at night, I don't like walking in the lot After class, I don't like the parking lot.~~ When I leave my night class or the shopping mall late the walk to the car is scary. ~~Most parking lots have large lights which make me feel at least a little better.~~ I feel least safe in our apartment building's laundry room ... It is a depressing place ... far down a tunnel-like hallway in the basement ... pipes making noises ... a creaky service elevator or cement steps the only ways out....

_____   Dangerous Places
Highways
Parking lots
Feel frightened in our laundry room
Big crowds—concerts, movies
Closed-in places
Subway stations
Airplane
Elevators and escalators

_____   Dangerous Places

There are some places where I never feel completely safe. For example, I never feel safe in subway stations. The people in subway stations often look tired and angry as they wait for trains that always seem late. There are no security people in my city's subway system, and this lack of humanity adds to my feeling that a fight could occur, that someone could be mugged, or that someone could harass me. I also feel unsafe in large, dark parking lots. When I leave my night class a little late, or I am one of the few leaving the mall at 10 p.m., I dread the walk to my car. I am afraid that someone may be lurking behind another car, ready to jump out at me. And I fear that my car will not start, leaving me stuck in the dark parking lot. The place where I feel least safe is the basement laundry room in our apartment building. No matter what time I do my laundry, I seem to be the only person there. The room is a windowless cube, located at the end of a long dark tunnel of a hall on the bottom floor of my building. Moreover, the laundry room is a shadowy, damp space whose only exits are the creaking service elevator or a set of badly lit concrete steps. While I'm folding the clothes, I feel trapped. If anyone unfriendly came down those steps, I would have nowhere to go. The pipes in the room make sudden gurgles, clanks, and hisses, adding to my uneasiness. Places like subway stations, dark parking lots, and our laundry room give me the shivers.

_____   There are some places where I never feel completely safe. For example, I never feel safe in subway stations. The people in subway stations often look tired and angry as they wait for trains that always seem late. The lack of security people adds to my feeling that someone could harass me. I also feel unsafe in large, dark parking lots. When I leave my night class a little late or I leave the mall at 10 p.m., the walk to the car is scary. I'm afraid that someone may be behind a car. Also that my car won't start. The place where I feel least safe is the basement laundry room in our apartment building. No matter when I do the laundry, I'm the only person there. The room is a windowless cube with only a creaky elevator or set of dark stairs as exits. I feel trapped when I fold the clothes. The pipes in the room make frightening noises such as hisses and clanks. Places like subway stations, parking lots, and our laundry room give me the shivers.

——————— Some places seem dangerous and unsafe to me. For example, last night I stayed till 10:15 after night class and walked out to parking lot alone. Very scary. Also, other places I go to every day, such as places in my apartment building. Also frightened by big crowds and lonely subway stations.

Why was the parking lot scary?	What places in my building scare me?
Dark	Laundry room (especially)
Only a few cars	Elevators
No one else in lot	Lobby at night sometimes
Could be someone behind a car	Outside walkway at night
Cold	

2   Parking lots
3   Laundry room
1   Subway stations

Activity 3: Identifying Changes between Drafts

The author of "Dangerous Places" in Activity 2 made a number of editing changes between the second draft and the final draft. Compare the two drafts and identify five of the changes in the spaces provided below.

1. _____

2. _____

3. _____

4. _____

5. _____

A Review of the Chapter

Fill in the missing words in the following summary of this chapter.

Having the Right Attitude: Some people feel that if one is to be a good writer, writing must come easily. This idea is false and can interfere with the ability to make progress in writing. A more realistic and productive attitude includes the understanding that, for most people, writing is _____. In addition, it helps to realize that, like driving or typing, writing is a _____ that can be learned with lots of _____.

Writing for a Specific Purpose and Audience: The three most common purposes of writing are to _____, to _____, and to _____. In this book, you will have a lot of practice in writing to persuade people and some practice in writing to provide information.

Your main audience in class is your _____. But he or she is really a symbol for a general audience of well-educated adults. Writing for this audience should be clear and well organized.

This book will also give you practice in writing for a specific audience. That practice will help you develop the knack of choosing the words and tone of voice that suit specific purposes and people.

Knowing or Discovering Your Subject: It is best to write about a subject that _____ you and that you know something about, either directly or indirectly. When you must write on a topic about which you have little or no background, you should do _____ to gain the necessary knowledge. The library is one good place to do that.

There are times, however, when you won't know your exact subject until after you have written for a while. Writing will help you think about and explore your material. On occasion you will write for a page or two and discover that it will make sense to change the _____ of your paper.

As you work on a paper, remember that it is not necessary to write a paper straight through from _____ to end. You should proceed in whatever way seems easiest, including starting at the middle or even the end. Make whatever adjustments are needed to reach your goal of a paper that makes and _____ a point.

Prewriting: There are five prewriting techniques.

1. One technique, called _____, is a process of generating ideas by asking questions about your subject. Such questions include *What? When?* and *Why?*

2. Freewriting is a second prewriting technique. It involves writing on your topic for ten minutes without _____ or worrying about being correct. In this process, your thoughts about your paper often become clearer.

3. Making a _____ is a third excellent prewriting technique for getting started on a paper. The goal is to generate many possible details for your paper and maybe even ways of developing that paper.

4. Diagramming, also known as _____ or _____, is a fourth prewriting activity. Here you use lines, boxes, arrows, and circles to show relationships among the ideas and details that come to you.

5. The fifth and most helpful technique for writing a good paper is preparing a scratch outline. It is an excellent follow-up to the other prewriting techniques. Sometimes you may even skip the other techniques and concentrate on this one. In a scratch outline, you think about the specific point you will make in your paper, the exact _____ that will support that point, and the exact _____ in which you will arrange those items.

Outlining: Often the best way to write an effective paragraph is to _____ it. Outlining develops your ability to think clearly and logically. It helps you to see and work with the fundamental ideas of a paper, and it helps you to focus on producing a paper that is unified, well supported, and well organized.

Writing, Revising, Editing, and Proofreading: Writing a paper is usually a step-by-step process. It *begins* with prewriting, during which you accumulate raw material. In the *second stage*, you shape your paper by *writing and revising it* several times. Finally, you *edit and proofread*. Editing involves checking your paper for mistakes in sentence _____. Proofreading involves checking the final copy of your paper for mistakes in _____ or _____.

THE FIRST AND SECOND STEPS IN WRITING

This chapter will show you how to

- **Begin a paper by making a point of some kind**
- **Provide specific evidence to support that point**
- **Write a simple paragraph**

The four basic steps in writing an effective paragraph are as follows:

1. Make a single clear point: **unity**
2. Support the point with specific evidence: **support**
3. Organize and connect the specific evidence: **coherence**
4. Write clear, error-free sentences: **sentence skills**

These steps lead to success in achieving the four goals or bases in effective writing, as noted on the inside front cover.

This chapter will present the first two steps, and the chapter that follows (see page 71) will present the last two.

Step 1: Make a Point

Your first step in writing is to decide what point you want to make and to write that point in a single sentence. The point is commonly known as a *topic sentence*. As a guide to yourself and to the reader, put that point in the first sentence of your paragraph. *Everything else in the paragraph* should then *develop* and *support in specific ways the single point given in the first sentence.*

Activity: Identifying a Clear Starting Point

Read the two paragraphs below, written by students on the topic "Cheating in Everyday Life." Which paragraph starts with a clear, single point and goes on to support that point? Which paragraph fails to start with a clear point and rambles on in many directions, introducing a number of ideas but developing none of them?

Paragraph A

Cheating

Cheating has always been a part of life, and it will be so in the future. An obvious situation is that students have many ways of cheating in school. This habit can continue after school is over and become part of their daily lives. There are steps that can be taken to prevent cheating, but many teachers do not seem to care. Maybe they are so burned out by their jobs that they do not want to bother. The honest student is often the one hurt by the cheating of others. Cheating at work occurs also. This cheating may be more dangerous, because employers watch out for it more. Businesses have had to close down because cheating by employees took away a good deal of their profits. A news story recently concerned a server who was fired for taking a steak home from the restaurant where he worked, but his taking the steak may have been justified. Cheating in the sense of being unfaithful to a loved one is a different story because emotions are involved. People will probably never stop cheating unless there is a heavy penalty to be paid.

Paragraph B

Everyday Cheating

Cheating is common in everyday life. For one thing, cheating at school is common. Many students will borrow a friend's homework and copy it in their own handwriting. During a test, students will use a tiny sheet of answers stored in their pockets or sit near a friend to copy answers. People also cheat on the job. They use the postal meter at work for personal mail or take home office supplies such as tape, paper, or pens. Some people who are not closely supervised or who are out on the road may cheat an employer by taking dozens of breaks or using work time for personal chores. Finally, many people cheat when they deal with large businesses. For instance, few customers will report an incorrect bill in their favour. Visitors in a hotel may take home towels, and restaurant patrons may take home silverware. A customer in a store may change price tags because "This is how much the shirt cost last month." For many people, daily cheating is an acceptable way to behave.

Complete the following statement: Paragraph _____ is effective because it makes a clear, single point in the first sentence and goes on in the remaining sentences to support that single point.

Paragraph B starts with a *single idea* — that people cheat in everyday life — and then supports that idea with several different examples. But paragraph A does not begin by making a definite point. Instead, we get two broad, obvious statements — that cheating "has always been a part of life" and "will be so in the future." Because the author has not focused on a clear, single point, what happens in this paragraph is inevitable.

The line of thought in paragraph A swerves about like a car without a steering wheel. In the second sentence, we read that "students have many ways of cheating in school," and we think for a moment that this will be the author's point: he or she will give us supporting details about different ways students cheat in school. But the next sentence makes another point: that after school is over, students may continue to cheat as "part of their daily lives." We therefore expect the author to give us details backing up the idea that students who cheat continue to cheat after they leave or finish school. However, the next sentence makes two additional points: "There are steps that can be taken to prevent cheating, but many teachers do not seem to care." These are two more ideas that could be — but are not — the focus of the paragraph. By now we are not really surprised at what happens in the following sentences. Several more points are made: "The honest student is often the one hurt by the cheating of others," cheating at work "may be more dangerous," an employee who stole a steak "may have been justified," and cheating by being unfaithful is different "because emotions are involved." *No single idea is developed; the result is confusion.*

Step 2: Support the Point with Specific Evidence

The first essential step in writing effectively is to *start with a clearly stated point.* The second basic step is to *support that point with specific evidence.* Following are the two examples of supported points that you've already read.

Point 1

I've decided not to go out with Tony any more.

Support for Point 1

1. Late for our date
2. Bossy
3. Abrupt

Point 2

Cheating is common in everyday life.

Support for Point 2

1. At school
    a. Copying homework
    b. Cheating on tests
2. At work
    a. Using postage meter
    b. Stealing office supplies
    c. Taking breaks and doing errands on company time
3. With large businesses
    a. Not reporting error on bill
    b. Stealing towels and silverware
    c. Switching price tags

The supporting evidence is needed so that we can *see and understand for our-selves* that each writer's point is sound. By providing us with particulars about Tony's actions, the first writer shows why she has decided not to go out with him any more. We can see that she has made a sound point. Likewise, the author of "Everyday Cheating" has supplied specific supporting examples of how cheating is common in everyday life. That paragraph, too, has provided the evidence that is needed for us to understand and agree with the writer's point.

Activity: Distinguishing "Showing" from "Telling"

Both of the paragraphs that follow resulted from an assignment to "Write a paper that details your reasons for being in college." Both writers make the point that they have various reasons for attending college. Which paragraph then goes on to provide plenty of specific evidence to back up its point? Which paragraph is vague and repetitive and lacks the concrete details needed to show us exactly why the author decided to attend college?

A well-known piece of advice to writers is "*Show*, don't tell."

Hint: Imagine that you were asked to make a short film based on each paragraph. Which one suggests specific pictures, locations, words, and scenes you could shoot?

Paragraph A

Reasons for Going to College

I decided to attend college for various reasons. One reason is self-respect. For a long time now, I have felt little self-respect. I spent a lot of time doing nothing, just hanging around or getting into trouble, and eventually I began to feel bad about it. Going to college is a way to start feeling better about myself. By accomplishing things, I will improve my self-image. Another reason for going to college is that things happened in my life that made me think about a change. For one thing, I lost the part-time job I had. When I lost the job, I realized I would have to do something in life, so I thought about school. I was in a rut and needed to get out of it but did not know how. But when something happens out of your control, then you have to make some kind of decision. The most important reason for college, though, is to fulfil my dream. I know I need an education, and I want to take the courses I need to reach the position that I think I can handle. Only by qualifying yourself can you get what you want. Going to college will help me fulfil this goal. These are the main reasons why I am attending college.

Paragraph B

Why I'm in School

There are several reasons I'm in school. First of all, my father's attitude made me want to succeed in school. One night last year, after I had come in at 3 a.m., my father said, "Mickey, you're a bum. When I look at my son, all I see is a good-for-nothing bum." I was angry, but I knew my father was right in a way. I had spent the last two years working odd jobs at a pizza place and luncheonette, taking "uppers" and "downers" with my friends. That night, though, I decided I would prove my father wrong. I would go to college and be a success. Another reason I'm in college is my girlfriend's encouragement. Marie has already been in school for a year, and she is doing well in her computer courses. Marie helped me fill out my application and register for courses. She even lent me sixty-five dollars for textbooks. On her day off, she lets me use her car so I don't have to take the college bus. The main reason I am in college is to fulfil a personal goal: I want to finish something for the first time in my life. For example, I quit high school in the eleventh grade. Then I enrolled in a government job-training program, but I dropped out after six months. I tried to get a high school equivalency diploma, but I started missing classes and eventually gave up. Now I am in a special program where I will earn my high school degree by completing a series of five courses. I am determined to accomplish this goal and to then go on and work for a degree in hotel management.

Complete the following statement: Paragraph _____ provides clear, vividly detailed reasons why the writer decided to attend college.

Paragraph B is the one that solidly backs up its point. The writer gives us specific reasons he is in school. On the basis of such evidence, we can clearly understand his opening point. The writer of paragraph A offers only vague, general reasons for being in school. We do not get specific examples of how the writer was "getting into trouble," what events occurred that forced the decision, or even what kind of job he or she wants to qualify for. We sense that the feeling expressed is sincere, but without the benefit of particular examples, we cannot really see why the writer decided to attend college.

THE GOAL: SPECIFIC DETAILS

1   The *point* that opens a paper is a general statement.
2   The *evidence* that supports a point is made up of specific details, reasons, examples, and facts.

Specific details have two key functions. First of all, details *excite the reader's interest.* They make writing a pleasure to read, for we all enjoy learning particulars about other people—what they do and think and feel. Second, details *support and explain a writer's point;* they give the evidence needed for us to see and understand a general idea. For example, the writer of "Good-Bye, Tony" provides details that make vividly clear her decision not to see Tony any more. She specifies the exact time Tony was supposed to arrive (8:30) and when he actually arrived (9:20). She mentions the kind of film she wanted to see (a new Steve Martin movie) and the one that Tony took her to instead (*The Night of the Living Dead*). She tells us what she may have wanted to do after the movie (have a hamburger or a drink) and what Tony did instead (went necking); she even specifies the exact location of the place Tony took her (a back road near Oakcrest High School). She explains precisely what happened next (Tony "cut his finger on a pin I was wearing") and even mentions specifically (disinfectant and a bandage) the treatments he planned to use.

The writer of "Why I'm in School" provides equally vivid details. He gives clear *reasons* for being in school:

1.   His father's attitude

2. His girlfriend's encouragement

3. His wish to fulfil a personal goal

He *backs up each reason with specific details*. His details give us many sharp pictures. For instance, we hear the exact words his father spoke: "Mickey, you're a bum." He tells us exactly how he was spending his time ("working odd jobs at a pizza parlour and luncheonette, taking 'uppers' and 'downers' with my friends"). He describes how his girlfriend helped him (filling out the college application, lending money and her car). Finally, instead of stating generally that "you have to make some kind of decision," as the writer of "Reasons for Going to College" does, he specifies that he has a strong desire to finish college because he dropped out of many schools and programs in the past: high school, a job-training program, and a high school equivalency course.

In both "Good-Bye, Tony" and "Why I'm in School," then, the vivid, exact details capture our interest and enable us to share in the writer's experience. We see people's actions and hear their words; the details provide pictures that make each of us feel "I am there." The particulars also allow us to understand each writer's point clearly. We are *shown* exactly why the first writer has decided not to see Tony any more and exactly why the second writer is attending college.

Activity: Identifying Specific Supporting Information

Each of the five points below is followed by two selections. Write *S* (for *specific*) in the space next to the selection that provides specific support for the point. Write *NS* (for *not specific*) in the space next to the selection that lacks supporting details.

1. My two-year-old son was in a stubborn mood today.

   _____ a. When I asked him to do something, he gave me nothing but trouble. He seemed determined to make things difficult for me, for he had his mind made up.

   _____ b. When I asked him to stop playing in the yard and come indoors, he looked me square in the eye and shouted "No!" and then spelled it out, "N ... O!"

2. The prices in the amusement park were outrageously high.

   _____ a. The food seemed to cost twice as much as it would in a supermarket and was sometimes of poor quality. The rides also cost a lot, and so I had to tell the children that they were limited to a certain number of them.

   _____ b. The cost of the log flume, a ride that lasts roughly 3 minutes, was $4.75 a person. Then I had to pay $1.50 for a 250 ml soft drink and $3.25 for a hot dog.

3. My brother-in-law is accident-prone.

_____ a. Once he tried to open a tube of permanent glue with his teeth. When the cap came loose, glue squirted out and sealed his lips shut. They had to be pried open in a hospital emergency room.

_____ b. Even when he does seemingly simple jobs, he seems to get into trouble. This can lead to hilarious, but sometimes dangerous, results. Things never seem to go right for him, and he often needs the help of others to get out of one predicament or another.

4. The so-called "bargains" at the yard sale were junk.

_____ a. The tables at the yard sale were filled with useless stuff no one could possibly want. They were the kinds of things that should be thrown away, not sold.

_____ b. The "bargains" at the yard sale included two headless dolls, blankets filled with holes, scorched pot holders, and a plastic Christmas tree with several branches missing.

5. The key to success in college is organization.

_____ a. Knowing what you're doing, when you have to do it, and so on is a big help for a student. A system is crucial in achieving an ordered approach to study. Otherwise, things become very disorganized, and it is not long before grades will begin to drop.

_____ b. Organized students never forget paper or exam dates, which are marked on a calendar above their desks. And instead of having to cram for exams, they study their clear, neat classroom and textbook notes on a daily basis.

Comments: The specific support for the first point is answer _b_. The writer does not just tell us that the little boy was stubborn but provides an example that shows us. In particular, the detail of the son's spelling out "N ... O!" makes his stubbornness vividly real for the reader. For the second point, answer _b_ gives specific prices ($4.75 for a ride, $1.50 for a soft drink, and $3.25 for a hot dog) to support the idea that the amusement park was expensive. For the third point, answer _a_ vividly backs up the idea that the brother-in-law is accident-prone by detailing an accident with permanent glue. The fourth point is supported by answer _b_, which lists specific examples of useless items that were offered for sale—from headless dolls to a broken plastic Christmas tree. We cannot help agreeing with the writer's point that the items were not bargains but junk. The fifth point is backed up by answer _b_, which identifies two specific strategies of organized students: they mark important dates on calendars above their desks, and they take careful notes and study them on a daily basis.

In each of the five cases, then, specific evidence is presented to enable us to *see for ourselves* that the writer's point is valid.

THE GOAL: ENOUGH SPECIFIC SUPPORT

One of the most common and most serious problems in students' writing is inadequate development. You must provide *enough* specific details to support fully a point you are making. You could not, for example, submit a paragraph about how your brother-in-law is accident-prone and provide only a short example. You would have to add several other examples or provide an extended example of your brother-in-law's ill luck. Without such additional support, your paragraph would be underdeveloped.

At times, students try to disguise an undersupported point by using repetition and wordy generalities. You saw this, for example, in the paragraph titled "Reasons for Going to College" on page 47. Be prepared to do the plain hard work needed to ensure that each of your paragraphs has full and solid support.

Activity: Identifying Adequate Development

The following paragraphs were written on the same topic, and each has a clear opening point. Which one is adequately developed? Which one has only several particulars and uses mostly vague, general, wordy sentences to conceal the fact that it is starved for specific details?

Paragraph A

Abuse of Public Parks

Some people abuse public parks. Instead of using the park for recreation, they go there, for instance, to clean their cars. Park caretakers regularly have to pick up the contents of dumped ashtrays and car litter bags. Certain juveniles visit parks with cans of spray paint to deface buildings, fences, fountains, and statues. Other offenders are those who dig up and cart away park flowers, shrubs, and trees. One couple were even arrested for stealing park sod, which they were using to fill in their back lawn. Perhaps the most widespread offenders are the people who use park tables and benches and fireplaces but do not clean up afterward. Picnic tables are littered with trash, including crumpled bags, paper plates smeared with ketchup, and paper cups half-filled with stale pop. On the ground are empty beer bottles, dented pop cans, and sharp metal pull tabs. Parks are made for people, and yet-- ironically--their worst enemy is "people pollution."

Paragraph B

Mistreatment of Public Parks

Some people mistreat public parks. Their behaviour is evident in many ways, and the catalogue of abuses could go on almost without stopping. Different kinds of debris are left by people who have used the park as a place for attending to their automobiles. They are not the only individuals who mistreat public parks, which should be used with respect for the common good of all. Many young people come to the park and abuse it, and their offences can occur in any season of the year. The reason for their inconsiderate behaviour is best known only to themselves. Other visitors have a lack of personal cleanliness in their personal habits when they come to the park, and the park suffers because of it. Such people seem to have the attitude that someone else should clean up after them. It is an undeniable fact that people are the most dangerous thing that parks must contend with.

Complete the following statement: Paragraph _____ provides an adequate number of specific details to support its point.

Paragraph A offers a series of well-detailed examples of how people abuse parks. Paragraph B, on the other hand, is underdeveloped. Paragraph B speaks only of "different kinds of debris," while paragraph A refers specifically to "dumped ashtrays and car litter bags"; paragraph B talks in a general way of young people abusing the park, while paragraph A supplies such particulars as "cans of spray paint" and defacing "buildings, fences, fountains, and statues." And there is no equivalent in paragraph B for the specifics in paragraph A about people who steal park property and litter park grounds. In summary, paragraph B lacks the full, detailed support needed to develop its opening point convincingly.

■ Review Activity

To check your understanding of the chapter so far, answer the following questions.

1. It has been observed: "To write well, the first thing you must do is decide what nail you want to drive home." What is meant by *nail?*

   _____

2. How do you "drive home the nail" in a paper?

   _____

3. What are the two reasons for using specific details in your writing?

   a. _____

   b. _____

Practice in Making and Supporting a Point

You now know the two most important steps in competent writing: (1) making a point and (2) supporting that point with specific evidence. The purpose of this section is to expand and strengthen your understanding of these two basic steps.

You will first work through a series of activities on *making* a point:

1 Identifying Common Errors in Topic Sentences
2 Understanding the Two Parts of a Topic Sentence
3 Writing a Topic Sentence: I
4 Writing a Topic Sentence: II

You will then sharpen your understanding of specific details by working through a series of activities on *supporting* a point:

5 Making Words and Phrases Specific
6 Making Sentences Specific
7 Providing Specific Evidence
8 Identifying Adequate Supporting Evidence
9 Adding Details to Complete a Paragraph

Finally, you will practise writing a paragraph of your own:

10 Writing a Simple Paragraph

1 IDENTIFYING COMMON ERRORS IN TOPIC SENTENCES

When writing a point, or topic sentence, people sometimes make mistakes that undermine their chances of producing an effective paper. One mistake is to substitute an *announcement of the topic* for a true topic sentence. Other mistakes include *writing statements that are too broad or too narrow*. On the following page are examples of all three errors, along with contrasting examples of effective topic sentences.

Announcement

My Ford Escort is the concern of this paragraph.

The statement above is a simple announcement of a subject, rather than a topic sentence in which an idea or point of view is expressed about the subject.

Statement That Is Too Broad

Many people have problems with their cars.

The statement above is too broad to be supported adequately with specific details in a single paragraph.

Statement That Is Too Narrow

My car is a Ford Escort.

The statement above is too narrow to be expanded into a paragraph. Such a narrow statement is sometimes called a *dead-end statement* because there is no place to go with it. It is a simple fact that does not need or call for any support.

Effective Topic Sentence

I hate my Ford Escort.

The statement above expresses an opinion that could be supported in a paragraph. The writer could offer a series of specific supporting reasons, examples, and details to make it clear why he or she hates the car.

Here are additional examples:

Announcements

The subject of this paper will be my apartment.
I want to talk about increases in the divorce rate.

Statements That Are Too Broad

The places where people live have definite effects on their lives.
Many people have trouble getting along with others.

Statements That Are Too Narrow

I have no hot water in my apartment at night.
Almost one of every two marriages ends in divorce.

Effective Topic Sentences

My apartment is a terrible place to live.
The divorce rate is increasing for several reasons.

Activity 1: Distinguishing between Announcements and Topic Sentences

In each pair of sentences below, write *A* beside the sentence that only *announces* a topic. Write *OK* beside the sentence that *presents an idea* about the topic.

1. _____ a. This paper will deal with flunking math.

_____ b. I flunked math last semester for several reasons.

2. _____ a. I am going to write about my job as a gas station attendant.

_____ b. Working as a gas station attendant was the worst job I ever had.

3. _____ a. Obscene phone calls are the subject of this paragraph.

_____ b. People should know what to do when they receive an obscene phone call.

4. _____ a. In several ways, my college library is inconvenient to use.

_____ b. This paragraph will deal with the college library.

5. _____ a. My paper will discuss the topic of procrastinating.

_____ b. The following steps will help you stop procrastinating.

Activity 2: Distinguishing between Too-Narrow Statements and Adequate Topic Sentences

In each pair of sentences below, write *TN* beside the statement that is *too narrow* to be developed into a paragraph. (Such a narrow statement is also known as a *dead-end sentence.*) Write *OK* beside the statement in each pair that calls for support or development of some kind.

1. _____ a. I do push-ups and sit-ups each morning.

_____ b. Exercising every morning has had positive effects on my health.

2. _____ a. Farid works nine hours a day and then goes to school three hours a night.

_____ b. Farid is an ambitious man.

3. _____ a. I started college after being away from school for seven years.

_____ b. Several of my fears about returning to school have proved to be groundless.

4. _____ a. Parts of the NFB film *Get a Job* are interesting to students.

_____ b. Our class watched the NFB film *Get a Job* yesterday.

5. _____ a. My brother was depressed yesterday for several reasons.

_____ b. Yesterday my brother had to pay fifty-two dollars for a motor tune-up.

Activity 3: Distinguishing between Broad Statements and Adequate Topic Sentences

In each pair of sentences below, write *TB* beside the statement that is *too broad* to be supported adequately in a short paper. Write *OK* beside the statement that makes a limited point.

1. _____ a. Professional football is a dangerous sport.

   _____ b. Professional sports are violent.

2. _____ a. Married life is the best way of living.

   _____ b. Teenage marriages often end in divorce for several reasons.

3. _____ a. Aspirin can have several harmful side effects.

   _____ b. Drugs are dangerous.

4. _____ a. I've always done poorly in school.

   _____ b. I flunked math last semester for several reasons.

5. _____ a. Computers are changing our society.

   _____ b. Using computers to teach schoolchildren is a mistake.

2 UNDERSTANDING THE TWO PARTS OF A TOPIC SENTENCE

As stated earlier, the point that opens a paragraph is often called a *topic sentence*. When you look closely at a point, or topic sentence, you can see that it is made up of two parts:

1 The *limited topic*

2 The writer's *attitude* about the limited topic

The writer's attitude or point of view or idea is usually expressed in a *key word* or *words*. All the details in a paragraph should support the idea expressed in the key words. In each of the topic sentences below, a single line appears under the topic and a double line under the idea about the topic (expressed in a key word or words):

My girlfriend is very aggressive.

Highway accidents are often caused by absentmindedness.

The kitchen is the most widely used room in my house.

Voting should be required by law in Canada.

My pickup truck is the most reliable vehicle I have ever owned.

In the first sentence, the topic is *girlfriend*, and the key word that expresses the writer's idea about his topic is that his girlfriend is *aggressive*. In the second sentence, the topic is *highway accidents*, and the key word that determines the focus of the paragraph is that such accidents are often caused by *absent-mindedness*. Notice each topic and key word or words in the other three sentences as well.

Activity: Finding Topic and Point of View

For each point below, draw a single line under the topic and a double line under the idea about the topic.

1. Billboards should be abolished.
2. My boss is an ambitious woman.
3. The middle child is often a neglected member of the family.
4. The apartment needed repairs.
5. Television commercials are often insulting.
6. My parents have rigid racial attitudes.
7. The language in many movies today is offensive.
8. Home-owners today are more energy-conscious than ever before.
9. My friend Crystal, who is only nineteen, is extremely old-fashioned.
10. Looking for a job can be a degrading experience.
11. Certain regulations in the school cafeteria should be strictly enforced.
12. My car is a temperamental machine.
13. Living in a one-room apartment has its drawbacks.
14. The city's traffic-light system has both values and drawbacks.
15. Consumers' complaints can often have positive results.

3   WRITING A TOPIC SENTENCE: I

Activity: Writing an Appropriate Topic Sentence

The activity on the following pages will give you practice in writing an accurate point, or topic sentence—one that is neither too broad nor too narrow for the supporting material in a paragraph. Sometimes you will construct your topic sentence after you have decided what details you want to discuss. An added value of this activity is that it shows you how to write a topic sentence that will exactly match the details you have developed.

1. ***Topic sentence:*** _____

    _____

    a. Some are caused by careless people tossing matches out of car windows.
    b. A few are started when lightning strikes a tree.
    c. Some result from campers who fail to douse cooking fires.
    d. The majority of forest fires are deliberately set by arsonists.

2. ***Topic sentence:*** _____

    _____

    a. We had to wait a half hour even though we had reserved a table.
    b. Our appetizers and main courses all arrived at the same time.
    c. The server ignored our requests for more water.
    d. The wrong desserts were delivered to us.

3. ***Topic sentence:*** _____

    _____

    a. My phone goes dead at certain times of the day.
    b. When I talk long distance, I hear conversations in the background.
    c. The line to the phone service centre is busy for hours.
    d. My telephone bill includes three calls I never made.

4. ***Topic sentence:*** _____

    _____

    a. The crowd scenes were crudely spliced from another film.
    b. Mountains and other background scenery were just painted cardboard cutouts.
    c. The "sync" was off, so that you heard voices even when the actors' lips were not moving.
    d. The so-called monster was just a spider that had been filmed through a magnifying lens.

5. ***Topic sentence:*** _____

_____

a. In early grades we had spelling bees, and I would be among the first ones sitting down.
b. In grade six English, my teacher kept me busy diagramming sentences on the board.
c. In grade ten we had to recite poems, and I always forgot my lines.
d. In grade twelve, my compositions had more red correction marks than anyone else's.

4 WRITING A TOPIC SENTENCE: II

Often you will start with a general topic or a general idea of what you want to write about. You may, for example, want to write a paragraph about some aspect of school life. To come up with a point about school life, begin by limiting your topic. One way to do this is to make a list of all the limited topics you can think of that fit under the general topic.

Activity: Developing Your Point

On the following pages are five general topics and a series of limited topics that fit under them. Make a point out of one of the limited topics in each group.

Hint: To create a topic sentence, ask yourself, "What point do I want to make about _____ (*my limited topic*)?"

Example Recreation

- Movies
- Dancing
- TV shows
- Reading
- Sports parks

Your point: *Sports parks today have some truly exciting games.*

1. Your school

   - Instructor
   - Cafeteria
   - Specific class
   - Particular room or building
   - Particular policy (attendance, grading, etc.)
   - Class-mate

   Your point: _____

2. Job

   - Pay
   - Boss
   - Working conditions
   - Duties
   - Co-workers
   - Customers or clients

   Your point: _____

3. Money

   - Budgets
   - Credit cards
   - Dealing with a bank
   - School expenses
   - Ways to get it
   - Ways to save it

   Your point: _____

4. Cars

   - First car
   - Driver's test
   - Road conditions
   - Accident
   - Mandatory speed limit
   - Safety problems

   Your point: _____

5. Sports

- A team's chances
- At your school
- Women's teams
- Recreational versus spectator
- Favourite team
- Outstanding athlete

Your point: _____

5   MAKING WORDS AND PHRASES SPECIFIC

To be an effective writer, you must use specific, rather than general, words. Specific words create pictures in the reader's mind. They help capture interest and make your meaning clear. Your writing, when you are specific, *shows*, rather than *tells* your reader what you see in *your* "mind's eye."

Activity: Using Specific Words

This activity will give you practice at replacing vague, indefinite words with sharp, specific words. Insert three or more specific words to replace the general word or words underlined in each sentence. Make changes in the wording of a sentence as necessary.

Example   My bathroom cabinet contains <u>many drugs</u>.

My bathroom cabinet contains aspirin, antibiotics,

tranquillizers, and codeine cough medicine.

1. At the shopping centre, we visited <u>several stores</u>.

   _____

   _____

2. Sunday is my day to take care of <u>chores</u>.

   _____

   _____

3. Crystal enjoys <u>various activities</u> in her spare time.

   _____

   _____

4. I spent most of my afternoon doing <u>homework</u>.

    _____

    _____

5. We returned home from vacation to discover that <u>several pests</u> had invaded the house.

    _____

    _____

6 MAKING SENTENCES SPECIFIC

Again, you will practise replacing vague, indefinite writing with lively, image-filled writing that captures your reader's interest and makes your meaning clear. Compare the following sentences:

General	*Specific*
The boy came down the street.	Fabio ran down Woodlawn Avenue.
A bird appeared on the grass.	A blue jay swooped down on the frost-covered lawn.
She stopped the car.	Wanda slammed on the brakes of her car.

The specific sentences create clear pictures in your reader's mind. The details *show* readers exactly what has happened.

Here are four ways to make your words and sentences specific:

1 Use exact names.

She loves her *motorbike*.
Crystal loves her *Honda*.

2 Use lively verbs.

The garbage truck *went* down Front Street.
The garbage truck *rumbled* down Front Street.

3 Use descriptive words (modifiers) before nouns.

A girl peeked out the window.
A *chubby, six-year-old* girl peeked out the *dirty kitchen* window.

4   Use words that relate to the five senses: sight, hearing, taste, smell, and touch.

That woman is a karate expert.
That *slight, silver-haired* woman is a karate expert. (*Sight*)

When the dryer stopped, a signal sounded.
When the *whooshing* dryer stopped, a *loud buzzer* sounded. (*Hearing*)

Crystal offered me an orange slice.
Crystal offered me a *sweet, juicy* orange slice. (*Taste*)

The real estate agent opened the door of the closet.
The real estate agent opened the door of the *cedar-scented* closet. (*Smell*)

I pulled the blanket around me to fight off the wind.
I pulled the *scratchy* blanket around me to fight off the *chilling* wind. (*Touch*)

Activity: Adding Specific Details

With the help of the methods described above, add specific details to any eight
of the ten sentences that follow. Use a separate sheet of paper.

Examples   The person got out of the car.

The elderly man painfully lifted himself out of the white

station wagon.

The fans enjoyed the victory.

Many of the ten thousand fans stood, waved blankets, and

cheered wildly when Barnes scored the winning touchdown.

1. The lunch was not very good.
2. The animal ran away.
3. An accident occurred.
4. The instructor came into the room.
5. The machine did not work.
6. The crowd grew restless.
7. I relaxed.
8. The room was cluttered.
9. The child threw the object.
10. The driver was angry.

7   PROVIDING SPECIFIC EVIDENCE

Activity: Adding Supporting Details

Provide three details that logically support each of the following points, or topic sentences. Your details can be drawn from your own experience, or they can be invented. In each case, the details should show in a specific way what the point expresses in only a general way. State your details briefly in several words rather than in complete sentences.

Example   Steve had several ways of passing time during the dull lecture.

Shielded his eyes with his hand and dozed awhile.

Read the sports magazine he had brought to class.

Made an elaborate drawing on a page of his notebook.

1.   I could tell I was coming down with flu.

2.   The food at the cafeteria was terrible yesterday.

3.   I had car problems recently.

4.   When your money gets tight, there are several ways to economize.

5.   Some people have dangerous driving habits.

8 IDENTIFYING ADEQUATE SUPPORTING EVIDENCE

Activity: Identifying Adequate Development

Two of the following paragraphs provide sufficient details to support their topic sentences convincingly. Write *AD*, for *adequate development*, beside those paragraphs. There are also three paragraphs that, for the most part, use vague, general, or wordy sentences as a substitute for concrete details. Write *U*, for *underdeveloped*, beside those paragraphs.

_____ 1.

My Husband's Stubbornness

My husband's worst problem is his stubbornness. He simply will not let any kind of weakness show. If he isn't feeling well, he refuses to admit it. He will keep on doing whatever he is doing and will wait until the symptoms get almost unbearable before he will even hint that anything is the matter with him. Then things are so far along that he has to spend more time recovering than he would if he had a different attitude. He also hates to be wrong. If he is wrong, he will be the last to admit it. This happened once when we went shopping, and he spent an endless amount of time going from one place to the next. He insisted that one of them had a fantastic sale on things he wanted. We never found a sale, but the fact that this situation happened will not change his attitude. Finally, he never listens to anyone else's suggestions on a car trip. He always knows he's on the right road, and the results have led to a lot of time wasted getting back in the right direction. Every time one of these incidents happens, it only means it is going to happen again in the future.

_____ 2.

Street Hockey: Tradition or Torture?

Because ball hockey has always been popular with boys and girls in Red Deer, Alberta, we feel we have a tradition to keep up, but it's becoming an increasingly dangerous pastime. Games are constantly interrupted by cars and trucks. This fall, one of the new girl players, who was captain of her school's field hockey team, believed she had to prove herself to us. Unaware of the amount of traffic on seemingly quiet streets, she ploughed forward, head down, eyes focused on the ball, and nearly wound up as the hood ornament on a minivan. Late-night drinking drivers make street hockey even more hazardous. Bottles thrown out the windows shatter on the pavement, and large chunks of glass get picked up by hockey sticks as we chase the ball. Two players ended up in Emergency, one with a dangerous cut over his eye, the other with six stitches in his forearm, both injuries caused by flying glass. The most dangerous incident, though, had nothing to do with traffic; it was a combination of ordinary carelessness and modern lawn-care. A wild shot sent the ball onto someone's newly treated front yard. Our forward sprinted to retrieve the ball, tripped over the "dangerous chemical" sign, and fell face-forward into damp grass, freshly soaked in weed-killer. He turned out to be violently allergic to the ingredients, and went into something like an asthma attack. We had to call 911 for paramedics with inhalers and oxygen. So, a traditional teenage prairie sport has lost some of its appeal these days and, in fact, has become more of a hazard than a tradition for its players.

_____   3.   Attitudes about Food

Attitudes about food that we form as children are not easily changed. In some families, food is love. Not all families are like this, but some children grow up with this attitude. Some families think of food as something precious and not to be wasted. The attitudes children pick up about food are hard to change in adulthood. Some families celebrate with food. If a child learns an attitude, it is hard to break this later. Someone once said: "As the twig is bent, so grows the tree." Children are very impressionable, and they can't really think for themselves when they are small. Children learn from the parent figures in their lives, and later from their peers. Some families have healthy attitudes about food. It is important for adults to teach their children these healthy attitudes. Otherwise, the children may have weight problems when they are adults.

_____   4.   Qualities in a Friend

There are several qualities I look for in a friend. A friend should give support and security. A friend should also be fun to be around. Friends can have faults, like anyone else, and sometimes it is hard to overlook them. But a friend can't be dropped because he or she has faults. A friend should stick by you, even in bad times. There is a saying that "a friend in need is a friend indeed." I believe this means that there are good friends and fair-weather friends. The second type is not a true friend. He or she is the kind of person who runs when there's trouble. Friends don't always last a lifetime. Someone you believed to be your best friend may lose contact with you if you move to a different area or go around with a different group of people. A friend should be generous and understanding. A friend does not have to be exactly like you. Sometimes friends are opposites, but they still like each other and get along. Since I am a very quiet person, I can't say that I have many friends. But these are the qualities I believe a friend should have.

_____   5.   Schoolyard Cardsharks

My daughter's school playground is an odd location for an evenings-only men's club and casino. Every spring, as dusk gathers over Halifax, under the arc lights provided for the safety of children using the equipment and ballfield, a group of gentlemen with certain peculiar habits gather to socialize. The members of this society have a uniform: ballcaps worn back-to-front, XXLL-size T-shirts, and immense, unlaced, brand-name running shoes.

Sheltering in the lee of the wooden "climbing castle," they arrange their chosen furniture, worn folding chairs stolen from the neighbourhood's front porches. Next, raised ritual handgrips are exchanged, and the fraternal greetings are heard: "How the f--- are ya?" "So where were ya last night?" As a rough circle is formed by the players in their chairs, packs of Export "A" and Players emerge from pockets and sleeves, and the sacramental beverages of Molson Ex and Gatorade are in readiness for the tense action to follow. Finally, the stakes are agreed upon, and the equipment is carefully set on a pilfered card-table or picnic bench: two dog-eared decks of playing cards. Is their game five-card stud, or blackjack, deuces wild? No, it's euchre or hearts ... the same games their grandparents are playing in their retirement homes. Youth and age meet in strange ways, and strange locations.

9 ADDING DETAILS TO COMPLETE A PARAGRAPH

Activity: Adding Specific Supporting Details

Each of the following paragraphs needs specific details to back up its supporting points. In the spaces provided, add a sentence or two of realistic details for each supporting point. The more specific you are, the more convincing your details are likely to be. Use your own paper, if you require more space.

1.

A Pushover Instructor

We knew after the first few classes that the instructor was a pushover. First of all, he didn't seem able to control the class.

_____

_____

_____

In addition, he made some course requirements easier when a few

students complained. _____

_____

_____

_____

Finally, he gave the easiest quiz we had ever taken. _____

_____

_____

_____

2.

Helping a Parent in College

There are several ways a family can help a parent who is attending college. First, family members can take over some of the household chores that the parent usually does. _____

_____

_____

_____

_____

Also, family members can make sure that the student has some quiet study time. _____

_____

_____

_____

_____

Third, families can take an interest in the student's problems and accomplishments. _____

_____

_____

_____

_____

10   WRITING A SIMPLE PARAGRAPH

You know now that an effective paragraph does two essential things: (1) it makes a point, and (2) it provides specific details to support that point. You have considered a number of paragraphs that were effective because they followed these two basic steps or ineffective because they failed to follow them.

You are ready, then, to write a simple paragraph of your own. Choose one of the three assignments below, and follow carefully the guidelines provided.

■ Assignment 1

Turn back to the activity on page 64 and select the point for which you have the best supporting details. Develop the point into a paragraph by following these steps:

a   If necessary, rewrite the point so that the first sentence is more specific or suits your purpose more exactly. For example, you might want to rewrite the second point so that it includes a specific time and place: "Dinner at the Union Building Cafeteria was terrible yesterday."

b   Provide several sentences of information to develop each of your three supporting details fully. Make sure that all the information in your paragraph truly supports your point. As an aid, use the paragraph form on page 557.

c   Use the words *First of all*, *Second*, and *Finally* to introduce each of your three supporting details.

d   Conclude your paragraph with a sentence that refers to your opening point. This last sentence "rounds off" the paragraph and lets the reader know that your discussion is complete. For example, the second paragraph about cheating on page 44 begins with "Cheating is common in everyday life." It closes with a statement that refers to, and echoes, the opening point: "For many people, daily cheating is an acceptable way to behave."

e   Supply a title based on the point. For instance, the fourth point might have the title "Ways to Economize."

Use the following list to check your paragraph for each of the above items:

Yes   *No*

_____   _____   Do you begin with a point?

_____   _____   Do you provide relevant, specific details that support the point?

_____   _____   Do you use the words *First of all*, *Second*, and *Finally* to introduce each of your three supporting details?

_____   _____   Do you have a closing sentence?

_____   _____   Do you have a title based on the point?

_____   _____   Are your sentences clear and free from obvious errors?

■ Assignment 2

In this chapter you have read two paragraphs (pages 47–48) on reasons for being in college. For this assignment, write a paragraph describing your own reasons for being in college. You might want to look first at the following list of common reasons students give for going to school. Use the ones that apply to you (making them as specific as possible) or supply your own. Select three of your most important reasons for being in school and generate specific supporting details for each reason.

Before starting, reread paragraph B on pages 47–48. *You must provide comparable specific details of your own.* Make your paragraph truly personal; do not fall back on vague generalities like those in paragraph A on page 47. Use the checklist for Assignment 1 as a guideline as you work on the paragraph.

Apply in My Case	*Reasons Students Go to College*
_____	■ To have some fun before getting a job
_____	■ To prepare for a specific career
_____	■ To please their families
_____	■ To educate and enrich themselves
_____	■ To be with friends who are going to college
_____	■ To take advantage of an opportunity they didn't have before
_____	■ To find a husband or wife
_____	■ To see if college has anything to offer them
_____	■ To do more with their lives than they've done so far
_____	■ To take advantage of provincial or federal assistance programs or other special funding
_____	■ To earn the status that they feel comes with a college degree
_____	■ To get a new start in life

■ Assignment 3

Write a paragraph about stress in your life. Choose three of the following areas of stress and provide specific examples and details to develop each area.

Stress at school

Stress at work

Stress at home

Stress with a friend or friends

Use the checklist for Assignment 1 as a guideline while working on the paragraph.

Some Suggestions on What to Do Next

1 Work through the next chapter in Part One: "The Third and Fourth Steps in Writing" (pages 71–90).

2 Read "Providing Examples" (pages 125–133) in Part Two and do the first writing assignment.

3 Work through "Using the Dictionary" (page 376) and "Improving Spelling" (page 385) in Part Four.

4 Do the introductory projects in Part Five and begin working on the sentence skills you need to review.

THE THIRD AND FOURTH STEPS IN WRITING

This chapter will show you how to

- **Organize specific evidence in a paper by using a clear method of organization**
- **Connect the specific evidence by using transitions and other connecting words**
- **Write clear, error-free sentences by referring to the rules in Part Four of this book**

The third and fourth steps in effective writing are

3 Organize and connect the specific evidence: **coherence**

4 Write clear, error-free sentences: **sentence skills**

You know from the previous chapter that the first two steps in writing an effective paragraph are stating a point and supporting it with specific evidence. The third step is organizing and connecting the specific evidence. Most of this chapter will deal with the chief ways to organize and connect the supporting information in a paper. Practice with, and success in organizing and connecting, your supporting evidence leads to achieving the third goal or base in effective writing: coherence. The chapter will then look briefly at the sentence skills that make up the fourth step in writing a successful paper.

Step 3: Organize and Connect the Specific Evidence

At the same time that you are generating the specific details needed to support a point, you should be thinking about ways to organize and connect those details. All the details in your paper must *cohere*, or *stick together;* when they do, your reader is able to move smoothly and clearly from one bit of supporting information to the next. This chapter will discuss the following ways to organize and connect supporting details:

1 Common methods of organization

2 Transitions

3 Other connecting words

COMMON METHODS OF ORGANIZATION: TIME ORDER AND EMPHATIC ORDER

Time order and *emphatic order* are common methods used to organize the supporting material in a paper. You will learn more specialized methods of development in Part Two of the book.

Time order simply means that details are listed as they occur in time. *First* this is done; *next* this; *then* this; *after* that, this; and so on. Here is a paragraph that organizes its details through time order:

How I Relax

The way I relax when I get home from school on Thursday night is, first of all, to put my three children to bed. Next, I run hot water in the tub and put in lots of perfumed bubble bath. As the bubbles rise, I undress and get into the tub. The water is relaxing to my tired muscles, and the bubbles are tingly on my skin. I lie back and put my feet on the water spigots, with everything but my hair under the water. I like to stick my big toe up the spigot and spray water over the tub. After about ten minutes of soaking, I wash myself with scented soap, get out and dry myself off, and put on my nightgown. Then I go downstairs and make myself two ham, lettuce, and tomato sandwiches on white bread and pour myself a tall glass of iced tea with plenty of sugar and ice cubes. I carry these into the living room and turn on the television. To get comfortable, I sit on the couch with a pillow behind me and my legs under me. I enjoy watching a video or a late movie. The time is very peaceful after a long, hard day of housecleaning, cooking, washing, and attending night class.

Fill in the missing words: "How I Relax" uses the following words to help show time order: _____, _____, _____, _____, and _____.

Emphatic order is sometimes described as "save-the-best-till-last" order. It means that the most interesting or important detail is placed in the last part of a paper. (In cases where all the details seem equal in importance, the writer should impose a personal order that seems logical or appropriate to the details in question.) *The last position* in a paper is *the most emphatic position* because the reader is most likely to remember the last thing read. *Finally*, *last of all*, and *most important* are typical words showing emphasis. The following paragraph organizes its details through emphatic order.

Tabloid TV

"Tab TV" shows, or what used to be called interview shows, are so popular today that they threaten staple daytime soaps for viewer ratings, and have changed news magazine programs into celebrity confessionals. The old National Enquirer slogan, "Enquiring minds want to know," has turned Canadians and Americans into nations of televoyeurs, who apparently want to know all about demented relationships, teenage pimps, and drug-addicted family pets. First, TV guides and network promos hype these shows day and night: Rolonda has "Teen Romance," and Gerry Springer referees brawls between transvestites who can't stay faithful. Canadian networks have Camilla Scott's teen tramps and seasoned streetwalkers telling all, and Dini Petty blending celebrity recipes with scandalous audience confessions. These shows' popularity and broadcast frequency achieve three things: ease of accessibility to an incredibly wide audience, increased fascination with the grubby details of previously unknown lives, and networks lining up to create more "tab TV." Next, let's look at our appetite: what makes us "want to know." We love gossip — the lower, the better — so these shows cater to what used to be called human interest issues, and do humans ever have a lot of interests they'll discuss in front of millions! Printed tabs prefer celebrity misdemeanours, but TV tabs let us watch and listen to the heartaches and brawls of ordinary folks; perhaps these tales are more appealing because of their recognizable everyday quality. It's hard to resist the chance to wallow in someone else's misery or filthy behaviour. Chances are, ultimately, as we channel-surf in search of diversion or information, Geraldo or Ricki will get us. We wouldn't dare to goad even a close friend for that kind of detail. That kind of detail, in live action, may be the most important clue to the popularity of "tab TV." In the 1950s, the very respectable Walter Cronkite let us experience history by interviewing actors playing Napoleon and Julius Caesar on a show called You Are There, and in the sixties, Andy Warhol said that in the future everyone would be famous for fifteen minutes. Well, courtesy of "tab TV," we are there, and more and more of us are achieving fifteen minutes of fame.

Fill in the missing words: The paragraph lists a total of _____ different reasons people watch "tab TV." The writer of the paragraph feels that the most important

reason is _____.

He or she signals this reason by using the emphasis words _____.

Some paragraphs use a *combination of time order and emphatic order.* For example, "Good-Bye, Tony" on page 5 includes time order: it moves from the time Tony arrived to the end of the evening. In addition, the writer uses emphatic order, ending with her most important reason (signalled by the words "most of all") for not wanting to see Tony any more.

TRANSITIONS

Transitions are *signal words* that help readers *follow the direction* of the writer's thought. They show the relationship between ideas, connecting one thought with the next. They can be compared to signs on the road that guide travellers.

To see the value of transitions, look at the following pairs of examples. Put a check beside the example in each pair that is easier and clearer to read and understand.

1. _____ a. Our building manager recently repainted our apartment. He replaced our faulty air conditioner.

   _____ b. Our building manager recently repainted our apartment. Also, he replaced our faulty air conditioner.

2. _____ a. I carefully inserted a disk into the computer. I turned on the power button.

   _____ b. I carefully inserted a disk into the computer. Then I turned on the power button.

3. _____ a. Movie-goers usually dislike film monsters. Film-goers pitied King Kong and even shed tears at his death.

   _____ b. Movie-goers usually dislike film monsters. However, film-goers pitied King Kong and even shed tears at his death.

You should have checked the second example in each pair. The transitional words in those sentences — *Also, Then,* and *However* — make the relationship between the sentences clear. Like all effective transitions, they help connect the writer's thoughts.

In the following box are common transitional words and phrases, grouped according to the kind of signal they give readers. Note that certain words provide more than one kind of signal. In the paragraphs you write, you will most often use addition signals: words like *first of all*, *also*, *another*, and *finally* will help you move from one supporting reason or detail to the next.

Transitions

Addition signals: first of all, for one thing, second, the third reason, also, next, another, and, in addition, moreover, furthermore, finally, last of all

Time signals: first, then, next, after, as, before, while, meanwhile, now, during, finally

Space signals: next to, across, on the opposite side, to the left, to the right, in front, in back, above, below, behind, nearby

Change-of-direction signals: but, however, yet, in contrast, otherwise, still, on the contrary, on the other hand

Illustration signals: for example, for instance, specifically, as an illustration, once, such as

Conclusion signals: therefore, consequently, thus, then, as a result, in summary, to conclude, last of all, finally

---

Activity: Finding Transition Signals

1. Underline the three *addition* signals in the following selection:

> I am opposed to provincial lotteries for a number of reasons. First of all, by supporting lotteries, provinces are supporting gambling. I don't see anything morally wrong with gambling, but it is a known cause of suffering for many people who do it to excess. Provinces should be concerned with relieving suffering, not causing it. Another objection I have to the lotteries is the kind of advertising they do on television. The commercials promote the lotteries as an easy way to get rich. In fact, the odds against getting rich are astronomical. Last, the lotteries take advantage of the people who can least afford them. Studies have shown that people with lower incomes are more likely to play the lottery than people with higher incomes. This is the harshest reality of the lotteries: provinces are encouraging people of limited means not to save their money but to throw it away on a government-supported pipe dream.

2. Underline the four *time* signals in the following selection:

    It is often easy to spot bad drivers on the road because they usually make more than one mistake: they make their mistakes in series. First, for example, you notice that someone is tailgating you. Then, almost as soon as you notice, this driver has passed you in a no-passing zone. That's two mistakes already in a matter of seconds. Next, almost invariably, you see the driver speed down the road and pass someone else. Finally, as you watch in disbelief, glad that he or she is out of your way, the same driver speeds through a red light or cuts across oncoming traffic in a wild left turn.

3. Underline the three *space* signals in the following selection:

    Standing in the burned-out shell of my living room was a shocking experience. Above my head were charred beams, all that remained of our ceiling. In front of me, where our television and stereo had once stood, were twisted pieces of metal and chunks of blackened glass. Strangely, some items seemed little damaged by the fire. For example, I could see the TV tuner knob and a dusty CD under the rubble. I walked through the gritty ashes until I came to what was left of our couch. Behind the couch had been a wall of family photographs. Now, the wall and the pictures were gone. I found only a water-logged scrap of my wedding picture.

4. Underline the four *change-of-direction* signals in the following selection:

    In some ways, train travel is superior to air travel. People always marvel at the speed with which airplanes can zip from one end of the country to another. Trains, on the other hand, definitely take longer. But sometimes longer can be better. Travelling across the country by train allows you to experience the trip more completely. You get to see the cities and towns, mountains and prairies that too often pass by unnoticed when you fly. Another advantage of train travel is comfort. Travelling by plane means wedging yourself into a narrow seat with your knees bumping the back of the seat in front of you and being handed a "snack" consisting of a bag of ten roasted peanuts. In contrast, the seats on most trains are spacious and comfortable, permitting even the most long-legged traveller to stretch out and watch the scenery just outside the window. And when train travellers grow hungry, they can get up and stroll to the dining car, where they can order anything from a simple snack to a gourmet meal. There's no question that train travel is definitely slow and old-fashioned compared with air travel. However, in many ways it is much more civilized.

5. Underline the three *illustration* signals in the following selection:

    Status symbols are all around us. The cars we drive, for instance, say something about who we are and how successful we have been. The auto makers depend on this perception of automobiles, designing their commercials to show older, well-established people driving Cadillacs and young, fun-loving people driving to the beach in sports cars. Television, too, has become something of a status symbol. Specifically, schoolchildren are often rated by their class-mates according to whether or not their family has all the cable television stations. Another example of a status symbol is the home computer. This device, not so long ago considered a novelty, is now considered as common as the television set itself. Being without a PC today is like having a car without whitewalls in the fifties.

6.   Underline the *conclusion* signal in the following selection:

A hundred years ago, miners used to bring caged canaries down into the mines with them to act as warning signals. If the bird died, the miner knew that the oxygen was running out. The smaller animal would be affected much more quickly than the miners. In the same way, animals are acting as warning signals to us today. Baby birds die before they can hatch because pesticides in the environment cause the adults to lay eggs with paper-thin shells. Fish die when lakes are contaminated with acid rain or poisonous mercury. The dangers in our environment will eventually affect all life on earth, including humans. Therefore, we must pay attention to these early warning signals. If we don't, we will be as foolish as a miner who ignored a dead canary--and we will die.

OTHER CONNECTING WORDS

In addition to transitions, there are three other kinds of connecting words that help tie together the specific evidence in a paper: repeated words, pronouns, and synonyms. Each will be discussed in turn.

Repeated Words

Many of us have been taught by English instructors — correctly so — not to repeat ourselves in our writing. On the other hand, repeating key words can help tie a flow of thought together. In the selection that follows, the word *retirement* is repeated to remind readers of the key idea on which the discussion is centred. Underline the word the five times it appears.

Oddly enough, retirement can pose more problems for the spouse than for the retired person. For a person who has been accustomed to a demanding job, retirement can mean frustration and a feeling of uselessness. This feeling will put pressure on the spouse to provide challenges at home equal to those of the workplace. Often, these tasks will disrupt the spouse's well-established routine. Another problem arising from retirement is filling up all those empty hours. The spouse may find himself or herself in the role of social director or tour guide, expected to come up with a new form of amusement every day. Without sufficient challenges or leisure activities, a person can become irritable and take out the resulting boredom and frustration of retirement on the marriage partner. It is no wonder that many of these partners wish their spouses would come out of retirement and do something--anything--just to get out of the house.

Pronouns

Pronouns (*he, she, it, you, they, this, that,* and others) are words that take the place of nouns. They are another way to connect ideas as you develop a paper. Using pronouns to take the place of other words or ideas can help you avoid needless repetition. (Be sure, though, to use pronouns with care in order to avoid the unclear or inconsistent pronoun references described on pages 295–302 of this book.) Underline the eight pronouns in the passage below, noting at the same time the words that the pronouns refer to.

> A professor of nutrition at a major university recently advised his* students that they could do better on their* examinations by eating lots of sweets. He told them that the sugar in cakes and candy would stimulate their* brains to work more efficiently, and that if the sugar was eaten for only a month or two, it would not do them any harm.

Synonyms

Using synonyms — words that are alike in meaning — can also help move the reader clearly from one thought to the next. In addition, the use of synonyms increases variety and interest by avoiding needless repetition of the same words. Underline the three words used as synonyms for *fallacies* in the following selection.

> There are many fallacies about suicide. One false idea is that a person who talks about suicide never follows through. The truth is that about three out of every four people who commit suicide notify one or more other persons ahead of time. Another misconception is that a person who commits suicide is poor or downtrodden. Actually, poverty appears to be a deterrent to suicide rather than a predisposing factor. A third myth about suicide is that people bent on suicide will eventually take their lives one way or another, whether or not the most obvious means of suicide is removed from their reach. In fact, since an attempt at suicide is a kind of cry for help, removing

---

* The pronouns marked with asterisks are *possessive* pronouns. Such words do not replace a noun; rather, they indicate possession.

a convenient means of taking one's life, such as a gun, shows people bent on suicide that someone cares enough about them to try to prevent it.

Activity: Finding Effective Repetition, Pronoun Substitutes, and Synonyms

Read the selection below and then answer the questions about it that follow.

My Worst Experience of the Week

[1]The registration process at McKenzie College was a nightmare. [2]The night before registration for my course officially began, I went to bed anxious about the whole thing, and nothing that happened the next day eased any of my tension. [3]First, even though I had paid my registration fee early last spring, the staff in the registration office had no record of my payment. [4]For some bizarre reason, they wouldn't accept the receipt I had. [5]Consequently, I had to stand in a special numbered line for two hours, waiting for someone to give me a paper which stated that I had, in fact, paid my registration fee. [6]The need for this new receipt seemed ridiculous to me, since, all along, I had proof that I had paid. [7]I was next told that I had to see my program co-ordinator in the International Business Faculty and that this faculty was in Section C, Phase 2, of the Champlain Building. [8]I had no idea what or where the Champlain Building was. [9]But, finally, I found the ugly cinder-block structure. Then I began looking for Section C and Phase 2. [10]When I found these, everyone there was a member of the Communications Department. [11]No one seemed to know where International Business had gone. [12]Finally, one instructor said she thought International Business was in Section A. [13]"And where is Section A?" I asked. [14]"I don't know," the teacher answered. "I'm new here." [15]She saw the bewildered look on my face and said sympathetically, "You're not the only one who's confused." [16]I nodded and walked numbly away. [17]I felt as if I were fated to spend the rest of the semester trying to complete the registration process, and I wondered if I would ever become an official college student.

Questions

1. How many times is the key idea *registration* repeated? _____

2. Write here the pronoun that is used for *staff in the registration office* (sentence 4): _____; *Section C, Phase 2* (sentence 10): _____; *instructor* (sentence 15): _____.

3. Write here the words that are used as a synonym for *receipt* (sentence 5):

    _____;

the words that are used as a synonym for *Champlain* (sentence 9):

_____ ;

the word that is used as a synonym for *instructor* (sentence 14):

_____ .

Step 4: Write Clear, Error-Free Sentences

The fourth step in writing an effective paper is to follow the agreed-upon rules, or conventions, of written English. These conventions — or, as they are called in this book, *sentence skills* — must be followed if your sentences are to be clear and error-free. Here are some of the most important of these skills.

1 Write complete sentences rather than fragments.

2 Do not write run-on sentences.

3 Use verb forms and tenses correctly and consistently.

4 Make sure that subjects and verbs agree.

5 Use pronoun forms and types correctly.

6 Use adjectives and adverbs correctly.

7 Eliminate faulty modifiers and faulty parallelism.

8 Use correct paper format.

9 Use capital letters where needed.

10 Use numbers and abbreviations correctly.

11 Use the following punctuation marks correctly: apostrophes, quotation marks, commas, colons, semi-colons, dashes, hyphens, parentheses.

12 Use the dictionary as necessary.

13 Eliminate spelling errors.

14 Use words accurately by developing your vocabulary and distinguishing between commonly confused words.

15 Choose words effectively to avoid slang, clichés, and wordiness.

16 Vary your sentences.

17 Edit and proofread to eliminate careless errors.

This list may *look* intimidating, but you and your instructor may already be working on individual items from the list. You should refer to Part Four for clear explanations or for answers to your questions. Sentence skills are explained in detail, and activities are provided, in Part Four. Introductory projects will help you determine which skills you need to work on. Your instructor will also identify such skills in marking your papers and may use the correction symbols shown on the inside back cover. Note that the correction symbols, and also the checklist of sentence skills on the inside front cover, include page references, so that you can turn quickly to those skills that give you problems.

■ Review Activity

Complete the following statements.

1. The four steps in writing a paper are:

    a. _____

    b. _____

    c. _____

    d. _____

2. *Time order* means _____

    _____

3. *Emphatic order* means _____

    _____

4. _____ are signal words that help readers follow the direction of a writer's thought.

5. In addition to transitions, three other kinds of connecting words that help link sentences and ideas are repeated words, _____, and

    _____.

Practice in Organizing and Connecting Specific Evidence

You now know the third step in effective writing: organizing the specific evidence used to support the main point of a paper. You also know that the fourth step — writing clear, error-free sentences — is treated in detail in Part Four of the book. This section will expand and strengthen your understanding of the third step in writing. You can achieve the third base, or goal, of effective writing: **coherence**.

You will work through the following series of activities:

1 Organizing through Time Order
2 Organizing through Emphatic Order
3 Organizing through a Combination of Time Order and Emphatic Order
4 Identifying Transitions
5 Providing Transitions
6 Identifying Transitions and Other Connecting Words

1 ORGANIZING THROUGH TIME ORDER

Activity: Placing Ideas in Time Order

The following is a list of sentences in scrambled order, which could form a coherent paragraph if set in chronological, or time, order. Read the sentences through, then recopy them onto your own sheet of paper, leaving two lines between each sentence. Cut the sentences into one-sentence strips, so that you can change their sequence.

Now move the sentences around on your desk until their order makes sense to you. Number each sentence in time order, and transfer your numbers to the spaces provided below.

_____ The table is right near the garbage pail.

_____ So you reluctantly select a gluelike tuna-fish sandwich, a crushed apple pie, and watery hot coffee.

_____ You sit at the edge of the table, away from the garbage pail, and gulp down your meal.

_____ Trying to eat in the cafeteria is an unpleasant experience.

_____ Suddenly you spot a free table in the corner.

_____ With a last swallow of the lukewarm coffee, you get up and leave the cafeteria as rapidly as possible.

_____ Flies are flitting in and out of the pail.

_____ By the time it is your turn, the few things that are almost good are gone.

_____ There does not seem to be a free table anywhere.

_____ Unfortunately, there is a line in the cafeteria.

_____ The submarine sandwiches, coconut-custard pie, and iced tea have all disappeared.

_____ You hold your tray and look for a place to sit down.

_____ You have a class in a few minutes, and so you run in to grab something to eat quickly.

2 ORGANIZING THROUGH EMPHATIC ORDER

Activity: Placing Ideas in Emphatic Order

Follow the same procedure as described above for the sentences out of time order. These sentences should be rearranged into order of importance, or emphatic order. Start with what seems to be the least important detail and end with the most important item.

_____ The people here are all around my age and seem to be genuinely friendly and interested in me.

_____ The place where I live has several important advantages.

_____ The schools in this neighbourhood have a good reputation, so I feel that my daughter is getting a good education.

_____ The best thing of all about this area, though, is the school system.

_____ Therefore, I don't have to put up with public transportation or worry about how much it's going to cost to park each day.

_____ The school also has an extended day-care program, so I know my daughter is in good hands until I come home from work.

_____ First of all, I like the people who live in the other apartments near mine.

_____ Another positive aspect of this area is that it's close to where I work.

_____ That's more than I can say for the last place I lived, where people stayed behind locked doors.

_____ The office where I'm a receptionist is only a six-block walk from my house.

_____ In addition, I save a lot of wear and tear on my car.

3 ORGANIZING THROUGH A COMBINATION OF TIME ORDER AND EMPHATIC ORDER

Activity: Combining Time and Emphatic Order

Follow the same *read, rewrite, cut, and unscramble* technique for the following group of sentences. This time, use a combination of time and emphatic order to arrange the sentence sequence. Write the number *1* beside the point that all the other sentences seem to support. Then number the supporting sentences in terms of occurrence in time and relative importance. Pay close attention to transitional words and phrases; this will help you to organize and connect the supporting sentences.

_____ I did not see the spider but visited my friend in the hospital, where he suffered through a week of nausea and dizziness because of the poison.

_____ We were listening to the radio when we discovered that nature was calling.

_____ As I got back into the car, I sensed, rather than felt or saw, a presence on my left hand.

_____ After my two experiences, I suspect that my fear of spiders will be with me until I die.

_____ The first experience was when my best friend received a bite from a poisonous spider.

_____ I looked down at my hand, but I could not see anything because it was so dark.

_____ I had two experiences when I was sixteen that are the cause of my *arachniphobia*, or terrible and uncontrollable fear of spiders.

_____ We stopped the car at the side of the road, walked into the woods a few feet, and watered the leaves.

_____ My friend then entered the car, putting on the dashboard light, and I almost passed out with horror.

_____ I saw the bandage on his hand and the puffy swelling when the bandage was removed.

_____ Then it flew off my hand and into the dark bushes nearby.

_____ I sat in the car for an hour afterward, shaking and sweating and constantly rubbing the fingers of my hand to reassure myself that the spider was no longer there.

_____ But my more dramatic experience with spiders happened one evening when another friend and I were driving around in his car.

_____ Almost completely covering my fingers was a monstrous brown spider, with white stripes running down each of a seemingly endless number of long, furry legs.

_____ Most of all, I saw the ugly red scab on his hand and the yellow pus that continued oozing from under the scab for several weeks.

_____ I imagined my entire hand soon disappearing as the behemoth relentlessly devoured it.

_____ At the same time I cried out "Arghh!" and flicked my hand violently back and forth to shake off the spider.

_____ For a long, horrible second it clung stickily, as if intertwined for good among the fingers of my hand.

4   IDENTIFYING TRANSITIONS

Activity: Finding Different Types of Transitions

Locate the major transitions used in the following two selections. Then write the transitions in the spaces provided. Mostly you will find _addition_ words such as _another_ and _also_. You will also find several _change-of-direction_ words such as _but_ and _however_.

1.   Watching TV Football

   Watching a football game on television may seem like the easiest thing in the world. However, like the game of football itself, watching a game correctly is far more complicated than it appears. First is the matter of the company. The ideal number of people depends on the size of your living room. Also, at least one of your companions should be rooting for the opposite team. There's nothing like a little rivalry to increase the enjoyment of a football game. Next, you must attend to the refreshments. Make sure to have on hand plenty of everyone's favourite drinks, along with the essential chips, dips, and pretzels. You may even want something more substantial on hand, like sandwiches or pizza. If you do, make everyone wait until the moment of kick-off before eating. Waiting will make everything taste much better. Finally, there is one last piece of equipment you should have on hand: a football. The purpose of this object is not to send lamps hurtling from tables or to smash the television screen, but to toss around--outside--during half-time. If your team happens to be getting trounced, you may decide not to wait until half-time.

   a. _____

   b. _____

   c. _____

   d. _____

   e. _____

2.   Avoidance Tactics

Getting down to studying for an exam or writing a paper is hard, and
so it is tempting for students to use one of the following five avoidance
tactics in order to put the work aside. For one thing, students may say to
themselves, "I can't do it." They adopt a defeatist attitude at the start and
give up without a struggle. They could get help with their work by using
such college services as tutoring programs and skills labs. However, they
refuse even to try. A second avoidance technique is to say, "I'm too busy."
Students may take on an extra job, become heavily involved in social
activities, or allow family problems to become so time-consuming that they
cannot concentrate on their studies. Yet if college really matters to a
student, he or she will make sure that there is enough time to do the
required work. Another avoidance technique is expressed by the phrase
"I'm too tired." Typically, sleepiness occurs when it is time to study or go to
class and then vanishes when the school pressure is off. This sleepiness is a
sign of work avoidance. A fourth excuse is to say, "I'll do it later." Putting
things off until the last minute is practically a guarantee of poor grades on
tests and papers. When everything else--watching TV, calling a friend, or
even cleaning the oven--seems more urgent than studying, a student may
simply be escaping academic work. Last, some students avoid work by
saying to themselves, "I'm here, and that's what counts." Such students live
under the dangerous delusion that, since they possess a college ID, a
parking sticker, and textbooks, the course work will somehow take care of
itself. But once a student has a college ID in a pocket, he or she has only
just begun. Doing the necessary studying, writing, and reading will bring
real results: good grades, genuine learning, and a sense of accomplishment.

a. _____

b. _____

c. _____

d. _____

e. _____

f. _____

g. _____

h. _____

5   PROVIDING TRANSITIONS

Activity: Adding Appropriate Transitions

In the spaces provided, add logical transitions to tie together the sentences and ideas in the following paragraphs. Use the words in the boxes that precede each paragraph.

1.

however	a second	last of all
for one thing	also	on the other hand

Why School May Frighten a Young Child

Schools may be frightening to young children for a number of reasons.

_____, the regimented environment may be a new and disturbing experience. At home children may have been able to do what

they wanted when they wanted to do it. In school, _____, they are given a set time for talking, working, playing, eating, and even

going to the toilet. _____ source of anxiety may be the public method of discipline that some teachers use. Whereas at home children are scolded in private, in school they may be held up to embarrassment and ridicule in front of their peers. "Bonnie," the teacher may say, "why are you the only one in the class who didn't do your homework?" Or, "David, why are you the only one who can't work quietly at your seat?" Children may

_____ be frightened by the loss of personal attention. Their little discomforts or mishaps, such as tripping on the stairs, may bring instant sympathy from a parent; in school, there is often no one to notice, or the teacher is frequently too busy to care and just says, "Go do your

work. You'll be all right." _____, a child may be scared by the competitive environment of the school. At home, one hopes, such

competition for attention is minimal. In school, _____, children may vie for the teacher's approving glance or tone of voice, or for stars on a paper, or for favoured seats in the front row. For these and other reasons, it is not surprising that children may have difficulty adjusting to school.

2.

for example	finally	first of all
but	such as	as a result
	another	

Job Burnout

Job burnout has several causes. _____, successful workers may be given more to do just because they do their jobs well. Soon they become overloaded and must work even harder just to keep up with the pace. The work load becomes impossible, and exhaustion sets in.

_____ cause of burnout is conflicting demands. Many

career women, _____, find themselves trapped between one set of expectations in the workplace and another at home. They are expected to perform competently for eight hours a day and then come home to cook a gourmet meal or help a child or spouse with a problem.

_____, certain occupations entail a high risk of burnout.

People in the service professions, _____ nurses, social workers, and teachers, begin their careers filled with idealism and

commitment. _____ the long hours, heavy case loads or enrolments, and miles of red tape become overwhelming, and the rewards--

the few people they can help--are all too few. _____, burnout for these people is almost inevitable.

6   IDENTIFYING TRANSITIONS AND OTHER CONNECTING WORDS

Activity: Creating Coherence with Connecting Words

The selections on the following page use *transitions*, *repeated words*, *synonyms*, and *pronouns* to help tie ideas together. The connecting words you are to identify have been underlined. In the space provided, write *T* for *transition*, *RW* for *repeated word*, *S* for *synonym*, or *P* for *pronoun*.

_____   1. I decided to pick up a course change form from the registrar's office. However, I changed my mind when I saw the long line of students waiting there.

_____ 2. We absorb radiation from many sources in our environment. Our colour television sets and microwave ovens, among other things, give off low-level <u>radiation</u>.

_____ 3. I checked my car's tires, oil, water, and belts before the trip. But the ungrateful <u>machine</u> blew a gasket about fifty kilometres from home.

_____ 4. At the turn of the century, bananas were still an oddity in North America. Some people even attempted to eat <u>them</u> with the skins on.

_____ 5. Many researchers believe that people have weight set-points their bodies try to maintain. This may explain why many dieters return to their original <u>weight</u>.

_____ 6. Women's clothes, in general, use less material than men's clothes. Yet women's <u>garments</u> are usually more expensive than men's.

_____ 7. In England, drivers use the left-hand side of the road. <u>Consequently</u>, steering wheels are on the right-hand side of their cars.

_____ 8. At the end of the rock concert, thousands of fans held up lighters in the darkened arena. The sea of lights signalled that the <u>fans</u> wanted an encore.

_____ 9. The temperance movement in this country sought to ban alcohol. Drinking <u>liquor</u>, movement leaders said, led to violence, poverty, prostitution, and insanity.

_____ 10. Crawling babies will often investigate new objects by putting them in their mouths. <u>Therefore</u>, parents should be alert for any pins, tacks, or other dangerous items on floors and carpets.

_____ 11. One technique that advertisers use is to have a celebrity endorse a product. The consumer <u>then</u> associates the star qualities of the celebrity with the product.

_____ 12. Canning vegetables is easy and economical. <u>It</u> can also be very dangerous.

_____ 13. For me, apathy quickly sets in when the weather becomes hot and humid. This <u>listlessness</u> disappears when the humidity decreases.

_____ 14. Establishing credit is important for a woman. A good <u>credit</u> history is often necessary when applying for a loan or charge account.

_____ 15. The restaurant table must have had uneven legs. Every time we tried to eat, <u>it</u> wobbled like a seesaw.

Some Suggestions on What to Do Next

1 Work through the final chapter in Part One: "Four Bases for Evaluating Writing."

2 Read "Explaining a Process" (pages 134–141) in Part Two and do the first writing assignment.

3 Read "Vocabulary Development" (page 394) in Part Four.

4 Continue your review of sentence skills in Part Four. If you plan to make a general review of all the skills, here is an appropriate sequence to follow: (1) Paper Format, (2) Capital Letters, (3) Subjects, Objects, and Verbs, (4) Sentence Fragments, (5) Run-On Sentences, (6) Standard English Verbs, (7) Irregular Verbs, (8) Subject–Verb Agreement, (9) Apostrophes, (10) Commas, (11) Quotation Marks, (12) Sentence Variety.

FOUR BASES FOR EVALUATING WRITING

This chapter will show you how to evaluate a paper for

- **Unity**
- **Support**
- **Coherence**
- **Sentence skills**

In the preceding two chapters, you learned four essential steps in writing an effective paper. The box below shows how these steps lead to four goals, bases, or standards you can use in evaluating a paper.

Four Steps ⟶	*Four Bases* ⟶	*Four Goals Defined*
1 If you make one point and stick to that point,	your writing will have *unity*.	**Unity:** a single main idea pursued and supported by the points and details of your writing
2 If you back up the point with specific evidence,	your writing will have *support*.	**Support:** for each supporting point, specific and definite details
3 If you organize and connect specific evidence,	your writing will have *coherence*.	**Coherence:** supporting points and details organized and connected clearly
4 If you write clear, error-free sentences,	your writing will reflect effective *sentence skills*.	**Sentence Skills:** sentence structure, grammar, spelling, and punctuation free of errors

This chapter will discuss the four bases of unity, support, coherence, and sentence skills and will show how these four bases can be used to evaluate writing.

Base 1: Unity

Activity: Discovering the Elements of Unity

The following two paragraphs were written by students on the topic "Why Students Drop Out of College." Read them and decide which one makes its point more clearly and effectively, and why.

Paragraph A

Why Students Drop Out

Students drop out of college for many reasons. First of all, some students are bored in school. These students may enter college expecting nonstop fun or a series of fascinating courses. When they find out that college is often routine, they quickly lose interest. They do not want to take dull required courses or spend their nights studying, and so they drop out. Students also drop out of college because the work is harder than they thought it would be. These students may have made decent grades in high school simply by showing up for class. In college, however, they may have to prepare for two-hour exams, write fifteen-page term papers, or make detailed presentations to a class. The hard work comes as a shock, and students give up. Perhaps the most common reason students drop out is that they are having personal or emotional problems. Younger students, especially, may be attending college at an age when they are also feeling confused, lonely, or depressed. These students may have problems with room-mates, family, boyfriends, or girlfriends. They become too unhappy to deal with both hard academic work and emotional troubles. For many types of students, dropping out seems to be the only solution they can imagine.

Paragraph B

Student Dropouts

There are three main reasons students drop out of college. Some students, for one thing, are not really sure they want to be in school and lack the desire to do the work. When exams come up, or when a course requires a difficult project or term paper, these students will not do the required studying or research. Eventually, they may drop out because their grades are so poor they are about to flunk out anyway. Such students sometimes come back to school later with a completely different attitude about school. Other students drop out for financial reasons. The pressures of paying tuition, buying textbooks, and possibly having to support themselves can be overwhelming. These students can often be helped by the school because financial aid is available, and some schools offer work-study programs.

Finally, students drop out because they have personal problems. They cannot concentrate on their courses because they are unhappy at home, they are lonely, or they are having trouble with boyfriends or girlfriends. Instructors should suggest that such troubled students see counsellors or join support groups. If instructors would take a more personal interest in their students, more students would make it through troubled times.

Fill in the blanks: Paragraph _____ makes its point more clearly and effectively because _____

_____

_____ .

UNDERSTANDING UNITY

Paragraph A is more effective because it is *unified*. All the details in this paragraph are *on target;* they support and develop the *single point* expressed in the first sentence — that there are many reasons students drop out of college. On the other hand, paragraph B contains some details irrelevant to the opening point — that there are three main reasons students drop out. These details should be omitted in the interest of paragraph unity. Go back to paragraph B and cross out the sections that are off target — the sections that do not support the opening idea.

You should have crossed out the following sections: "Such students sometimes ... attitude about school"; "These students can often ... work–study programs"; and "Instructors should suggest ... through troubled times."

The difference between these two paragraphs leads us to the first base, or standard, of effective writing: *unity. To achieve unity is to have all the details in your paper related to the single point expressed in the topic sentence, the first sentence.* Each time you think of something to put in, ask yourself whether it relates to your main point. If it does not, leave it out. For example, if you were writing about a certain job as the worst job you ever had and then spent a couple of sentences talking about the interesting people that you met there, you would be missing the first and most essential base of good writing. (The pages ahead will consider the other three bases that you must touch in order to "score" in your writing.)

CHECKING FOR UNITY

To check a paper for *unity*, ask yourself these questions:

1   Is there a clear opening statement of the point of the paper?

2   Is all the material on target in support of the opening point?

Base 2: Support

Activity: Discovering Effective Supporting Details

The following student paragraphs were written on the topic "A Quality of Some Person You Know." Both are unified, but one communicates more clearly and effectively. Which one, and why?

Paragraph A

My Quick-Tempered Father

My father is easily angered by normal everyday mistakes. One day my father told me to wash the car and cut the grass. I did not hear exactly what he said, and so I asked him to repeat it. Then he went into a hysterical mood and shouted, "Can't you hear?" Another time he asked my mother to go to the store and buy groceries with a fifty-dollar bill, and he told her to spend no more than twenty dollars. She spent twenty-two dollars. As soon as he found out, he immediately took the change from her and told her not to go anywhere else for him; he did not speak to her the rest of the day. My father even gives my older brothers a hard time with his irritable moods. One day he told them to be home from their dates by midnight; they came home at 12:15 a.m. He informed them that they were grounded for three weeks. To my father, making a simple mistake is like committing a crime.

Paragraph B

My Generous Grandfather

My grandfather is the most generous person I know. He has given up a life of his own in order to give his grandchildren everything they want. Not only has he given up many years of his life to raise his children properly, but he is now sacrificing many more years to his grandchildren. His generosity is also evident in his relationship with his neighbours, friends, and the members of his church. He has been responsible for many good deeds and has always been there to help all the people around him in times of trouble. Everyone knows that he will gladly lend a helping hand. He is so generous that you almost have to feel sorry for him. If one day he suddenly became selfish, it would be earthshaking. That's my grandfather.

Fill in the blanks: Paragraph _____ makes its point more clearly and effectively

because _____

_____

_____ .

UNDERSTANDING SUPPORT

Paragraph A is more effective, for it offers specific examples that show us the writer's father in action. We see for ourselves why the writer describes the father as quick-tempered. The second writer, on the other hand, gives us no specific evidence. This writer tells us repeatedly that the grandfather is generous but never *shows* us examples of that generosity. Just how, for instance, did the grandfather sacrifice his life for his children and grandchildren? Did he hold two jobs so that his son could go to college, or so that his daughter could have her own car? Does he give up time with his wife and friends to travel every day to his daughter's house to baby-sit, go to the store, and help with the dishes? Does he wear threadbare suits and coats and eat Hamburger Helper and other inexpensive meals (with no desserts) so that he can give money to his children and toys to his grandchildren? We want to *see* and *judge for ourselves* whether the writer is making a valid point about the grandfather, but without specific details we cannot do so. In fact, we have almost no picture of him at all.

Consideration of these two paragraphs leads us to the second base of effective writing: *support*. After realizing the importance of specific supporting details, one student writer revised a paper she had done on a restaurant job as the worst job she ever had. In the revised paper, instead of talking about "unsanitary conditions in the kitchen," she referred to such specifics as "green mould on the bacon" and "ants in the potato salad." All your papers should *show*, not tell, and should include many vivid details!

CHECKING FOR SUPPORT

To check a paper for *support*, ask yourself these questions:

1 Is there *specific* evidence to support the opening point?
2 Is there *enough* specific evidence?

Base 3: Coherence

Activity: Discovering Methods of Creating Coherence

The following two paragraphs were written on the topic "The Best or Worst Job You Ever Had." Both are *unified* and both are *supported*. However, one communicates more clearly and effectively. Which one, and why?

Paragraph A

Pantry Helper

My worst job was as a pantry helper in one of Vancouver's well-known restaurants. I had an assistant from three to six in the afternoon who did little but stand around and eat the whole time she was there. She kept an ear open for the sound of the back door opening, which was a sure sign the boss was coming in. The boss would testily say to me, "You've got a lot of things to do here, Ray. Try to get a move on." I would come in at two o'clock to relieve the woman on the morning shift. If her day was busy, that meant I would have to prepare salads, slice meat and cheese, and so on. Orders for sandwiches and cold platters would come in and have to be prepared. The worst thing about the job was that the heat in the kitchen, combined with my nerves, would give me an upset stomach by seven o'clock almost every night. I might be going to the storeroom to get some supplies, and one of the servers would tell me he or she wanted a bacon, lettuce, and tomato sandwich on white toast. I would put the toast in and head for the supply room, and a server would holler out that the customer was in a hurry. Bluebottle flies would come in through the torn screen in the kitchen window and sting me. I was getting paid only $3.60 an hour. At five o'clock when the dinner rush began, I would be dead tired. Roaches scurried in all directions whenever I moved a box or picked up a head of lettuce to cut.

Paragraph B

My Worst Job

The worst job I ever had was as a server at the Westside Inn. First of all, many of the people I waited on were rude. When a baked potato was hard inside or a salad was flat or their steak wasn't just the way they wanted it, they blamed me, rather than the kitchen. Or they would ask me to pick up their forks, or chase flies from their tables, or even take their children to the bathroom. Also, I had to contend with not only the customers but the kitchen staff as well. The cooks and bussers were often undependable and surly. If I didn't treat them just right, I would wind up having to apologize to customers because their meals came late or their water glasses weren't filled. Another reason I didn't like the job was that I was always moving. Because of the constant line at the door, as soon as one group left, another would take its place. I usually had only a twenty-minute lunch break and a ten-minute break in almost nine hours of work. I think I could have put up with the job if I had been able to pause and rest more often. The last and most important reason I hated the job was my boss. She played favourites with the servers, giving some the best-tipping repeat customers and preferences on holidays. She would hover around during my break to make sure I didn't take a second more than the allotted time. And even when I helped out by working through a break, she never had an appreciative word but would just tell me not to be late for work the next day.

Fill in the blanks: Paragraph _____ makes its point more clearly and effectively because _____

_____

_____ .

UNDERSTANDING COHERENCE

Paragraph B is more effective because the material is *organized clearly* and logically. Using emphatic order, the writer gives us a list of four reasons why the job was so bad: rude customers, unreliable kitchen staff, constant motion, and — most of all — an unfair boss. Further, the writer includes transitional words that act as signposts, making movement from one idea to the next easy to follow. The major transitions are *First of all*, *Also*, *Another reason*, and *The last and most important reason.*

While paragraph A is unified and supported, the writer does not have any clear and consistent way of organizing the material. Partly, emphatic order is used, but this is not made clear by transitions or by saving the most important reason for last. Partly, time order is used, but it moves inconsistently from two to seven to five o'clock.

These two paragraphs lead us to the third base of, or goal for, effective writing: *coherence*. The supporting ideas and sentences in a composition must be organized so that they cohere or "stick together." As has already been mentioned, key techniques for tying material together are

1. clear method of organization (such as time order or emphatic order)
2. transitions, and
3. other connecting words.

CHECKING FOR COHERENCE

To check a paper for coherence, ask yourself these questions:

1 Does the paper have a clear method of organization?

2 Are transitions and other connecting words used to tie together the material?

Base 4: Sentence Skills

Activity: Recognizing Sentence Errors

Two versions of a student's paragraph are given below. Both are *unified*, *supported*, and *organized*, but one version communicates more clearly and effectively. Which one, and why?

Paragraph A

Falling Asleep Anywhere

[1]There are times when people are so tired that they fall asleep almost anywhere. [2]For example, there is a lot of sleeping on the bus or train on the way home from work in the evenings. [3]A man will be reading the newspaper, and seconds later it appears as if he is trying to eat it. [4]Or he will fall asleep on the shoulder of the stranger sitting next to him. [5]Another place where unplanned naps go on is the lecture hall. [6]In some classes, a student will start snoring so loudly that the professor has to ask another student to shake the sleeper awake. [7]A more embarrassing situation occurs when a student leans on one elbow and starts drifting off to sleep. [8]The weight of the head pushes the elbow off the desk, and this momentum carries the rest of the body along. [9]The student wakes up on the floor with no memory of getting there. [10]The worst time to fall asleep is when driving a car. [11]Police reports are full of accidents that occur when people lose consciousness and go off the road. [12]If the drivers are lucky, they are not seriously hurt. [13]One woman's car, for instance, went into the river. [14]She woke up in four feet of water and thought it was raining. [15]When people are really tired, nothing will stop them from falling asleep--no matter where they are.

Paragraph B

Falling Asleep Anywhere

[1]There are times when people are so tired that they fall asleep almost anywhere. [2]For example, on the bus or train on the way home from work. [3]A man will be reading the newspaper, seconds later it appears as if he is trying to eat it. [4]Or he will fall asleep on the shoulder of the stranger sitting next to him. [5]Another place where unplanned naps go on are in the lecture hall. [6]In some classes, a student will start snoring so loudly that the professor has to ask another student to shake the sleeper awake. [7]A more embarrassing situation occurs when a student leans on one elbow and starting to drift off to sleep. [8]The weight of the head push the elbow off the

desk, and this momentum carries the rest of the body along. ⁹The student wakes up on the floor with no memory of getting there. ¹⁰The worst time to fall asleep is when driving a car. ¹¹Police reports are full of accidents that occur when people conk out and go off the road. ¹²If the drivers are lucky they are not seriously hurt. ¹³One womans car, for instance went into the river. ¹⁴She woke up in four feet of water. ¹⁵And thought it was raining. ¹⁶When people are really tired, nothing will stop them from falling asleep-- no matter where they are.

Fill in the blanks: Paragraph _____ makes its point more clearly and effectively because _____

_____

_____.

UNDERSTANDING SENTENCE SKILLS

Paragraph A is more effective because it incorporates *sentence skills*, the fourth base of competent writing. See now if you can identify the ten sentence-skills mistakes in paragraph B. Do this, first of all, by going back and underlining the ten spots in paragraph B that differ in wording or punctuation from paragraph A. Then try to identify the ten sentence-skills mistakes by circling what you feel is the correct answer in each of the ten statements below.

Note: Comparing paragraph B with the correct version may help you guess correct answers even if you are not familiar with the names of certain skills.

1. In word group 2, there is a
    a. missing comma
    b. missing apostrophe
    c. sentence fragment
    d. dangling modifier

2. In word group 3, there is a
    a. run-on
    b. sentence fragment
    c. mistake in subject–verb agreement
    d. mistake involving an irregular verb

3. In word group 5, there is a
    a. sentence fragment
    b. spelling error
    c. run-on
    d. mistake in subject–verb agreement

4. In word group 7, there is a
    a. misplaced modifier
    b. dangling modifier
    c. mistake in parallelism
    d. run-on

5. In word group 8, there is a
   a. nonstandard English verb
   b. run-on
   c. comma mistake
   d. missing capital letter

6. In word group 11, there is a
   a. mistake involving an
      irregular verb
   b. sentence fragment
   c. slang phrase
   d. mistake in subject–verb
      agreement

7. In word group 12, there is a
   a. missing apostrophe
   b. missing comma
   c. mistake involving an
      irregular verb
   d. sentence fragment

8. In word group 13, there is a
   a. mistake in parallelism
   b. mistake involving an
      irregular verb
   c. missing apostrophe
   d. missing capital letter

9. In word group 13, there is a
   a. missing comma around an
      interrupter
   b. dangling modifier
   c. run-on
   d. cliché

10. In word group 15, there is a
    a. missing quotation mark
    b. mistake involving an
       irregular verb
    c. sentence fragment
    d. mistake in pronoun point
       of view

You should have chosen the following answers:

| 1. c | 3. d | 5. a | 7. b | 9. a |
| 2. a | 4. c | 6. c | 8. c | 10. c |

Part Four of this book explains these and other sentence skills. You should review all the skills carefully. Doing so will ensure that you know the most important rules of grammar, punctuation, and usage — rules needed to write clear, error-free sentences.

CHECKING FOR SENTENCE SKILLS

Sentence skills are summarized in the chart on the following page and on the inside front cover of the book.

A Summary of the Four Bases of Effective Writing

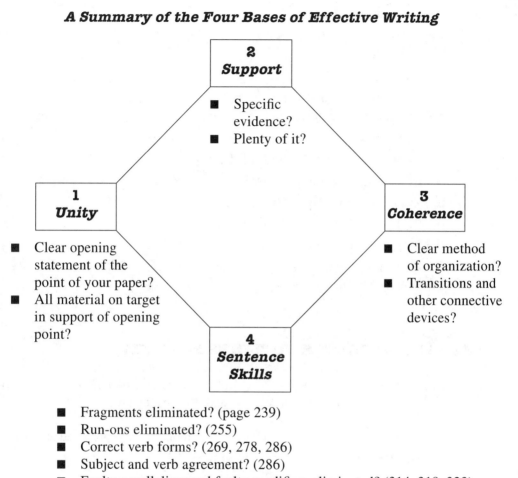

2
Support

■ Specific evidence?
■ Plenty of it?

1
Unity

■ Clear opening statement of the point of your paper?
■ All material on target in support of opening point?

3
Coherence

■ Clear method of organization?
■ Transitions and other connective devices?

4
Sentence Skills

■ Fragments eliminated? (page 239)
■ Run-ons eliminated? (255)
■ Correct verb forms? (269, 278, 286)
■ Subject and verb agreement? (286)
■ Faulty parallelism and faulty modifiers eliminated? (314, 318, 323)
■ Faulty pronouns eliminated? (295)
■ Capital letters used correctly? (332)
■ Punctuation marks where needed?
  (a) Apostrophes (344)   (d) Colons; semi-colons (372–373)
  (b) Quotation marks (353)   (e) Dashes; hyphens (373, 374)
  (c) Commas (361)   (f) Parentheses (374–375)
■ Correct paper format? (327)
■ Needless words eliminated? (412–413)
■ Correct word choices? (408)
■ Possible spelling errors checked? (385, 391–392, 398)
■ Careless errors eliminated through proofreading? (32, 427)
■ Sentences varied? (417)

Practice in Using the Four Bases: Evaluating and Revising

You are now familiar with four bases, or standards, of effective writing: *unity*, *support*, *coherence*, and *sentence skills*. In this closing section, you will expand and strengthen your understanding of the four bases as you work through the following activities:

1 Evaluating Scratch Outlines for Unity
2 Evaluating Paragraphs for Unity
3 Evaluating Paragraphs for Support
4 Evaluating Paragraphs for Coherence
5 Revising Paragraphs for Coherence
6 Evaluating Paragraphs for All Four Bases: Unity, Support, Coherence, and Sentence Skills

1   EVALUATING SCRATCH OUTLINES FOR UNITY

The best time to check a paper for unity is *when it is in outline form*. A scratch outline, as explained on page 23, is one of the best techniques for getting started with a paper.

Look at the following scratch outline that one student prepared and then corrected for unity:

I had a depressing weekend.

1. Hay fever bothered me
2. Had to pay seventy-seven-dollar car bill
3. ~~Felt bad~~
4. Boyfriend and I had a fight
5. ~~Did poorly in my math test today as a result~~
6. My mother yelled at me unfairly

Four reasons support the opening statement that the writer was depressed over the weekend. The writer crossed out "Felt bad" because it was not a specific reason for her depression. (Saying that she felt bad is only another way of saying that she was depressed.) She also crossed out the item about the day's math test because the point she is supporting is that she was depressed over the weekend.

Activity: Checking for Unifying Details

Cross out the items that do not support the opening point in each outline. These items must be omitted in order to achieve paragraph unity.

1. The cost of raising a child keeps increasing.
   a. School taxes get higher every year.
   b. A pair of children's shoes will probably cost $200 by the year 2000.
   c. Overpopulation is a worldwide problem.
   d. Providing nutritious food is more costly because of inflated prices.
   e. Children should work at age sixteen.
2. My father's compulsive gambling hurt our family life.
   a. We were always short of money for bills.
   b. Luckily, my father didn't drink.
   c. My father ignored his children to spend time at the race-track.
   d. Gamblers Anonymous can help compulsive gamblers.
   e. My mother and father argued constantly.
3. There are several ways to get better mileage in your car.
   a. Check air pressure in tires regularly.
   b. Drive at the ninety kilometre per hour speed limit.
   c. Orange and yellow cars are the most visible.
   d. Avoid jackrabbit starts at stop signs and traffic lights.
   e. Always have duplicate ignition and trunk keys.
4. My swimming instructor helped me overcome my terror of the water.
   a. He talked with me about my fears.
   b. I was never good at sports.
   c. He showed me how to hold my head under water and not panic.
   d. I held on to a floating board until I was confident enough to give it up.
   e. My instructor was on the swimming team at his college.
5. Fred Wilkes is the best candidate for provincial premier.
   a. He has fifteen years' experience in provincial parliament.
   b. His son is a professional football player.
   c. He has helped stop air and water pollution in the province.
   d. His opponent has been divorced.
   e. He has brought new industries and jobs to the province.

2 EVALUATING PARAGRAPHS FOR UNITY

Activity: Omitting Nonsupporting Details

Each of the following five paragraphs contains *sentences that are off target* — sentences that do not support the opening point — and so the paragraphs are *not unified*. In the interest of paragraph unity, such sentences must be omitted.

Cross out the irrelevant sentences and write the numbers of those sentences in the spaces provided. The number of spaces will tell you the number of irrelevant sentences in each paragraph.

1.   A Kindergarten Failure

[1]In kindergarten I experienced the fear of failure that haunts many schoolchildren. [2]My moment of panic occurred on my last day in kindergarten at Laurier Public School in Dauphin, Manitoba. [3]My family lived in Manitoba for three years before we moved to Toronto, where my father was a Human Resources manager for The Co-operators Insurance Company. [4]Our teacher began reading a list of names of all those students who were to line up at the door in order to visit the grade one classroom. [5]Our teacher was a pleasant-faced woman who had resumed her career after raising her own children. [6]She called off every name but mine, and I was left sitting alone in the class while everyone else left, the teacher included. [7]I sat there in absolute horror. [8]I imagined that I was the first kid in human history who had flunked things like crayons, sandbox, and sliding board. [9]Without getting the teacher's permission, I got up and walked to the bathroom and threw up into a sink. [10]Only when I ran home in tears to my mother did I get an explanation of what had happened. [11]Since I was to go to a separate school in the fall, I had not been taken with the other children to meet the grade one teacher at the public school. [12]My moment of terror and shame had been only a misunderstanding.

The numbers of the irrelevant sentences: _____ _____

2.   How to Prevent Cheating

[1]Instructors should take steps to prevent students from cheating on exams. [2]To begin with, instructors should stop re-using old tests. [3]A test that has been used even once is soon known on the student grapevine. [4]Students will check with their friends to find out, for example, what was on Dr. Thompson's biology final last term. [5]They may even manage to find a copy of the test itself, "accidentally" not turned in by a former student of Dr. Thompson's. [6]Instructors should also take some common-sense precautions at test time. [7]They should make students separate themselves--by at least one seat--during an exam, and they should watch the class closely. [8]The best place for the instructor to sit is in the rear of the room, so that a student is never sure if the instructor is looking at him or her. [9]Last of all, instructors must make it clear to students that there will be stiff penalties for cheating. [10]One of the problems with our school systems is a lack of discipline. [11]Instructors never used to give in to students' demands or put up with bad behaviour, as they do today. [12]Anyone caught cheating should immediately receive a zero for the exam. [13]A person even suspected of cheating should

be forced to take an alternative exam in the instructor's office. [14]Because cheating is unfair to honest students, it should not be tolerated.

The numbers of the irrelevant sentences: _____ _____

3. A Dangerous Cook

[1]When my friend Tom sets to work in the kitchen, disaster often results. [2]Once he tried to make toasted cheese sandwiches for us by putting slices of cheese in the toaster along with the bread; he ruined the toaster. [3]Unfortunately, the toaster was a fairly new one that I had just bought for him three weeks before, on his birthday. [4]On another occasion, he had cut up some fresh beans and put them in a pot to steam. [5]I was really looking forward to the beans, for I eat nothing but canned vegetables in my dormitory. [6]I, frankly, am not much of a cook either. [7]The water in the Teflon pan steamed away while Tom was on the telephone, and both the beans and the Teflon coating in the pan were ruined. [8]Finally, another time Tom made spaghetti for us, and the noodles stuck so tightly together that we had to cut off slices with a knife and fork. [9]In addition, the meatballs were burned on the outside but almost raw inside. [10]The tomato sauce, on the other hand, turned out well. [11]For some reason, Tom is very good at making meat and vegetable sauces. [12]Because of Tom's kitchen mishaps, I never eat at his place without an antacid tablet in my pocket, or without money in case we have to go out to eat.

The numbers of the irrelevant sentences:

_____ _____ _____ _____ _____

4. Why Adults Visit Amusement Parks

[1]Adults visit amusement parks for several reasons. [2]For one thing, an amusement park is a place where it is acceptable to "pig out" on junk food. [3]At the park, everyone is drinking pop and eating popcorn, ice cream, or hot dogs. [4]No one seems to be on a diet, and so buying all the junk food you can eat is a guilt-free experience. [5]Parks should provide stands where healthier food, such as salads or cold chicken, would be sold. [6]Another reason people visit amusement parks is to prove themselves. [7]They want to visit the park that has the newest, scariest ride in order to say that they went on the Parachute Drop, the seven-story Elevator, the Water Chute, or the Death Slide. [8]Going on a scary ride is a way to feel courageous and adventurous without taking much of a risk. [9]Some rides, however, can be dangerous. [10]Rides that are not properly inspected or maintained have killed people all over the country. [11]A final reason people visit amusement parks is to escape from everyday pressures. [12]When people are poised at the top of a gigantic roller coaster, they are not thinking of bills, work, or personal problems. [13]A scary ride empties the mind of all worries--except

making it to the bottom alive. [14]Adults at an amusement park may claim they have come for their children, but they are there for themselves as well.

The numbers of the irrelevant sentences: _____   _____   _____

5.   My Colour Television

[1]My colour television has given me nothing but heartburn. [2]I was able to buy it a little over a year ago because I had my relatives give me money for my birthday instead of a lot of clothes that wouldn't fit. [3]My first dose of stomach acid came when I bought the set. [4]I let a salesclerk fool me into buying a discontinued model. [5]I realized this a day later, when I saw newspaper advertisements for the set at seventy-five dollars less than I had paid. [6]The set worked so beautifully when I first got it home that I would keep it on until stations signed off for the night. [7]Fortunately, I didn't get any channels showing all-night movies, or I would never have gotten to bed. [8]Then I started developing a problem with the set that involved static noise. [9]For some reason, when certain shows switched into a commercial, a loud buzz would sound for a few seconds. [10]Gradually, this sound began to appear during a show, and to get rid of it, I had to click the dial to another channel and click it back. [11]Sometimes this technique would not work, and I had to pick up the set and shake it to remove the buzzing sound. [12]I actually began to build up my arm muscles shaking my set; I could feel the new muscles working whenever I shot a basketball. [13]When neither of these methods removed the static noise, I would sit popping Tums and wait for the sound to go away. [14]Eventually I wound up slamming the set with my hand again, and it stopped working altogether. [15]My trip to the repair shop cost me $62. [16]The set is working well now, but I keep expecting more trouble.

The numbers of the irrelevant sentences: _____   _____   _____   _____

3   EVALUATING PARAGRAPHS FOR SUPPORT

Activity: Checking for Adequate Support

The five paragraphs that follow lack sufficient supporting details. Identify the spot or spots where more specific details are needed in each paragraph.

1.   Chicken: Our Best Friend

[1]Chicken is the best-selling meat today for a number of good reasons. [2]First of all, its reasonable cost puts it within everyone's reach. [3]Chicken is popular, too, because it can be prepared in so many different ways. [4]It can, for example, be cooked by itself, in spaghetti sauce, or with noodles and gravy. [5]It can be baked, boiled, broiled, or fried. [6]Chicken is also convenient. [7]Last and most important, chicken has a high nutritional value. [8]Two

hundred and fifty grams of chicken contain twenty-eight grams of protein, which is almost half the recommended daily dietary allowance.

Fill in the blanks: The first spot where supporting details are needed occurs after sentence number _____. The second spot occurs after sentence number _____.

2.

A Car Accident

[1]I was on my way home from work when my terrible car accident took place. [2]As I drove my car around the curve of the expressway exit, I saw a number of cars ahead of me, backed up because of a red light at the main road. [3]I slowly came to a stop behind a dozen or more cars. [4]In my rear-view mirror, I then noticed a car coming up behind me that did not slow down or stop. [5]I had a horrible, helpless feeling as I realized the car would hit me. [6]I knew there was nothing I could do to signal the driver in time, nor was there any way I could get away from the car. [7]Minutes after the collision, I picked up my glasses, which were on the seat beside me. [8]My lip was bleeding, and I got out a tissue to wipe it. [9]The police arrived quickly, along with an ambulance for the driver of the car that hit me. [10]My car was so damaged that it had to be towed away. [11]Today, eight years after the accident, I still relive the details of the experience whenever a car gets too close behind me.

Fill in the blank: The point where details are clearly needed occurs after sentence number _____.

3.

Tips on Bringing Up Children

[1]In some ways, children should be treated as mature people. [2]For one thing, adults should not use baby talk with children. [3]Using real words with children helps them develop language skills more quickly. [4]Baby talk makes children feel patronized, frustrated, and confused, for they want to understand and communicate with adults by learning their speech. [5]So animals should be called cows and dogs, not "moo-moos" and "bow-wows." [6]Second, parents should be consistent when disciplining children. [7]For example, if a parent tells a child, "You cannot have dessert unless you put away your toys," it is important that the parent follow through on the warning. [8]By being consistent, parents will teach children responsibility and give them a stable centre around which to grow. [9]Finally, and most important, children should be allowed and encouraged to make simple decisions. [10]Parents will thus be helping their children prepare for the complex decisions that they will have to deal with in later life.

Fill in the blank: The spot where supporting details are needed occurs after sentence number _____.

4.

Telephone Answering Machines

¹Telephone answering machines are beginning to annoy me. ²First of all, I am so surprised when a machine answers the phone that I become tongue-tied or flustered. ³As the metallic voice says, "Please leave your message when you hear the tone," my mind goes blank. ⁴I don't like to hang up, but I know I'll sound like a fool when the owner plays back the message: "Uh, uh, Dr. Spencer, uh, I wanted to make an appointment, uh, wait a minute, for the fifth, no the second, uh, I'm not sure...." ⁵Another problem I have with the machines is that they can malfunction. ⁶I sometimes call big catalogue companies to place orders, and the order is taken by a recording machine. ⁷Just as I'm trying to say, "Two blouses, number B107, size 10," the machine clicks off. ⁸When I call back, another mix-up will occur. ⁹Above all, I dislike the so-called funny tapes that some people now use to answer their phones. ¹⁰One of my co-workers recently bought an answering machine and uses one of these tapes. ¹¹Answering machines seem to be in use everywhere, but I would rather talk to a human voice any time.

Fill in the blanks: The first spot where supporting details are needed occurs

after sentence number _____. The second spot occurs after sentence number

_____.

5.

Being on TV

¹People act a little strangely when a television camera comes their way. ²Some people behave as if a crazy puppet-master is pulling their strings. ³Their arms jerk wildly about, and they begin jumping up and down for no apparent reason. ⁴Often they accompany their body movements with loud screams, squeals, and yelps. ⁵Another group of people engage in an activity known as the cover-up. ⁶They will be calmly watching a sports game or other televised event when they realize the camera is focused on them. ⁷The camera operator can't resist zooming in for a close-up of these people. ⁸Then there are those who practise their funny faces on the unsuspecting public. ⁹They take advantage of the television time to show off their talents, hoping to get that big break that will carry them to stardom. ¹⁰Finally, there are those who pretend they are above reacting for the camera. ¹¹They wipe all expression from their faces and appear to be interested in something else. ¹²Yet if the camera stays on them long enough, they will slyly check to see if they are still being watched. ¹³Everybody's behaviour seems to be slightly strange in front of a TV camera.

Fill in the blanks: The first spot where supporting details are needed occurs

after sentence number _____. The second spot occurs after sentence number

_____.

4   EVALUATING PARAGRAPHS FOR COHERENCE

Activity: Discovering Elements of Coherence

Answer the questions about coherence that follow each of the two paragraphs below.

1.   Why I Have a Home Security Service

> ¹I invested in a home security service for several reasons. ²Most important, I have been frightened by a person who, every few nights for the past several weeks, has been lingering at the edge of my front lawn late at night. ³This person stands, or slowly wanders back and forth under the street-lights. ⁴As if this isn't enough, every time I see this figure, then wait for him to disappear, my phone rings, then no one speaks. ⁵I decided, after finding out the calls couldn't be traced, to look into home security services. ⁶Crime is increasing in my neighbourhood. ⁷One neighbour's house was vandalized while she was at work; the thieves not only stole her appliances but also spray-painted obscene messages on her living-room walls and slashed her furniture. ⁸Not long after this incident, an elderly woman from the apartment house on the corner was robbed and beaten when she answered her doorbell. ⁹Someone claiming to be from the provincial gas company grabbed her purse and threw her to the floor, breaking her hip. ¹⁰I started thinking about my security about a year ago when I was watching the local Calgary news one night. ¹¹It seemed every news story involved violence--rapes, murders, and robberies--inflicted on people "trapped" in their homes, with no form of security protection. ¹²I wondered if some of the victims in the stories would still be alive if a light-motion sensor, video monitor, or 911 alarm system had been in place. ¹³As time passed, I became more convinced that I should install a good security system in the house.

   a.   What words show emphasis in sentence 2? _____

   b.   What is the number of the sentence to which the transition *In addition* could be added? _____

   c.   In sentence 8, to whom does the pronoun *her* refer? _____

   d.   How many times is the key word *security* repeated in the paragraph?

   _____

   e.   The paragraph should use emphatic order. Write a *1* before the reason that is slightly less important than the other two, a *2* before the second-most-important reason, and a *3* before the most important reason.

   _____ Stranger near property and phone calls

   _____ Crime increase in neighbourhood

   _____ News stories about crime victims

2.   Joining a Health Club

¹You should do some investigating before you decide to join a health club. ²Make sure that the contract you sign is accurate. ³Check the agreement to be certain that the fees listed are correct, that the penalties for breaking the contract are specified, and that no hidden charges are included. ⁴As soon as you begin thinking about joining a health club, make a list of your needs and requirements. ⁵Decide if you want (or will ever use) facilities such as a swimming pool, jogging track, steam room, weight machines, racquetball courts, or a bar and lounge. ⁶Your requirements will determine what kind of club you should join and where you will truly get your money's worth. ⁷After you have decided what type of exercise club is best for you, visit some local clubs and check out the facilities. ⁸Make sure that the equipment is in good order, that the changing rooms and exercise areas are clean, and that there are enough instructors for everyone. ⁹Talk to some of the members to see if they are satisfied with the club and its management. ¹⁰Ask them if they have had any problems with contracts, the club's hours, or lack of equipment. ¹¹Once you have found the best club, you are ready to sign a membership contract.

a. What is the number of the sentence to which the word *Also* could be added? _____

b. To whom does the pronoun *them* in sentence 10 refer? _____

c. What is a synonym for *contract* in sentence 3? _____

d. What is the number of a sentence to which the words *For example* could be added? _____

e. The paragraph should use time order. Put a *1* before the step that should come first, a *2* before the intermediate step, and a *3* before the final step.

_____ Make sure the contract is accurate.

_____ Make a list of your needs and requirements.

_____ Visit some local clubs to check facilities.

5 REVISING PARAGRAPHS FOR COHERENCE

The two paragraphs in this section begin with a clear point, but the supporting material that follows the point is not coherent. Read each paragraph and the comments that follow it on how to organize and connect the supporting material. Then do the activity provided in each case.

Paragraph 1

A Difficult Period

Since I arrived on the West Coast in midsummer, I have had the most difficult period of my life. I had to look for an apartment. I found only one place that I could afford, but the owner said I could not move in until it was painted. When I first arrived in Vancouver, my thoughts were to stay with my father and stepmother. I had to set out looking for a job so that I could afford my own place, for I soon realized that my stepmother was not at all happy having me live with them. A three-week search led to a job shampooing rugs for a house-cleaning company. I painted the apartment myself, and at least that problem was ended. I was in a hurry to get settled because I was starting school at the University of British Columbia in September. A transportation problem developed because my stepmother insisted that I return my father's bike, which I was using at first to get to school. I had to rely on a bus that often arrived late, with the result that I missed some classes and was late for others. I had already had a problem with registration in early September. My counsellor had made a mistake with my classes, and I had to register all over again. This meant that I was one week late for class. Now I'm riding to school with a class-mate and no longer have to depend on the bus. My life is starting to order itself, but I must admit that at first I thought it was hopeless to stay here.

Comments on Paragraph 1: The writer of this paragraph has provided a good deal of specific evidence to support the opening point. The evidence, however, needs to be organized. Before starting the paragraph, the writer should have decided to arrange the details by using time order. He or she could then have listed in a scratch outline the exact sequence of events that made for such a difficult period.

Activity 1: Discovering Time Sequence

Here is a list of the various events described by the writer of paragraph 1. Number the events in the correct time sequence by writing a *1* in front of the first event that occurred, a *2* in front of the second event, and so on.

Since I arrived on the West Coast in midsummer, I have had the most difficult period of my life.

———— I had to search for an apartment I could afford.

———— I had to find a job so that I could afford my own place.

———— My stepmother objected to my living with her and my father.

_____ I had to paint the apartment before I could move in.

_____ I had to find an alternative to unreliable bus transportation.

_____ I had to re-register for my courses because of a counsellor's mistake.

Your instructor may now have you rewrite the paragraph on separate paper. If so, be sure to use time signals such as *first, next, then, during, when, after,* and *now* to help guide your reader from one event to the next.

Paragraph 2

Childhood Cruelty

When I was in grade school, my class-mates and I found a number of excuses for being cruel to a boy named Andy Poppovian. Sometimes Andy gave off a strong body odour, and we knew that several days had passed since he had taken a bath. Andy was very slow in speaking, as well as very careless in personal hygiene. The teacher would call on him during a math or grammar drill. He would sit there silently for so long before answering that she sometimes said, "Are you awake, Andy?" Andy had long fingernails that he never seemed to cut, with black dirt caked under them. We called him "Poppy," or we accented the first syllable in his name and mispronounced the rest of it and said to him, "How are you today, POP-o-van?" His name was funny. Other times we called him "Popeye," and we would shout at him, "Where's your spinach today, Popeye?" Andy always had sand in the corners of his eyes. When we played tag games at recess, Andy was always "it" or the first one who was caught. He was so physically slow that five guys could dance around him and he wouldn't be able to touch any of them. Even when we tried to hold a regular conversation with him about sports or a teacher, he was so slow in responding to a question that we got bored talking with him. Andy's hair was always uncombed, and it was often full of white flakes of dandruff. Only when Andy died suddenly of spinal meningitis in grade seven did some of us begin to realize and regret our cruelty toward him.

Comments on Paragraph 2: The writer of this paragraph provides a number of specifics that support the opening point. However, the supporting material has not been organized clearly. Before writing this paragraph, the author should have (1) decided to arrange the supporting evidence by using *emphatic order* and (2) listed in a scratch outline the reasons for the cruelty to Andy Poppovian and the supporting details for each reason. The writer could also have determined which reason to use in the emphatic final position of the paper.

Activity 2: Creating an X-Ray or Skeleton Outline

Create a clear outline for paragraph 2 by filling in the scheme below. The outline is partially completed.

When I was in elementary school, my class-mates and I found a number of excuses for being cruel to a boy named Andy Poppovian.

Reason   1. Physically slow _____

Details   a. _____

          b. Five guys could dance around him. _____

Reason   2. _____

Details   a. _____

          b. Sand in eyes _____

          c. _____

          d. _____

Reason   3. Funny name _____

Details   a. _____

          b. _____

Reason   4. _____

Details   a. _____

          b. In regular conversation _____

Your instructor may have you rewrite the paragraph on separate paper. If so, be sure to introduce each of the four reasons with *transitions* such as *First*, *Second*, *Another reason*, and *Finally*. You may also want to use repeated words, pronouns, and synonyms to help tie your sentences together.

6   EVALUATING PARAGRAPHS FOR ALL FOUR BASES: UNITY, SUPPORT, COHERENCE, AND SENTENCE SKILLS

Activity

In this activity, you will evaluate paragraphs in terms of all four bases: *unity, support, coherence,* and *sentence skills*. Evaluative comments follow each paragraph below. Circle the letter of the statement that best applies in each case.

1.   André's Poutine Palace

There are a number of advantages to eating at André's. The first advantage is that the meals are moderate in price. Another reason is that the surroundings are clean, and the people are pleasant. Also, I have a variety of dinners to choose from. The last and main advantage is that I don't have to plan and prepare the meal.

   a.   The paragraph is not unified.
   b.   The paragraph is not adequately supported.
   c.   The paragraph is not well organized.
   d.   The paragraph does not show a command of sentence skills.
   e.   The paragraph is well written in terms of the four bases.

2.   A Frustrating Moment

A frustrating moment happened to me several days ago. When I was shopping. I had picked up a tube of toothpaste and a jar of skin cream. After the cashier rang up the purchases, which came to $4.15. I handed her $10. Then got back my change, which was only $0.85. I told the cashier that she had made a mistake. Giving me change for $5 instead of $10. But she insist that I had only gave her $5, I became very upset and insist that she return the rest of my change. She refused to do so instead she asked me to step aside so she could wait on the next customer. I stood very rigid, trying not to lose my temper. I simply said to her, I'm not going to leave here, Miss, without my change for $10. Giving in at this point a bell was rung and the manager was summoned. After the situation was explain to him, he ask the cashier to ring off her register to check for the change. After doing so, the cashier was $5 over her sale receipts. Only then did the manager return my change and apologize for the cashier mistake.

   a.   The paragraph is not unified.
   b.   The paragraph is not adequately supported.
   c.   The paragraph is not well organized.
   d.   The paragraph does not show a command of sentence skills.
   e.   The paragraph is well written in terms of the four bases.

3.   Asking Men Out

There are several reasons I have trouble asking guys to go out with me. I have asked some of the fellows in my classes out and have been turned down. This is one reason that I can't talk to them. At one time I was very shy and quiet, and people sometimes didn't even know I was present. I can talk to boys and men now as friends, but as soon as I want to ask them out, I usually start to become quiet, and a little bit of shyness comes out. When I get up the nerve finally, the guy sometimes turns me down, and I swear that I will never ask another one out again. I feel sure I will get a refusal, and I have no confidence in myself. Also, my friends mock me, though they aren't any better than I am. It can become discouraging when your girlfriends get on you. Sometimes I just stand there and wait to hear what line the fellow will use. The one they use a lot is "I like you as a friend, Terri, and it's better to stay that way." Sometimes I want to have the line on a tape recorder, so they won't have to waste their breath on me. All my past experiences with boys and men have been just as bad. One guy used me to make his old girlfriend jealous. Then when he succeeded, he started going out with her again. I had a bad experience when I asked a man I knew to the end-of-semester Turn-About Dance. I spent a lot of money on the evening. Two days later, he told me that he was going steady with another girl. I feel that when I meet someone male I have to be sure I can trust him. I don't want him to turn on me.

a. The paragraph is not unified.

b. The paragraph is not adequately supported.

c. The paragraph is not well organized.

d. The paragraph does not show a command of sentence skills.

e. The paragraph is well written in terms of the four bases.

4.

A Change in My Writing

A technique in my present English class has corrected a writing problem that I've always had. In past English courses, I had major problems with commas in the wrong places, bad spelling, capitalizing the wrong words, sentence fragments, and run-on sentences. I never had any big problems with unity, support, or coherence, but the sentence skills were another matter. They were like little bugs that always appeared to infest my writing. My present instructor asked me to rewrite papers, just concentrating on sentence skills. I thought that the instructor was crazy because I didn't feel that rewriting would do any good. I soon became certain that my instructor was out of his mind, for he made me rewrite my first paper four times. It was very frustrating, for I became tired of doing the same paper over and over. I wanted to curse at my instructor when I'd show him each new draft and he'd find skills mistakes and say "Rewrite." Finally, my papers began to improve and the sentence skills began to fall into place. I was able to see them and correct them before turning in a paper, whereas I couldn't before. Why or how this happened I don't know, but I think that rewriting helped a lot. It took me most of the semester, but I stuck it out and the work paid off.

a. The paragraph is not unified.

b. The paragraph is not adequately supported.

c. The paragraph is not well organized.

    d.   The paragraph does not show a command of sentence skills.

    e.   The paragraph is well written in terms of the four bases.

5.

Luck and Me

    I am a very lucky young man, which has not been the case with the rest of my family. Sometimes when I get depressed, which is too frequently, it's hard to see just how lucky I am. I'm lucky that I'm living in Canada, where I'm free. I'm allowed to worship the way I want to, and that is very important to me. Without a belief in God a person cannot live with any real certainty in life. My family cares about me, though maybe not as much as I would like. My relationship with my girlfriend is a source of good fortune for me. She gives me security and that's something I need a lot. Even with these positive realities in my life, I still seem to find time for insecurity, worry, and, worst of all, depression. At times in my life I have had bouts of terrible luck. But overall, I'm a very lucky guy. I plan to further develop the positive aspects of my life and try to eliminate the negative ones.

    a.   The paragraph is not unified.

    b.   The paragraph is not adequately supported.

    c.   The paragraph is not well organized.

    d.   The paragraph does not show a command of sentence skills.

    e.   The paragraph is well written in terms of the four bases.

Some Suggestions on What to Do Next

1   Read "Providing Examples" (pages 125–133) or "Narrating an Event" (pages 190–197) in Part Two and do the writing assignments given. Then go on to the other types of paragraph development in Part Two.

2   When you have mastered the different types of paragraph development, you may want to work through "Writing the Essay" in Part Three and do one or more of the writing assignments.

3   Continue review of sentence skills in Part Four.

PART TWO

PARAGRAPH
DEVELOPMENT

PREVIEW

Part Two introduces you to paragraph development and gives you practice in the following common types of paragraph development:

Providing Examples
Explaining a Process
Examining Cause and Effect
Comparing or Contrasting
Defining a Term
Dividing and Classifying
Describing a Scene or Person
Narrating an Event
Arguing a Position

After a brief explanation of each type of paragraph development, student paragraphs illustrating each type are presented, followed by questions about those paragraphs. The questions relate to the standards of effective writing described in Part One. You are then asked to write your own paragraph. In each case, writing assignments progress from personal-experience topics to more formal and objective topics. The final assignment, "Writing about a Reading Selection," asks you first to read one of the professional essays in Part Five that illustrates a particular type of development. At times, topic sentences are suggested, so that you can concentrate on (1) making sure your evidence is on target in support of your opening idea, (2) providing plenty of specific supporting details to back up your point, and (3) organizing your supporting material clearly.

INTRODUCTION TO PARAGRAPH DEVELOPMENT

Nine Patterns of Paragraph Development

Traditionally, all writing has been divided into the following forms:

- Exposition

  Examples   Comparison or contrast

  Process   Definition

  Cause and effect   Division and classification

- Description
- Narration
- Argumentation or persuasion

In *exposition*, the writer provides information about and explains a particular subject. Patterns of development in exposition include (1) giving examples, (2) detailing the process of doing or making something, (3) analyzing causes or effects, (4) comparing or contrasting, (5) defining a term or concept, and (6) dividing something into parts or grouping it into categories. In this part of the book, each of the *six patterns of exposition* is presented in a separate chapter.

There are also individual chapters devoted to (7) *description*, (8) *narration*, and (9) *argument*. A *description* is a verbal picture of a person, place, or thing. In *narration*, a writer tells the story of something that happened. *Argumentation* or *persuasion* is an attempt to prove a point or defend an opinion.

You will have a chance, then, to learn how nine different patterns can help organize material in your papers. Each of the nine patterns has its own internal logic and provides its own special strategies for imposing order on your ideas.

As you practise each pattern, you should keep the following two points in mind:

■ In each paragraph that you write, one pattern will predominate, but very often one or more additional patterns may also be involved. For instance, "Good-Bye, Tony" — a paragraph you have already read (page 5) — presents a series of *causes* leading to an *effect:* that the writer will not go out with Tony again. But the writer also presents examples to explain each of the causes (Tony was late, he was bossy, he was abrupt). And there is an element of *narration,* as the writer presents examples that occur from the beginning to the end of the date.

■ More important, a paragraph you write in almost any pattern will probably involve some form of *argumentation.* You will advance a point and then go on to support your point. To convince the reader that your thesis or main idea is valid, you may use a series of *examples,* or *narration,* or *description,* or some other pattern of organization. Among the paragraphs you will read in Part Two, one writer supports the point that a certain pet shop is depressing by providing a number of descriptive details. Another writer labels a certain experience in his life as a "heartbreak" and then uses a narrative to demonstrate the truth of his statement. A third writer advances the opinion that good horror movies can be easily distinguished from bad horror movies and then supplies comparative information about both to support her claim. Much of your writing, in short, will have the purpose of persuading your reader that the idea you have advanced is valid.

Writer, Purpose, and Audience

As was noted in "Important Factors in Writing" in Part One, the purpose of most writing is to inform, entertain, or persuade; in this book, most of your writing will involve some form of persuasion or information. The audience for your writing is primarily your instructors and sometimes other students—who are really a symbol for any general audience of educated adults. Sometimes, however, you must write for *more specific audiences;* therefore, it is important to develop the skills of

1. choosing appropriate words
2. adopting an appropriate tone of voice
3. for a particular purpose and particular readers

This part of the book, then, includes assignments that ask you to write with a *very specific purpose in mind* and *for a very specific audience.* You will be asked, for example, to imagine yourself as a TV critic addressing parents at a school, as a graduate of a local high school advising a counsellor there about a drug problem, as an aide at a day-care centre preparing instructions for children, as an apartment tenant complaining to an owner about neighbours, or as a client of a video dating service introducing himself or herself to potential dates. Through these and other assignments, you will learn how to adjust your style and tone of voice to a given writing situation.

Tools for Paragraph Development

USING PART TWO: THE PROGRESSION IN EACH CHAPTER

After each type of essay development is explained, student papers illustrating that type are presented, followed by questions about the papers. The questions relate to *unity*, *support*, and *coherence* — the principles of effective writing explained earlier in the book. You are then asked to write your own essay. In most cases, the first assignment is fairly structured and provides a good deal of guidance for the writing process. The other assignments offer a wide choice of writing topics. One assignment requires writing with a specific purpose and for a specific audience, and one assignment relates to the reading selections in Part Five.

USING PEER REVIEW

In addition to having your instructor as an audience for your writing, you will benefit by having another student in your class as an audience. On the day a paper is due, or on a day when you are writing papers in class, your instructor may ask you to pair up with another student. That student will read your paper, and you will read his or her paper.

Ideally, read the other paper aloud while your peer listens. If that is not practical, read it in a whisper while your peer looks on. As you read, both you and your peer should look and listen for spots where the paper does not read smoothly and clearly. Check or circle the trouble spots where your reading snags.

Your peer should then read your paper, marking possible trouble spots while doing so. Then each of you should do the following three things.

1 Identification

On a separate sheet of paper, write at the top the title and author of the paper you have read. Underneath that, write your name as the reader of the paper.

2 Scratch or Skeleton Outline

"X-ray" the paper for its inner logic by making up a scratch or skeleton outline. The skeleton outline need be no more than twenty words or so, but it should show clearly the logical foundation, the "bones" on which the paper is built. It should identify and summarize the overall point of the paper and the three areas of support for the main point.

Your outline can look as follows.

Point: _____

Support:

(1) _____

(2) _____

(3) _____

For example, here is a scratch outline of the paper on a new puppy in the house on pages 142–143:

Point: A new puppy can have drastic effects in a house.

Support:

(1) Keeps family awake at night

(2) Destroys possessions

(3) Causes arguments

3 Comments

Under the outline, write the heading "Comments." Here is what you should comment on:

■ Look at the spots where your reading of the paper snagged: Are words missing or misspelled? Is there a lack of parallel structure (see pages 323–326)? Are there punctuation mistakes? Is the meaning of a sentence confused? Try to figure out what the problems are and suggest ways of fixing them.

■ Are there spots in the paper where you see problems with *unity*, *support*, or *organization?* If so, offer comments. For example, you might say, "More details are needed in the first supporting paragraph," or "Some of the details in the last supporting paragraph don't really back up your point."

■ Finally, make note of something you really liked about the paper, such as good use of transitions or an especially realistic or vivid specific detail.

After you have completed your evaluation of the paper, give it to your peer. Your instructor may provide you with the option of rewriting a paper in light of this feedback. Whether or not you rewrite, be sure to hand in the peer evaluation form with your paper.

USING A PERSONAL CHECKLIST

After you have completed a paper, there are three ways you should check it yourself. You should *always* do the first two checks, which take only a couple of minutes. Ideally, you should take the time to do the detailed final check as well.

1 Read the paper *out loud*. If it does not sound right — that is, if it does not read smoothly and clearly — then make the changes needed to ensure that it does.

2 Make sure you can answer clearly and concisely two basic questions: "What is the point of my essay? What are the three distinct bits of support for my point?"

3 Last, evaluate your paper in terms of the detailed checklist given on the following page. The checklist is also reproduced on the inside front cover of this book.

Checklist of the Four Bases in Effective Writing

Use the questions below as a guide in both writing and evaluating a paper. Numbers in parentheses refer to the pages that explain each skill.

Base 1: Unity

- Clear opening statement of the point of your paper? (pages 43–45; 53–56)
- All material on target in support of opening point? (92–93; 102–106)

Base 2: Support

- *Specific* evidence? (45–51; 61–64; 94–95)
- Plenty of it? (51–52; 65–68; 106–108)

Base 3: Coherence

- Clear method of organization? (72–74; 81–86; 95–97; 110–113)
- Transitions and other connective devices? (74–77; 87–89)

Base 4: Sentence Skills

- Fragments eliminated? (239)
- Run-on sentences eliminated? (255)
- Correct verb forms? (269; 278; 286)
- Subject and verb agreement? (286)
- Faulty modifiers and faulty parallelism eliminated? (314; 318; 323)
- Faulty pronouns eliminated? (295)
- Capital letters used correctly? (332)
- Punctuation marks where needed?
  - **a** Apostrophes (344)
  - **b** Quotation marks (353)
  - **c** Commas (361)
  - **d** Colons; semi-colons (372–373)
  - **e** Dashes; hyphens (373; 374)
  - **f** Parentheses (374–375)
- Correct paper format? (327)
- Needless words eliminated? (412–413)
- Correct word choices? (408)
- Possible spelling errors checked? (385; 391–392; 398)
- Careless errors removed through editing and through proofreading? (32; 427)
- Sentences varied? (417)

PROVIDING
EXAMPLES

In our daily conversations, we often provide *examples* — that is, details, particulars, specific instances — to explain statements that we make. In the box below are several statements and supporting examples:

Statement	**Examples**
The IGA was crowded today.	There were at least four carts waiting at each of the check-out counters, and it took me forty-five minutes to get through a line.
The corduroy shirt I bought is poorly made.	When I washed it, the colours began to fade, one button cracked and another fell off, a shoulder seam opened, and the sleeves shrank almost two inches.
My son Peter is unreliable.	If I depend on him to turn off a pot of beans in ten minutes, the family is likely to eat burned beans. If I ask him to turn down the thermostat before he goes to bed, the heat is likely to stay on all night.

In each case, the examples help us *see for ourselves* the truth of the statement that has been made. In paragraphs, too, explanatory examples help the audience fully understand a point. Lively, specific examples also add interest to a paper.

In this chapter, you will be asked to provide a series of examples to support a topic sentence. Providing examples to support a point is one of the most common and simplest methods of paragraph development. First read the paragraphs ahead; they all use examples to develop their points. Then answer the questions that follow.

PARAGRAPHS TO CONSIDER

Inconsiderate Drivers

[1]Some people are inconsiderate drivers. [2]In the city, they will at times stop right in the middle of the street while looking for a certain home or landmark. [3]If they had any consideration for the cars behind them, they would pull over to the curb first. [4]Other drivers will suddenly slow down unexpectedly at a city intersection to make a right or left turn. [5]The least they could do is use their turn signals to let those behind them know in advance of their intention. [6]On the highway, a common example of inconsiderateness is night drivers who fail to turn off their high beams, creating glare for cars approaching in the other direction. [7]Other rude highway drivers move to the second or passing lane and then stay there, making it impossible for cars behind to go around them. [8]Yet other drivers who act as if they have special privileges are those who do not wait their turn in bottleneck situations where the cars in two lanes must merge alternately into one lane. [9]Perhaps the most inconsiderate drivers are those who throw garbage out their windows, creating litter that takes away some of the pleasure of driving and that must be paid for with everyone's tax dollars.

The Cruelty of Children

[1]Children can be very cruel. [2]For one thing, they start very early to use words that wound. [3]Three-year-olds in nursery school, for example, call each other "dum-dum" or "weirdo," and slightly older children use nicknames like "fatty" or "four-eyes" to tease their school-mates. [4]Children who are just a bit older learn facts about other kids from their parents, and use those facts to make someone break down and cry. [5]Children also attack each other physically. [6]For instance, whenever a group of elementary-school children come home from school, there is a lot of pushing, tripping, punching, and pinching. [7]An argument may end in shoving and hair-pulling. [8]But far worse than harsh words or physical violence is the emotional hurt that children can cause their class-mates by their cruelty. [9]By junior high school days, for example, young teenagers start to shut out the people they do not like. [10]They ignore the kids whose looks, clothes, interests, or finances differ from their own. [11]Popular kids form groups, and the unpopular ones are left to face social isolation, loneliness, and depression. [12]Many adults think that childhood is an ideal time, but terribly cruel things can happen then.

An Egotistical Neighbour

[1]I have an egotistical neighbour named Alice. [2]If I tell Alice how beautiful I think the dress she is wearing is, she will take the time to tell

me the name of the store where she bought it, the type of material that was used in making it, and the price. ³Alice is also egotistical when it comes to her children. ⁴Because they are hers, she thinks they just have to be the best children on the block. ⁵I am wasting my time by trying to tell her I have seen her kids expose themselves on the street or take things from parked cars. ⁶I do not think parents should praise their children too much. ⁷Kids have learned how to be good at home and simply awful when they are not at home. ⁸Finally, Alice is quick to describe the furnishings of her home for someone who is meeting her for the first time. ⁹She tells how much she paid for the panelling in her dining room. ¹⁰She mentions that she has two colour television sets and that they were bought at an expensive furniture store. ¹¹She lets the person know that the sound system in her living room cost more than a thousand dollars, and that she has such a large collection of CDs that she would not be able to play them all in one week. ¹²Poor Alice is so self-centred that she never realizes how boring she can be.

■ Questions

About Unity

1. Which two sentences in "An Egotistical Neighbour" are irrelevant to the point

   that Alice is egotistical? (*Write the sentence numbers here.*) _____   _____

About Support

2. In "Inconsiderate Drivers," how many examples are given of inconsiderate drivers?

   _____ one _____ two _____ four _____ six

3. After which sentence in "The Cruelty of Children" are specific details needed?

   _____

About Coherence

4. What are the three main transition words used in "The Cruelty of Children"?

   a. _____

   b. _____

   c. _____

5. What are the two main transition words in "An Egotistical Neighbour"?

   a. _____

   b. _____

6. Which two paragraphs clearly use emphatic order to organize their details, saving for last what the writers regard as their most important examples?

   _____

   _____

WRITING AN EXAMPLES PARAGRAPH

■ Writing Assignment 1

The assignment here is to complete an unfinished paragraph (opposite page), which has as its topic sentence, "My husband, Roger, is a selfish person." Provide the supporting details needed to fill out the examples of Roger's selfishness. The first example has been done for you.

How to Proceed: To do this assignment, first jot down on separate paper a couple of answers for each of the following questions.

a What specific vacations did the family go on because Roger wanted to go? Give places, length of stay, time of year. What vacations has the family never gone on (for example, to visit the wife's relatives), even though the wife wanted to?

b What specific items has Roger bought for himself (rather than for the whole family's use) with leftover budget money?

c What chores and duties involved in the everyday caring for the children has Roger never done?

Note: Your instructor may ask you to work with one or two other students in generating the details needed to develop the three examples in the paragraph. Each group may then be asked to read their details aloud, with the class deciding which details are the most effective for each example.

Here and in general in your writing, try to generate *more* supporting material than you need. You are then in a position to choose the *most convincing* details for your paper. Now take your best details, reshape them as needed, and use them to complete the paragraph about Roger.

A Selfish Person

My husband, Roger, is a selfish person. For one thing, he refuses to move out of the city, even though it is a bad place to raise the children. We inherited some money when my parents died, and it might be enough for a down payment on a small house in a nearby town. But Roger says he would miss his buddies in the neighbourhood.

Also, when we go on vacation, we always go where Roger wants to go.

_____

_____

_____

_____

_____

_____

Another example of Roger's selfishness is that he always spends any budget money that is left over.

_____

_____

_____

_____

_____

_____

Finally, Roger leaves all the work of caring for the children to me.

_____

_____

_____

_____

_____

_____

■ **Writing Assignment 2**

Write a paragraph about one quality of a person you know well. The person might be a member of your family, a friend, a room-mate, a boss or supervisor, a neighbour, an instructor, or someone else. Listed on the next page are some descriptive words that can be applied to people. They are only suggestions; you can write about any other specific quality.

Honest	Hard-working	Jealous
Bad-tempered	Supportive	Materialistic
Ambitious	Suspicious	Sarcastic
Bigoted	Open-minded	Self-centred
Considerate	Lazy	Spineless
Argumentative	Independent	Good-humoured
Soft-hearted	Stubborn	Co-operative
Energetic	Flirtatious	Disciplined
Patient	Irresponsible	Sentimental
Reliable	Stingy	Defensive
Generous	Trustworthy	Dishonest
Persistent	Aggressive	Insensitive
Shy	Courageous	Unpretentious
Sloppy	Compulsive	Neat

How to Proceed

a **Prewrite.** Two good prewriting methods are *listing examples* and *asking yourself questions about your topic.*

Make a list of examples that will support your topic sentence. For example, if you decide to write about your brother's irresponsibility, jot down several examples of times when he showed this quality. Part of your list might look like this:

```
Lost rent money
Forgot to return borrowed textbooks
Didn't show up for big family dinner
Left dog alone in the apartment for two days
Left my bike out in the rain
Missed conference with instructor
```

Another way to get started is to ask yourself questions about your topic and write down the answers. Again, if you were writing about your brother's irresponsibility, you might ask yourself questions such as these:

How has Bill been irresponsible?
What are examples of times he has shown this quality?
What happened on these occasions?
Who was involved?
What were the results of his actions?

The answers to these questions should serve as an excellent source of details for the paragraph.

b **Group details.** Then prepare a scratch outline made up of the strongest examples from the prewriting material you generated above. Note that as you make this outline, you should *group related details together*. For example, the items in the list about the irresponsible brother might be categorized as follows:

At apartment
Lost rent money
Left dog alone in apartment

At home
Missed family dinner
Left bike in rain

At school
Didn't return textbooks
Missed conference

c **Write a topic sentence.** Next, write out your topic sentence. This first sentence should *tell the name* of the person you are writing about, *your relationship* to the person, and the *specific quality* you are focusing on. For example, you might write, "Linda is a flirtatious girl I know at school," or "Stubbornness is Uncle Carl's outstanding characteristic."

Do not make the mistake of beginning with more than one quality ("I have a cousin named Alan who is soft-hearted and generous") or with a general quality ("My boss is a good person"). Focus on *one specific quality*.

d **Develop specific details.** Develop your examples with specific details. Remember that you don't want to *tell* us about the person; rather, you want to *show* the person to us by detailing words, actions, or both. You might want to go back and reread the examples provided in "An Egotistical Neighbour."

e **Revise your details.** As you are writing drafts of your paragraph, ask yourself repeatedly: "Do my examples truly show that my subject has a certain quality?" Your aims in this assignment are twofold: (1) to provide *specific* details for the quality in question and (2) to provide *enough* specific details so that you solidly support your point.

f **Edit for sentence skills.** When you are satisfied that you have provided effective examples, edit your paragraph carefully for the sentence-skills mistakes listed on the inside front cover. In addition, make sure you can answer *Yes* to the questions on unity, support, and coherence.

■ Writing Assignment 3

Write a paragraph that uses examples to develop one of the following statements or a related statement of your own.

1. _____ is a distracting place to try to study.
2. The daily life of a student is filled with conflicts.
3. Abundant evidence exists that Canada has become a health-conscious nation.
4. Despite modern appliances, many household chores are still drudgery.
5. One of my instructors, _____, has some good (*or* unusual) teaching techniques.
6. Wasted electricity is all around us.
7. Life in Canada (or your city or town) is faster-paced than ever before.
8. Violence on television is widespread.
9. Women today (*or* men today) are wearing some ridiculous fashions.
10. Some students here at _____ do not care about learning (*or* are overly concerned about grades).

Be sure to choose examples that truly support your point. They should be relevant facts, statistics, personal experiences, or incidents you have heard or read about. Organize your paragraph by grouping several examples that support your point. Save the most vivid, convincing, or important example for last.

■ Writing Assignment 4

Imagine that you are a television critic and are still living near the high school you attended. The principal is planning a special parents' evening and would like you to make a speech on the topic "Television and the Responsible Parent." You accept the invitation and decide to organize your talk around this thesis: "There are three television programs that represent worthwhile viewing for families." Write a one-paragraph summary of your talk.

To make an outline for your speech, think of three programs you would recommend for viewing by all members of a family. Write down the titles of the programs, and then list under each the specific features that made you choose that show.

■ Writing Assignment 5

Writing about a Reading Selection: Read Mary Curran's selection "The True Meaning of Literacy" on pages 501–502. Then write a paragraph in which you give a series of examples which support your agreement or disagreement with one of the points in Curran's article.

You might begin with a topic sentence such as the following:

> I can relate to the pleasure Mary Curran's students found in writing personal letters to her, and I strongly agree with her point that casual writing increases a student's confidence in his or her ability to write.
>
> a. Example 1
> b. Example 2
> c. Example 3

Your supporting examples might come from your own classroom experiences or from those of friends or family.

Alternatively, you could write a paragraph in which you disagree with one of Mary Curran's views, again giving a series of examples to back up your viewpoint. For instance:

> I disagree with Curran's view that Canadian education puts too much emphasis on practical goals and accurate marking in the teaching of writing.
>
> a. Example 1
> b. Example 2
> c. Example 3

To get started, reread Curran's article and note ideas or examples you can think of which support or refute the author's points. Eventually, you'll find that there is one point in particular for which you have more evidence than for some of the others. Write that point on a fresh piece of paper, and note all the examples you can generate for that point. Select your strongest examples, decide on your order of presentation (remembering to save your strongest point for the final, or most emphatic, position), and begin the first draft of your paragraph.

The hints on "How to Proceed" on pages 130–132 may help you as you work on your paragraph.

EXPLAINING A PROCESS

Every day we perform many activities that are processes — that is, series of steps carried out in a definite order. Many of these processes are familiar and automatic: for example, tying shoelaces, changing bed linen, using a vending machine, and starting a car. We are thus seldom aware of the sequence of steps making up each activity. In other cases, such as when we are asked for directions to a particular place or when we try to read and follow the directions for a new board game, we may be painfully conscious of the whole series of steps involved in the process.

In this section, you will be asked to write a process paragraph — one that explains clearly how to do or make something, or, alternatively, how something is done or made. "How to" process writing is sometimes called *prescriptive process writing;* it *prescribes* a way of doing something, or gives a set of instructions. "How to" process writing speaks actively and directly to the reader, saying: "Do this...." Process writing which explains or describes *how something is done* is sometimes called *descriptive process writing.* This type of process writing *describes* the stages by which something was achieved or completed; it explains a finished procedure or product, and it does not always address the reader actively or directly. To prepare for this assignment, you should first read the student process papers below and then respond to the questions that follow.

Note: In process writing, where you are often giving instruction, the pronoun *you* can appropriately be used. Two of the model paragraphs here use *you* — as indeed does much of this book, which gives instruction on how to write effectively. *Except for writing process paragraphs or essays, though, do not use* you *in your writing.*

PARAGRAPHS TO CONSIDER

Prescriptive Process Paragraphs

Sneaking into the House at Night

[1]The first step I take is bringing my key along with me. [2]Obviously, I don't want to have to knock on the door at 1:30 in the morning and rouse my parents out of bed. [3]Second, I make it a point to stay out past midnight. [4]If I come in before then, my father is still up. [5]I find it hard to face his disapproving look after a night out. [6]All I need in my life right now is for him to make me feel guilty. [7]Trying to make it as a college student is as much as I'm ready to handle. [8]Next, I am careful to be very quiet upon entering the house. [9]This involves lifting the front door up slightly as I open it, so that it does not creak. [10]It also means treating the floor and steps to the second floor like a minefield, stepping carefully over the spots that squeak. [11]Finally, I stop briefly in the bathroom without turning on the light and then tiptoe to my room, put my clothes in a pile on a chair, and slip quietly into bed. [12]With my careful method of sneaking into the house at night, I have avoided some major hassles with my parents.

How to Harass an Instructor

[1]You can use a number of time-proven techniques to harass an instructor. [2]First of all, show up late for class, so that you can interrupt the beginning of the instructor's presentation. [3]Saunter in nonchalantly and try to find a seat by a friend. [4]In a normal tone of voice, speak some words of greeting to your friends as you sit down, and scrape your chair as loudly as possible while you make yourself comfortable in it. [5]Then just sit there and do anything but pay attention. [6]When the instructor sees that you are not involved in the class, he or she may pop a quick question, probably hoping to embarrass you. [7]You should then say, in a loud voice, "I DON'T KNOW THE ANSWER." [8]This declaration of ignorance will throw the instructor off guard. [9]If the instructor then asks you why you don't know the answer, say "I don't even know what page we're on" or "I thought the assignment was boring, so I didn't do it." [10]Give the impression that there is no sane reason why you should be expected to know the answer. [11]After the instructor calls on someone else, get up loudly from your seat, walk to the front of the classroom, and demand to be excused for an emergency meeting in the washroom. [12]Stay at least fifteen minutes and take your time coming back. [13]If the instructor asks you where you've been when you re-enter the room, simply ignore the question and go to your seat. [14]Flop into your chair, slouching back and extending your legs as far out as possible. [15]When the instructor informs you of the assignment that the class is working on, heave an exaggerated sigh and very slowly open up your book and start turning the pages. [16]As soon as he or she stops looking at

you, rest your elbows on the desk, hold your pencil between your fingertips, and gaze off into space. [17]The instructor will look at you and wonder whether it wouldn't have been better to go into business instead of education.

Merging with Supertraffic

[1]If you want to drive on any Canadian expressway, throughway, or freeway and live to tell your tale, be prepared for treacherous supertraffic, and the steps you must follow to merge with it, as you approach the on-ramp. [2]To begin, you must prepare yourself mentally as you approach the signage for the ramp. [3]Do not give in to panic as you spot the sign alerting you to the five kilometres before your turn-off. [4]Instead, as you signal and try to ease over in the right direction, repeat to yourself, in a calm tone of voice, "Other drivers do not want to kill me. [5]They are sane people. [6]Someone will let me in that lane." [7]Next, as you actually complete the successful crossing of two to three lanes, you should practise the technique of simultaneously looking in three directions at once. [8]In each moment, look ahead at the ramp you must enter, check your rear-view for tailgaters, and lift your eyes to the volume of the traffic flow on your six-lane goal. [9]Following this, you will now be dealing with those six lanes of supertraffic. [10]Try to maintain the speed at which you are comfortable. [11]Do not slow down to check out orange construction signs or stalled cars. [12]This will merely create a massive pile-up behind you. [13]Finally, the trickiest point is to actually enter the lane in which you want to drive. [14]At some point, you have become aware of how much traffic there is in those six lanes, and how likely you are to reach either the centre or fast lane; you have to make a move, usually across two lanes of transport trucks. [15]You can use your directional signals, although these will have little effect on most drivers. [16]The best way to continue the merging or lane-changing process is to check your rear-view mirror until you spot a timid-looking driver slightly behind you, or a transport driver who hasn't yet geared up to full speed. [17]These will slow down as you cross their lanes and make the successful transition into the next-fastest lane. [18]Never cut across in front of a black number-modelled Euro-import or in front of one of the "carboyz" in a Trans Am. [19]Such people will speed up, not slow down. [20]These instructions should enable you either to enter the centre lane or to join those stuck at a slightly higher speed in the "fast lane." [21]Congratulations! You are now part of supertraffic.

A Descriptive Process Paragraph

The No-Fear Approach to Horror Movies

[1]A number of steps can be taken to allow enjoyment of a horror movie without fear. [2]If, like me, you usually cringe and occasionally want to leave during <u>Feast of the Dead, Part XV</u>, there are several fool-proof steps, tried

and tested repeatedly by the writer to ensure that future gore-and-splatter experiences are actually enjoyable. [3]First, before going to the movie, magazines and TV shows which deal with preproduction tricks, special effects, and computerized dummies should be examined. [4]The exploding heads and guts you will see will become what they are: plastic, chemical, and computer-generated hoaxes. [5]Next, your viewing companions should be chosen with care. [6]What you seek are people who laugh loudly and frequently during the really scary parts of any horror movie. [7]You will find it difficult to scream or want to vomit while your friends are laughing uproariously. [8]Peer pressure and the infectious nature of laughter are excellent fear-suppressants. [9]Finally, the purchase of a lot of complicated, hard-to-manage food is very important. [10]Lap-placement, sharing your hoard, and the noise produced by trying to finish all those nachos, extra-greasy bags of popcorn, and melting ice cream bars result in enough distractions to keep you from ever paying much attention to the movie screen. [11]These three techniques are guaranteed by my personal testing to produce an evening of fearless horror.

Note: This paragraph *describes* a method or procedure. The writer is reviewing a set of experiences he or she has undergone, and is *describing* how these have worked. For students in technical or mechanical courses, *descriptive* process writing, which explains *how* something is done, is extremely useful.

■ Questions

About Unity

1. Which paragraph lacks a topic sentence?

   _____

2. Which two sentences in "Sneaking into the House at Night" should be eliminated in the interest of paragraph unity? (*Write the sentence numbers here.*)

   _____   _____

About Support

3. After which sentence in "How to Harass an Instructor" are supporting details needed? _____

4. Summarize the four steps in the process of merging with supertraffic.

   a. _____

   b. _____

   c. _____

   d. _____

About Coherence

5. Do these paragraphs use time order or emphatic order?

   _____

6. List the three main transition words in "The No-Fear Approach to Horror Movies."

   a. _____   c. _____

   b. _____

WRITING A PROCESS PARAGRAPH

■ Writing Assignment 1

Choose one of the topics below to write about in a process paper.

> How to change a car or bike tire
> How to bathe a dog or cat
> How to get rid of house or garden pests such as mice, ants, or wasps
> How to fall asleep (if you need to and can't)
> How to play a simple game like checkers, tic-tac-toe, or an easy card game
> How to load a van
> How to learn a song
> How to live on a limited budget
> How to shorten a skirt or pants
> How to plant a garden
> How to take care of plants
> How to fix a leaky faucet, a clogged drain, or the like
> How to build a campfire
> How to make your house look lived in when you are away
> How to study for an important exam
> How to paint a ceiling
> How to conduct a yard or garage sale
> How to wash dishes efficiently, clean a bathroom, do laundry, or the like

How to Proceed

a   Begin by prewriting. Freewrite for ten minutes on the topic you have chosen. Do not worry about spelling, grammar, organization, or other matters of correct form. Just write whatever comes into your head regarding the topic. Keep writing for more than ten minutes if added details about the topic occur to you. This freewriting will give you a base of raw material that you can draw on in the next phase of your work on the paragraph. After freewriting, you should have a sense of whether there is enough material available for you to write a process paragraph about the topic. If so, continue as explained below. If not, choose another topic and freewrite about *it* for ten minutes.

b **Write a clear, direct topic sentence about the process** you are going to describe. In your topic sentence, you can (1) say that it is important for your audience to know about the process ("Knowing how to study effectively for a major exam can mean the difference between passing and failing a course"), or (2) state your opinion of the process ("My technique for building a campfire is almost foolproof").

c **List all the steps** you can think of that may be part of the process. Don't worry, at this point, about how each step fits or whether certain steps overlap. Here, for example, is the list prepared by the author of "Sneaking into the House at Night":

Quiet on stairs	Lift up front door
Come in after Dad's asleep	Late dances on Saturday night
House is freezing at night	Don't turn on bathroom light
Bring key	Avoid squeaky spots on floor
Know which steps to avoid	Get into bed quietly

d **Number your items in time order**; strike out items that do not fit in the list; add others that come to mind. Thus:

~~Quiet on stairs~~

2 Come in after Dad's asleep

~~House is freezing at night~~

1 Bring key

5 Know which steps to avoid

3 Lift up front door

~~Late dances on Saturday night~~

6 Don't turn on bathroom light

4 Avoid squeaky spots on floor

8 Get into bed quietly

7 *Undress quietly*

e **Use your list as a guide to write the first rough draft** of your paper. As you write, try to think of additional details that will support your opening sentence. Do not expect to finish your paper in one draft. You should, in fact, be ready to write a series of lists and drafts as you work toward the goals of unity, support, and coherence.

f **Keep the point of view in your paragraph consistent.** For example, if you begin to write "How *I* got rid of mice" (first person), do not switch suddenly to "*You* must buy the right traps" (second person). Write your paragraph either from the first-person point of view (*I-we*) *or* from the second-person point of view (*you*). As noted at the beginning of this chapter, do not hesitate to use the second-person *you* point of view. A process paragraph in which you give instructions is one of the few situations in formal writing where the second-person *you* is acceptable.

g **Be sure to use some transitions** such as *first*, *next*, *also*, *then*, *after*, *now*, *during*, and *finally* so that your paper moves smoothly and clearly from one step in the process to the next.

h **Refer to the checklist** on the inside front cover while working on your paper, to make sure you can answer *Yes* to the questions about unity, support, and coherence. Also, refer to the checklist when you edit the next-to-final draft of your paper for sentence-skills mistakes, including spelling.

■ Writing Assignment 2

For this assignment, you will be working with more general topics than those in Writing Assignment 1. You will find, in many cases, that you must invent your own steps in a particular process. You will also have to make decisions about how many steps to include and what order to place them in.

How to break a bad habit such as smoking, overeating, or excessive drinking
How to improve a course you have taken
How to make someone you know happy
How to go about meeting people
How to discipline a child
How to improve the place where you work
How to show appreciation to others
How to make someone forgive you
How to con an instructor
How to make yourself depressed
How to get over a broken relationship
How to procrastinate
How to flirt

■ Writing Assignment 3

Everyone is an expert at something. Write a process paragraph on some skill that you can perform very well. The skill might be, for example, "refereeing a game," "fishing for perch," "playing third base," "putting up a tent," "making an ice cream soda," "becoming a long-distance runner," or "fine-tuning a car engine." Write

from the point of view that "This is how _____ should be done."

■ Writing Assignment 4

Option 1:   You have a part-time job helping out in a day-care centre. The direc-tor, who is pleased with your work and wants to give you more responsibility, has assigned you to be in charge of a group activity (for example, an exercise session, an alphabet lesson, or a valentine-making project). But before you actually begin the activity, the director wants to see a summary of how you would go about it. What advance preparation would be needed, and what exactly would you be doing throughout the time of the project? Write a paragraph explaining the steps you would follow in conducting the activity. For assistance, consider the passages about *descriptive* process writing on page 134 and the example on pages 136–137.

Option 2:   Alternatively, write an explanation you might give to one of the children on how to do a simple classroom task — serving juice and cookies, get-ting ready for nap time, watering a plant, putting toys or other classroom mate-rials away, or any other task you choose. Explain each step of the task in a way that a child would understand.

■ Writing Assignment 5

Writing about a Reading Selection: Read the selection titled "Power Learning" on pages 477–482. Then write a process paragraph or essay on how you could go about improving your study skills. Your topic sentence or thesis might be, "To become a better student, I will take the following steps to strengthen my time control, my classroom note-taking, and my textbook study."

To get started, read through "Power Learning" again and jot down a list of all the suggestions that will be helpful for you. Then pull out the five or six that seem most important. Next, put the steps into a sequence: put hints on time con-trol first, hints on note-taking second, and hints on textbook study third. Then prepare a rough draft of your paper in which you present each step and explain briefly why it is valuable for you. Use transitions and synonyms such as *One step*, *Another way*, *A third study aid*, *Next*, *A fifth means*, and *Last* as you develop your ideas.

EXAMINING CAUSE AND EFFECT

What caused Pat to drop out of school? Why are soap operas so popular? Why does our football team do so poorly each year? How has retirement affected Dad? What effects does divorce have on children? Every day we ask questions similar to these and look for answers. We realize that many actions do not occur without causes, and we realize also that a given action can have a series of effects — for good or bad. By examining the causes or effects of an action, we seek to understand and explain things that happen in our lives.

In this section, you will be asked to do some detective work by examining the causes of something or the effects of something. First read the three paragraphs that follow and answer the questions about them. Each of the three paragraphs supports its opening point by explaining a series of causes or a series of effects.

PARAGRAPHS TO CONSIDER

New Puppy in the House

[1]Buying a new puppy can have drastic effects on a quiet household. [2]For one thing, the puppy keeps the entire family awake for at least two solid weeks. [3]Every night when the puppy is placed in its box, it begins to howl, yip, and whine. [4]Even after the lights go out and the house quiets down, the puppy continues to moan. [5]Since it is impossible to sleep while listening to a heartbroken, trembling "Woo-wooo," the family soon begins to suffer the effects of loss of sleep. [6]Everyone becomes hostile, short-tempered, depressed, and irritable. [7]A second effect is that the puppy tortures the family by destroying its material possessions. [8]Every day something different is damaged. [9]Family members find chewed belts and shoes, gnawed table legs, and leaking sofa cushions. [10]In addition, the puppy usually ruins the wall-to-wall carpeting and makes the house smell like a public washroom at a big-city bus station. [11]Worst of all, though, the puppy causes family arguments. [12]Parents argue with children about who is supposed to feed and walk the dog. [13]Children argue among themselves about whose turn it is to play with the puppy. [14]Everyone argues about

whose idea it was to get the puppy in the first place. [15]These continual arguments, along with the effects of sleeplessness and the loss of valued possessions, seriously disrupt a household. [16]Only when the puppy gets a bit older will the house be peaceful again.

My Car Accident

[1]Several factors caused my recent car accident. [2]First of all, because a heavy snow and freezing rain had fallen the day before, the road that I was driving on was hazardous. [3]The road had been ploughed but was dangerously icy in spots where dense clusters of trees kept the early morning sun from hitting the road. [4]Second, despite the slick patches, I was stupidly going along at about one hundred kilometres an hour instead of driving more cautiously. [5]I have a daredevil streak in my nature and sometimes feel I want to become a stock-car racer after I finish school, rather than an accountant as my parents want me to be. [6]Another factor contributing to my accident was a dirty green Chevy van that suddenly pulled onto the road from a small intersecting street about fifty metres ahead of me. [7]The road was a sheet of ice at that point, but I was forced to apply my brake and also swing my car into the next lane. [8]Unfortunately, the fourth and final cause of my accident now presented itself. [9]The rear of my Honda Civic was heavy because I had a barbell set in the backseat. [10]I was selling the fairly new weight-lifting set to someone at school, since the weights had failed to build up my muscles immediately and I had gotten tired of practising with them. [11]The result of all the weight in the rear was that after I passed the van, my car spun completely around on the slick road. [12]For a few horrifying, helpless moments, I was sliding down the highway backwards at nearly a hundred kilometres an hour, with no control whatsoever over the car. [13]Then, abruptly, I slid off the road, thumping into a high-ploughed snowbank. [14]I felt stunned for a moment but then also relieved. [15]I saw a telephone pole about three metres to the right of me and realized that my accident could have been really disastrous.

Why I Stopped Smoking

[1]For one thing, I realized that my cigarette smoke bothered others, particularly my wife and children, irritating their eyes and causing them to cough and sneeze. [2]Also, cigarettes are a messy habit. [3]Our house was littered with ashtrays piled high with butts, matchsticks, and ashes, and the children were always knocking them over. [4]Cigarettes are expensive, and I estimated that the carton a week that I was smoking cost me about $1,500 a year. [5]Another reason I stopped was that the message about cigarettes being harmful to health finally got through to me. [6]A heavy smoker I know from work is in Victoria Hospital now with lung cancer. [7]Cigarettes were also inconvenient. [8]Whenever I smoked, I would have to drink something to

wet down my dry throat, and that meant I had to keep going to the bathroom all the time. ⁹I sometimes seemed to spend whole weekends doing nothing but smoking, drinking, and going to the bathroom. ¹⁰Most of all, I resolved to stop smoking because I felt exploited. ¹¹I hated the thought of wealthy, greedy corporations making money off my sweat and blood. ¹²The rich may keep getting richer, but--at least regarding cigarettes--with no thanks to me.

■ Questions

About Unity

1. Which two sentences in "My Car Accident" are not on target in support of the opening idea and so should be omitted? (*Write the sentence numbers here.*) _____ _____

2. Which paragraph lacks a topic sentence?

   _____

About Support

3. How many causes are given to support the opening idea in "My Car Accident"?

   _____ one _____ two _____ three _____ four

   In "Why I Stopped Smoking"?

   _____ one _____ two _____ three _____ four _____ five _____ six

4. How many effects of bringing a new puppy into the home are given in "New Puppy in the House"?

   _____ one _____ two _____ three _____ four

About Coherence

5. What are the five major transition words used in "Why I Stopped Smoking"?

   a. _____ c. _____ e. _____

   b. _____ d. _____

6. What words signal the most important effect in "New Puppy in the House"?

   _____

Activity 1: Discovering Cause and Effects

Complete the following outline of "Why I Stopped Smoking." The effect is that the author stopped smoking; the causes are what make up the paragraph. Summarize each in a few words. The first cause and details are given for you as an example.

Point

There are a number of reasons why I stopped smoking.

1. Reason: <u>Bothered others</u>

   Details: <u>Eye irritations, coughing, sneezing</u>

2. Reason: _____

   Details: _____

3. Reason: _____

   Details: _____

4. Reason: _____

   Details: _____

5. Reason: _____

   Details: _____

6. Reason: _____

   Details: _____

Activity 2: Distinguishing between Main Points and Supporting Details

When you make a point in a paragraph or an essay, you should have two "categories" or levels of information to back up your main point. In cause–effect formats, the distinction between these two types of information is especially clear: You have (1) *reasons* why you have made a statement, and a second, or supporting level of information to back up or clarify your reasons. These secondary pieces of information, vital to your readers' understanding of your reasons, are (2) *details*.

The following exercise presents you with a scrambled list of both *reasons* and *supporting details*. You will learn to distinguish between *reasons* that help you to make your point and *details* that support, clarify, and go with each one of the reasons.

Rewrite the following list of sentences onto a piece of your own paper, or process them, leaving at least two lines between each sentence. Cut out each sentence so that it forms a strip of paper.

Now, look for the sentences which make up the *reasons* that support the point "why people enjoy eating at Burger Village." Mark these sentences with the letters *a*, *b*, *c*, and *d*, in what you feel is their order of importance. Arrange the sentence strips you feel are *supporting details* for each of these points by numbering them (*a*) *1*, (*a*) *2*, on your desk under strips *a*, *b*, and so on.

You are now ready to fill in the outline structure below. Summarize the reasons and details in a few words, rather than writing them out completely.

Point

There are a number of reasons why people enjoy eating at Burger Village.

Reasons and Details

An order is ready no more than three minutes or so after it is placed.

A host is present in the dining room to help parents with children.

The workers wear clean uniforms, and their hands are clean.

There are french fries in two sizes.

The host hands out moistened cloths to wash the children after they eat.

The waiting line moves quickly.

Customers can order hamburgers or fish, chicken, or ham sandwiches.

The host helps with the children's coats and gets a highchair for the baby.

The place is clean.

There are several flavours of milk shakes and several kinds of soft drinks, as well as coffee and hot chocolate.

Someone is always sweeping the floor, collecting trays, and wiping off tables.

The kitchen area is all clean and polished stainless steel.

The service is fast and convenient.

The host gives the children small cups to drink from and special hats.

There is a variety of items on the menu.

Orders come packaged in bags or boxes for easy carrying out.

Outline

a. _____

    (1) _____

    (2) _____

    (3) _____

b. _____

    (1) _____

    (2) _____

    (3) _____

c. _____

    (1) _____

    (2) _____

    (3) _____

d. _____

    (1) _____

    (2) _____

    (3) _____

WRITING A CAUSE–EFFECT PARAGRAPH

■ Writing Assignment 1

Listed below are topic sentences and brief outlines for three cause or effect paragraphs. Choose one of them to develop into a paragraph.

Option 1

Topic sentence: There are several reasons why some high school graduates are unable to read.

    a. Failure of parents (cause)

    b. Failure of schools (cause)

    c. Failure of students themselves (cause)

Option 2

Topic sentence: Attending college has changed my personality in positive ways.

    a. More confident (effect)

    b. More knowledgeable (effect)

    c. More assertive (effect)

Option 3

Topic sentence: Living with room-mates (or family) makes attending college difficult.

    a. Late night hours (cause)

    b. More temptations to cut class (cause)

    c. More distractions from studying (cause)

How to Proceed

a **Begin by prewriting.** On separate paper, make a list of details that might go under each of the supporting points. Provide more details than you can actually use. Here, for example, are some of the details generated by the writer of "New Puppy in the House" while working on the paragraph:

```
Whines and moans
Arguments about walking dog
Arguments about feeding dog
Purchase collar, leash, food
Chewed belts and shoes
Arguments about playing with dog
Loss of sleep
Visits to vet
Short tempers
Accidents on carpet
Chewed cushions and tables
```

b **Edit and select details.** Decide which details you will use to develop the paragraph. Also, number the details in the order in which you will present them. Here is how the writer of "New Puppy in the House" made decisions about details:

```
2   Whines and moans
6   Arguments about walking dog
6   Arguments about feeding dog
    Purchase collar, leash, food
4   Chewed belts and shoes
6   Arguments about playing with dog
1   Loss of sleep
    Visits to vet
3   Short tempers
5   Accidents on carpet
4   Chewed cushions and tables
```

Notice that the writer has put the same number in front of certain details that go together. For example, there is a "4" in front of "Chewed belts and shoes" and also in front of "Chewed cushions and tables."

c **Keep checking your material** as you are working on your paper, to make sure it is unified, supported, and coherent.

d **Edit the next-to-final draft** of your paper for sentence-skills mistakes, including spelling.

■ **Writing Assignment 2**

Below are ten topic sentences for a cause or effect paper. In scratch outline form on separate paper, provide brief supporting points for five of the ten statements.

List the Causes

1. There are several reasons so many accidents occur on _____ (*name a local road, highway, or intersection*).

2. _____ is (*or* is not) a good instructor (*or* employer), for several reasons.

3. _____ is a sport that cannot be appreciated on television.

4. _____ is the most difficult course I have ever taken.

5. For several reasons, many students live at home while going to school.

List the Effects

6. Watching too much TV can have a bad effect on students.

7. When I heard the news that _____, I was affected in various ways.

8. Conflicts between parents can have harmful effects on a child.

9. Breaking my bad habit of _____ has changed my life (*or* would change my life).

10. My fear of _____ has affected my everyday life.

Decide which of your outlines would be most promising to develop into a paragraph. Make sure that your causes or effects are logical ones that truly support the point in the topic sentence. Then follow the directions on "How to Proceed" in Writing Assignment 1.

■ **Writing Assignment 3**

Most of us criticize others readily, but we find it more difficult to give compliments. For this assignment, write a one-paragraph letter praising someone. The letter may be to a person you know (parent, relative, friend); to a public figure (actor, politician, leader, sports star, and so on); or to a company or organization (for example, the manufacturer of a product you own, a newspaper, a TV network, or a government agency).

To start, make a list of reasons why you admire the person or organization. Here are examples of reasons for praising an automobile manufacturer:

My car's dependability
Prompt action on a complaint
Well-thought-out design
Friendly dealer service

Here are reasons for admiring a parent:

Sacrifices you made
Patience with me
Your sense of humour
Your fairness
Your encouragement

Then follow the suggestions on "How to Proceed" in Writing Assignment 1.

■ Writing Assignment 4

Option 1: Assume that there has been an alarming increase in drug abuse among the students at the high school you attended. What might be the causes of this increase? Spend some time thinking about several possible causes. Then, as a concerned member of the local community, write a letter to the high school guidance counsellor explaining the reasons for the increased drug abuse. Your purpose in the letter is to provide helpful information that the counsellor may be able to use in dealing with the problem.

Option 2: Your room-mate has been complaining that it's impossible to succeed in Mr. X's class because the class is too stressful. You volunteer to attend the class and see for yourself. Afterward, you decide to write a letter to the instructor, calling attention to the stressful conditions in the class and suggesting concrete ways that he or she could deal with these conditions. Write this letter, dealing with the causes and effects of stress in the class.

■ Writing Assignment 5

Writing about a Reading Selection: Read the selection titled "Truth or Consequences" by Laura J. Turner on pages 471–473. Each of us lies sometimes. The reasons for our lies may be major or minor, and may have consequences for ourselves or for others which may be significant or insignificant. Think of a lie which you told consciously; think about the *reasons* you told the lie, and about the *effects* that lie had on you or on others. Write a paragraph which begins by relating the lie that you told, and your feelings about why you did so. Your topic sentence might be something like "I always regretted lying to my mother about my boyfriend's _____ habits, and there are three reasons why I told her that story." As you develop each *reason* or *cause* for your decision, use signal words like *One*, *Another*, and *Finally* to introduce and to emphasize the order of your reasons. Conclude with your most important point.

As an alternative, you could write about the consequences, or *effects*, of the lie that you told. Once again, be sure to include effects and supporting details in order of importance.

COMPARING OR CONTRASTING

Comparison and contrast are two thought processes we constantly perform in everyday life. When we *compare* two things, we show how they are similar; when we *contrast* two things, we show how they are different. We might compare or contrast two brand-name products (for example, Guess versus Silver jeans), two television shows, two cars, two instructors, two jobs, two friends, or two courses of action we could take in a given situation. The purpose of comparing or contrasting is to understand each of the two things more clearly and, at times, to make judgements about them.

In this section, you will be asked to write a paper of comparison or contrast. First, however, you must learn the two common methods of developing a comparison or contrast paragraph. Read the two paragraphs that follow and try to explain the difference in the two methods of development.

PARAGRAPHS TO CONSIDER

Last Dance

¹My graduation dance was nothing like what I had expected it to be. ²From the start of grade twelve, I had pictured getting dressed in a blue gown that my aunt would make and that would cost five hundred dollars in any store. ³No one else would have a gown as attractive as mine. ⁴I imagined my boyfriend coming to the door with a lovely blue corsage, and I pictured myself happily inhaling its perfume all evening long. ⁵I saw us setting off for the evening in his brother's Lincoln Continental. ⁶We would make a flourish as we swept in and out of a series of parties before the dance. ⁷Our evening would be capped by a delicious steak dinner and by dancing closely together into the early morning hours. ⁸The formal was held on May 17, 1996, at the Riding Club on the Pembina Highway. ⁹However, because of sickness in her family, my aunt had no time to finish my gown and I had to buy an ugly pink one at the last minute for eighty dollars. ¹⁰My corsage of yellow carnations looked terrible on my pink gown, and I

do not remember its having any scent. [11]My boyfriend's brother was out of town, and I stepped outside to the stripped-down Chevy that he used at races on weekends. [12]We went to one party where I drank a lot of wine that made me sleepy and upset my stomach. [13]After we arrived at the dance, I did not have much more to eat than a roll and some celery sticks. [14]Worst of all, we left early without dancing because my boyfriend and I had had a fight several days before and at the time we did not really want to be with each other.

Computer versus Typewriter

[1]The Macintosh computer that I use at school is dramatically different from the family typewriter that I have at home. [2]First of all, the computer with its word processing program is easy to use. [3]On the screen in front of me, I can see an entire rough draft of a paragraph as I'm working on it. [4]When I'm using the typewriter, in contrast, all that I have to look at is the rough draft that's on a sheet of paper next to the typewriter. [5]I have to keep looking back and forth between that and the draft I'm typing out. [6]Second, the computer is quick. [7]In a moment or two I can easily delete sentences from the paragraph or insert new sentences into it. [8]I can move a sentence from one part of the paragraph to the next, and I can make corrections in spelling or wording with a few strokes on the keyboard. [9]But with the typewriter, there is no quick way to make a correction, delete a sentence, add a sentence, or move a sentence around. [10]Every time I want to make a change, I have to use an eraser or correction fluid, or I have to type a new draft of the paragraph. [11]Finally, the computer offers helpful options. [12]At any point I can give it a command to check my spelling in the paper that I'm writing. [13]I can also have it analyze my grammatical style and make suggestions for improvements. [14]I can ask it to count the number of words in my paper. [15]I can have it change my margins and spaces between lines, and I can order it to number the pages of my paper as it prints them out. [16]The typewriter, on the other hand, offers not a single one of these options. [17]With the computer, I feel that I'm on the cutting edge of technology; with the typewriter, I feel that I'm back in the Stone Age.

Complete this comment: The difference in the methods of contrast in the two paragraphs is _____

_____

_____

_____ .

Compare your answer with the following explanation of the two methods of development used in comparison or contrast paragraphs.

METHODS OF DEVELOPMENT

There are two common methods of development in a comparison or contrast paper. Details can be presented in a *one-side-at-a-time* or a *point-by-point* format.

One Side at a Time

Look at the outline of "Last Dance":

    a. Expectations (*first half of paper*)
        (1) Gown (expensive, blue)
        (2) Corsage (lovely, fragrant, blue)
        (3) Car (Lincoln Continental)
        (4) Partying (much)
        (5) Dinner (shrimp)
        (6) Dancing (all night)
    b. Reality (*second half of paper*)
        (1) Gown (cheap, pink)
        (2) Corsage (wrong colour, no scent)
        (3) Car (stripped-down Chevy)
        (4) Partying (little)
        (5) Dinner (roll and celery sticks)
        (6) Dancing (didn't because of quarrel)

The first half of the paragraph explains fully *one side* of the contrast; the second half of the paragraph deals entirely with *the other side*. In using this method, be sure to follow the same order of points of contrast (or comparison) for each side.

Point by Point

Now look at the outline of "Computer versus Typewriter":

    a. Easy
        (1) Computer
        (2) Typewriter
    b. Quick
        (1) Computer
        (2) Typewriter
    c. Helpful options
        (1) Computer
        (2) Typewriter

The outline shows how the computer and the typewriter are contrasted *point by point*. First, the writer compares the ease of using the computer with the awkwardness of using the typewriter; next, the writer compares the speed of the computer with the slowness of the typewriter; finally, the writer compares the handy options on the computer with the lack of such options on the typewriter.

When you begin a comparison or contrast paper, you should decide right away whether you are going to use the one-side-at-a-time format or the point-by-point format. An outline is an essential step in helping you decide which format will be more workable for your topic.

Activity 1: Outlining to Determine Method of Development

Complete the partial outlines provided for the two paragraphs that follow.

1.   How My Parents' Divorce Changed Me

> In the three years since my parents' divorce, I have changed from a spoiled brat to a reasonably normal college student. Before the divorce, I expected my mother to wait on me. She did my laundry, cooked and cleaned up after meals, and even straightened up my room. My only response was to complain if the meat was too well done or if the sweater I wanted to wear was not clean. In addition, I expected money for anything I wanted. Whether it was an expensive bowling ball or a new school jacket, I expected Mom to hand over the money. If she refused, I would get it from Dad. However, he left when I was fifteen, and things changed. When Mom got a full-time job to support us, I was the one with the free time to do housework. Now, I did the laundry, started the dinner, and cleaned not only my own room but the whole house. Fortunately, Mom was tolerant. She did not even complain when my first laundry project left us with streaky blue underwear. Also, I no longer asked her for money, since I knew there was none to spare. Instead, I got a part-time job on weekends to earn my own spending money. Today I have my own car that I am paying for, and I am putting myself through college. Things have been hard sometimes, but I am glad not to be that spoiled kid any more.

Topic sentence: In the three years since my parents' divorce, I have changed from a spoiled brat to a reasonably normal college student.

a. Before the divorce

    (1) _____

    (2) _____

b. After the divorce

    (1) _____

    (2) _____

Complete the following statement: Paragraph 1 uses a _____ method of development.

2. Good and Bad Horror Movies

A good horror movie is easily distinguished from a bad one. A good horror movie, first of all, has both male and female victims. Both sexes suffer terrible fates at the hands of monsters and maniacs. Therefore, everyone in the audience has a chance to identify with the victim. Bad horror movies, on the other hand, tend to concentrate on women, especially half-dressed ones. These movies are obviously prejudiced against half the human race. Second, a good horror movie inspires compassion for its characters. For example, the audience will feel sympathy for the Wolfman's victims and also for the Wolfman, who is shown to be a sad victim of fate. In contrast, a bad horror movie encourages feelings of aggression and violence in viewers. For instance, in the Halloween films, the murder scenes use the murderer's point of view. The effect is that the audience stalks the victims along with the killer and feels the same thrill he does. Finally, every good horror movie has a sense of humour. In Dracula, the Count says meaningfully at dinner, "I don't drink wine" as he stares at a young woman's juicy neck. Humour provides relief from the horror and makes the characters more human. A bad horror movie, though, is humourless and boring. One murder is piled on top of another, and the characters are just cardboard figures. Bad horror movies may provide cheap thrills, but the good ones touch our emotions and live forever.

Topic sentence: A good horror movie is easily distinguished from a bad one.

a. Kinds of victims

    (1) _____

    (2) _____

b. Effect on audience

    (1) _____

    (2) _____

c. Tone

    (1) _____

    (2) _____

Complete the following statement: Paragraph 2 uses a _____ method of development.

Activity 2: Ordering Supporting Points

Write the number *1* beside the point that is supported by all the other scrambled sentences in the list below. Then number the rest of the sentences in a logical order. To do this, you will have to decide whether the sentences should be arranged according to a *one-side-at-a-time* order or *point-by-point* order.

A Change in Attitude

_____ Eventually I could not find a dress or pair of slacks in my wardrobe that I could wear while still continuing to breathe.

_____ In the evening when I got hungry, I made myself tomato, lettuce, and onion salad with vinegar dressing.

_____ I have kicked my chocolate habit, saved my clothes wardrobe, and enabled myself to breathe again.

_____ I also could seldom resist driving over to the nearby Snack Shack in the evening to get a large chocolate shake.

_____ For dessert at lunch I had an orange or other fruit.

_____ I gobbled chocolate bars during breaks at work, had chocolate cake for dessert at lunch, and ate chocolate-covered truffles in the evening.

_____ At this point I began using will-power to control my urge for chocolate.

_____ As a result, the twelve pounds that I didn't want dropped off steadily and eventually disappeared.

_____ When the pounds began to multiply steadily, I tried to console myself.

_____ I have been able to lose weight by changing my attitude about chocolate.

_____ I said, "Well, that's only three pounds; I can lose that next week."

_____ Also, I made myself go and step on the bathroom scale whenever I got the urge to drive over to the Snack Shack.

_____ There was a time when I made chocolate a big part of my daily diet.

_____ Instead of eating chocolate bars on my break, I munched celery and carrots.

Complete the following statement: The sentences can be organized using

_____ order.

ADDITIONAL PARAGRAPHS TO CONSIDER

Read these additional paragraphs of comparison or contrast and then answer the questions that follow.

My Broken Dream

[1]When I became a police officer in my town, the job was not as I had dreamed it would be. [2]I began to dream about being a police officer at about age ten. [3]I could picture myself wearing a handsome blue uniform and having an impressive-looking badge on my chest. [4]I could also picture myself

driving a powerful patrol car through town and seeing everyone stare at me with envy. [5]But most of all, I dreamed of wearing a gun and using all the equipment that "TV cops" use. [6]I just knew everyone would be proud of me. [7]I could almost hear the guys on the block saying, "Boy, Devon made it big. [8]Did you hear he's a cop?" [9]I dreamed of leading an exciting life, solving big crimes, and meeting lots of people. [10]I just knew that if I became a cop everyone in town would look up to me. [11]However, when I actually did become a police officer, I soon found out that it was not as I had dreamed it would be. [12]My first disappointment came when I was sworn in and handed a well-used, baggy uniform. [13]My disappointment continued when I was given a badge that looked like something pulled out of a Cracker Jack box. [14]I was assigned a beat-up old junker and told that it would be my patrol car. [15]It had a striking resemblance to a car that had lost a demolition derby at a stock-car raceway. [16]Disappointment seemed to continue. [17]I soon found out that I was not the envy of all my friends. [18]When I drove through town, they acted as if they had not seen me. [19]I was told I was crazy doing this kind of job by people I thought would look up to me. [20]My job was not as exciting as I had dreamed it would be either. [21]Instead of solving robberies and murders every day, I found that I spent a great deal of time comforting a local resident because a neighbourhood dog had watered his favourite bush.

Two Views on Toys

[1]There is a vast difference between children and adults where presents are concerned. [2]First, there is the matter of taste. [3]Adults pride themselves on taste, while children ignore the matter of taste in favour of things that are fun. [4]Adults, especially grandparents, pick out tasteful toys that go unused, while children love the cheap playthings advertised on television. [5]Then, of course, there is the matter of money. [6]The new games on the market today are a case in point. [7]Have you ever tried to lure a child away from some expensive game in order to get him or her to play with an old-fashioned game or toy? [8]Finally, there is a difference between an adult's and a child's idea of what is educational. [9]Adults, filled with memories of their own childhoods, tend to be fond of the written word. [10]Today's children, on the other hand, concentrate on anything electronic. [11]These things mean much more to them than to adults. [12]Next holiday season, examine the toys that adults choose for children. [13]Then look at the toys the children prefer. [14]You will see the difference.

Rusty and Zena

[1]Like his wife Zena, Rusty has a good sense of humour. [2]Also, they are both short, dark-haired, and slightly pudgy. [3]Both Rusty and Zena can be charming when they want to be, and they seem to handle small crises in a calm, cool way. [4]A problem such as an overflowing washer, a stalled car, or a sick child is not a cause for panic; they seem to take such events in

stride. ⁵Unlike Zena, though, Rusty tends to be disorganized. ⁶He is late for appointments and unable to keep important documents--bank records, receipts, and insurance papers--where he can find them. ⁷And unlike Zena, Rusty tends to hold a grudge. ⁸He is slow to forget a cruel remark, a careless joke, or an unfriendly slight. ⁹Also, Rusty enjoys swimming, camping, and tennis, unlike Zena, who is an indoors type.

■ Questions

About Unity

1. Which paragraph lacks a topic sentence?

    _____

2. Which paragraph has a topic sentence that is too broad?

    _____

About Support

3. Which paragraph contains virtually no specific details?

    _____

4. Which paragraph do you feel offers the most effective details?

    _____

About Coherence

5. What method of development (one-side-at-a-time or point-by-point) is used in "My Broken Dream"?

    _____

    In "Two Views on Toys"?

    _____

6. Which paragraph offers specific details but lacks a clear, consistent method of development?

    _____

WRITING A COMPARISON OR CONTRAST PARAGRAPH

■ Writing Assignment 1

Below are topic sentences and supporting points for three contrast paragraphs. Choose one of the three to develop into a paragraph.

Option 1

Topic sentence: I abused my body when I was twenty, but I treat myself much differently at the age of thirty.

a. At twenty, I was a heavy smoker....
    Now, instead of smoking, I ...
b. At twenty, I had a highly irregular diet....
    Today, on the other hand, I eat ...
c. Finally, at twenty, I never exercised....
    Today, I work out regularly....

Option 2

Topic sentence: Dating is still somewhat easier for boys than it is for girls.

a. A boy can take the initial step of asking for a date without seeming too aggressive....
    In contrast, a girl ...
b. The boy is usually in charge of deciding where to go and what to do....
    The girl, on the other hand, has to live with the choices....
c. At the end of the night, the boy has an idea of the moves he is planning to make, if any....
    But the girl may wait nervously to see what will happen....

Option 3

Topic sentence: My sociology instructor teaches a class quite differently from my psychology instructor.

a. For one thing, Ms. X demands many hours of homework each week....
    In contrast, Mr. Y does not believe in much work outside class....
b. In addition, Ms. X gives difficult tests—with no study aids....
    Mr. Y's tests, on the other hand, are easy....
c. Finally, Ms. X keeps every class strictly on the subject of the day....
    But Mr. Y will wander off onto any topic that snags his interest....

How to Proceed

a   **Begin by prewriting.** To develop some supporting details for the paragraph, freewrite for five minutes on the topic sentence you have chosen.

b **Ask yourself questions.** Add to the material you have written by asking yourself questions. If you were writing about how you treat your body differently at thirty, for example, you might ask yourself:

How many cigarettes did I smoke at twenty?
What have I substituted for cigarettes?
What kinds of food did I eat?
How regularly did I eat?
What foods do I eat today?
Why didn't I exercise at twenty?
What made me decide to start exercising?
What kind of exercises do I do?
How often do I exercise?

Write down whatever answers occur to you for these and other questions. As with the freewriting, do not worry at this stage about writing correctly. Instead, concentrate on getting down all the information you can think of that supports each point.

c **Go through all the material you have accumulated.** Perhaps some of the details you have written down may help you think of even better details that would fit. If so, write them down.

d **Use contrast and linking transitions.** As you work on the drafts of your paper, use words such as *in contrast*, *but*, *on the other hand*, and *however* to tie your material together.

e **Edit for sentence and spelling errors.** Be sure to edit the next-to-final draft of your paper for sentence-skills mistakes, including spelling.

■ Writing Assignment 2

Write a comparison or contrast paragraph on one of the twenty topics below.

Two holidays	Two jobs
Two instructors	Two characters in the same
Two children	movie or TV show
Two kinds of eaters	Two commercials
Two drivers	Two methods of studying
Two co-workers	Two cartoon strips
Two members of a team	Two cars
(or two teams)	Two friends
Two singers or groups	Two crises
Two animals	Two employees
Two parties	Two magazines

How to Proceed

a **Make two decisions.** You must begin by making two decisions: (1) what your topic will be and (2) whether you are going to do a comparison or a contrast paper. Many times, students choose to do essays centred on differences between two things. For example, you might write about how a math instructor you have in college differs from a math teacher you had in high school. You might discuss important differences between two co-workers or between two of your friends. You might contrast a factory job you had packing vegetables with a white-collar job you had as a salesperson in a clothing store.

b **Make an outline.** After you choose a tentative topic, write a simple topic sentence expressing it. Then see what kind of support you can generate for that topic. For instance, if you plan to contrast two cars, see if you can think of and jot down three distinct ways they differ. In other words, prepare a scratch outline. *An outline is an excellent prewriting technique to use when doing any paragraph; it is almost indispensable when planning a comparison or contrast paragraph.* For a model, look back at the outlines given on pages 27–29 and 154.

Keep in mind that this planning stage is probably the *single most important phase* of work you will do on your paper. Without clear planning, you are not likely to write an effective paragraph.

c **Decide on your method.** After you have decided on a topic and the main lines of support, you must decide whether to use a *one-side-at-a-time* or a *point-by-point* method of development. Both methods are illustrated in this chapter.

d **Freewrite** for about ten minutes on the topic you have chosen. Do not worry about punctuation, spelling, or other matters relating to correct form. Just get as many details as you can onto the page. You want a base of raw material that you can add to and select from as you now work on the first draft of your paper. After you do a first draft, put it aside for a day or at least several hours. You will then be ready to return with a fresh perspective on the material and build on what you have already done.

e **Add contrast and linking transitions** such as *first, in addition, also, in contrast, another difference, on the other hand, but, however,* and *most important* to link points together.

f **Refer to the checklist** on the inside front cover as you continue working on your paper. Make sure that you can answer *Yes* to the questions about unity, support, and coherence.

g **Edit.** Finally, use the checklist on the inside front cover to edit the next-to-final draft of your paper for sentence-skills mistakes, including spelling.

■ Writing Assignment 3

Write a contrast paragraph on one of the fifteen topics below.

Neighbourhood stores versus a shopping mall
Driving on an expressway versus driving on country roads
People versus *Maclean's* (or any other two popular magazines)
Camping in a tent versus camping in a recreational vehicle
Working parents versus stay-at-home parents
Last year's fashions versus this year's
Used car versus new car
Tapes versus CDs
PG-rated movies versus R-rated movies
News in a newspaper versus news on television
Yesterday's toys versus today's
Fresh food versus canned or frozen food
Winning locker room after a game versus losing one
Ad on television versus ad (for the same product) in a magazine
Amateur sport versus professional sport

Follow the directions on "How to Proceed" given in Writing Assignment 2.

■ Writing Assignment 4

You are living in an apartment building in which new tenants are making life unpleasant for you. Write a letter of complaint to the owner or caretaker comparing and contrasting life before and after the tenants arrived. You might want to focus on one or more of the following:

Noise level
Garbage
Safety hazards
Parking situation

■ Writing Assignment 5

Writing about a Reading Selection: Read the selection "Memoirs of a Book-Molesting Childhood" on pages 507–510. Then write a paragraph comparing or contrasting your own memories of reading, or of what books meant to you as a child.

To start, you may want to make up two lists: (1) your memories of learning to read, and your feelings about various experiences you had with reading and books during your earlier and later school and personal life, and (2) Adele Wiseman's memories of what reading meant to her, both inside and outside of school. Next, decide whether to use a side-by-side or point-by-point method of development.

Here is a side-by-side outline:

My memories of learning to read/books:	**Wiseman's memories:**
a. struggled in school/no one read at home	a. found it so easy/envied others reading
b. barely read assigned books/ liked comics & video games for escape	b. read to escape & for pleasure/ school arguments over her reading
c. now read some books for pleasure/TV & movies more meaningful to me	c. reading & storytelling are significant parts of her life experience

Here is a point-by-point outline:

a. Early memories & influence of parents
   — me: slow reader, no books at home, no one wrapped up in reading
   — AW: happy, absorbed reader/everyone around her involved in books and stories
b. Reading in school & attitudes to reading/books
   — me: lagged behind class for years, never found even Dr. Seuss fun/ preferred TV and video games
   — AW: loved reading so much that teachers and librarians were critical — she got lost in reading
c. Attitude toward reading today
   — me: realize I need it for college & work, read some Stephen King for enjoyment/still prefer TV & movies
   — AW: reading is a conscious part of her life/it keeps giving her pleasure; she's "addicted" to it

Once you have your outline, you should be ready to work on the first draft of your paper. Check the general guidelines on pages 160–162 while writing your paragraph.

DEFINING
A TERM

In talking with other people, we at times offer informal definitions to explain just what we mean by particular terms. Suppose, for example, we say to a friend, "Ted is an anxious person." We might then expand on our idea of *anxious* by saying, "He's always worrying about the future. Yesterday he was talking about how many bills he'll probably have this year. Then he was worrying about what he would ever do if he got laid off." *In a written definition, we make clear in a more complete and formal way our own personal understanding of a term.* Such a definition typically starts with one meaning of a term. The meaning is then illustrated with a series of examples or a story.

In this section, you will be asked to write a paragraph in which you define a term. The three student papers below are all examples of definition paragraphs. Read them and then answer the questions that follow.

PARAGRAPHS TO CONSIDER

Luck

¹Luck is putting $1.75 into a vending machine and getting the money back with your snacks. ²It is a teacher's decision to give a retest on a test where you first scored thirty. ³Luck refers to moments of good fortune that happen in everyday life. ⁴It is not going to the dentist for two years and then going and finding out that you do not have any cavities. ⁵It is calling up a plumber to fix a leak on a day when the plumber has no other work to do. ⁶Luck is finding a used car for sale at a good price at exactly the time when your car rolls its last mile. ⁷It is driving into a traffic bottleneck and choosing the lane that winds up moving most rapidly. ⁸Luck is being late for work on a day when your boss arrives later than you do. ⁹It is having a new check-out aisle at the supermarket open up just as your cart arrives. ¹⁰The best kind of luck is winning a new colour TV set with a ticket for which you paid only a quarter.

Disillusionment

[1]Disillusionment is the feeling of having one of our most cherished beliefs stolen from us. [2]I learned about disillusionment firsthand the day Mr. Keller, our grade eight teacher, handed out the marks on our class biology projects. [3]I had worked hard to assemble what I thought was the best insect collection any school had ever seen. [4]For weeks, I had set up home-made traps around our house, in the woods, and in vacant lots. [5]At night, I would stretch a white sheet between two trees, shine a lantern on it, and collect the night-flying insects that gathered there. [6]With my own money, I had bought killing jars, insect pins, gummed labels, and display boxes. [7]I carefully arranged related insects together, with labels listing each scientific name and the place and date of capture. [8]Slowly and painfully, I wrote and typed the report that accompanied my project at the school science fair. [9]In contrast, my friend Eddie did almost nothing for his project. [10]He had his father, a doctor, build an impressive maze complete with live rats and a sign that read, "You are the trainer." [11]A person could lift a little plastic door, send a rat running through the maze, and then hit a button to release a pellet of rat food as a reward. [12]This exhibit turned out to be the most popular one at the fair. [13]I felt sure that our teacher would know that Eddie could not have built it, and I was certain that my hard work would be recognized and rewarded. [14]Then the grades were finally handed out, and I was crushed. [15]Eddie had gotten an A plus, but my grade was a B. [16]I suddenly realized that honesty and hard work don't always pay off in the end. [17]The idea that life is not fair, that sometimes it pays to cheat, hit me with such force that I felt sick. [18]I will never forget that moment.

A Bird Course

[1]A bird course is any college course that is so easy that even a bird could fly through it with an A grade. [2]A student who is taking a heavy schedule, or who does not want four or five especially difficult courses, will try to sandwich in a bird course. [3]A student can find out about such a course by consulting other students, since word of a genuine bird course spreads like wildfire. [4]Or a student can study the university's calendar for tell-tale course titles like "The Art of Self-Expression," "History of the Comic Book," or "Watching Television Creatively." [5]In an advanced course such as microbiology, though, a student had better be prepared to spend a good deal of time during the semester on that course. [6]Students in a bird course can attend the classes while half-asleep, hung-over, or wearing stereo earphones or sunglasses; they will still pass. [7]The course exams (if there are any) would not challenge a five-year-old. [8]The course lectures usually consist of information that anyone with common sense knows anyway. [9]Attendance may be required, but participation or involvement in the class is not. [10]The main requirement for passing is that a student's body is there, warming a

seat in the classroom. [11]There are no difficult labs or special projects, and term papers are never mentioned. [12]Once safely registered for such a course, all the students have to do is sit back and watch the credits accumulate on their transcripts.

■ Questions

About Unity

1. Which paragraph places its topic sentence within the paragraph rather than, more appropriately, at the beginning?

   _____

2. Which sentence in "A Bird Course" should be omitted in the interest of paragraph unity? (*Write the sentence number here.*) _____

About Support

3. Which two paragraphs develop their definitions through a series of short examples?

   _____

   _____

4. Which paragraph develops its definition through a single extended example?

   _____

About Coherence

5. Which paragraph uses emphatic order, saving its best detail for last?

   _____

6. Which paragraph uses time order to organize its details?

   _____

WRITING A DEFINITION PARAGRAPH

■ Writing Assignment 1

Following are a topic sentence and three supporting points for a paragraph that defines the term *TV addict*. Using separate paper, plan out and write the secondary supporting details and closing sentence needed to complete the paragraph. Refer to the suggestions on the next page on "How to Proceed."

Topic sentence: Television addicts are people who will watch all the programs they can, for as long as they can, rather than do anything else.

a. TV addicts, first of all, will watch anything on the tube, no matter how bad it is....

b. In addition, addicts watch TV more hours than normal people do....

c. Finally, addicts feel that TV is more important than any other activities or events that might be going on....

How to Proceed

a **Begin by prewriting.** Prepare examples for each of the three qualities of a TV addict. For each quality, you should have at least two or three sentences that provide either an extended example or shorter examples of this quality in action.

b **Generate supporting details.** To generate these details, ask yourself the following questions:

What are some examples of terrible shows that I (or people I know) watch just because the television is turned on?

What are some examples of how much I (or people I know) watch TV?

What are some other activities or events that I (or people I know) give up in order to watch TV?

Write down quickly whatever answers occur to you. Do not worry about writing correct sentences; just concentrate on getting down all the details about television addicts that you can think of.

c **Draft your paragraph.** Draw from and add to this material as you work on the paragraph. Make sure that your paragraph is unified, supported, and coherent.

d **Edit.** Finally, edit the next-to-final draft of your paper for sentence-skills mistakes, including spelling.

■ Writing Assignment 2

Write an essay that defines one of the following terms. Each term refers to a certain kind of person.

Bigmouth	Clown	Good example
Charmer	Jellyfish	Hypocrite
Loser	Leader	Perfectionist
Lazybones	Nerd	Pack rat

Con artist	Good neighbour	Hard worker
Fair-weather friend	Optimist	Apple-polisher
Team player	Pessimist	Fusspot

How to Proceed

a **Classify your term or definition.** To write a topic sentence for your definition paragraph, your first step should be to *place the term in a class or category*. Then *describe what you feel are the special features that distinguish your term from all the other members of its class.*

In the sample topic sentences below, underline the class, or category, that the term belongs to and double-underline the distinguishing details of that class, or category. One is done for you as an example.

A klutz is a <u>person</u> who <u>stumbles through life</u>.
A worrywart is a person who sees danger everywhere.
The class clown is a student who gets attention in the wrong way.
A clothes-horse is a person who needs new clothes to be happy.

b **Develop your definition.** Use one of the following methods:

Examples. Give several examples that support your topic sentence.
Extended example. Use one longer example to support your topic sentence.
Contrast. Support your topic sentence by showing what your term is *not*. For instance, you may want to define a "fair-weather friend" by contrasting his or her actions with those of a true friend.

c **Write an outline.** Once you have created a topic sentence and decided how to develop your paragraph, write a scratch outline. This step is especially important if you are using a contrast method of development.

d **Check mechanics.** Be sure you touch the four bases of unity, support, coherence, and sentence skills in your writing.

■ Writing Assignment 3

Write an essay that defines one of the abstract terms below.

Persistence	Responsibility	Fear
Rebellion	Insecurity	Arrogance
Sense of humour	Assertiveness	Conscience
Escape	Jealousy	Class
Danger	Nostalgia	Innocence

Curiosity	Gentleness	Freedom
Common sense	Depression	Violence
Family	Obsession	Shyness
Practicality	Self-control	

As a guide in writing your paper, use the suggestions on "How to Proceed" in Writing Assignment 2. Remember to place your term in a class, or category, and to describe what *you* feel are the distinguishing features of that term. Three examples follow.

Laziness is a quality that doesn't deserve its bad reputation.

Jealousy is the emotion that hurts the most.

Persistence is the quality of not giving up even during rough times.

■ Writing Assignment 4

Option 1: At the place where you work, one employee has just quit, creating a new job opening. Since you have been working there for a while, your boss has asked you to write a job description of the position. That description, which is really a detailed definition of the job, will be sent to employment services. These services will be responsible for interviewing candidates. Choose any position you know about, and write a job description for it. First give the purpose of the job, and then list its duties and responsibilities. Finally, give the qualifications for the position.

Option 2: Alternatively, imagine that a new worker has been hired, and your boss has asked you to explain "team player" to him or her. The purpose of your explanation will be to give the newcomer an idea of the teamwork that is expected in this workplace. Write a paragraph that defines in detail what your boss means by *team player*. Use examples or one extended example to illustrate your general statements.

■ Writing Assignment 5

Writing about a Reading Selection: Read the selection titled "What Good Families Are Doing Right" on pages 453–461. Then write a definition paragraph on the hallmarks of a *bad* family. Your topic sentence might be, "A bad family is one that is _____, _____, and _____."

To get started, you should first *reread* the features of a good family explained in the selection. Doing so will help you think about what qualities are found in a bad family. Prepare a list of as many bad qualities as you can think of. Then go through the list and decide upon the qualities that seem most characteristic of a bad family.

Next, spend some time thinking of and jotting down *examples* of each of these qualities. You'll note that the selection provides examples of the hallmarks of a good family; your goal will be to provide examples of the hallmarks of a bad family. Your examples can be drawn from your own experience or observation, or they can be hypothetical examples—examples that you invent but that you feel are realistic. Perhaps your examples will be composites of several bad families or of behaviours that may occur at different times in any family.

Finally, *decide on the order* in which to present these qualities, keeping in mind that you will want to end with the most telling quality. And remember that you will want to *use transition words and synonyms* such as *The first hallmark*, *Another quality*, *A third feature*, and so on.

You should now be ready to write the first draft of your paper.

DIVIDING AND CLASSIFYING

If you were doing the laundry, you would probably begin by separating the clothing into piles. You might put all the whites in one pile and all the colours in another. You might put all cottons in one pile, polyesters in another, silks in a third, and so on. Or you might divide and classify the laundry not according to colour or fabrics but on the basis of use. You might put bath towels in one pile, bed sheets in another, personal garments in a third, and so on. Sorting clothes in various ways is just one small example of how we spend a great deal of time organizing our environment in one manner or another.

In this section, you will be asked to write a paragraph in which you divide or classify a subject according to a single principle. To prepare for this assignment, first read the division and classification paragraphs below and then work through the questions and the activity that follow.

PARAGRAPHS TO CONSIDER

Automobile Drivers

[1]One type of automobile driver is the slowpoke. [2]A man who is a slowpoke, for instance, will drive sixty kilometres per hour in a ninety-kilometre zone. [3]He will slow down and start signalling for a left-hand turn three blocks before making it. [4]Or his car will slow down while he is in avid conversation with other people in the car, or while he fiddles with the tape-deck, or while he looks at construction sites, or as he struggles to open the wrapping of his Harvey's burger. [5]A second type is the high-speed driver. [6]A woman who is a high-speed driver, for example, will limit her speed only when she suspects that the provincial police or radar traps are nearby. [7]The provincial police must develop a system to ensure that they begin to catch this kind of driver. [8]She typically speeds past cars on the left and right sides, weaving in and around them sharply, and she closely tailgates a car that holds her up until it shifts to another lane. [9]She races to get through yellow or just-red lights at highway and city intersections, and she speeds down city streets, oblivious to the possibility that people may emerge from

between parked cars or that someone may open a car door. [10]The final type is the sensible-speed driver who, road conditions being normal, maintains the posted speed limits and drives at a consistent and moderate rate. [11]If these drivers do change their rate, they do so because they are driving defensively. [12]They are speeding up to pass the driver in front, who is creeping along to look at the pumpkins on display at a roadside stand. [13]Or they are slowing down to allow the speed demon who has tried passing to get back in lane and out of the path of an oncoming truck.

Studying for a Test

[1]The time a student spends studying for a test can be divided into three distinct phases. [2]Phase 1, often called the "no problem" phase, runs from the day the test is announced to approximately forty-eight hours before the dreaded exam is passed out. [3]During phase 1, the student is carefree, smiling, and kind to helpless animals and small children. [4]When asked by class-mates if he or she has studied for the test yet, the reply will be an assured "No problem." [5]During phase 1, no actual studying takes place. [6]Phase 2 is entered two days before the test. [7]For example, if the test is scheduled for 9 a.m. Friday, phase 2 begins at 9 a.m. Wednesday. [8]During phase 2, again, no actual studying takes place. [9]Phase 3, the final phase, is entered twelve hours before "zero hour." [10]This is the acute phase, characterized by sweaty palms, nervous twitches, and confused mental patterns. [11]For a test at nine o'clock on Friday morning, a student begins exhibiting these symptoms at approximately nine o'clock on Thursday night. [12]Phase 3 is also termed the "shock" phase, since the student is shocked to discover the imminent nature of the exam and the amount of material to be studied. [13]During this phase, the student will probably be unable to sleep and will mumble meaningless phrases like "$a^2 + c^2$." [14]This phase will not end until the exam is over. [15]If the cram session has worked, the student will fall gratefully asleep. [16]On waking up, he or she will be ready to go through the whole cycle again with the next test.

The Dangers of Tools

[1]Tools can be divided into three categories according to how badly people can injure themselves with them. [2]The first group of tools causes dark-purple bruises to appear on the user's feet, fingers, or arms. [3]Hammers are famous for this, as millions of cartoons and comic strips have shown. [4]Mallets and crowbars, too, can go a bit off target and thud onto a bit of exposed flesh. [5]But first-class bruises can also be caused by clamps, pliers, vise grips, and wrenches. [6]In a split second, any one of these tools can lash out and badly squeeze a stray finger. [7]Later, the victim will see blue-black blood forming under the fingernail. [8]The second type of tool usually attacks by cutting or tearing. [9]Saws seem to enjoy cutting through human flesh as

well as wood. [10]Keeping a hand too close to the saw, or using a pair of knees as a saw-horse, will help the saw satisfy its urge. [11]Planes, chisels, and screwdrivers also cut into skin. [12]And the utility knife--the kind with a razor blade projecting from a metal handle--probably cuts more people than it does linoleum. [13]The most dangerous tools, however, are the mutilators, the ones that send people directly to the emergency room. [14]People were definitely not made to handle monster tools like chain saws, table saws, power drills, and power hammers. [15]Newspapers are filled with stories of shocking accidents people have had with power tools. [16]In summary, if people are not careful, tools can definitely be hazardous to their health.

■ Questions

About Unity

1. Which paragraph lacks a topic sentence? _____

2. Which sentence in "Automobile Drivers" should be omitted in the interest of
    paragraph unity? (*Write the sentence number here.*) _____

About Support

3. Which of the three phases in "Studying for a Test" lacks specific details?

    _____

4. After which sentence in "The Dangers of Tools" are supporting details
    needed? _____

About Coherence

5. Which paragraph uses time order to organize its details?

    _____

6. Which paragraph uses emphatic order to organize its details?

    _____

7. What words in the emphatic-order paragraph signal the most important detail?

    _____

Activity: Identifying Unified Groups of Items

This activity will sharpen your sense of the classifying process. In each of the following ten groups, cross out the one item that has not been classified on the same basis as the other three. Also, indicate in the space provided the single principle of classification used for the three items. Note the examples.

Examples Water
a. Cold
~~b. Lake~~
c. Hot
d. Lukewarm
Unifying principle:

Temperature

Household pests
~~a. Mice~~
b. Ants
c. Roaches
d. Flies
Unifying principle:

Insects

1. Eyes
   a. Blue
   b. Near-sighted
   c. Brown
   d. Hazel
   Unifying principle:

   _____

5. College classes
   a. Enjoy
   b. Dislike
   c. Tolerate
   d. Morning
   Unifying principle:

   _____

2. Mattresses
   a. Double
   b. Twin
   c. Queen
   d. Firm
   Unifying principle:

   _____

6. Wallets
   a. Leather
   b. Plastic
   c. Stolen
   d. Fabric
   Unifying principle:

   _____

3. Zoo animals
   a. Flamingo
   b. Peacock
   c. Polar bear
   d. Ostrich
   Unifying principle:

   _____

7. Newspaper
   a. Wrapping garbage
   b. Editorials
   c. Making paper planes
   d. Covering floor while painting
   Unifying principle:

   _____

4. Vacation
   a. Summer
   b. Holiday
   c. Seashore
   d. Weekend
   Unifying principle:

   _____

8. Students
   a. Undergraduate
   b. Transfer
   c. Postgraduate
   d. Doctoral
   Unifying principle:

   _____

9. Exercise
   a. Running
   b. Swimming
   c. Gymnastics
   d. Fatigue
   Unifying principle:

   _____

10. Leftovers
    a. Cold chicken
    b. Feed to dog
    c. Reheat
    d. Use in a stew
    Unifying principle:

    _____

WRITING A DIVISION AND CLASSIFICATION PARAGRAPH

■ Writing Assignment 1

Below are four possible division and classification writing assignments, along with possible divisions. Choose *one* of them to develop into a paragraph.

Option 1

Supermarket shoppers
a. Slow, careful shoppers
b. Average shoppers
c. Rushed, hurried shoppers

Option 2

Eaters
a. Super-conservative eaters
b. Typical eaters
c. Adventurous eaters

Option 3

Methods of housekeeping
a. Never clean
b. Clean regularly
c. Clean constantly

Option 4

Attitudes toward money
a. Tight-fisted
b. Sometimes splurge
c. Spendthrift

How to Proceed

a **Freewrite.** Begin by prewriting. To develop some ideas for the paragraph, freewrite for five or ten minutes on your topic.

b **Ask questions.** To add to the material you have written, ask yourself questions. If you are writing about supermarket shoppers, for example, you might ask:

How do the three kinds of shoppers pick out the items they want?
How many aisles will each type of shopper visit?
Which shoppers bring lists, calculators, coupons, and so on?
How much time does it take each type of shopper to finish shopping?

Write down whatever answers occur to you for these and other questions. As with freewriting, do not worry at this stage about writing correctly. Instead, concentrate on getting down all the information you can think of that supports each of the three points.

c **Evaluate and order your details.** Now go through all the material you have accumulated. Perhaps some of the details you have written down may help you think of even better details that would fit. If so, write them down. Then make decisions about the exact information you will use to support each point. Number the details *1, 2, 3,* and so on, in the order you will present them.

d **Check mechanics.** As you work on the drafts of your paragraph, make sure that it touches the bases of unity, support, and coherence.

e **Edit.** Finally, edit the next-to-final draft of your paper for sentence-skills mistakes, including spelling.

■ Writing Assignment 2

Write a division and classification essay on one of the following subjects:

Instructors	Drivers
Sports fans	Mothers or fathers
Eating places	Women's or men's magazines
Attitudes toward life	Presents
Commercials	Neighbours
Employers	Rock, pop, or country singers
Jobs	Amusement parks or rides
Bars	Guests or company
Family get-togethers	Ways to get an A (or F) in a course
Shoes	Car accessories

How to Proceed

a **Choose a single principle for dividing your subject.** The first step in writing a division and classification paragraph is to divide your tentative topic into three reasonably complete parts. *Always use a single principle of division when you form your three parts.* For example, if your topic was "Automobile Drivers" and you divided them into slow, moderate, and fast drivers, your single basis for division would be "rate of speed." It would be illogical, then, to have as a fourth type "teenage drivers" (the basis of such a division would be "age") or "female drivers" (the basis of such a division would be "sex"). You could probably classify automobile drivers on the basis of age or sex or another division, for almost any subject can be analyzed in more than one way. What is important, however, is that in any single paper you *choose only one basis for division and stick to it*. Be consistent.

In "Studying for a Test," the writer divides the process of studying into three time phases: from the time the test is announced to forty-eight hours before the test; the day and a half before the test; and the final twelve hours before the test. In "The Dangers of Tools," the single basis for dividing tools into three categories is the kind of injury each type inflicts: bruises, cuts, and major injuries.

b **Make a clear outline.** To ensure a clear three-part division in your own paragraph, fill in the outline below before starting your paper and make sure you can answer *Yes* to the questions that follow. You should expect to do a fair amount of thinking before coming up with a logical plan for your paper.

Topic: _____
Three-part division of the topic:

(1) _____

(2) _____

(3) _____

Is there a single basis of division for the three parts? _____

Is the division reasonably complete? _____

c **Check mechanics.** Refer to the checklist of the four bases on the inside front cover while writing the drafts of your paper. Make sure you can answer *Yes* to the questions about unity, support, coherence, and sentence skills. Also, use the checklist when you edit the next-to-final draft of your paper for sentence-skills mistakes, including spelling.

■ Writing Assignment 3

There are many ways you could classify the students around you. Choose one of your courses and write a division and classification paragraph on the students in that class. You might want to categorize the students according to one of the principles of division below:

Attitude toward the class	Attendance
Participation in the class	Level of confidence
Method of taking notes in class	Performance during oral reports,
Method of taking a test in class	speeches, presentations, lab sessions
Punctuality	

Of course, you may use any other principle of division that seems appropriate. Follow the steps listed in "How to Proceed" for Writing Assignment 2.

■ Writing Assignment 4

You are teaching a class in safe driving at a high school, and part of today's lecture is about types of drivers to avoid. For this part of your presentation, write a paragraph dividing the category "unsafe drivers" into three or more types according to their driving habits. For each type, include both a description and suggestions to your students on how to avoid an accident with this type of driver.

■ Writing Assignment 5

Writing about a Reading Selection: Read Jim Maloney's selection titled "Why Should We Hire You?" on pages 493–496. Maloney describes three types of attitudes prevalent among students: (1) the belief that job interviews will be automatically available; (2) the assumption that a diploma is "a guarantee" of entry into a chosen career; (3) the realization that career preparation begins during the first few semesters of college.

Choose the classification which most closely resembles your own view, and defend your position with three distinct supporting examples. Choose your specific supporting material from your own experience or from references to Professor Maloney's essay.

DESCRIBING A SCENE OR PERSON

When you describe something or someone, you give your readers a picture in words. To make this "word picture" as vivid and real as possible, you must observe and record *specific details* that *appeal to your readers' senses* (sight, hearing, taste, smell, and touch). More than any other type of writing, a descriptive paragraph needs sharp, colourful details.

Here is a description in which only the sense of sight is used:

A rug covers the living-room floor.

In contrast, here is a description rich in sense impressions:

A thick, reddish-brown shag rug is laid wall to wall across the living-room floor. The long, curled fibres of the shag seem to whisper as you walk through them in your bare feet, and when you squeeze your toes into the deep covering, the soft fibres push back at you with a spongy resiliency.

Sense impressions include sight (*thick, reddish-brown shag rug*; *laid wall to wall*; *walk through them in your bare feet*; *squeeze your toes into the deep covering*; *push back*), hearing (*whisper*), and touch (*bare feet, soft fibres, spongy resiliency*). *The sharp, vivid images* provided by the sensory details give us a clear picture of the rug and enable us to share in the writer's experience.

In this section, you will be asked to describe a person, place, or thing for your readers through the use of words rich in sensory details. To help you prepare for the assignment, first read the three paragraphs ahead and then answer the questions that follow.

PARAGRAPHS TO CONSIDER

An Athlete's Room

[1] As I entered the bright, cheerful space, with its beige walls and practical, flat-pile carpet, I noticed a closet to my right with the door open. [2] On the shelf above the bunched-together clothes were a red baseball cap, a

fielder's glove, and a battered brown gym bag. ³Turning from the closet, I noticed a single bed with its wooden headboard against the far wall. ⁴The bedspread was a brown, orange, and beige print of basketball, hockey, and baseball scenes. ⁵A lamp shaped like a baseball and a copy of <u>Sports Illustrated</u> were on the top of a nightstand to the left of the bed. ⁶A sports schedule and several yellowing newspaper clippings were tacked to the cork bulletin board on the wall above the nightstand. ⁷A desk with a bookcase top stood against the left wall. ⁸I walked toward it to examine it more closely. ⁹As I ran my fingers over the items on the dusty shelves, I noticed some tarnished medals and faded ribbons for track accomplishments. ¹⁰These lay next to a heavy gold trophy that read, "MVP: Pinewood Varsity Basketball." ¹¹I accidentally tipped an autograph-covered, slightly deflated basketball off one shelf, and the ball bounced with dull thuds across the width of the room. ¹²Next to the desk was a window with brightly printed curtains that matched the bedspread. ¹³Between the window and the left corner stood a dresser with one drawer half open, revealing a tangle of odd sweat socks and a few stretched-out T-shirts emblazoned with team insignias. ¹⁴As I turned to leave the room, I carefully picked my way around scattered pairs of worn-out sneakers.

A Depressing Place

¹The pet shop in the mall is a depressing place. ²A display window attracts passers-by who stare at the prisoners penned inside. ³In the right-hand side of the window, two puppies press their forepaws against the glass and attempt to lick the human hands that press from the outside. ⁴A cardboard barrier separates the dogs from several black-and-white kittens piled together in the opposite end of the window. ⁵Inside the shop, rows of wire cages line one wall from top to bottom. ⁶At first, it is hard to tell whether a bird, hamster, gerbil, cat, or dog is locked inside each cage. ⁷Only an occasional movement or clawing, shuffling sound tells visitors that living creatures are inside. ⁸Running down the centre of the store is a line of large wooden perches that look like coat racks. ⁹When customers pass by, the parrots and mynahs chained to these perches flutter their clipped wings in a useless attempt to escape. ¹⁰At the end of this centre aisle is a large plastic tub of dirty, stagnant-looking water containing a few motionless turtles. ¹¹The shelves against the left-hand wall are packed with all kinds of pet-related items. ¹²The smell inside the entire shop is an unpleasant mixture of strong chemical deodorizers, urine-soaked newspapers, and musty sawdust. ¹³Because so many animals are crammed together, the normally pleasant, slightly milky smell of the puppies and kittens is sour and strong. ¹⁴The droppings inside the uncleaned birdcages give off a dry, stinging odour. ¹⁵Visitors hurry out of the shop, anxious to feel fresh air and sunlight. ¹⁶The animals stay on.

Elaine

[1]Elaine, my brother's new girlfriend, is a cat-like creature. [2]Her face, with its wide forehead, sharp cheekbones, and narrow, pointed chin, resembles a triangle. [3]Elaine's skin is a soft, velvety brown. [4]Her large brown eyes slant upward at the corners, and she emphasizes their angle with a sweep of maroon eye shadow. [5]Elaine's habit of looking sidelong out of the tail of her eye makes her look cautious, as if she were expecting something to sneak up on her. [6]Her nose is small and flat. [7]The sharply outlined depression under it leads the observer's eye to a pair of red-tinted lips. [8]With their slight upward tilt at the corners, Elaine's lips make her seem self-satisfied and secretly pleased. [9]One reason Elaine may be happy is that she was recently asked to be in a local beauty contest. [10]Elaine's face is framed by a smooth layer of brown hair that always looks just combed. [11]Her long neck and slim body are perfectly in proportion with her face. [12]Elaine manages to look elegant and sleek no matter how she is standing or sitting, for her body seems to be made up of graceful angles. [13]Her slender hands are tipped with long, polished nails. [14]Her narrow feet are long, too, but they appear delicate even in flat-soled running shoes. [15]Somehow, Elaine would look perfect in a cat's jewelled collar.

The View from My Window

[1]I live in an old section of Montreal, and my friends think I never see anything "natural." [2]My closest friends at college live mainly in rural areas near school, and many grew up on farms. [3]They tell me about rich tastes of harvest fruits and vegetables, the soft or spiky feel of cows and horses, the aroma of fresh manure, and the silence of undisturbed snow on the winter fields. [4]But when I sit at my processor looking out my third-floor bay window, I see enough citified nature to take my mind off the machine on which I'm working. [5]My part of the city was built more than one hundred years ago, and all the trees are taller than the houses. [6]Before me I watch trees with characters all their own: the black branches of spreading maple leaning from the neighbour's lot bud all April with deep purple hints of spring, then shade my window with green summer leaves, and finally brighten my fall schoolwork sessions with scarlet and gold. [7]An immense pine looms on my right-hand view, and winter storms blanket its soft branches with softer coats of snow or with dangling daggers of ice. [8]Many of my neighbours are older people, who have great pride in their gardens. [9]Bushy yellow forsythia sparkle in spring, climbing rose-trellises bloom with brilliant reds and send delicate perfume through my open windows in the warm weather. [10]As a "starving student," I benefit even more directly from their gardening. [11]Delicious tomatoes, newly pulled earthy lettuce, and juicy peaches and apples come to me as fresh as they do to my country friends. [12]When I look out my window at the richly blooming late-summer gardens across the street, I realize how close to nature a city-dweller can be.

■ Questions

About Unity

1. Which paragraphs lack a topic sentence?

   _____

2. Which sentence in the paragraph on Elaine should be omitted in the interest
   of paragraph unity? (*Write the sentence number here.*) _____
   Which sentence in "The View from My Window" should be omitted in the
   interest of paragraph unity? (*Write the sentence number here.*) _____

About Support

3. Label as *sight*, *touch*, *taste*, *hearing*, or *smell* all the sensory details in the following sentences taken from the three paragraphs. The first one is done for
   you as an example.

                  touch   sight   sight

   a. I accidentally tipped an autograph-covered, slightly deflated basketball off
                     sight   hearing   sight
   one shelf, and the ball bounced with dull thuds across the width of the room.

   b. Because so many animals are crammed together, the normally pleasant,

       slightly milky smell of the puppies and kittens is sour and strong.

   c. Her slender hands are tipped with long, polished nails.

   d. As I ran my fingers over the items on the dusty shelves, I noticed some

       tarnished medals and faded ribbons for track accomplishments.

   e. Delicious tomatoes, newly pulled earthy lettuce, and juicy peaches and

       apples come to me as fresh as they do to my country friends.

4. After which sentence in "A Depressing Place" are specific details needed?

   _____

About Coherence

5. Spatial signals (*above*, *next to*, *to the right*, and so on) are often used to help
   organize details in descriptive paragraphs. List four space signals that appear
   in "An Athlete's Room":

   _____

   _____

_____

_____

6. The writer of "Elaine" organizes the details by observing Elaine in an orderly way. Which of Elaine's features is described first? _____

Which is described last? _____ Check the method of spatial organization that best describes the paragraph:

_____ Interior to exterior

_____ Near to far

_____ Top to bottom

WRITING A DESCRIPTIVE PARAGRAPH

■ Writing Assignment 1

Write a paragraph describing a special kind of room. Use as your topic sentence "I could tell by looking at the room that a _____ lived there." There are many kinds of people who could be the focus for such a paragraph. You can select any one of the following, or think of some other type of person.

Photographer	Music lover	Carpenter
Cook	TV addict	Baby
Student	Camper	Cat or dog lover
Musician	Grandparent	World traveller
Hunter	Model	Drug addict
Slob	Football player	Little boy or girl
Outdoors person	Actor	Alcoholic
Instructor	Prostitute	Rollerblader

How to Proceed

a List details about your topic. Begin by prewriting. After choosing a topic, spend a few minutes making sure it will work. Prepare a list of all the details you can think of that support the topic. For example, the writer of "An Athlete's Room" made this list:

Sports trophy
Autographed basketball
Sports Illustrated

Baseball lamp
Sports schedule
Medals and ribbons
Sports print on bedspread, curtains
Sweat socks, T-shirts
Baseball cap
Baseball glove
Gym bag
Sports clippings

If you don't have enough details, then choose another type of person, and check your new choice with a list of details before committing yourself to the topic.

b   Make your goals the four bases of effective writing. Keep all four in mind as you work on the paragraph.

Base 1: Unity. Everything in the paragraph should support your point. For example, if you are writing about an athlete's room, *all the details* should serve to show that the person who lives in the room is an athlete. Other details should be omitted.

TIP: After your paragraph is finished, imagine omitting the key word in your topic sentence. Your details alone should make it clear to the reader what word should fit in that empty space.

Base 2: Support. Description depends on the use of *specific* rather than *general* descriptive words. For example:

General	*Specific*
Old sports trophies	Tarnished medals and faded ribbons for track accomplishments
Ugly turtle tub	Large plastic tub of dirty, stagnant-looking water containing a few motionless turtles
Unpleasant smell	Unpleasant mixture of strong chemical deodorizers, urine-soaked newspapers, and musty sawdust
Nice skin	Soft, velvety brown skin

Remember that you want your readers to *experience* the room vividly as they read. Your words should be as detailed as a clear photograph and should give your readers a real feel for the room as well. Use *as many senses as possible* in describing the room. Chiefly you will use sight, but to some extent you may be able to use touch, hearing, taste, and smell as well.

Base 3: Coherence. *Organize* your descriptive paragraph by using *spatial order.* Spatial order means that you move from right to left or from larger items to smaller ones, just as a visitor's eye might move around a room. For instance, the writer of "An Athlete's Room" presents an orderly description in which the eye moves from right to left around the room. Here are *transition words* that will help you connect your sentences as you describe the room:

to the left	across from	on the opposite side
to the right	above	nearby
next to	below	

Such transitions will help prevent you—and your reader—from getting lost as the description proceeds.

Base 4: Sentence skills. In the later drafts of your paper, edit carefully for sentence-skills mistakes. Refer to the checklist of such skills on the inside front cover of the book.

■ Writing Assignment 2

Write a paragraph about a particular place that you can observe carefully or that you already know well. It might be one of the following or some other place:

Student lounge area	Hair salon
Car showroom	Doctor's or dentist's office
Gymnasium	Classroom
Fast-food restaurant	Bank
Inside of a car	Dressing room
Ladies' or men's room	Attic
Movie theatre	Street market
Auto repair garage	Place where you work
Record shop	Porch

How to Proceed

a **Create a dominant impression.** Remember that, like all paragraphs, a descriptive paper must have an opening point. This point, or topic sentence, should state a dominant impression about the place you are describing. In a single short sentence, state the place you want to describe and the dominant impression you want to make. The sentence can be refined later. For now, you just want to find and express a workable topic. You might write, for example, a sentence like one of the following:

The student lounge was hectic.
The record shop was noisy.

The car's interior was very clean.

The dressing room in the department store was stifling.

The dentist's office was soothing.

The movie theatre was freezing.

The gymnasium was tense.

The attic was gloomy.

The men's room was classy.

The office where I work was strangely quiet.

b **List supporting details.** Now make a list of all the details you can think of that support the general impression. For example, the writer of "A Depressing Place" made the list shown on the next page:

A Depressing Place
Puppies behind glass
Unpleasant smell
Chained birds
Rows of cages
Dirty tub of turtles
Stuffy atmosphere
Kittens in window
Sounds of caged animals
Droppings and urine on newspapers

c **Decide on a method of organization.** Organize your paper by using any one or a combination of the following methods.

In terms of physical order: That is, move from left to right, or far to near, or in some other consistent order.

In terms of size: That is, begin with large features or objects and work down to smaller ones.

In terms of a special order: Use a special order appropriate to the subject.

For instance, the writer of "A Depressing Place" organizes the paper in terms of physical order (from one side of the pet shop to the centre to the other side).

d **Use varied sense details.** Use as many senses as possible in describing a scene. Chiefly you will use sight, but to some extent you may be able to use touch, hearing, smell, and perhaps even taste as well. Remember that it is through the richness of your sense impressions that the reader will gain a picture of the scene.

e **Check mechanics.** As you are working on the drafts of your paper, refer to the checklist on the inside front cover. Make sure you can answer *Yes* to the questions about unity, support, coherence, and sentence skills.

■ Writing Assignment 3

Write a paragraph describing a person. Decide on a dominant impression you have about the person, and use only those details that will add to that impression. Here are some examples of people you might want to write about.

TV or movie personality	Co-worker
Instructor	Clergy member
Employer	Police officer
Child	Store owner or manager
Older person	Bartender
Close friend	Joker
Enemy	Neighbour

Before you begin, you may want to look carefully at the paragraph on Elaine given earlier in this chapter and at "How to Proceed" in Writing Assignment 2.

Here are some possible topic sentences. Your instructor may let you develop one of these or may require you to write your own.

Kate gives the impression of being permanently nervous.

The old man was as faded and brittle as a dying leaf.

The child was a cherubic little figure.

Our high school principal resembled a cartoon drawing.

The young woman seemed to belong to another era.

Our neighbour is a fussy person.

The rock singer seemed to be plugged in to some special kind of energy source.

The drug addict looked as lifeless as a corpse.

My friend Mike is a slow, deliberate person.

The owner of that grocery store seems burdened with troubles.

■ Writing Assignment 4

Option 1: You have succumbed to a free preview of a video dating service. Clients of this service are required to make a three-minute presentation, which will be recorded on videotape. In this presentation, clients describe the kind of person they would like to date. Write a one-paragraph description for your video presentation. Begin by brainstorming for a few minutes on what your "ideal date" would be like. Then arrange the details you come up with into some or all of the following categories:

■ **Character and personality** (Are his or her attitudes important to you? Do you prefer someone who's quiet or someone who's outgoing?)

■ *Interests* (Should your date have some of the same interests as you? If so, which ones?)

■ *Personal habits* (Do you care, for instance, if your date is a nonsmoker?)

■ *Physical qualities* (How might your ideal date look and dress?)

Option 2: Alternatively, write a similar presentation in which you describe *yourself*. Your aim is to present yourself as honestly as possible, so that interested members of the dating service will get a good sense of what you are like.

■ Writing Assignment 5

Writing about a Reading Selection: Read Tony Wong's article titled "Have You Seen My Missing Math Gene?" on pages 516–518. Then write a descriptive paragraph about some aspect of *you* that seems to be missing, or dormant, or undiscovered.

We all have some weak spots; some of these are serious, such as problems with will power, or low self-esteem, or petty dishonesty. Many of our "missing genes" may have more to do with "missing jeans": minor problems like forgetfulness, procrastination, untidiness, and the like. Are you always late for class? Can you make toast that isn't charcoal?

Your paragraph may be humorous or straightforward in approach. As Wong does, begin by describing specifically "what's missing" and by briefly recounting how this affects your day-to-day life. As you prewrite, think of some more vivid examples from your life, situations where your "missing _____ gene" caused misunderstandings or problems. Choose three strong examples, and use the liveliest descriptive verbs and adjectives possible to *show*, rather than *tell*, the reader what you felt. Use dialogue, or direct speech, to enliven your examples if it seems appropriate. Your purpose is to give a vivid impression of the people, objects, emotions, and events involved in describing your subject.

Before starting this paper, you may find it helpful to review the writing suggestions on pages 184–187.

NARRATING
AN EVENT

At times we make a statement clear by relating in detail something that has happened to us. In the story we tell, we present the details *in the order in which they happened*. A person might say, for example, "I was embarrassed yesterday," and then go on to illustrate the statement with the following narrative:

> I was hurrying across campus to get to a class. It had rained heavily all morning, so I was hopscotching my way around puddles in the pathway. I called to two friends ahead to wait for me, and right before I caught up to them, I came to a large puddle that covered the entire path. I had to make a quick choice of either stepping into the puddle or trying to jump over it. I jumped, wanting to seem cool since my friends were watching, but I didn't clear the puddle. Water splashed everywhere, drenching my shoes, socks, and pantlegs, and also spraying the pants of my friends as well. "Well done, Tran!" they said. I felt all the more embarrassed because I had tried to look so casual.

The speaker's details have made his moment of embarrassment vivid and real for us, and we can see and understand just why he felt as he did.

In this section, you will be asked to tell a story that illustrates some point. The paragraphs below all present narrative experiences that support a point. Read them and then answer the questions that follow.

PARAGRAPHS TO CONSIDER

Heartbreak

[1]Bonnie and I had gotten engaged in August, just before she left for Carleton University. [2]A week before Thanksgiving, I drove up to see her as a surprise. [3]When I knocked on the door of her dorm room, she was indeed surprised but not in a pleasant way. [4]She introduced me to her room-mate, who looked uncomfortable and quickly left. [5]I asked Bonnie how classes were going, and at the same time I tugged on the sleeve of my heavy

sweater in order to pull it off. [6]As I was pulling it off, a large poster caught my eye. [7]It was decorated with paper flowers and yellow ribbon, and it said, "Bonnie and Blake." [8]"What's going on?" I said. [9]I stood there stunned and then felt an anger that grew rapidly. [10]"Who is Blake?" I asked. [11]Bonnie laughed nervously and said, "What do you want to hear about--my classes or Blake?" [12]I don't really remember what she then told me, except that Blake was a second-year math major. [13]I felt a terrible pain in the pit of my stomach, and I wanted to rest my head on someone's shoulder and cry. [14]I wanted to tear down the sign and run out, but I did nothing. [15]Clumsily I pulled on my sweater again. [16]My knees felt weak, and I barely had control of my body. [17]I opened the room door, and suddenly more than anything I wanted to slam the door shut so hard that the dorm walls would collapse. [18]Instead, I managed to close the door quietly. [19]I walked away, understanding what was meant by a broken heart.

A Childhood Disappointment

[1]The time I almost won a car when I was ten years old was probably the most disappointing moment of my childhood. [2]One hot summer afternoon I was wandering around a local department store, waiting for my mother to finish shopping. [3]Near the toy department, I was attracted to a crowd of people gathered around a bright blue car that was on display in the main aisle. [4]A sign indicated that the car was the first prize in a sweepstakes celebrating the store's tenth anniversary. [5]The sign also said that a person did not have to buy anything to fill out an entry form. [6]White entry cards and shiny yellow pencils were scattered on a card table nearby, and the table was just low enough for me to write on, so I filled out a card. [7]Then, feeling very much like an adult, I slipped my card into the slot of a heavy blue wooden box that rested on another table nearby. [8]I then proceeded to the toy department, completely forgetting about the car. [9]However, about a month later, just as I was walking into the house from my first day back at school, the telephone rang. [10]When my mother answered it, a man asked to speak to a Michael Ingersoll. [11]My mother said, "There's a Michael Ingutta here, but not a Michael Ingersoll." [12]He asked, "Is this 862-9715 at 29 Ingutta Street?" [13]My mother said, "That's the right number, but this is 29 Ingersoll Street." [14]She then asked him, "What is this all about?" and he explained to her about the sweepstakes contest. [15]My mother then called me to ask if I had ever filled out an application for a sweepstakes draw. [16]I said that I had, and she told me to get on the phone. [17]The man by this time had realized that I had filled in my first name and street name on the line where my full name was to be. [18]He told me I could not qualify for the prize because I had filled out the application incorrectly. [19]For the rest of the day, I cried whenever I thought of how close I had come to winning the car. [20]I am probably fated for the rest of my life to think of the "almost" prize whenever I fill out any kind of contest form.

A Frustrating Job

[1]Working as a baby-sitter was the most frustrating job I ever had. [2]I discovered this fact when my sister asked me to stay with her two sons for the evening. [3]I figured I would get them dinner, let them watch a little TV, and then put them to bed early. [4]The rest of the night I planned to watch TV and collect an easy twenty dollars. [5]It turned out to be anything but easy. [6]First, right before we were about to sit down for a pizza dinner, Rickie let the parakeet out of its cage. [7]This bird is really intelligent and can repeat almost any phrase. [8]The dog started chasing it around the house, so I decided to catch it before the dog did. [9]Rickie and Jeff volunteered to help, following at my heels. [10]We had the bird cornered by the fireplace when Rickie jumped for it and knocked over the hamster cage. [11]Then the bird escaped again, and the hamsters began scurrying around their cage like crazy creatures. [12]The dog had disappeared by this point, so I decided to clean up the hamsters' cage and try to calm them down. [13]While I was doing this, Rickie and Jeff caught the parakeet and put it back in its cage. [14]It was time to return to the kitchen and eat cold pizza. [15]But upon entering the kitchen, I discovered why the dog had lost interest in the bird chase. [16]What was left of the pizza was lying on the floor, and tomato sauce was dripping from the dog's chin. [17]I cleaned up the mess and then served chicken noodle soup and ice cream to the boys. [18]Only at nine o'clock did I get the kids to bed. [19]I then returned downstairs to find that the dog had thrown up pizza on the living-room rug. [20]When I finished cleaning the rug, my sister returned. [21]I took the twenty dollars and told her that she should get someone else next time.

■ Questions

About Unity

1. Which paragraph lacks a topic sentence?

   _____

   Write a topic sentence for the paragraph:

   _____

   _____

   _____

2. Which sentence in "A Frustrating Job" should be omitted in the interest of paragraph unity? (*Write the sentence number here.*) _____

About Support

3. What is for you the best (most real and vivid) detail or image in the paragraph "Heartbreak"?

    _____

    _____

    What is the best detail or image in "A Childhood Disappointment"?

    _____

    _____

    What is the best detail or image in "A Frustrating Job"?

    _____

    _____

4. Which two paragraphs provide details in the form of the actual words used by the participants?

    _____

    _____

About Coherence

5. Do the three paragraphs use time order or emphatic order to organize details?

    _____

6. What are four transition words used in "A Frustrating Job"?

    a. _____

    b. _____

    c. _____

    d. _____

WRITING A NARRATIVE PARAGRAPH

■ Writing Assignment 1

Write an essay about an experience in which a certain emotion was predominant. The emotion might be fear, pride, satisfaction, embarrassment, or any of the following:

Frustration	Sympathy	Shyness
Love	Bitterness	Disappointment

Sadness	Violence	Happiness
Terror	Surprise	Jealousy
Shock	Nostalgia	Anger
Relief	Loss	Hate
Envy	Silliness	Nervousness

The experience should be *limited in time*. Note that the three paragraphs presented in this chapter all detail experiences that occurred within relatively short periods. One writer describes a heartbreaking surprise he received the day he visited his girlfriend; another describes the disappointing loss of a prize; the third describes a frustrating night of baby-sitting.

A good way to re-create an event is to *include some dialogue*, as the writers of two of the three paragraphs in this chapter have done. Repeating what you have said or what you have heard someone else say helps make the situation come alive. First, though, be sure to check the section on quotation marks on pages 353–360.

How to Proceed

a **Begin by prewriting.** Think of an experience or event in your life in which you felt a certain emotion strongly. Then spend ten minutes freewriting about the experience. Do not worry at this point about such matters as spelling or grammar or putting things in the right order; instead, just try to get down all the details you can think of that seem related to the experience.

b **Link the event and the emotion and list details.** This preliminary writing will help you decide whether your topic is promising enough to develop further. If it is not, choose another emotion. If it is, do two things:

   ■ First, write your topic sentence, underlining the emotion you will focus on. For example, "My first day in kindergarten was one of the scariest days of my life."

   ■ Second, make up a list of all the details involved in the experience. Then arrange these details in time order.

c **Draft details into sequence.** Using your list of details as a guide, prepare a rough draft of your paper. Use time signals such as *first, then, next, after, while, during,* and *finally* to help connect details as you move from the beginning to the middle to the end of your narrative.

d **Check mechanics.** As you work on the drafts of your paper, refer to the checklist on the inside front cover to make sure that you can answer *Yes* to the questions about unity, support, and coherence. Also use the checklist to edit the next-to-final draft of your paper for sentence-skills mistakes, including spelling.

■ **Writing Assignment 2**

Write a paper that shows, through some experience you have had, the truth or falsity of a popular belief. You might write about any one of the following statements or some other popular saying.

Every person has a price.

Haste makes waste.

Don't count your chickens before they're hatched.

A bird in the hand is worth two in the bush.

It isn't what you know, it's who you know.

Borrowing can get you into trouble.

What you don't know won't hurt you.

Keeping a promise is easier said than done.

You never really know people until you see them in an emergency.

If you don't help yourself, nobody will.

An ounce of prevention is worth a pound of cure.

Hope for the best but expect the worst.

Never give advice to a friend.

You get what you pay for.

A stitch in time saves nine.

A fool and his money are soon parted.

There is an exception to every rule.

Nice people finish last.

Absence makes the heart grow fonder.

Misery loves company.

Never put off till tomorrow what you can do today.

Beauty is only skin-deep.

Begin your narrative paragraph with a topic sentence that expresses your agreement or disagreement with a popular saying. For example, "My sister learned recently that 'Keeping a promise is easier said than done.'" Or "'Never give advice to a friend' is not always good advice, as I learned after helping a friend re-unite with her boyfriend."

Refer to the suggestions about "How to Proceed" on page 194 when doing your paper. Remember that the purpose of your story is to *support* your topic sentence. Feel free to select carefully from and even add to your experience so that the details truly support the point of your story.

■ Writing Assignment 3

Write an account of a memorable personal experience. Make sure that your narrative has a point, expressed in the first sentence of the paper. If necessary, tailor your narrative to fit your purpose. Use *time order* to organize your details (*first* this happened; *then* this; *after* that, this; *next*, this; and so on). Concentrate on providing *as many specific details as possible* so that the reader can really share your experience. Try to make it as vivid for the reader as it was for you when you first experienced it.

You might want to use one of the topics below, or a topic of your own choosing. Regardless, remember that your story must illustrate or support a point stated in the first sentence of your paper.

> The first time you felt grown-up
>
> A major decision
>
> A moment you knew you were happy
>
> The occasion of your best or worst date
>
> A time you took a foolish risk
>
> An argument you will never forget
>
> An incident that changed your life
>
> A time when you did or did not do the right thing
>
> Your best or worst holiday, birthday, or other special occasion
>
> A time you learned a lesson or taught one to someone else
>
> An occasion of triumph in sports or some other event

You may want to refer to the suggestions on "How to Proceed" in Writing Assignment 1.

■ Writing Assignment 4

Imagine that a younger brother or sister, or a young friend, has to make a difficult decision of some kind. Perhaps he or she must decide how to go about preparing for a job interview, whether or not to get help with a difficult class, or what to do about a co-worker who is taking money from the cash register. Write a narration from your own experience (or that of someone you know) that will teach a younger person something about the decision he or she must make. In your paragraph, include a comment or two about the lesson your story teaches. You may narrate an experience about any problem young people face, including any of those already mentioned or those listed below.

> Should he or she save a little from a weekly paycheque?
>
> Should he or she live at home or move to an apartment with some friends?

How should he or she deal with a group of friends who are involved with drugs, stealing, or both?

■ Writing Assignment 5

Writing about a Reading Selection: Read Maya Angelou's article "Adolescent Confusion" on pages 535–537. Most teenagers are, at times, as impulsive and unthinking as Angelou was. Write a narrative about a time during your teenage years when you did something impulsively, with little regard for the possible consequences — something which you later regretted. You may have committed this act because you, like Angelou, wanted to know about something or because you were pressured into it by others.

ARGUING
A POSITION

Most of us know someone who enjoys a good argument. Such a person usually challenges any sweeping statement we might make. "Why do you say that?" he or she will ask. "Give your reasons." Our questioner then listens carefully as we cite our reasons, waiting to see if we really do have solid evidence to support our point of view. Such a questioner may make us feel a bit nervous, but we may also feel grateful to him or her for helping us think through our opinions.

The ability to advance sound and compelling arguments is an important skill in everyday life. We can use persuasion to get an extension on a term paper, obtain a favour from a friend, or convince an employer that we are the right person for a job. Understanding persuasion based on clear, logical reasoning can also help us see through the sometimes faulty arguments advanced by advertisers, editors, politicians, and others who try to bring us over to their side.

In this section, you will be asked to argue a position and defend it with a series of solid reasons. You are in a general way doing the same thing — making a point and then supporting it — with all the paragraphs in the book. The difference here is that, in a more direct and formal manner, you will advance a point about which you feel strongly and seek to convince others to agree with you.

PARAGRAPHS TO CONSIDER

Let's Ban Formals

¹While many students regard "the Formal" as the peak event in high school life, I believe that high school formals should be banned. ²One reason is that even before the formal takes place, it causes problems. ³Teenagers are separated into "the ones who were asked" and "the ones who weren't." ⁴Being one of those who weren't asked can be heartbreaking to a sensitive young person. ⁵Another pre-formal problem is money. ⁶The price of the various items needed can add up quickly to a lot of money. ⁷The dance itself can be unpleasant and frustrating, too. ⁸At the beginning of the evening, the girls enviously compare dresses while the boys sweat nervously inside their

rented suits. [9]During the dance, the couples who have gotten together only to go to the formal have split up into miserable singles. [10]When the event draws to a close, the popular teenagers drive off happily to other parties while the less-popular ones head home, as usual. [11]Perhaps the main reason formals should be banned, however, is the drinking and driving that go on after the dance is over. [12]Teenagers pile into their cars on their way to "post-parties" and pull out the bottles and cans stashed under the seat. [13]By the time the big night is finally over, at 4 or 5 a.m., students are trying to weave home without encountering the police or a roadside tree. [14]Some of them do not make it, and grad formal night turns into tragedy. [15]For all these reasons, formals have no place in our schools.

A Terrible Vacation

[1]Despite much advertising to the contrary, taking a cruise is a terrible way to spend a vacation. [2]For one thing, there is too much food. [3]You are force-fed seven times a day: breakfast, midmorning snack, lunch, afternoon punch and pastries, dinner, the midnight buffet, and the 1:30 a.m. pizza in the disco. [4]Also, the servers will not take "no" for an answer when they bring the food to your table. [5]They think "no" means "give me a medium-sized portion." [6]Another problem with a cruise is that there is too little genuine exercise. [7]The swimming pool is the size of a large bathtub. [8]Three strokes bring you to the other side. [9]And if you want to jog around the deck, you will have to dodge flying ping-pong balls and leapfrog over the shuffleboard players as you go. [10]Finally, the shipboard activities are boring. [11]The big event of the afternoon is bingo, and at night, for excitement, there is the Queen's Plate, complete with little wooden horses and a social director throwing dice to see which one wins. [12]Many people are opposed to gambling anyway, and these games can be offensive to them. [13]If you try to start a conversation on deck with one of the other passengers, you will find that most of them have sent their minds on vacation along with their bodies. [14]All they are interested in is what kind of suntan lotion you are using or what you think will be served at the next meal. [15]You will soon give up and join them in the chief activity on board--staring at the ocean. [16]So the next time you look through your vacation folders, pick the mountains, the seashore--anything but a cruise ship. [17]This way, your vacation will expand your mind and your muscles but not your waistline.

Living Alone

[1]Living alone is quite an experience. [2]People who live alone, for one thing, have to learn to do all kinds of tasks by themselves. [3]They must learn--even if they have had no experience--to change fuses, put up curtains and shades, temporarily dam an overflowing toilet, cook a meal, and defrost a refrigerator. [4]When there is no father, husband, mother, or wife to depend

on, a person can't fall back on the excuse, "I don't know how to do that." [5]Those who live alone also need the strength to deal with people. [6]Alone, singles must face noisy neighbours, unresponsive property managers, dishonest repair people, and aggressive bill collectors. [7]Because there are no buffers between themselves and the outside world, people living alone have to handle every visitor--friendly or unfriendly--alone. [8]Finally, singles need a large dose of courage to cope with occasional panic and unavoidable loneliness. [9]That weird thump in the night is even more terrifying when there is no one in the next bed or the next room. [10]Frightening weather or unexpected bad news is doubly bad when the worry can't be shared. [11]Even when life is going well, little moments of sudden loneliness can send shivers through the heart. [12]Struggling through such bad times taps into reserves of courage that people may not have known they possessed. [13]Facing everyday tasks, confronting all types of people, and handling panic and loneliness can shape singles into brave, resourceful, and more independent people.

■ Questions

About Unity

1. The topic sentence in "Living Alone" is too broad. Circle the topic sentence below that states accurately what the paragraph is about.
   a. Living alone takes courage.
   b. Living alone can create feelings of loneliness.
   c. Living alone should be avoided.

2. Which sentence in "A Terrible Vacation" should be eliminated in the interest of paragraph unity? (*Write the sentence number here.*) _____

About Support

3. How many reasons are given to support the topic sentence in each paragraph?
   a. In "A Terrible Vacation"   _____ one _____ two _____ three _____ four
   b. In "Let's Ban Formals"   _____ one _____ two _____ three _____ four
   c. In "Living Alone"   _____ one _____ two _____ three _____ four

4. After which sentence in "Let's Ban Formals" are more specific details needed? _____

About Coherence

5. Which paragraph uses a combination of time and emphatic order to organize its details?

6. What are the three main transition words in "Living Alone"?

    a. _____   b. _____   c. _____

Activity: Creating a Skeleton Outline

Complete the "X-ray" or "skeleton" outline below of "A Terrible Vacation." Summarize in a few words the primary and secondary supporting material that fits under the topic sentence. Two items have been done for you as examples.

Topic sentence: Despite much advertising to the contrary, taking a cruise is a terrible way to spend a vacation.

    a. _____

        (1) _____

        (2) _____

    b. _____

        (1) _____

        (2) *Little room for jogging*

    c. _____

        (1) _____

        (2) *Dull conversations with other passengers*

        (3) _____

WRITING AN ARGUMENT PARAGRAPH

■ Writing Assignment 1

On separate paper, make up brief outlines for any *four* of the eight statements that follow. Note the example. Make sure that you have three *separate* and *distinct reasons* for each statement.

Example   Large cities should outlaw passenger cars.
        a. Cut down on smog and pollution
        b. Cut down on noise
        c. Create more room for pedestrians

1. Condoms should (*or* should not) be made available in schools.

2. _____ (*name a specific sports team*) should win its league championship.

3. Television is one of the best (*or* worst) inventions of this century.

4. _____ are the best (*or* worst) pets.

5. All cigarette and alcohol advertising should be banned.

6. Teenagers make poor parents.

7. _____ is one public figure today who can be considered a hero.

8. This college needs a better _____ (cafeteria *or* library *or* student centre *or* grading policy *or* attendance policy).

How to Proceed

a **Decide on the best topic and check the logic of your support.** Decide, perhaps through discussion with your instructor or class-mates, which of your outlines would be most promising to develop into a paragraph. Make sure that your supporting points are logical ones that actually back up your topic sentence. Ask yourself in each case, "Does this item truly support my topic sentence?"

b **Prewrite to generate details.** Now do some prewriting. Prepare a list of all the details you can think of that might support your point. To begin with, prepare more details than you can actually use. Here, for example, are details generated by the writer of "Let's Ban Formals" while working on the paragraph:

Car accidents (most important)	Waste of school money
Drinking after dance	Going with someone you don't like
Competition over dates	Licence to stay out all night
Preparation for formal cuts into school hours	Separates popular from unpopular
	Expenses
Rejection of not being asked	Parents' interference

c **Edit for best details and order details. Create an outline.** Decide which details you will use to develop your paragraph. Also, number the details in the order in which you will present them. (You may also want to make an outline of your paragraph at this point.) Because *emphatic order* (most important reason last) is the most effective way to organize an argument paragraph, be sure to save your most powerful reason for last. Here is how the writer of "Let's Ban Formals" made decisions about details:

8   Car accidents (most important)

7   Drinking after dance

3   Competition over dates

      ~~Preparation for formal cuts into school hours~~

1   Rejection of not being asked

      ~~Waste of school money~~

4   Going with someone you don't like

6   Licence to stay out all night

5   Separates popular from unpopular

2   Expenses

      ~~Parents' Interference~~

d   **Add specific details to each supporting reason.** Develop each reason with specific details. For example, in "Let's Ban Formals," notice how the writer explains how unpleasant the formal can be by describing boys "who sweat nervously" and one-night-only dates splitting up into "miserable singles." The writer also expands the idea of after-dance drinking by describing the "bottles and cans stashed under the seat" and the teenagers "trying to weave home."

e   **Check your draft for persuasiveness.** As you write, imagine that your audience is a jury that will ultimately render a verdict on your argument. Have you presented a convincing case? If *you* were on the jury, would you be favourably impressed with this argument?

f   **Keep checking your material** as you are working on the drafts of your paper, with the four bases of unity, support, coherence, and sentence skills in mind.

g   **Edit the next-to-final draft of your paper** for sentence-skills mistakes, including spelling.

■ Writing Assignment 2

Write a paragraph that uses *reasons* to develop a point of some kind. You may advance and defend a point of your own about which you feel strongly, or you could support any one of the following statements:

1. Junk food should be banned from school cafeterias.

2. Being young is better than being old.

3. Being old is better than being young.

4. Fall can be seen as the saddest season.

5. Many college instructors know their subjects, but some are poor teachers.

6. _____ is a sport that should be banned.

7. _____ is a subject that should be taught in every school.

8. Athletes at schools with national reputations in sports should be paid for their work.

9. _____ is the one material possession that is indispensable in everyday life.

10. A college diploma is (*or* is not) essential for an ambitious person.

Use the suggestions in "How to Proceed" on pages 202–203 as a guide in writing your paragraph.

■ Writing Assignment 3

Write a paragraph in which you take a stand on one of the controversial subjects below. As a lead-in to this writing project, your instructor might give the class a chance to "stand up for what they believe in." One side of the front of the room should be designated *strong agreement* and the other side *strong disagreement*, with the space between for varying intermediate degrees of agreement or disagreement. As the class stands in front of the room, the instructor will read one *value statement* at a time from the list below, and students will move to the appropriate spot depending on their degree of agreement or disagreement. Some time will be allowed for students, first, to discuss with those near them the reasons they are standing where they are, and second, to state to those on the other end of the scale the reasons for their position.

1. Students should not be required to attend high school.
2. Prostitution should be legalized.
3. Homosexuals and lesbians should not be allowed to teach in schools.
4. The death penalty should exist for certain crimes.
5. Abortion should be legal.
6. Federal prisons should be co-ed, and prisoners should be allowed to marry.
7. Parents of girls under eighteen should be informed if their daughters receive birth-control aids.
8. The government should set up centres where sick or aged persons can go voluntarily to commit suicide.
9. Anyone on welfare for over one year should be sent to a work training centre.
10. Parents should never hit their children.

Begin your paragraph by writing a sentence that expresses your attitude toward one of these value statements—for example, "I feel that prostitution should be legalized."

Outline the reason or reasons you hold the opinion that you do. Your support may be based on (1) your own experience, (2) the experience of someone you know, and/or (3) logic. For example, an outline of a paragraph based on one student's *logic* proceeded as follows:

I feel that prostitution should be legalized for the following reasons:

1. Prostitutes would then have to pay their fair share of income tax.
2. Government health centres would administer regular check-ups and thus help prevent the spread of sexually transmitted diseases.
3. Prostitutes would be able to work openly and independently and would not be subject to exploitation by others.
4. Most of all, prostitutes would no longer be so much regarded as social outcasts--an attitude that is psychologically damaging to those who may already have emotional problems.

Another outline, based on *experience*, proceeded as follows:

I do not feel that prostitution should be legalized, because of a woman I know who was once a prostitute.

1. The attention Linda received as a prostitute prevented her from seeing and working on her personal problems.
2. She became embittered toward all men, whom she always suspected of wanting to exploit her.
3. She developed a negative self-image and felt that no one could love her.

Use your outline as the basis for writing a paragraph. Be sure to refer to the suggestions on "How to Proceed" on pages 202–203.

■ Writing Assignment 4

You have finally met Mr. or Ms. Right—but your parents don't approve of him or her. Specifically, they are against your doing one of the following:

Continuing to see this person

Going steady

Moving in together

Getting married at the end of the school year

Write a letter to your parents explaining in a fully detailed way why you have made your choice. Do your best to convince them that it is a good choice.

■ Writing Assignment 5

Writing about a Reading Selection: Read Brian Preston's selection titled "Shots on Goal" on pages 440–443. Then write a persuasive paragraph in which you agree or disagree with one of the comments about Manon Rhéaume made by her coach, another player, one of the reporters, or the author himself. Your topic sentence may be simple and direct, like one of these:

> I strongly agree with Chris McSorley's point about Manon's being a "phenomenal athlete" because of her hard work and competence.

> I disagree totally with Alexei Yashin's mother when she states that women can understand hockey as well as men but they aren't as strong as men so they must be smarter.

Alternatively, you could develop your own paragraph about women in violent sports like hockey and wrestling. Your topic sentence might be like one of the following:

> We need the presence of female skill and technical intelligence in sports where brute strength has been the only selling point.

> Women should be too intelligent to lower themselves to beating each other up in sports where brutality is essential to ticket sales.

> Men may be afraid that women will show how violent they can be, if they become too successful in sports like hockey or boxing.

PART THREE

ESSAY DEVELOPMENT

PREVIEW

Part Three moves from the single-paragraph paper to the several-paragraph essay. The differences between a paragraph and an essay are explained and then illustrated with a paragraph that has been expanded into an essay. You are shown how to begin an essay, how to tie its supporting paragraphs together, and how to conclude it. Three student essays are presented, along with questions to increase your understanding of the essay form. Finally, directions on how to plan an essay are followed by a series of essay writing assignments.

WRITING THE ESSAY

What Is an Essay?

DIFFERENCES BETWEEN AN ESSAY AND A PARAGRAPH

An essay is simply a paper of several paragraphs, rather than one paragraph, supporting a single point. In an essay, subjects can and should be treated more fully than they would be in a single-paragraph paper.

The main idea or point developed in an essay is called the *thesis statement* (rather than, as in a paragraph, the *topic sentence*). The thesis statement appears in the introductory paragraph, and it is then developed in the supporting paragraphs that follow. A short concluding paragraph closes the essay.

THE FORM OF AN ESSAY

The diagram on the next page shows the form of an essay.

Introductory Paragraph

```
Introduction
Thesis sentence
Plan of development:
Points 1, 2, 3
```

The *introduction* attracts the reader's interest.

The *thesis sentence* states the main idea advanced in the paper.

The *plan of development* is a list of the points that support the thesis. The points are presented *in the order in which they will be developed* in the paper.

First Supporting Paragraph

```
Topic sentence (point 1)
Specific evidence
```

The *topic sentence* advances the first supporting point for the thesis, and the *specific evidence* in the rest of the paragraph develops that first point.

Second Supporting Paragraph

```
Topic sentence (point 2)
Specific evidence
```

The *topic sentence* advances the second supporting point for the thesis, and the *specific evidence* in the rest of the paragraph develops that second point.

Third Supporting Paragraph

```
Topic sentence (point 3)
Specific evidence
```

The *topic sentence* advances the third supporting point for the thesis, and the *specific evidence* in the rest of the paragraph develops that third point.

Concluding Paragraph

```
Summary, conclusion,
or both
```

A *summary* is a brief restatement of the thesis and its main points. A *conclusion* is a final thought or two stemming from the subject of the paper.

A MODEL ESSAY

Gene, the writer of the paragraph on working in an apple plant (page 36), later decided to develop his subject more fully. Here is the essay that resulted.

My Job in an Apple Plant

Introductory paragraph

[1] In the course of working my way through school, I have taken many jobs I would rather forget. [2] I have spent nine hours a day lifting heavy automobile and truck batteries off the end of an assembly line. [3] I have risked the loss of eyes and fingers working a punch press in a textile factory. [4] I have served as a ward aide in a mental hospital, helping care for brain-damaged men who would break into violent fits at unexpected moments. [5] But none of these jobs was as dreadful as my job in an apple plant in Prince Edward County. [6] The work was physically hard; the pay was poor; and, most of all, the working conditions were dismal.

First supporting paragraph

[7] First of all, the job made enormous demands on my strength and energy. [8] For ten hours a night, I took cartons that rolled down a metal track and stacked them onto wooden skids in a tractor trailer. [9] Each carton contained twelve heavy cans or bottles of apple juice. [10] A carton shot down the track about every fifteen seconds. [11] I once figured out that I was lifting an average of twelve tonnes of apple juice every night. [12] When a truck was almost filled, I or my partner had to drag fourteen bulky wooden skids into the empty trailer nearby and then set up added sections of the heavy metal track so that we could start routing cartons to the back of the empty van. [13] While one of us did that, the other performed the stacking work of two men.

Second supporting paragraph

[14] I would not have minded the difficulty of the work so much if the pay had not been so poor. [15] I was paid the minimum wage of that time, two dollars an hour, plus the minimum of a quarter extra for working the night shift. [16] Because of the low salary, I felt compelled to get as much overtime pay as possible. [17] Everything over eight hours a night was time-and-a-half, so I typically worked twelve hours a night. [18] On Friday I would sometimes work straight through until Saturday at noon--eighteen hours. [19] I averaged over sixty hours a week but did not take home much more than $100.

Third supporting paragraph

[20] But even more than the low pay, what upset me about my apple plant job was the working conditions. [21] Our humourless supervisor cared only about his production record for each night and tried to keep the assembly line moving at a break-neck pace. [22] During work I was limited to two ten-minute breaks and an unpaid half hour for lunch. [23] Most of my time was spent outside on the truck loading dock in near-zero-degree temperatures. [24] The steel floors of the trucks were like ice; the quickly penetrating cold made my feet feel like stone. [25] I had no shared interests with the man I loaded cartons with, and so I had to work without companionship on the job. [26] And after the production line shut down and most people left, I had

to spend two hours alone scrubbing clean the apple vats, which were coated with a sticky residue.

Concluding paragraph   [27]I stayed on the job for five months, all the while hating the difficulty of the work, the poor money, and the conditions under which I worked. [28]By the time I quit, I was determined never to do such degrading work again.

Important Points about the Essay

INTRODUCTORY PARAGRAPH

An introductory paragraph has certain purposes or functions and can be constructed using various methods.

Purposes of the Introduction

An introductory paragraph should do three things:

1   Attract the reader's *interest*. Using one of the suggested methods of introduction described below can help draw the reader into your paper.

2   Present a *thesis sentence* — a clear, direct statement of the *central idea* that you will develop in your paper. The thesis statement, like a topic sentence, should have a key word or words that reflect your *attitude* about the subject. For example, in the essay on the apple plant job, the key word is *dreadful*.

3   Indicate a *plan of development* — a *preview of the major points* that will support your thesis statement, listed *in the order in which they will be presented*. In some cases, the thesis statement and plan of development may appear in the same sentence. In some cases, also, the plan of development may be omitted.

Activity: Analyzing the Opening Paragraph

1.   In "My Job in an Apple Plant," which sentences are used to attract the reader's interest?

_____ Sentences 1 to 3   _____ 1 to 4   _____ 1 to 5

2.   The thesis in "My Job in an Apple Plant" is presented in

_____ Sentence 4   _____ Sentence 5   _____ Sentence 6

3.   The thesis is followed by a plan of development.

_____ Yes   _____ No

4. Which words in the plan of development announce the three major supporting points in the essay? Write them below.

a. _____

b. _____

c. _____

Common Methods of Introduction

Here are some common methods of introduction. Use any one method, or a combination of methods, to introduce your subject in an interesting way.

1 *Broad statement.* Begin with a broad, general statement of your topic and *narrow it down to your thesis statement.* Broad, general statements ease the reader into your thesis statement by providing a background for it. In "My Job in an Apple Plant," Gene writes generally on the topic of his worst jobs and then narrows down to a specific worst job.

2 *Contrast.* Start with an idea or situation that is the *opposite* of the one you will develop. This approach works because your readers will be surprised, and then intrigued, by the contrast between the opening idea and the thesis that follows it. Here is an example of a "contrast" introduction:

> When I was a girl, I never argued with my parents about differences between their attitudes and mine. My father would deliver his judgement on an issue, and that was usually the end of the matter. Discussion seldom changed his mind, and disagreement was not tolerated. But the situation is different with today's parents and children. My husband and I have to contend with radical differences between what our children think about a given situation and what we think about it. We have had disagreements with all three of our daughters, Stephanie, Diana, and Gisel.

3 *"Relevance."* Explain the importance of your topic. If you can convince your readers that the subject applies to them in some way, or is something they should know more about, they will want to continue reading. The introductory paragraph of "Consuming Canadians" (page 217) provides an example of a "relevance" introduction.

4 *Anecdote.* Use an incident or brief story. Stories are naturally interesting. They appeal to a reader's curiosity. In your introduction, an anecdote will grab the reader's attention right away. The story should be *brief* and should be *related to your central idea.* The incident in the story can be something that happened to you, something that you have heard about, or something that you have read about in a newspaper or magazine. Here is an example of a paragraph that begins with a story:

> The husky man pushes open the door of the bedroom and grins as he pulls out a .38 revolver. An elderly man wearing thin pyjamas looks at him and whimpers. In a feeble effort at escape, the old man slides out of his bed and moves to the door of the room. The husky man, still grinning, blocks his way. With the face of a small, frightened animal, the old man looks up and whispers, "Oh God, please don't hurt me." The grinning man then fires four times. The television movie cuts now to a soap commercial, but the little boy who has been watching the set has begun to cry. Such scenes of direct violence on television must surely be harmful to children for a number of psychological reasons.

5 *Questions.* Ask your readers one or more questions. These questions catch the readers' interest and make them want to read on. Here is an example of a paragraph that begins with questions:

> What would happen if we were totally honest with ourselves? Would we be able to stand the pain of our own self-deception? Would the complete truth be too much for us to bear? Such questions will probably never be answered, for in everyday life we protect ourselves from the onslaught of too much reality. All of us cultivate defence mechanisms that prevent us from seeing and hearing and feeling too much. Included among such defence mechanisms are rationalization, reaction formation, and substitution.

Note, however, that the thesis itself must *not* be a question.

6 *Quotation.* A quotation can be something you have read in a book or an article. It can also be something that you have heard: a popular saying or proverb ("Never give advice to a friend"); a current or recent advertising slogan ("Reach out and touch someone"); a favourite expression used by your friends or family ("My father always says …"). Using a quotation in your introductory paragraph lets you add someone else's voice to your own. Here is an example of a paragraph that begins with a quotation:

> "Evil," wrote Martin Buber, "is lack of direction." In my school days as a fatherless boy, with a mother too confused by her own life to really care for me, I strayed down a number of dangerous paths. Before my eighteenth birthday, I had been a car thief, a burglar, and a drug seller.

SUPPORTING PARAGRAPHS

Most essays have three supporting points, developed in three separate paragraphs. (Some essays will have two supporting points; others, four or more.) Each of the supporting paragraphs should begin with a topic sentence that states the point to be detailed in that paragraph. Just as the thesis provides a focus for the entire essay, the topic sentence provides a focus for each supporting paragraph.

Activity: Finding Topic Sentences

1. What is the topic sentence for the first supporting paragraph of "My Job in an Apple Plant"? (*Write the sentence number here.*) _____

2. What is the topic sentence for the second supporting paragraph? _____

3. What is the topic sentence for the third supporting paragraph? _____

TRANSITIONAL SENTENCES

In paragraphs, transitions and other connective devices (pages 74–79) are used to help link sentences. Similarly, in an essay *transitional sentences* are used to help tie the supporting paragraphs together. *Such transitional sentences usually occur near the end of one paragraph or the beginning of the next.*

In "My Job in an Apple Plant," the first transitional sentence is:

> I would not have minded the <u>difficulty</u> of the work so much if the <u>pay</u> had not been so poor.

In this sentence, the key word *difficulty* reminds us of the point of the first supporting paragraph, while *pay* tells us the point to be developed in the second supporting paragraph.

Activity

Here is the other transitional sentence in "My Job in an Apple Plant":

> But even more than the low pay, what upset me about my apple plant job were the working conditions.

Complete the following statement: In the sentence above, the key words

_____ *echo* the point of the second supporting paragraph, and

the key words _____ *announce* the topic of the third supporting paragraph.

CONCLUDING PARAGRAPH

The concluding paragraph often summarizes the essay by briefly restating the thesis and, at times, the main supporting points of the essay. Also, the conclusion brings the paper to a natural and graceful end, sometimes leaving the reader with a final thought on the subject.

Activity

1. Which sentence in the concluding paragraph of "My Job in an Apple Plant" restates the thesis and supporting points of the essay? _____

2. Which sentence contains the concluding thought of the essay? _____

Essays to Consider

Read the three student essays below and then answer the questions that follow.

Giving Up a Baby

¹As I awoke, I overheard a nurse say, "It's a lovely baby boy. ²How could a mother give him up?" ³"Be quiet," another voice said. ⁴"She's going to wake up soon." ⁵Then I heard the baby cry, but I never heard him again. ⁶Three years ago, I gave up my child to two strangers, people who wanted a baby but could not have one. ⁷I was in pain over my decision, and I can still hear the voices of people who said I was selfish or crazy. ⁸But the reasons I gave up my child were important ones, at least to me.

⁹I gave up my baby, first of all, because I was very young. ¹⁰I was only seventeen, and I was unmarried. ¹¹Because I was so young, I did not yet feel the desire to have and raise a baby. ¹²I knew that I would be a child raising a child and that, when I had to stay home to care for the baby, I would resent the loss of my freedom. ¹³I might also blame the baby for that loss. ¹⁴In addition, I had not had the experiences in life that would make me a responsible, giving parent. ¹⁵What could I teach my child, when I barely knew what life was all about myself?

¹⁶Besides my age, another factor in my decision was the problems my parents would have. ¹⁷I had dropped out of high school before graduation, and I did not have a job or even the chance of a job, at least for a while. ¹⁸My parents would have to support my child and me, possibly for years. ¹⁹My mom and dad had already struggled to raise their family and were not well off financially. ²⁰I knew I could not burden them with an unemployed teenager and her baby. ²¹Even if I eventually got a job, my parents would have to help raise my child. ²²They would have to be full-time baby-sitters while I tried to make a life of my own. ²³Because my parents are good people, they would have done all this for me. ²⁴But I felt I could not ask for such a big sacrifice from them.

²⁵The most important factor in my decision was, I suppose, a selfish one. ²⁶I was worried about my own future. ²⁷I didn't want to marry the baby's father. ²⁸I realized during the time I was pregnant that we didn't love each other. ²⁹My future as an unmarried mother with no education or skills would certainly have been limited. ³⁰I would be struggling to survive, and I would have to give up for years my dreams of getting a job and my

own car and apartment. ³¹It is hard to admit, but I also considered the fact that, with a baby, I would not have the social life most young people have. ³²I would not be able to stay out late, go to parties, or feel carefree and irresponsible, for I would always have an enormous responsibility waiting for me at home. ³³With a baby, the future looked limited and insecure.

³⁴In summary, thinking about my age, my responsibility to my parents, and my own future made me decide to give up my baby. ³⁵As I look back today at my decision, I know that it was the right one for me at the time.

Consuming Canadians

¹Almost all Canadians have become constant consumers. ²They may grocery shop daily, or check the flyers obsessively, or shuffle coupons like decks of cards. ³They cruise the malls, haunt the discount or "wholesale" outlets, or drive the shopping strips like starved cabbies after a fare. ⁴Shopping seems like an innocent pleasure, but look at how it dominates our lives. ⁵In reality, shopping, or consuming, has reached a point where it plays too large a part in daily life. ⁶It is a needless substitute for other activities, has affected children's attitudes and behaviour, and has created twin TV monsters: home shopping networks and infomercials.

⁷Constant food shopping in an era of refrigeration and two-career families is one of the most time-wasting and obvious signs of our consuming mania. ⁸Grocery stores, once ordinary and unglamorous, now issue "Special Reports" on hot new products that informed Canadians must buy and keep up on, for reasons of health, trendiness, or just plain indulgence. ⁹On a Saturday after one of these gussied-up flyers appears, the aisles of supermarkets are clogged with the carts of rampaging shoppers. ¹⁰In addition, back-up radio and TV advertisements blanket local stations during these promotions. ¹¹Grocery executives are interviewed seriously about the importance of their new items, and videotapes sold, showing shoppers the VP of Foodworld turning dog food into a gourmet delight with his or her special Dijon mustard. ¹²Moreover, the middles of most Saturday papers are now stuffed with as many as a dozen four-to-six-page flyers. ¹³Stimulated by all this promotion, Canadians, whether motivated by the desire for a bargain or by a yen for Quadruple-Chocolate Demonic Delight, hit the stores every day, not out of need, but because of carefully managed marketing strategies.

¹⁴Children absorb our attitudes toward shopping and our views of the importance of consumer products automatically. ¹⁵As early as age five or six, children want clothes from The Gap, Roots ballcaps, and Sailor Moon everything. ¹⁶Later, in high school, the trendily clad or neatly Ralph Laurened teenager is sometimes assumed to be a better student than his or her earringed or grunge-plaid-clad fellow student. ¹⁷Even grunge or "goth-wear" must be shopped for, and represent market-created consumer trends. ¹⁸The mall as social centre appears endlessly in movies like Clueless and TV shows aimed at adolescents: shopping, or "malling," dreaming about buying things, has replaced extra-curricular activities, studying, or just plain hanging around. ¹⁹Canada may be

the only country where our climate has helped to create "supermalls," with amusement parks, wave-pools, and anything any child or teenager could want.

[20]Our consuming craziness is especially evident in our television programming. [21]For one thing, we don't need to go out to shop. [22]We've gone beyond the humble and even the very fancy catalogue for the passive in-home shopper. [23]We can shop right from the potato position on the couch. [24]Besides the obnoxious infomercial, where some aging American celebrity lies about hair regrowth, we have entire cable networks devoted twenty-four hours a day to offering us everything from cubic zirconia to sticky pads to put under furniture feet. [25]Whether in Moose Jaw or Come-by-Chance, all we need is our credit card and a telephone. [26]Canada even has its own off-the-wall home shopping star, promoting a peculiar product: our future. [27]JoJo Simard, of the doggy-palace hairdo, is there for us, along with her "talented psychics," ready to take our money day or night. We'll buy nothing for something, apparently.

[28]Canadians truly have become crazed consumers. [29]Perhaps we feel inferior and want to keep up with trends we imagine our American neighbours enjoying. [30]Perhaps we want our children to have more than we did. [31]Perhaps our lives really are empty. [32]Whatever the reason, we're living to shop these days, any way we can.

An Interpretation of <u>Lord of the Flies</u>

[1]Modern history has shown us the evil that exists in human beings. [2]Assassinations are common, governments use torture to discourage dissent, and six million Jews were exterminated during World War II. [3]In <u>Lord of the Flies</u>, William Golding describes a group of schoolboys shipwrecked on an island with no authority figures to control their behaviour. [4]One of the boys soon yields to dark forces within himself, and his corruption symbolizes the evil in all of us. [5]First, Jack Merridew kills a living creature; then, he rebels against the group leader; and finally, he seizes power and sets up his own murderous society.

[6]The first stage in Jack's downfall is his killing of a living creature. [7]In Chapter 1, Jack aims at a pig but is unable to kill. [8]His upraised arm pauses "because of the enormity of the knife descending and cutting into living flesh, because of the unbearable blood," and the pig escapes. [9]Three chapters later, however, Jack leads some boys on a successful hunt. [10]He returns triumphantly with a freshly killed pig and reports excitedly to the others, "I cut the pig's throat." [11]Yet Jack twitches as he says this, and he wipes his bloody hands on his shorts as if eager to remove the stains. [12]There is still some civilization left in him.

[13]After the initial act of killing the pig, Jack's refusal to co-operate with Ralph shows us that this civilized part is rapidly disappearing. [14]With no adults around, Ralph has made some rules. [15]One is that a signal fire must be kept burning. [16]But Jack tempts the boys watching the fire to go hunting, and the fire goes out. [17]Another rule is that at a meeting, only the person holding a special seashell has the right to speak. [18]In Chapter 5, another

boy is speaking when Jack rudely tells him to shut up. ¹⁹Ralph accuses Jack of breaking the rules. ²⁰Jack shouts: "Bollocks to the rules! We're strong--we hunt! If there's a beast, we'll hunt it down! We'll close in and beat and beat and beat--!" ²¹He gives a "wild whoop" and leaps off the platform, throwing the meeting into chaos. ²²Jack is now much more savage than civilized.

²³The most obvious proof of Jack's corruption comes in Chapter 8, when he establishes his own murderous society. ²⁴Insisting that Ralph is not a "proper chief" because he does not hunt, Jack asks for a new election. ²⁵After he again loses, Jack announces, "I'm going off by myself.... Anyone who wants to hunt when I do can come too." ²⁶Eventually, nearly all the boys join Jack's "tribe." ²⁷Following his example, they paint their faces like savages, sacrifice to "the beast," brutally murder two of their schoolmates, and nearly succeed in killing Ralph as well. ²⁸Jack has now become completely savage--and so have the others.

²⁹Through Jack Merridew, then, Golding shows how easily moral laws can be forgotten. ³⁰Freed from grown-ups and their rules, Jack learns to kill living things, defy authority, and lead a tribe of murdering savages. ³¹Jack's example is a frightening reminder of humanity's potential for evil. ³²The "beast" the boys try to hunt and kill is actually within every human being.

■ Questions

1. In which essay does the thesis statement appear in the last sentence of the introductory paragraph?

   _____

2. In the essay on *Lord of the Flies*, which sentence of the introductory paragraph contains the plan of development? _____

3. Which method of introduction is used in "Giving Up a Baby"?
   a. General to narrow   c. Incident or story
   b. Stating importance of topic   d. Questions

4. Complete the following brief outline of "Giving Up a Baby": I gave up my baby for three reasons:

   a. _____

   b. _____

   c. _____

5. Which *two* essays use a transitional sentence between the first and second supporting paragraphs?

   _____

   _____

6. *Complete the following statement:* Emphatic order is shown in the last supporting paragraph of "Giving Up a Baby" with the words *most important fac-*

tor; in the last supporting paragraph of "Consuming Canadians" with the words _____; and in the last supporting paragraph of "An Interpretation of *Lord of the Flies*" with the words _____.

7. Which essay uses time order as well as emphatic order to organize its three supporting paragraphs? _____

8. List four major transitions used in the supporting paragraphs of "An Interpretation of *Lord of the Flies*."

   a. _____   c. _____

   b. _____   d. _____

9. Which *two* essays include a sentence in the concluding paragraph that summarizes the three supporting points?

   _____

   _____

10. Which essay includes two final thoughts in its concluding paragraph?

    _____

Planning the Essay

OUTLINING THE ESSAY

When you write an essay, advance planning is crucial for success. You should plan your essay by outlining in two ways:

1 Prepare a scratch outline. This should consist of a short statement of the thesis followed by the main supporting points for the thesis. Here is Gene's scratch outline for his essay on the apple plant:

Working at an apple plant was my worst job.
1. Hard work
2. Poor pay
3. Bad working conditions

Do not underestimate the value of this initial outline—or the work involved in achieving it. Be prepared to do a good deal of plain hard thinking at this first and most important stage of your paper.

2 Prepare a more detailed outline. The outline form that follows will serve as a guide. Your instructor may ask you to submit a copy of this form either before you actually write an essay or along with your finished essay.

FORM FOR PLANNING AN ESSAY

To write an effective essay, use a form like the one that follows.

Introduction

Opening remarks

Thesis statement _____

_____

Plan of development

Body

Topic sentence 1 _____

_____

Specific supporting evidence

Topic sentence 2 _____

_____

Specific supporting evidence

Topic sentence 3 _____

_____

Specific supporting evidence

Conclusion

Summary, closing remarks, or both

Essay Writing Assignments

Hints: Keep the following points in mind when writing an essay on any of the topics below.

1 Your first step must be to *plan your essay*. Prepare both a scratch outline and a more detailed outline, as explained on the preceding pages.

2 While writing your essay, *use the checklist below* to make sure your essay touches all four bases of effective writing.

Base 1: Unity

_____ Clearly stated thesis in the introductory paragraph of your paper

_____ All the supporting paragraphs on target in backing up your thesis

Base 2: Support

_____ Three separate supporting points for your thesis

_____ *Specific* evidence for each of the three supporting points

_____ *Plenty* of specific evidence for each supporting point

Base 3: Coherence

_____ Clear method of organization

_____ Transitions and other connecting words

_____ Effective introduction and conclusion

Base 4: Sentence Skills

_____ Clear, error-free sentences (use the checklist on the inside front cover of this book)

■ **1   Your House or Apartment**

Write an essay on the advantages *or* disadvantages (not both) of the house or apartment where you live. In your introductory paragraph, describe briefly the place you plan to write about. End the paragraph with your thesis statement and a plan of development. Here are some suggestions for thesis statements:

The best features of my apartment are its large windows, roomy closets, and great location.

The drawbacks of my house are its unreliable oil furnace, tiny kitchen, and old-fashioned bathroom.

An inquisitive owner, sloppy neighbours, and armies of ants came along with our rented house.

My apartment has several advantages, including friendly neighbours, lots of storage space, and a good security system.

■ 2 A Big Mistake

Write an essay about the biggest mistake you made within the past year. Describe the mistake and show how its effects have convinced you that it was the wrong thing to do. For instance, if you write about "taking on a full-time job while going to school" as your biggest mistake, show the problems it caused. (You might discuss such matters as low grades, constant exhaustion, and poor performance at work, for example.)

To get started, *make a list* of all the things you did last year that, with hindsight, now seem to be mistakes. Then choose the action that has had the most serious consequences for you. Make a brief outline to guide you as you write, as in the examples below.

Thesis: Separating from my husband was the worst mistake I made last year.
1. Children have suffered
2. Financial troubles
3. Loneliness

Thesis: Buying a used car to commute to school was the worst mistake I made last year.
1. Unreliable--late for class or missed class
2. Expenses for insurance, repairs
3. Led to an accident

■ 3 A Valued Possession

Write an essay about a valued material possession. Here are some suggestions:

Car	Appliance
Portable radio	CD player
TV set	Photograph album
Piece of furniture	Piece of clothing
Piece of jewellery	Stereo system (car or home)
Camera	Piece of hobby equipment

In your introductory paragraph, describe the possession: tell what it is, when and where you got it, and how long you have owned it. Your thesis statement should centre on the idea that there are several reasons this possession is so important to you. In each of your supporting paragraphs, provide details to back up one of the reasons.

For example, here is a brief outline of an essay written about a leather jacket:

Thesis: My favourite garment is my black leather jacket.
1. It is comfortable.
2. It wears well.
3. It makes me look and feel good.

■ 4 Summarizing a Selection

Write an essay in which you summarize three of the study skills described in the selection "Power Learning" on pages 477–482.

1. Summarizing involves condensing material by highlighting main points and key supporting details.
2. You can eliminate minor details and most examples given in the original material.
3. You should avoid using the exact language of the original material; put the ideas into your own words.

The introductory paragraph of the essay and suggested topic sentences for the supporting paragraphs are provided below. In addition to developing the supporting paragraphs, you should write a brief conclusion for the essay.

Introductory Paragraph

Using Study Skills

Why do some students in a college class receive A grades, while others get D's and F's? Are some people just naturally smarter? Are other students doomed to failure? Motivation--willingness to do the work--is a factor in good grades. But the main difference between successful and unsuccessful students is that the ones who do well have mastered the specific skills needed to handle college work. Fortunately, these skills can be learned by anyone. Doing well in college depends on knowing how to ... *[Complete this sentence with the three study skills you decide to write about.]*

Suggested Topic Sentences for the Supporting Paragraphs (Choose Any Three)

Time control is one aid to success as a student....
Another aid is the use of memory techniques....
Knowing how to concentrate is another essential skill....

Studying a textbook effectively is another key to success....

Perhaps the most crucial step of all is effective classroom note-taking....

■ 5 How Study Skills Help

You may already be practising some of the study skills described in "Power Learning" (pages 477–482). If so, write an essay on how study skills are helping you to succeed in school. Your thesis might be, "Study skills are helping me to succeed in college." You could organize the essay by describing, in separate paragraphs, how three different study skills have improved your work. Your topic sentences might be similar to these:

First of all, time control has helped me to make the best use of my time.

In addition, taking good notes in class has enabled me to do well in discussions and on tests.

Finally, I can study a textbook effectively now.

Alternatively, begin applying some of the techniques and be prepared to write an essay at a later time on how the study skills helped you become a better student. Or you might want to write about three study techniques of your own that have helped you succeed in your studies.

■ 6 Single Life

Write an essay on the advantages or drawbacks of single life. To get started, *make a list of all the advantages and drawbacks* you can think of for single life. Advantages might include:

Fewer expenses

Fewer responsibilities

More personal freedom

More opportunities to move or travel

Drawbacks might include:

Parental disapproval

Being alone at social events

No companion for shopping, movies, and so on

Sadness at holiday time

After you make up two lists, *select the thesis for which you feel you have more supporting material*. Then organize your material into a scratch outline. Be sure to include an introduction, a clear topic sentence for each supporting paragraph, and a conclusion.

Alternatively, write an essay on the advantages or drawbacks of married life. Follow the directions given above.

■ 7   Influences on Your Writing

Are you as good a writer as you want to be? Write an essay analyzing the reasons you have become a good writer or explaining why you are not as good as you'd like to be. Begin by considering some factors that may have influenced your level of writing ability.

> ***Your family background:*** Did you see people writing at home? Did your parents respect and value the ability to write?
>
> ***Your school experience:*** Did you have good writing teachers? Did you have a history of failure or success with writing? Was writing fun, or was it a chore? Did your school emphasize writing?
>
> ***Social influences:*** How did your school friends do at writing? What were your friends' attitudes toward writing? What feelings about writing did you pick up from TV or the movies?

You might want to organize your essay by describing the three greatest influences on your writing skill (or lack of writing skill). Show how each of these has contributed to the present state of your writing.

■ 8   A Major Decision

All of us come to various crossroads in our lives — times when we must make an important decision about which course of action to follow. Think about a major decision you have had to make (or one you are planning to make). Then write an essay on the reasons for your decision. In your introduction, describe the decision you reached. Each of the body paragraphs that follow should fully *explain one of the reasons for your decision.* Here are some examples of major decisions that often confront people:

> Enrolling in or dropping out of college
> Accepting or quitting a job
> Getting married or divorced
> Breaking up with a boyfriend or girlfriend
> Having a baby
> Moving away from home

Student papers on this topic include the essay on pages 216–217 and the paragraphs on pages 47–48.

■ 9   Reviewing a TV Show or Movie

Write an essay about a television show or movie you have seen very recently. The thesis of your essay will be that the show (or movie) has *both* good and bad features. (If you are writing about a TV series, be sure that you evaluate only one episode.)

In your first supporting paragraph, briefly summarize the show or movie. Don't get bogged down in small details here; just describe briefly the major characters and give the highlights of the action.

In your second supporting paragraph, explain what you feel are the best features of the show or movie. Listed below are some examples of good features you might write about:

Suspenseful, ingenious, or realistic plot

Good acting

Good scenery or special effects

Surprise ending

Good music

Believable characters

In your third supporting paragraph, explain what you feel are the worst features of the show or movie. Here are some possibilities:

Farfetched, confusing, or dull plot

Poor special effects

Bad acting

Cardboard characters

Unrealistic dialogue

Remember to cover only a few features in each paragraph; do not try to include everything.

Note: Titles of movies or TV shows are either underlined or printed in italics.

■ 10   Good Qualities

We are often quick to point out a person's flaws, saying, for example, "That instructor is conceited," "My boss has no patience," or "My sister is lazy." We are usually equally hard on ourselves; we constantly analyze our own faults. We rarely, though, spend as much time thinking about another person's, or our own, good qualities. Write an essay on the good qualities of a particular person. The person might be an instructor, a job supervisor, a friend, a relative, some other person you know well, or even yourself.

In your introductory paragraph, give some brief background information about the person you are describing. And include in your thesis statement a plan of development that names the three qualities you will write about. Here are several suggestions:

Patience, fairness, and kindness are my boss's best qualities.

My boyfriend is hard-working, ambitious, and determined.

Our psychology instructor has a good sense of humour, a strong sense of justice, and a genuine interest in his students.

When planning your paper, you may find it helpful to look at the positive qualities included in the list on page 130.

■ 11 Your High School

Imagine that you are an outside consultant called in as a neutral observer to examine the high school you attended. After your visit, you must send the school board a five-paragraph letter in which you describe the most striking features (good, bad, or a combination of both) of the school and the evidence for each of these features.

In order to write the letter, you may want to think about the following features of your high school:

Attitude of the teachers, student body, or administration

Condition of the buildings, classrooms, recreational areas, and so on

Curriculum

How classes are conducted

Extra-curricular activities

Crowded or uncrowded conditions

Be sure to include an introduction, a clear topic sentence for each supporting paragraph, and a conclusion.

PART FOUR

SENTENCE
SKILLS

PREVIEW

As explained in Part One, there are four steps, or bases, in effective writing. Part Four is concerned with the *fourth step: the ability to write clear, error-free sentences*. Important sentence skills appear under the general headings "Grammar," "Mechanics," "Punctuation," and "Word Use." "Word Use" includes a chapter on sentence variety which helps develop your sense of the various options and methods available for composing sentences. Finally, there is a "Practice" section which provides editing tests to reinforce many basic writing skills and to give you some experience in proofreading.

SUBJECTS, VERBS, AND OBJECTS

The basic building blocks of English sentences are subjects and verbs. Understanding them is an important first step toward mastering a number of sentence skills.

Every sentence has a subject and a verb. Who or what the sentence speaks about is called the <u>subject</u>; what the sentence says about the subject is called the <u>verb</u>.

The <u>children</u> <u>laughed</u>.

Several <u>branches</u> <u>fell</u>.

Most <u>students</u> <u>passed</u> the test.

That <u>man</u> <u>is</u> a crook.

A SIMPLE WAY TO FIND A SUBJECT

To find a subject, ask *who* or *what* the sentence is about. As shown below, your answer is the subject.

Who is the first sentence about? <u>Children</u>

What is the second sentence about? Several <u>branches</u>

Who is the third sentence about? Most <u>students</u>

Who is the fourth sentence about? That <u>man</u>

Nouns: The Words that Name Persons, Places, Ideas, and Things

The words in the four examples listed above—*children*, *branches*, *students*, and *man*—are called *nouns*. The word "noun" comes from the Latin word *nomen*, meaning "name"; therefore, a noun is a word that *names* an object, a place, a person, or another living thing. *Proper nouns* are those which are used for people's names, or for place names, such as *Mr. Almeida* or *Windsor*. Another type of noun is the *abstract noun*, which identifies an idea, condition, or state of being: i.e., *truth*, *beauty*, or *honesty*. Various texts may use different terms for these types of nouns, but the important fact is that a noun *names* something, someone, or an idea.

Subjects May Be Nouns, Pronouns, or Phrases

The *who* or *what* that a sentence is about may be tricky to find at first, but identifying the subject by a "tag," or its grammatical name, may help you. Look at the examples which follow.

1. The <u>professor</u> broke her piece of chalk.
   (The subject is a *noun*.)
2. <u>She</u> broke her piece of chalk.
   (The subject is a *pronoun*.*)
3. <u>The woman at the front of the classroom</u> broke her piece of chalk.
   (The subject is a *phrase*. The *simple subject* is the *noun* "woman.")

Activity: Identifying Different Types of Subjects

Find and underline the subjects of each of the following sentences. In the space in front of each sentence, specify whether the subject is a *noun* (N), a *pronoun* (P), or a *phrase* (PH).

_____ 1. The sun cast a golden light on the tall buildings.

_____ 2. He laboured over the old car until it was a work of art.

_____ 3. The door blew open in the wind.

_____ 4. Several lightning-struck tree branches broke in the storm.

_____ 5. They worked well together on the brainstorming exercise.

A SIMPLE WAY TO FIND A VERB

To find a verb, ask what the sentence *says about* the subject. As shown below, your answer is the verb.

What does the first sentence *say about* the children? They <u>laughed</u>.

What does the second sentence *say about* the branches? They <u>fell</u>.

---

* A pronoun is a word which "stands for" or "stands in place of" a *noun*.

What does the third sentence *say about* the students? They <u>passed</u>.

What does the fourth sentence *say about* that man? He <u>is</u> (a crook).

A second way to find the verb is to put *I*, *you*, *he*, *she*, *it*, or *they* in front of the word you think is a verb. If the result makes sense, you have a verb. For example, you could put *they* in front of *laughed* in the first sentence above, with the result, *they laughed*, making sense. Therefore you know that *laughed* is a verb. You could use *they* or *he* to test the other verbs as well.

Finally, it helps to remember that *most verbs show action*. In the sentences already considered, the three action verbs are *laughed*, *fell*, and *passed*. Certain other verbs, known as *linking verbs*, do not show action. They do, however, give information about the subject. In "That man is a crook," the linking verb *is* tells us that the man is a crook. Other common linking verbs include *am*, *are*, *was*, *were*, *feel*, *appear*, *look*, *become*, and *seem*.

Activity: Finding Subjects and Verbs

In each of the following sentences, draw one line under the subject and two lines under the verb.

1. The heavy purse cut into my shoulder.
2. Small stones pinged onto the windshield.
3. The test directions confused the students.
4. Cotton shirts feel softer than polyester ones.
5. The fog rolled into the cemetery.
6. Sparrows live in the eaves of my porch.
7. A horsefly stung her on the ankle.
8. Every other night, garbage trucks rumble down my street on their way to the river.
9. The family played badminton and volleyball, in addition to a game of softball, at the picnic.
10. With their fingers, the children drew pictures on the steamed window.

MORE ABOUT SUBJECTS AND VERBS

1   A pronoun (a word like *he*, *she*, *it*, *we*, *you*, or *they* used in place of a noun) can serve as the subject of a sentence. For example:

<u>He</u> <u>seems</u> like a lonely person.
<u>They</u> both <u>like</u> to gamble.

Without a surrounding context (so that we know who *He* or *They* refers to), the sentences may not seem clear, but they *are* complete.

2 A sentence may have more than one verb, more than one subject, or several subjects and verbs:

My heart skipped and pounded.
The radio and CD player were stolen from the car.
Dave and Ellen prepared the report together and presented it to the class.

3 Certain types of verbs, sometimes called *transitive verbs*, mainly verbs of action, may have what is called an *object*. The *object*, which may be a noun, pronoun, or phrase, *receives the action of the verb*. Here, indicated with a wavy underline, are some examples of objects of verbs.

The famished dog eagerly ate its dinner.
Enzo worked hard and finished his assignments.
Together, they achieved a great many tasks.

4 Some verbs, including the verb *to be*, never have an object. Such verbs generally do not show action; instead, they are *linking verbs* which describe states of being or of observing things. Examples of these verbs, sometimes called *intransitive verbs*, are *to seem*, *to become*, and *to appear*. The words following such verbs do not *receive* the action of a verb; instead, they often *describe* the subject of the sentence. These words which follow verbs of appearance and condition may be called *predicates*. Look at the examples which follow:

Andrea seemed sleepy and fatigued.
The weather appeared changeable.
Psychology and Marketing became my favourite courses.
He is a very cranky dog.

5 The subject of a sentence never appears within a prepositional phrase. A prepositional phrase is simply a group of words that begins with a preposition. Following is a list of common prepositions:

about	before	by	inside	over
above	behind	during	into	through
across	below	except	of	to
among	beneath	for	off	toward
around	beside	from	on	under
at	between	in	onto	with

Cross out prepositional phrases when looking for the subject of a sentence.

~~Under my pillow~~ I found a quarter left by the Tooth Fairy.

One ~~of the yellow lights at the school crossing~~ began flashing.

The comics section ~~of the newspaper~~ disappeared.

~~In spite of my efforts,~~ Bob dropped out of school.

~~During a rainstorm,~~ I sat in my car reading magazines.

6 Prepositions, like transitive verbs, may have *objects*. Because these *objects of prepositions* are often nouns, they may be easily confused with the subjects of sentences. In the examples above, where the prepositional phrases are crossed out, the *object* of each preposition is the *noun*, *pronoun*, or *phrase* which follows it. For example:

under *my pillow*	in spite of *my efforts*
of *the yellow lights*	during *a rainstorm*
of *the newspaper*	

To find the *object of a preposition*, say the preposition aloud, or to yourself. Then ask "about *what?*" or "behind *what?*" The "what," whether it is a *noun*, *pronoun*, or *phrase*, will be the *object of the preposition*.

7 *Many verbs consist of more than one word.* Here, for example, are some of the many forms of the verb *smile*. The extra words used with *smile* are called "helping (auxiliary)" verb parts.

smile	smiled	should smile
smiles	were smiling	will be smiling
does smile	have smiled	can smile
is smiling	had smiled	could be smiling
are smiling	had been smiling	must have smiled

Notes

a Words like *not, just, never, only,* and *always* are *not* part of the verb, although they may appear within the verb.

Larry <u>did</u> not <u>finish</u> the paper before class.

The road <u>was</u> just <u>completed</u> only last week.

b   The form of a verb beginning with the word *to* is called the *infinitive form.* Although this form indicates action, it is *never* used as the main verb in a sentence. *Infinitive* refers to the word *infinite*, meaning *having no limits.* The infinitive form (for example, *to do, to make, to begin*) is the source, or beginning point, for all other forms of any verb. All verb forms used as main verbs in sentences *have limits;* they are altered or *limited* by some change to show time (tense), relation to subject (person and number), and so on. The infinitive form never changes, but is used in combination with other *finite verb forms* as in the examples shown.

I was beginning *to understand* calculus when the lecture ended.
Maria swerved *to avoid* the oncoming truck.

c   *Present participles* and *gerunds* sound like exotic animals. In fact, they are simply two uses of the "-ing" form of any verb. Present *part*iciples are only *parts* of a verb form; their name should help you remember this fact. A present participle *must* be used with a "helping" or auxiliary verb: for example, "I *am making* the cat's breakfast."

■   *Participles* are sometimes used to describe things in English: for example, "He had a *winning* way about him." In these cases, they act as *adjectives.*

■   *Gerunds* are the same "-ing" forms used as *nouns* (or as subjects or objects) in sentences: for example, "*Winning* was the only thing that mattered to him."

The following examples may help you to see the difference between *participles used as part of a verb form* and *participles mistakenly used as a complete verb.* You will also see an example of the *gerund verb form* in its use as a noun/subject.

Being part of a huge crowd in the mosh-pit at the concert. (This is *not* a sentence, because a *present participle*, or only *part* of a verb, has been used.)

Being part of a huge crowd in the mosh-pit at the concert was a disgusting experience. (This is a sentence, because it contains a *finite*, or "real," non-partial verb form: *was*.)

In the following examples, the gerund is the subject of a sentence.

Leaving was my only reasonable choice.
Feeding the cat is an unpleasant chore.

Activity 1: Finding Subjects and Complete Verbs

Draw a single line under the subjects and a double line under the verbs in the following sentences. Be sure to include all parts of the verb.

1. A burning odour from the wood saw filled the room.
2. At first, sticks of gum always feel powdery on your tongue.
3. Vampires and werewolves are repelled by garlic.
4. Three people in the long bank line looked impatiently at their watches.
5. The driving rain had pasted wet leaves all over the car.
6. She has decided to buy a condominium.
7. The trees in the mall were glittering with tiny white lights.
8. The puppies slipped and tumbled on the vinyl kitchen floor.
9. Tanya and Luis ate at a pizza place and then went to a movie.
10. We have not met our new neighbours in the apartment building.

Activity 2: Finding Verbs and Identifying Objects

Draw a wavy line under the objects of the verbs in the following sentences. Draw a double line under the verb of each sentence. Indicate in the space in front of each sentence whether the object of the verb is a *noun* (*N*), a *pronoun* (*P*), or a *phrase* (*PH*).

_____ 1. The cat eagerly ate the tuna.

_____ 2. The instructor, new and nervous in his job, created more confusion than he'd imagined possible.

_____ 3. Assignments such as Tim received in Statistics class frightened him.

_____ 4. The vampire bit her neck with great gusto.

_____ 5. Carpet and upholstery shampoo cannot work miracles.

_____ 6. Li understood her essay's shortcomings perfectly.

_____ 7. Crystal and Tony's co-operation has helped them both.

_____ 8. New ideas don't always make life easier for everyone.

_____ 9. Vacations can upset young children.

_____ 10. Being late for class always irritated Enzo.

■ Review Test 1

Draw a single line under subjects and a double line under verbs. Crossing out prepositional phrases may help you find the subjects.

1. A cloud of fruit flies hovered over the bananas.
2. Candle wax dripped onto the table and hardened into pools.
3. Nick and Chan are both excellent soccer players.

4. The leaves of my dying rubber plant resembled limp brown rags.

5. During the first week of vacation, Ken slept until noon every day.

6. They have just decided to go on a diet together.

7. Psychology and word processing are my favourite subjects.

8. The sofa in the living room has not been cleaned for over a year.

9. The water stains on her suede shoes did not disappear with brushing.

10. Fred stayed in bed too long and, as a result, arrived late for work.

■ Review Test 2

In the sentences that follow, draw a single line under a *predicate*, a wavy line under the *object* of a verb, and a double line under the *verb* of each sentence. In the space provided, identify a *predicate* with the letters *PR* and an *object* with the letter *O*.

_____   1. For Jim, narrow spaces between desks are troublesome because of his wheel-chair.

_____   2. Sometimes our pet causes more trouble than any child.

_____   3. Peanut butter, bacon, and banana sandwiches were Elvis' favourite snack.

_____   4. The vampire stroked his gleaming patent-leather hair.

_____   5. Aliens appear as pale cat-like creatures.

_____   6. Mulder and Scully made a mess out of their investigation.

_____   7. Cats seem to be animals that like to lurk.

_____   8. Earthworms disgust me.

_____   9. Tony and Crystal appeared happy, but they were both seething with anger.

_____   10. They destroyed the tranquillity of the woods with their chainsaws.

SENTENCE FRAGMENTS

WHAT ARE SENTENCE FRAGMENTS?

Every sentence must have a subject and a verb and must express a complete thought. A word group that lacks a subject or a verb and that does not express a complete thought is a *fragment*. The most common types of fragments are:

1   Dependent-word fragments
2   *-ing* and *to* fragments
3   Added-detail fragments
4   Missing-subject fragments

Once you understand the specific kind or kinds of fragments that you might write, you should be able to eliminate them from your writing. The following pages explain all four fragment types.

DEPENDENT-WORD FRAGMENTS

Some word groups that begin with a dependent word are fragments. Here is a list of common dependent words:

Dependent Words		
after	if, even if	when, whenever
although, though	in order that	where, wherever
as	since	whether
because	that, so that	which, whichever
before	unless	while
even though	until	who, whoever
how	what, whatever	whose

Whenever you start a sentence with one of these words, you must be careful that a fragment does not result.

The word group beginning with the dependent word *After* in the example below is a fragment.

After I learned the price of new cars. I decided to keep my old Buick.

A *dependent statement*—one starting with a dependent word like *After*—cannot stand alone. It depends on another statement to complete the thought. "After I learned the price of new cars" is a dependent statement. It leaves us hanging. We expect in the same sentence to find out *what happened after* the writer learned the price of new cars. When a writer does not follow through and complete a thought, a fragment results.

To correct the fragment, simply follow through and complete the thought:

After I learned the price of new cars, I decided to keep my old Buick.

Remember, then, that *dependent statements by themselves are fragments.* They must be *attached to a statement that makes sense standing alone.*

Here are two other examples of dependent-word fragments:

My daughter refused to stop smoking. <u>Unless I quit also.</u>

Bill asked for a loan. <u>Which he promised to pay back in two weeks.</u>

"Unless I quit also" is a fragment; it does not make sense standing by itself. We want to know in the same statement *what would not happen unless* the writer quit also. The writer must complete the thought. Likewise, "Which he promised to pay back in two weeks" is not in itself a complete thought. We want to know in the same statement what *which* refers to.

Correcting a Dependent-Word Fragment

In *most* cases you can correct a dependent-word fragment by *attaching it to the sentence that comes after it or the sentence that comes before it*:

After I learned the price of new cars, I decided to keep my old Buick.
(*The fragment has been attached to the sentence that comes after it.*)

My daughter refused to quit smoking unless I quit also.
(*The fragment has been attached to the sentence that comes before it.*)

Bill asked for a loan which he promised to pay back in two weeks.
(*The fragment has been attached to the sentence that comes before it.*)

Another way of correcting a dependent-word fragment is simply *to eliminate the dependent word by rewriting the sentence*:

I learned the price of new cars and decided to keep my old Buick.

She wanted me to quit also.

He promised to pay it back in two weeks.

Do not use this second method of correction too frequently, however, for it may cut down on interest and variety in your writing style.

Notes

1 Use a comma if a dependent-word group comes at the beginning of a sentence (see also page 363):

After I learned the price of new cars, I decided to keep my old Buick.

However, do not generally use a comma if the dependent-word group comes at the end of a sentence:

My daughter refused to stop smoking unless I quit also.
Bill asked for a loan which he promised to pay back in two weeks.

2 Sometimes the dependent words *who*, *that*, *which*, or *where* appear not at the very start, but near the start, of a word group. A fragment often results:

The town council decided to put more lights on South Street. <u>A place where several people have been harassed.</u>

"A place where several people have been harassed" is not in itself a complete thought. We want to know in the same statement *where the place was* that several people were harassed. The fragment can be corrected by attaching it to the sentence that comes before it:

The town council decided to put more lights on South Street, a place where several people have been harassed.

Activity 1: Adding Dependent Clauses to Complete Thoughts

Turn each of the following dependent-word groups into a sentence by adding a complete thought. Put a comma after the dependent-word group if a dependent word starts the sentence.

Examples   Although I arrived in class late
  Although J arrived in class late, J still did well on the test.

The little boy who plays with our daughter
  The little boy who plays with our daughter just came down with the German measles.

1. Because the weather is bad

_____

_____

2. If I lend you twenty dollars

    _____

    _____

3. The car that we bought

    _____

    _____

4. Since I was tired

    _____

    _____

5. Before the instructor entered the room

    _____

    _____

Activity 2: Correcting Dependent-Word Fragments

Underline the dependent-word fragment or fragments in each of the five items below. Then correct each fragment by attaching it to the sentence that comes before or the sentence that comes after it—whichever sounds more natural. Put a comma after the dependent-word group *if it starts the sentence.*

1. Whenever our front and back doors are open. The air current causes the back door to slam shut. The noise makes everyone in the house jump.

    _____

    _____

2. Bill always turns on the radio in the morning to hear the news. He wants to be sure that World War III has not started. Before he gets on with his day.

    _____

    _____

3. Since the line at the Department of Motor Vehicles crawls at a snail's pace. Fred waited two hours there. When there was only one person left in front of him. The office closed for the day.

    _____

    _____

    _____

4. My dog ran in joyous circles on the wide beach. Until she found a dead fish. Before I had a chance to drag her away. She began sniffing and nudging the smelly remains.

    _____

    _____

    _____

5. When the air-conditioner broke down. The temperature was over thirty degrees. I then found an old fan. Which turned out to be broken also.

    _____

    _____

    _____

-ING AND *TO* FRAGMENTS (PARTICIPIAL AND INFINITIVE FRAGMENTS

When an *-ing* word appears at or near the start of a word group, a fragment may result. Such fragments often lack a subject and part of the verb. Underline the word groups in the examples below that contain *-ing* words. Each is a fragment.

Example 1

I spent almost two hours on the phone yesterday. Trying to find a garage to repair my car. Eventually I had to have it towed to a garage in another town.

Example 2

Maggie was at first very happy with the blue sports car she had bought for only five hundred dollars. Not realizing until a week later that the car averaged ten kilometres per litre of gas.

Example 3

He looked forward to the study period at school. It being the only time he could sit unbothered and dream about his future. He imagined himself as a lawyer with lots of money and women to spend it on.

People sometimes write *-ing* fragments because they think the subject in one sentence will work for the next word group as well. Thus, in the first example, the writer thinks that the subject *I* in the opening sentence will also serve as the subject for "Trying to find a garage to repair my car." But the subject must actually be *in* the sentence.

Correcting *-ing* Fragments

1 Attach the *-ing* fragment to the sentence that comes before it or the sentence that comes after it, whichever makes sense. Example 1 could read: "I spent two hours on the phone yesterday, trying to find a garage to repair my car."

2 Add a subject and change the *-ing* verb part to the correct form of the verb. Example 2 could read: "She realized only a week later that the car averaged ten kilometres per litre of gas."

3 Change *being* to the correct form of the verb *be* (*am, are, is, was, were*). Example 3 could read: "It was the only time he could sit unbothered and dream about his future."

Correcting *to* Fragments

When *to* appears at or near the start of a word group, a fragment sometimes results:

I plan on working overtime. To get this job finished. Otherwise, my boss may get angry at me.

The second word group here is a fragment and can be corrected by adding it to the preceding sentence:

I plan on working overtime to get this job finished.

Activity 1: Correcting *-ing* Fragments

Underline the *-ing* fragment in each of the three items that follow. Then make it a sentence by rewriting it, using the method described in parentheses.

Example A thunderstorm was brewing. A sudden breeze shot through the windows. <u>Driving the stuffiness out of the room.</u>
(Add the fragment to the preceding sentence.)
A sudden breeze shot through the windows, driving the

stuffiness out of the room.

(In the example, a comma is used to set off "driving the stuffiness out of the room," which is extra material placed at the end of the sentence.)

1. Sweating under his heavy load. Brian staggered up the stairs to his apartment. He felt as though his legs were crumbling beneath him.
(Add the fragment to the sentence that comes after it.)

_____

_____

2. He works ten hours a day. Then going to class for three hours. It is no wonder he writes sentence fragments.
   (Correct the fragment by adding the subject *he* and changing *going* to the proper form of the verb, *goes*.)

   _____

   _____

3. Carla loved the movie *Gone with the Wind*, but Fabio hated it. His chief objection being that it lasted four hours.
   (Correct the fragment by changing *being* to the proper verb form, *was*.)

   _____

   _____

Activity 2: Correcting *-ing* and *to* Fragments

Underline the *-ing* or *to* fragment or fragments in each of the five items that follow. Then rewrite each, correcting the fragments by using one of the three methods of correction described on page 245.

1. A mysterious package arrived on my porch yesterday. Bearing no return address. I half expected to find a bomb inside.

   _____

   _____

2. Jack bundled up and went outside on the bitterly cold day. To saw wood for his fireplace. He returned half frozen with only two logs.

   _____

   _____

3. Looking tired and drawn. The little girl's parents sat in the waiting room. The operation would be over in a few minutes.

   _____

   _____

4. Sighing with resignation. Jill switched on her television set. She knew that the picture would be snowy and crackling with static. Her house being in a weak reception area.

   _____

   _____

   _____

5. Jabbing the ice with a screwdriver. Bill attempted to speed up the defrosting process in his freezer. However, he used too much force. The result being a freezer compartment riddled with holes.

_____

_____

_____

_____

ADDED-DETAIL FRAGMENTS

Added-detail fragments lack a subject and a verb. They often begin with one of the following words:

also	except	including
especially	for example	such as

See if you can locate and underline the one added-detail fragment in each of the examples that follow:

Example 1

I love to cook and eat Italian food. Especially spaghetti and lasagna. I make everything from scratch.

Example 2

The class often starts late. For example, yesterday at quarter after nine instead of at nine sharp. Today the class started at five after nine.

Example 3

He failed a number of courses before he earned his diploma. Among them, English 100, Economics, and General Biology.

People often write added-detail fragments for much the same reason they write *-ing* fragments. They think the subject and verb in one sentence will serve for the next word group as well. But the subject and verb must be in *each* word group.

Correcting Added-Detail Fragments

1   Attach the fragment to the complete thought that precedes it. Example 1 could read: "I love to cook and eat Italian food, especially spaghetti and lasagna."

2   Add a subject and a verb to the fragment to make it a complete sentence. Example 2 could read: "The class often starts late. For example, yesterday it began at quarter after nine instead of at nine sharp."

3   Change words as necessary to make the fragment part of the preceding sentence. Example 3 could read: "Among the courses he failed before he earned his diploma were English 100, Economics, and General Biology."

Activity 1: Correcting Sentence Fragments

Underline the fragment in each of the three items below. Then make it a sentence by rewriting it, using the method described in parentheses.

Example   I am always short of pocket money. Especially for everyday items like magazines and pop. Luckily my friends often have change.
(Add the fragment to the preceding sentence.)

I am always short of pocket money, especially for everyday

items like magazines and pop.

1.   Nina is trying hard for a promotion. For example, through night classes and an assertiveness training course. She is also working overtime for no pay.
(Correct the fragment by adding the subject and verb *she is taking*.)

2.   I could feel Bill's anger building. Like a land mine ready to explode. I was silent because I didn't want to be the one to set it off.
(Add the fragment to the preceding sentence.)

3.   We went on vacation without several essential items. Among other things, our sneakers and fleece jackets.
(Correct the fragment by adding the subject and verb *we forgot*.)

Activity 2: Making Added-Detail Fragments into Sentences

Underline the added-detail fragment in each of the five items below. Then rewrite that part of the item needed to correct the fragment. Use one of the three methods of correction described above.

1. It's always hard for me to get up for work. Especially on Mondays after a holiday weekend. However, I always wake up early on free days.

   _____

   _____

2. Tony has enormous endurance. For example, the ability to run seven kilometres in the morning and then play basketball all afternoon.

   _____

   _____

3. A counsellor gives you a chance to talk about your problems. Whether with your family or the boss at work. You learn how to cope better with life.

   _____

   _____

4. Fred and Maria do most of their shopping through mail-order catalogues. Especially the Sears and Tilley Endurables catalogues.

   _____

   _____

5. One of my greatest joys in life is eating desserts. Such as cherry cheesecake and vanilla cream puffs. Almond fudge cake makes me want to dance.

   _____

   _____

MISSING-SUBJECT FRAGMENTS

In each example below, underline the word group in which the subject is missing.

Example 1

The truck skidded on the icy highway. But missed a telephone pole on the side of the road.

Example 2

Michelle tried each of the appetizers on the table. And then found that, when the dinner arrived, her appetite had gone.

People write missing-subject fragments because they think the subject in one sentence will apply to the next word group as well. But the *subject*, as well as the *verb*, must be *in each word group* to make it a sentence.

Correcting Missing-Subject Fragments

1 Attach the fragment to the preceding sentence. Example 1 could read: "The truck skidded on the icy highway but missed a telephone pole on the side of the road."

2 Add a subject (which can often be a pronoun standing for the subject in the preceding sentence). Example 2 could read: "She then found that, when the dinner arrived, her appetite had gone."

Activity: Correcting Missing-Subject Fragments

Underline the missing-subject fragment in each of the following three items. Then rewrite that part of the item needed to correct the fragment. Use one of the two methods of correction described above.

1. I tried on an old suit hanging in our basement closet. And discovered, to my surprise, that it was too tight to button.

_____

_____

_____

2. When Mary had a sore throat, friends told her to gargle with salt water. Or suck on an ice cube. The worst advice she got was to avoid swallowing.

_____

_____

_____

3. One of my elementary school teachers embarrassed us with her sarcasm. Also, seated us in rows from the brightest student to the dumbest. I can imagine the pain the student in the last seat must have felt.

_____

_____

_____

> ### A Review: How to Check for Sentence Fragments
>
> **1** Read your paper aloud from the *last* sentence to the *first*. You will be better able to see and hear whether each word group you read is a complete thought.
>
> **2** Ask yourself of any word group you think is a fragment: Does this contain a subject and a verb and express a complete thought?
>
> **3** More specifically, be on the lookout for the most common fragments:
>
> - Dependent-word fragments (starting with words like *after*, *because*, *since*, *when*, and *before*)
> - *-ing* and *to* fragments (*-ing* or *to* at or near the start of a word group)
> - Added-detail fragments (starting with words like *for example*, *such as*, *also*, and *especially*)
> - Missing-subject fragments (a verb is present but not the subject)

■ Review Test 1

Turn each of the following word groups into a complete sentence. Use the spaces provided.

Example   With sweaty palms

<u>With sweaty palms, I walked in for the job interview.</u>

Even when it rains

<u>The football teams practise even when it rains.</u>

1. When the alarm sounded

_____

2. In order to save some money

_____

3. Was late for the game

_____

4. To pass the course

_____

5. Peter, who is very impatient

_____

6. During the holiday season

_____

7. The store where I worked

_____

8. Before the movie started

_____

9. Down in the basement

_____

10. Feeling very confident

_____

■ Review Test 2

Each word group in the student paragraph below is numbered. In the space provided, write _C_ if a word group is a _complete sentence;_ write _F_ if it is a _fragment._ You will find seven fragments in the paragraph.

A Disastrous First Date

1. _____
2. _____
3. _____
4. _____
5. _____
6. _____
7. _____
8. _____
9. _____
10. _____
11. _____
12. _____
13. _____
14. _____
15. _____
16. _____
17. _____
18. _____
19. _____
20. _____

[1]My first date with Donna was a disaster. [2]I decided to take her to a small Italian restaurant. [3]That my friends told me had reasonable prices. [4]I looked over the menu and realized I could not pronounce the names of the dishes. [5]Such as "veal piccante," and "fettucini Alfredo." [6]Then, I noticed a burning smell. [7]The candle on the table was starting to blacken. [8]And scorch the back of my menu. [9]Trying to be casual, I quickly poured half my glass of water on the menu. [10]When the server returned to our table. [11]He asked me if I wanted to order some wine. [12]I ordered a bottle of Baby Duck. [13]The only wine that I had heard of and could pronounce. [14]The server brought the wine, poured a small amount into my glass, and waited. [15]I said, "You don't have to stand there. We can pour the wine ourselves." [16]After the server put down the wine bottle and left. [17]Donna told me I was supposed to taste the wine. [18]Feeling like a complete fool. [19]I managed to get through the dinner. [20]However, for weeks afterward, I felt like jumping out a tenth-storey window.

On a separate sheet of paper, correct the fragments you have found. Attach each fragment to the sentence that comes before or after it, or make whatever other change is needed to turn the fragment into a sentence.

■ Review Test 3

Underline the two fragments in each of the five items below. Then rewrite the item in the space provided, making the changes needed to correct the fragments.

Example   The people at the diner save money. <u>By watering down the coffee.</u> <u>Also, using the cheapest grade of hamburger.</u> Few people go there any more.

     The people at the diner save money by watering down the

     coffee. Also, they use the cheapest grade of hamburger.

1. Gathering speed with enormous force. The plane was suddenly in the air. Then it began to climb sharply. And several minutes later levelled off.

2. Before my neighbours went on vacation. They asked me to watch their house. I agreed to check the premises once a day. Also, to take in their mail.

3. Running untouched into the end zone. The halfback raised his arms in triumph. Then he slammed the football to the ground. And did a little victory dance.

4. It's hard to keep up with bills. Such as the telephone, gas, and hydro. After you finally mail the cheques. New ones seem to arrive a day or two later.

5. While a woman ordered ten kilos of cold cuts. Customers at the deli counter waited impatiently. The woman explained that she was in charge of a school picnic. And apologized for taking up so much time.

_____

_____

_____

■ Review Test 4

Write quickly for five minutes about what you like to do in your leisure time. Don't worry about spelling, punctuation, finding exact words, or organizing your thoughts. Just focus on writing as many words as you can without stopping.

Your challenge is to write a paragraph containing _at least_ five sentence fragments. Try _not_ to make these fragments obvious.

Exchange paragraphs with the student next to you. Have that student find and indicate your "intentional fragments," then mark your paragraph, after correcting the fragments.

RUN-ON SENTENCES

Introductory Project

A *run-on sentence* (or *run-on*) occurs when two sentences are run together with no adequate sign given to mark the break between them. Shown below are four run-on sentences and four correctly marked sentences. See if you can complete the statement that explains how each run-on is corrected.

1. He is the meanest little kid on his block he eats only the heads of animal crackers. *Run-on*

    He is the meanest little kid on his block. He eats only the heads of animal crackers. *Correct*

    The run-on has been corrected by using a _____ and a capital letter to separate the two complete thoughts.

2. Fred Grimaldi likes to gossip about other people, he doesn't like them to gossip about him. *Run-on*

    Fred Grimaldi likes to gossip about other people, but he doesn't like them to gossip about him. *Correct*

    The run-on has been corrected by using a joining word, _____, to connect the two complete thoughts.

3. The chain on my bike likes to chew up my pants, it leaves grease marks on my ankle as well. *Run-on*

    The chain on my bike likes to chew up my pants; it leaves grease marks on my ankle as well. *Correct*

    The run-on has been corrected by using a _____ to connect the two closely related thoughts.

4. The window shade snapped up like a gunshot, her cat leaped a metre off the floor. *Run-on*

    When the window shade snapped up like a gunshot, her cat leaped a metre off the floor. *Correct*

    The run-on has been corrected by using the subordinating word _____ to connect the two closely related thoughts.

Answers are on page 551.

WHAT ARE RUN-ONS?

A *run-on* is two complete thoughts that are run together with no adequate sign given to mark the break between them.* Some run-ons have no punctuation at all to mark the break between the thoughts. Such run-ons are known as *fused sentences:* they are fused or joined together as if they were only one thought.

Fused Sentence

My grades are very good this semester my social life rates only a C.

Fused Sentence

Our father was a madman in his youth he would do anything on a dare.

In other run-ons, known as *comma splices*, a comma is used to connect or "splice" together the two complete thoughts. However, a comma alone is not enough to connect two complete thoughts. Some stronger connection than a comma alone is needed.

Comma Splice

My grades are very good this semester, my social life rates only a C.

Comma Splice

Our father was a madman in his youth, he would do anything on a dare.

Comma splices are the most common kind of run-on mistake. Students sense that some kind of connection is needed between two thoughts, and so put a comma at the dividing point. But the comma alone is not sufficient, and a stronger, clearer mark between the two thoughts is needed.

CORRECTING RUN-ONS

Here are four common methods of correcting a run-on:

1 *Use a period and a capital letter to break the two complete thoughts into separate sentences.*

* *Note:* Some instructors refer to each complete thought in a run-on as an *independent clause.* A *clause* is simply a group of words having a subject and a verb. A clause may be *independent* (expressing a complete thought and able to stand alone) or *dependent* (not expressing a complete thought and not able to stand alone). A run-on is two independent clauses that are run together with no adequate sign given to mark the break between them.

My grades are very good this semester. My social life rates only a C.
Our father was a madman in his youth. He would do anything on a dare.

2 *Use a comma plus a joining word (and, but, for, or, nor, so, yet) to connect the two complete thoughts.*

My grades are very good this semester, but my social life rates only a C.
Our father was a madman in his youth, for he would do anything on a dare.

3 *Use a semi-colon to connect the two complete thoughts.*

My grades are very good this semester; my social life rates only a C.
Our father was a madman in his youth; he would do anything on a dare.

4 *Use subordination.*

Although my grades are very good this semester, my social life rates only a C.
Because my father was a madman in his youth, he would do anything on a dare.

The following pages will give you practice in all four methods of correcting a run-on. The use of subordination will be explained further on page 419, in a section of the book that deals with sentence variety.

Method 1: Period and a Capital Letter

One way of correcting a run-on is to use a period and a capital letter at the break between the two complete thoughts. Use this method especially if (1) *the thoughts are not closely related*, or (2) *another method would make the sentence too long*.

Activity 1: Correcting Fused Sentences

Locate the split in each of the following run-ons. Each is a *fused sentence*—that is, each consists of two sentences that are fused or joined together with no punctuation at all between them. Reading each sentence aloud will help you "hear" where a major break or split in the thought occurs. At such a point, your voice will probably drop and pause.

Correct the run-on sentence by putting a period at the end of the first thought and a capital letter at the start of the next thought.

Example   Maria Grimaldi shuffled around the apartment in her slippers. Her husband couldn't stand their slapping sound on the floor.

1. The goose down jacket was not well-made little feathers leaked out of the seams.

2. Tranh cringed at the sound of the dentist's drill it buzzed like a twenty-kilo mosquito.

3. Last summer no one swam in the lake a little boy had dropped his pet piranhas into the water.

4. A horse's teeth never stop growing they will eventually grow outside the horse's mouth.

5. Kim's doctor told her he was an astrology nut she did not feel good about learning that.

6. Ice water is the best remedy for a burn using butter is like adding fat to a flame.

7. In the apartment the air was so dry that her skin felt parched the heat was up to thirty degrees.

8. My parents bought me an ant farm it's going to be hard to find tractors that small.

9. Lobsters are cannibalistic this is one reason they are hard to raise in captivity.

10. Julia placed an egg timer next to the phone she did not want to talk more than three minutes on her long-distance calls.

Activity 2: Correcting Run-On Sentences

Locate the split in each of the following run-ons. Some of the run-ons are *fused sentences*, and some of them are *comma splices*—run-ons spliced or joined together only with a comma. Correct each run-on by putting a period at the end of the first thought and a capital letter at the start of the next thought.

1. A bird got into the house through the chimney we had to catch it before our cat did.

2. Some so-called health foods are not so healthy, many are made with oils that raise cholesterol levels.

3. We sat only three metres from the magician, we still couldn't see where all the birds came from.

4. Juan needs only five hours of sleep each night his wife needs at least seven.

5. Our image of dentistry will soon change dentists will use lasers instead of drills.

6. Cheri entered her apartment and jumped with fright someone was leaving through her bedroom window.

7. There were several unusual hair styles at the party one woman had bright green braids.

8. Jon saves all of his magazines, once a month, he takes them to a nursing home.

9. The doctor seemed to be in a rush, I still took time to ask all the questions that were on my mind.

10. When I was little, my brother tried to feed me flies, he told me they were raisins.

A Warning: Words That Can Lead to Run-Ons: People often write run-on sentences when the second complete thought begins with one of the following words. Remember to be on the alert for run-on sentences whenever you use one of these words in writing a paper.

I	we	there	now
you	they	this	then
he, she, it		that	next

Activity: Writing Follow-Up Sentences

Write a second sentence to go with each of the sentences that follow. Start the second sentence with the word shown at the left. Your sentences can be serious or playful.

Example **She** Jackie works for the phone company. _She climbs telephone poles in all kinds of weather._

It 1. The alarm clock is unreliable. _____

_____

He 2. My uncle has a peculiar habit. _____

_____

Then 3. Crystal studied for the math test for two hours. _____

_____

It 4. I could not understand why the car would not start. _____

_____

There 5. We saw all kinds of litter on the highway. _____

_____

Method 2: Comma and a Joining Word

Another way of correcting a run-on sentence is to use a comma plus a joining word to connect the two complete thoughts. Joining words (also called *conjunctions*) include *and, but, for, or, nor, so,* and *yet.* Here is what the four most common joining words mean:

and   in addition to, along with

His feet hurt from the long hike, and his stomach was growling.

(*And* means "in addition": His feet hurt from the long hike; *in addition*, his stomach was growling.)*

but   however, except, on the other hand, just the opposite

I remembered to get the cocoa, but I forgot the marshmallows.

(*But* means "however": I remembered to get the cocoa; *however*, I forgot the marshmallows.)*

for   because, the reason why, the cause for something

She was afraid of not doing well in the course, for she had always had bad luck with English before.

(*For* means "because" or "the reason": She was afraid of not doing well in the course; *the reason* was that she had always had bad luck with English before.)

Note: If you are not comfortable using *for,* you may want to use *because* instead of *for* in the activities that follow. If you do use *because,* omit the comma before it.

so   as a result, therefore

The windshield wiper was broken, so she was in trouble when the rain started.

(*So* means "as a result": The windshield wiper was broken; *as a result*, she was in trouble when the rain started.)*

_____

* The use of semi-colons with adverbial conjunctions is discussed on pages 262–263.

Activity 1: Inserting Appropriate Conjunctions

Insert the joining word (*and*, *but*, *for*, *so*) that logically connects the two thoughts in each sentence.

1. The couple wanted desperately to buy the house, _____ they did not qualify for a mortgage.

2. A lot of men today get their hair styled, _____ they use perfume and other cosmetics as well.

3. Devon asked his wife if she had any bandages, _____ he had just sliced his finger with a paring knife.

4. He failed the vision part of his driver's test, _____ he did not get his driver's licence that day.

5. The restaurant was beautiful, _____ the food was overpriced.

Activity 2: Adding Complete and Related Thoughts

Add a complete and closely related thought to go with each of the following statements. Use a comma plus the joining word at the left when you write the second thought.

> **Example** *for* Vicky spent the day walking barefoot, *for the heel of one of her shoes had come off.*

but 1. She wanted to go to the party _____

_____

and 2. Tony washed his car in the morning _____

_____

so 3. The day was dark and rainy _____

_____

for 4. I'm not going to eat in the school cafeteria any more _____

_____

but 5. I asked my brother to get off the telephone _____

_____

Method 3: Semi-Colon

A third method of correcting a run-on sentence is to use a semi-colon to mark the break between two thoughts. A *semi-colon* (;) is made up of a period above a comma and is sometimes called a *strong comma*. The semi-colon signals more of a pause than a comma alone but not quite the full pause of a period. The semi-colon is like "punctuation glue"; it can *join* two *equal* parts of a sentence.

Semi-Colon Alone: Here are some earlier sentences that were connected with a comma plus a joining word. Notice that a semi-colon, unlike the comma alone, can be used to *connect* the two complete thoughts in each sentence:

> A lot of men today get their hair styled; they use perfume and other cosmetics as well.
>
> She was afraid of not doing well in the course; she had always had bad luck with English before.
>
> The restaurant was beautiful; the food was overpriced.

Use of the semi-colon can add to sentence variety. For some people, however, the semi-colon is a confusing mark of punctuation. Keep in mind that if you are not comfortable using it, you can and should use one of the first two methods of correcting a run-on sentence.

Activity: Using a Semi-Colon to Join Two Complete Thoughts

Insert a semi-colon where the break occurs between the *two complete thoughts* in each of the following sentences.

Example   I missed the bus by seconds; there would not be another for half an hour.

1. I spend eight hours a day in a windowless office it's a relief to get out in the open air after work.
2. The audience howled with laughter the comedian enjoyed a moment of triumph.
3. It rained all week parts of the highway were flooded.
4. Tony never goes to a certain gas station any more he found out that the service manager overcharged him for a valve job.
5. The washer shook and banged with its unbalanced load then it began to walk across the floor.

Semi-Colon with a Transitional Word: A semi-colon is sometimes used with a transitional word and a comma to join two complete thoughts:

> We were short of money; *therefore,* we decided not to eat out that weekend.
>
> The roots of a geranium have to be crowded into a small pot; *otherwise,* the plants may not flower.
>
> I had a paper to write; *however,* my brain had stopped working for the night.

On the following page is a list of common transitional words (also known as *adverbial conjunctions*). Brief meanings are given for most of the words.

Transitional Word or Phrase	Meaning
however	but
nevertheless	however
on the other hand	however
instead	as a substitute
meanwhile	in the intervening time
otherwise	under other conditions
indeed	in fact
in addition	and, as well
also	in addition
moreover	in addition
furthermore	in addition
as a result	so
thus	as a result
consequently	as a result
therefore	as a result

Activity 1: Using Transitional Words and Semi-Colons

Choose a logical transitional word from the list in the box and write it in the space provided. Put a semi-colon *before* the connector and a comma *after* it.

Example   Exams are over _____; however,_____ I still feel tense and nervous.

1. I did not understand her point _____ I asked her to repeat it.

2. With his thumbnail, Tony tried to split open the cellophane covering on the

    box of crackers _____ the cellophane refused to tear.

3. Post offices are closed for today's holiday _____ no mail will
    be delivered.

4. They decided not to go to the movie _____ they went to play
    miniature golf.

5. I had to skip lunch _____ I would be late for class.

Activity 2: Using Semi-Colons and Commas

Punctuate each sentence by using a semi-colon and a comma.

Example   My brother's asthma was worsening; as a result, he quit the soccer team.

1. Bill ate an entire pizza for supper in addition he had a big chunk of pound cake for dessert.
2. The man leaned against the building in obvious pain however no one stopped to help him.
3. Our instructor was absent therefore the test was postponed.
4. I had no time to process the paper instead I printed it out neatly in black ink.
5. Crystal loves the velvety texture of cherry jelly moreover she loves to squish it between her teeth.

Method 4: Subordination

A fourth method of joining related thoughts is to use subordination. *Subordination is a way of showing that one thought in a sentence is not as important as another thought.*

Here are three earlier sentences that have been rewritten so that one idea is subordinated to (made less important than) the other idea:

When the window shade snapped up like a gunshot, her cat leaped two metres off the floor.

Because it rained all week, parts of the highway were flooded.

Although my grades are very good this year, my social life rates only a C.

Notice that when we subordinate, we use dependent words like *when*, *because*, and *although*. Here is a brief list of common dependent words:

Common Dependent Words		
after	before	unless
although	even though	until
as	if	when
because	since	while

Subordination is explained further on page 419.

Activity: Choosing Dependent Words and Subordinating

Choose a logical dependent word from the box above and write it in the space provided.

Example _____*Because*_____ I had so much to do, I never even turned on the TV last night.

1. _____ we emerged from the darkened theatre, it took several minutes for our eyes to adjust to the light.

2. _____ "All Natural" was printed in large letters on the yogurt carton, the fine print listing the ingredients told a different story.

3. I can't study for the test this weekend _____ my boss wants me to work overtime.

4. _____ the vampire movie was over, my children were afraid to go to bed.

5. _____ you have a driver's licence and two major credit cards, that store will not accept your cheque.

A Review: How to Check for Run-Ons

1 To see if a sentence is a run-on, read it aloud and listen for a break marking two complete thoughts. Your voice will probably drop and pause at the break.

2 To check an entire paper, read it aloud from the *last* sentence to the *first*. Doing so will help you hear and see each complete thought.

3 Be on the lookout for words that can lead to run-on sentences:

I	he, she, it	they	this	next
you	we	there	that	then

4 Correct run-on sentences by using one of the following methods:

- Period and capital letter
- Comma and joining word (*and, but, for, or, nor, so, yet*)
- Semi-colon alone or with a transitional word
- Subordination

■ Review Test 1: Run-Ons

Some of the run-ons that follow are fused sentences, having no punctuation between the two complete thoughts; others are comma splices, having only a comma between the two complete thoughts. Correct the run-ons by using one of the following three methods:

■ Period and a capital letter
■ Comma and a joining word
■ Semi-colon

Do not use the same method of correction for every sentence.

Example   Three people did the job, ^but^ I could have done it alone.

1. The impatient driver tried to get a jump on the green light he kept edging his car into the intersection.

2. The course on the history of UFOs sounded interesting, it turned out to be very dull.

3. That clothing store is a strange place to visit you keep walking up to dummies that look like real people.

4. Everything on the menu of the Pancake House sounded delicious they wanted to order the entire menu.

5. Bill pressed a cold washcloth against his eyes, it helped relieve his headache.

6. Craig used to be a fast-food junkie now he eats only vegetables and sunflower seeds.

7. I knew my term paper was not very good, I placed it in a shiny plastic cover to make it look better.

8. Crystal enjoys watching a talk show, Tony prefers watching a late movie.

9. My boss does not know what he is doing half the time then he tries to tell me what to do.

10. In the next minute, approximately 100 people will die, more than 240 babies will be born.

■ Review Test 2: Using Subordination

Correct the run-on in each sentence by using subordination. Choose from among the following dependent words:

after	before	unless
although	even though	until
as	if	when
because	since	while

Example My eyes have been watering all day, I can tell the pollen count is high.

Because my eyes have been watering all day, I can tell the

pollen count is high.

1. There are a number of suits and jackets on sale, they all have very noticeable flaws.

   _____

   _____

2. Rust has eaten a hole in the muffler, my car sounds like a motorcycle.

   _____

   _____

3. I finished my household chores, I decided to do some shopping.

   _____

   _____

4. The power went off for an hour during the night, all the clocks in the house must be reset.

   _____

   _____

5. Electric cars eliminate exhaust pollution, the limited power of the car's battery is a serious problem.

   _____

   _____

■ Review Test 3

Write quickly for five minutes about what you did this past weekend. Don't worry about spelling, punctuation, finding exact words, or organizing your thoughts. Just focus on writing as many words as you can without stopping.

Your challenge is to use five "intentional run-ons." Be clever in your use of run-ons, so that when you hand your paper to the student next to you, he or she will be challenged by finding and identifying your "intentional run-ons."

STANDARD
ENGLISH
VERBS

Introductory Project

Underline what you think is the correct form of the verb in each of the sentences below:

As a boy, he (enjoy, enjoyed) watching nature shows on television.
He still (enjoy, enjoys) watching such shows today as an adult.

When my car was new, it always (start, started) in the morning.
Now it (start, starts) only sometimes.

A couple of years ago, when Julio (cook, cooked) dinner, you needed an antacid tablet.
Now, when he (cook, cooks), neighbours invite themselves over to eat with us.

On the basis of the above examples, see if you can complete the following statements:

1. The first example in each pair refers to a (past, present) action, and

    the regular verb has an _____ ending.

2. The second example in each pair refers to a (past, present) action, and

    the regular verb has an _____ ending.

Answers are on page 551.

Many people have grown up in communities where nonstandard verb forms are used in everyday life. Such forms include *I thinks*, *he talk*, *it done*, *we has*, *you was*, and *she don't*. Community dialects have richness and power but are a drawback in college and the business world, where standard English verb forms must be used. Standard English helps ensure clear communication among English-speaking people everywhere, and it is especially important in the world of work.

This chapter compares community dialect and standard English forms of one regular verb and three common irregular verbs.

REGULAR VERBS: NONSTANDARD/DIALECT AND STANDARD FORMS

The chart below compares the community dialect (nonstandard) and the standard English forms of the regular verb *to smile*.

TO SMILE

Nonstandard/ *Community Dialect*		*Standard English*	
(Do *not* use in your writing)		(Use for clear communication)	
Present tense			
I smiles	we smiles	I smile	we smile
you smiles	you smiles	you smile	you smile
he, she, it smile	they smiles	he, she, it smiles	they smile
Past tense			
I smile	we smile	I smiled	we smiled
you smile	you smile	you smiled	you smiled
he, she, it smile	they smile	he, she, it smiled	they smiled

One of the most common nonstandard forms results from dropping the endings of regular verbs. For example, people might say "David never *smile* any more" instead of "David never *smiles* any more." Or they will say "Before he lost his job, David *smile* a lot" instead of "Before he lost his job, David *smiled* a lot." To avoid such nonstandard usage, memorize the forms shown above for the regular verb *to smile*. Then use the activities that follow to help make the inclusion of verb endings a writing habit.

Present Tense Endings: Third-Person Forms

The verb ending -*s* or -*es* is needed with a regular verb in the present tense when the subject is *he, she, it,* or *any one person or thing.* Consider the following examples of present tense endings.

He	He yell*s.*
She	She throw*s* things.
It	It really anger*s* me.
One person	Their son storm*s* out of the house.
One person	Their frightened daughter crouch*es* behind the bed.
One thing	At night the house shake*s.*

Activity 1: Correcting Verb Forms

All but one of the ten sentences that follow need -*s* or -*es* verb endings. Cross out the nonstandard verb forms and write the standard forms in the spaces provided. Mark the one sentence that needs no change with a *C* for *correct.* One example is given for you.

Example _____*wants*_____ Pat always want the teacher's attention.

_____ 1. That newspaper print nothing but bad news.

_____ 2. The gourmet ice cream bar sell for almost two dollars.

_____ 3. Pat gossip about me all the time.

_____ 4. Whole-wheat bread taste better to me than rye bread.

_____ 5. Bob weaken his lungs by smoking so much.

_____ 6. The sick baby scream whenever her mother puts her down.

_____ 7. You make me angry sometimes.

_____ 8. Paul drive twenty-five miles to work each day.

_____ 9. She live in a rough section of town.

_____ 10. Maria relax by drinking a glass of wine every night.

Activity 2: Adding Present-Tense Endings

Rewrite the short selection below, adding present tense -*s* or -*es* verb endings wherever needed.

The man lounge on his bed and watch a spider as it crawl across the ceiling. It come closer and closer to a point directly above his head. It reach the point and stop. If it drop now, it will fall right into his mouth. For a while he attempt to ignore the spider. Then he move nervously off the bed.

_____

_____

_____

_____

_____

_____

_____

Past-Tense Endings

The verb ending -*d* or -*ed* is needed with a regular verb in the past tense.

A midwife deliver*ed* my baby.
The visitor puzzl*ed* over the campus map.
The children watch*ed* cartoons all morning.

Activity 1: Adding Past-Tense Endings

All but one of the ten sentences that follow need -*d* or -*ed* verb endings. Cross out the nonstandard verb forms and write the standard forms in the spaces provided. Mark the one sentence that needs no change with a *C*.

Example   _____*failed*_____ This morning I fail a chemistry quiz.

_____ 1. The customer twist his ankle on the restaurant's slippery steps.

_____ 2. The Vietnamese student struggle with the new language.

_____ 3. The sick little boy start to cry again.

_____ 4. The tired mother turned on the TV for him.

_____ 5. I miss quite a few days of class early in the semester.

_____ 6. The weather forecaster promise blue skies, but rain began early this morning.

_____ 7. Sam attempt to put out the candle flame with his finger.

_____ 8. However, he end up burning himself.

_____ 9. Carlo thread the film through the reels of the projector.

_____ 10. As Alice was about to finish work last night, a man came into the restaurant and order two dozen hamburgers.

Activity 2: Using Past Tenses Correctly

Rewrite the short selection below, adding past tense *-d* or *-ed* verb endings wherever needed.

> I smoke for two years and during that time suffer no real side effects. Then my body attack me. I start to have trouble falling asleep, and I awaken early every morning. My stomach digest food very slowly, so that at lunchtime I seem to be still full with breakfast. My lips and mouth turn dry and I swallow water constantly. Also, mucous fill my lungs and I cough a lot. I decide to stop smoking when my wife insist I take out more life insurance for our family.

_____

_____

_____

_____

_____

_____

_____

_____

_____

_____

_____

THREE COMMON IRREGULAR VERBS: NONSTANDARD/DIALECT AND STANDARD FORMS

The following charts compare nonstandard dialect and standard English forms of the common irregular verbs *to be*, *to have*, and *to do*. (For more on irregular verbs, see pages 278–285.)

TO BE

Nonstandard/ Community Dialect		Standard English	
(Do *not* use in your writing)		(Use for clear communication)	

Present tense

~~I be (or is)~~	~~we be~~	I am	we are
you be	you be	you are	you are
~~he, she, it be~~	~~they be~~	he, she, it is	they are

Past tense

~~I were~~	~~we was~~	I was	we were
you was	you was	you were	you were
~~he, she, it were~~	~~they was~~	he, she it, was	they were

TO HAVE

Nonstandard/ Community Dialect		Standard English	
(Do *not* use in your writing)		(Use for clear communication)	

Present tense

~~I has~~	~~we has~~	I have	we have
you has	you has	you have	you have
~~he, she, it have~~	~~they has~~	he, she, it has	they have

Past tense

~~I has~~	~~we has~~	I had	we had
you has	you has	you had	you had
~~he, she, it have~~	~~they has~~	he, she, it had	they had

TO DO

Nonstandard/ Community Dialect		Standard English	
(Do *not* use in your writing)		(Use for clear communication)	

Present tense

~~I does~~	~~we does~~	I do	we do
you does	you does	you do	you do
~~he, she~~, it do	they ~~does~~	he, she, it does	they do

Past tense

~~I done~~	~~we done~~	I did	we did
you done	you done	you did	you did
~~he, she~~, it done	they ~~done~~	he, she, it did	they did

Note: Many people have trouble with one negative form of *to do*. They will say, for example, "He don't agree" instead of "He doesn't agree," or they will say "The door don't work" instead of "The door doesn't work." Be careful to avoid the common mistake of using *don't* instead of *doesn't*.

Activity 1: Choosing Standard Verb Forms

Underline the standard form of *to be*, *to have*, or *to do*.

1. When Walt (have, has) his own house, he will install built-in stereo speakers in every room.
2. The children (is, are) ready to go home.
3. Whenever we (do, does) the laundry, our clothes are spotted with blobs of undissolved detergent.
4. Tony and Crystal (was, were) ready to leave for the movies when the baby began to wail.
5. Our art class (done, did) the mural on the wall of the cafeteria.
6. If Maryanne (have, has) the time, she will help us set up the projector and tape the wires to the floor.
7. Kurt (be, is) the best ping-pong player in the college.
8. That mechanic always (do, does) a good job when he fixes my car.

9. The mice in our attic (have, has) chewed several holes in our ceiling.

10. The science instructor said that the province of British Columbia (be, is) ready for a major earthquake any day.

Activity 2: Using Standard Verb Forms

Fill in each blank with the standard form of *to be*, *to have*, or *to do*.

1. My car _____ a real personality.

2. Its behaviour _____ almost human.

3. On cold mornings, it _____ not want to start.

4. Like me, the car _____ a problem dealing with freezing weather.

5. I don't want to get out of bed, and my car _____ not like leaving the garage.

6. Also, we _____ the same feeling about rainstorms.

7. I hate driving to school in a downpour and so _____ the car.

8. When the car _____ stopped at a light, it stalls.

9. The habits my car _____ may be annoying.

10. But they _____ understandable.

■ Review Test 1

Underline the standard verb form.

1. Martin (argue, argues) just to hear himself talk.

2. Those shoppers (do, does) not seem to know their way around the market; they keep retracing their steps.

3. The cheap ballpoint pen (leak, leaked) all over the lining of my handbag.

4. Pat (bag, bagged) the dirty laundry and threw it into the car.

5. If you (has, have) any trouble with the assignment, give me a call.

6. Whenever the hairdresser (do, does) my hair, she cuts one side shorter than the other.

7. Crystal often (watch, watches) TV after her parents have gone to bed.

8. Two of the players (was, were) suspended from the league for ten games for using drugs.

9. Jeannie (has, have) only one eye; she lost the other years ago after falling on some broken glass.

10. I remember how my wet mittens (use, used) to steam on the hot school radiator.

■ Review Test 2

Cross out the two nonstandard verb forms in each sentence below. Then write the standard English verbs in the spaces provided.

Example   _____is_____   When our teacher be angry, his eyelid begin to twitch.
   _____begins_____

_____   _____   1. My mother work for the local newspaper; she take classified ads over the phone.

_____   _____   2. Last week the city tow away my car; this morning I paid sixty dollars and pick it up from the towing company.

_____   _____   3. When my wife be late for work, she rush around the house like a speeded-up cartoon character.

_____   _____   4. Henry love to go camping until two thieves in the campground remove his cooler, stove, and sleeping bag from his tent.

_____   _____   5. If the baby have a bad cold, I takes her into a steamy bathroom for a while to ease her breathing.

_____   _____   6. Although my little girls knows they shouldn't tease the cat, they often dresses up the animal in doll clothes.

_____   _____   7. When my brothers watches their favourite _Star Trek_ reruns, they knows exactly what Captain Kirk is going to say next.

_____   _____   8. Last week my cousin attempt to sell some time-share property to me, but I refuse to listen to him.

_____   _____   9. I show the receipt to the manager to prove that the clerk had accidentally over-charge me.

_____   _____   10. As far as our son be concerned, oatmeal taste like soggy cardboard.

IRREGULAR VERBS

Introductory Project

You may already have a sense of which common English verbs are regular and which are not. To test yourself, fill in the past tense* and past participle† of the verbs below. Five are regular verbs and so take -d or -ed in the past tense and past participle. Five are irregular verbs and will probably not sound right when you try to add -d or -ed. Write I for irregular in front of these verbs. Also, see if you can write in their irregular verb forms. (The item at the top is an example.)

Present	Past	Past Participle
shout	shouted	shouted
1. crawl		
2. bring		
3. use		
4. do		
5. give		
6. laugh		
7. go		
8. scare		
9. dress		
10. see		

Answers are on page 551.

---

* The *past tense* is the form of the verb used *alone* with a noun or pronoun subject: "Tony made...."

† The *past participle* is the form of the verb which must be used with a "helping verb," a form of the verb *to have:* "Tony *has made*...."

A BRIEF REVIEW OF REGULAR VERBS

Every verb has four principal parts: present tense, past tense, past participle, and present participle. These parts can be used to build all the verb *tenses* (the *times* shown by a verb).

The past and past participle of a regular verb are formed by adding *-d* or *-ed* to the present. The *past participle* is the form of the verb used with the helping verbs *have*, *has*, or *had* (or some form of *be* with passive verbs).* The *present participle* is formed by adding *-ing* to the present. Here are the principal forms of some regular verbs:

Present Tense	*Past Tense*	*Past Participle*	*Present Participle*
crash	crashed	crashed	crashing
shiver	shivered	shivered	shivering
kiss	kissed	kissed	kissing
apologize	apologized	apologized	apologizing
tease	teased	teased	teasing

Most verbs in English are regular.

LIST OF IRREGULAR VERBS

Irregular verbs have irregular forms in the past tense and past participle. For example, the past tense of the irregular verb *know* is *knew;* the past participle is *known*.

Almost everyone has some degree of trouble with irregular verbs. When you are unsure about the form of a verb, you can check the list of irregular verbs on the following pages. (The present participle is not shown on this list because it is formed simply by adding *-ing* to the present or base form of the verb.) Or you can check a dictionary, which gives the principal parts of irregular verbs.

* *Passive verb forms* are those in which the subject *does not perform the action* after the verb. Here are some examples:

1. Tony *was kissed* repeatedly by Crystal when he returned safely.
2. Jim *has been teased* unmercifully about his bright-blue hair.
3. Sheila *will be given* an award for safe driving.

Present Tense	Past Tense	Past Participle
arise	arose	arisen
awake	awoke	awoken
be (am, are, is)	was (were)	been
become	became	become
begin	began	begun
bend	bent	bent
bite	bit	bitten
blow	blew	blown
break	broke	broken
bring	brought	brought
build	built	built
burst	burst	burst
buy	bought	bought
catch	caught	caught
choose	chose	chosen
come	came	come
cost	cost	cost
cut	cut	cut
do (does)	did	done
draw	drew	drawn
drink	drank	drunk
drive	drove	driven
eat	ate	eaten
fall	fell	fallen
feed	fed	fed
feel	felt	felt
fight	fought	fought
find	found	found
fly	flew	flown
freeze	froze	frozen
get	got	got *or* gotten
give	gave	given
go (goes)	went	gone
grow	grew	grown

Present Tense	*Past Tense*	*Past Participle*
have (has)	had	had
hear	heard	heard
hide	hid	hidden
hold	held	held
hurt	hurt	hurt
keep	kept	kept
know	knew	known
lay	laid	laid
lead	led	led
leave	left	left
lend	lent	lent
let	let	let
lie	lay	lain
lose	lost	lost
make	made	made
meet	met	met
pay	paid	paid
ride	rode	ridden
ring	rang	rung
run	ran	run
say	said	said
see	saw	seen
sell	sold	sold
send	sent	sent
shake	shook	shaken
shrink	shrank	shrunk
shut	shut	shut
sing	sang	sung
sit	sat	sat
sleep	slept	slept
speak	spoke	spoken
spend	spent	spent
stand	stood	stood
steal	stole	stolen

Present Tense	Past Tense	Past Participle
stick	stuck	stuck
sting	stung	stung
swear	swore	sworn
swim	swam	swum
take	took	taken
teach	taught	taught
tear	tore	torn
tell	told	told
think	thought	thought
wake	woke	woken
wear	wore	worn
win	won	won
write	wrote	written

Activity 1: Choosing Correct Verb Forms

Cross out the incorrect verb form in each of the following sentences. Then write the correct form of the verb in the space provided.

Example   ___drew___   The little boy ~~drawed~~ on the marble table with permanent ink.

_____   1. Tomatoes were once thought to be poisonous, and they were growed only as ornamental shrubs.

_____   2. Jong has rode the bus to school for two years while saving for a car.

_____   3. My cats have tore little holes in all my good wool sweaters.

_____   4. The pipes in the bathroom freezed last winter, and they burst when they thawed.

_____   5. Every time my telephone has rang today, there has been bad news on the line.

_____   6. Only seven people have ever knowed the formula for Coca-Cola.

_____   7. Amy blowed up animal-shaped balloons for her son's birthday party.

_____   8. I shaked the bottle angrily until the ketchup began to flow.

_____   9. While waiting for the doctor to arrive, I sitted in a plastic chair for over two hours.

_____   10. The pile of bones on the plate showed how much chicken the family had ate.

Activity 2: Using Three Verb Forms

For each of the italicized verbs, fill in the three missing forms in the following order:

a Present tense, which takes an -*s* ending when the subject is *he, she, it*, or any *one person or thing* (see page 271)

b Past tense

c Past participle—the form that goes with the helping verb *have, has*, or *had*

Example   My uncle likes to *give* away certain things. He (*a*) _____*gives*_____ old, threadbare clothes to the Salvation Army. Last year he (*b*) _____*gave*_____ me a worthless television set in which the picture tube was burned out. He has (*c*) _____*given*_____ away stuff that a junk dealer would reject.

1. I like to *freeze* Caramilk bars. A Caramilk bar (*a*) _____ in half an hour. Once I (*b*) _____ a bottle of Pepsi. I put it in the freezer to chill and then forgot about it. Later I opened the freezer and discovered that it had (*c*) _____ and exploded.

2. I *know* the boy in the red trunks. He (*a*) _____ me, too. I (*b*) _____ his brother before I met him. I have (*c*) _____ him since boyhood.

3. An acquaintance of mine is a shoplifter, although he knows it's wrong to *steal*. He (*a*) _____ candy bars from supermarkets. Last month he (*b*) _____ a walkman and was caught by a detective. He has (*c*) _____ pants and shirts by wearing several layers of clothes out of a store.

4. I *go* to parties a lot. Often Camille (*a*) _____ with me. She (*b*) _____ with me just last week. I have (*c*) _____ to parties every Friday for the past month.

5. My brother likes to *throw* things. Sometimes he (*a*) _____ socks into his dresser drawer. In high school he (*b*) _____ footballs while quarterbacking the team. And he has (*c*) _____ baseballs in our backyard for as long as I can remember.

6. I *see* her every weekend. She (*a*) _____ her other friends during the week. We first (*b*) _____ each other on a cold Saturday night last winter, when we went for supper at an Indian restaurant. Since then we have (*c*) _____ each other every weekend except when my car was broken down.

7. I often *lie* down for a few minutes after a hard day's work. Sometimes my cat (*a*) _____ down near me. Yesterday was Saturday, so I (*b*) _____ in bed all morning. I probably would have (*c*) _____ in bed all afternoon, but I wanted to get some planting done in my vegetable garden.

8. I *do* not understand the assignment. It simply (*a*) _____ not make sense to me. I was surprised to learn that Elaine (*b*) _____ understand it. In fact, she had already (*c*) _____ the assignment.

9. I often find it hard to *begin* writing a paper. The assignment that I must do (*a*) _____ to worry me while I'm watching television, but I seldom turn off the set. Once I waited until the late movie had ended before I (*b*) _____ to write. If I had (*c*) _____ earlier, I would have gotten a decent night's sleep.

10. Maria likes to *eat*. She (*a*) _____ as continuously as some people smoke. Once she (*b*) _____ a large package of cookies in half an hour. Even if she has (*c*) _____ a heavy meal, she often starts munching snacks right afterward.

■ Review Test 1

Underline the correct verb in the parentheses.

1. I (shaked, shook) the bottle of medicine before I took a teaspoon of it.

2. Tyrone came into the gym and (began, begun) to practise on the parallel bars.

3. Over half the class has (taken, took) this course on a pass-fail basis.

4. Even though my father (teached, taught) me how to play baseball, I never enjoyed any part of the game.

5. Because I had (lended, lent) him the money, I had a natural concern about what he did with it.

6. The drugstore clerk (gave, gived) him the wrong change.

7. Crystal (brang, brought) a sweatshirt with her, for she knew the mountains got cold at night.

8. My sister (was, be) at school when a stranger came asking for her at our home.

9. The mechanic (did, done) an expensive valve job on my engine without getting my permission.

10. The basketball team has (broke, broken) the school record for most losses in one year.

11. Someone (leaved, left) his books in the classroom.

12. That sweater was (tore, torn) during the soccer game.

13. If I hadn't (threw, thrown) away the receipt, I could have got my money back.

14. I would have (become, became) very angry if you had not intervened.

15. As the flower pot (fell, falled) from the windowsill, the little boy yelled, "Bombs away!"

■ Review Test 2

Write short sentences that use the form requested for the following irregular verbs.

Example   Past tense of *to grow*   _I grew ten centimetres in one year._

1. Past tense of *to know* _____

2. Past tense of *to take* _____

3. Past participle of *to give* _____

4. Past participle of *to write* _____

5. Past tense of *to bring* _____

6. Past participle of *to speak* _____

7. Present tense of *to begin* _____

8. Past tense of *to go* _____

9. Past participle of *to see* _____

10. Past tense of *to drive* _____

SUBJECT–VERB AGREEMENT

A verb must *agree* with its subject *in number*. A *singular subject* (one person or thing) takes a singular verb. A *plural subject* (more than one person or thing) takes a plural verb. Mistakes in subject–verb agreement are sometimes made in the following situations (each situation is explained on the following pages):

1   When words come between the subject and the verb

2   When a verb comes before the subject

3   With compound subjects

4   With indefinite pronouns

WORDS BETWEEN SUBJECT AND VERB

Words that come between the subject and the verb do not change subject–verb agreement. In the sentence

The mean <u>cockroaches</u> behind my stove <u>get</u> high on bug spray.

the subject (<u>cockroaches</u>) is plural and so the verb (<u>get</u>) is plural. The words *behind my stove* that come between the subject and verb do not affect subject–verb agreement.

To help find the subject of certain sentences, you should cross out prepositional phrases (see page 235):

<u>Nell</u>, ~~with her three dogs close behind~~, <u>runs</u> around the park every day.

The <u>seams</u> ~~in my new coat~~, <u>have split</u> after only two wearings.

Activity: Verb Number Agreement

Underline the subject and cross out any words that come between the subject and the verb. Then double-underline the verb choice in parentheses that you believe is correct.

1.   The decisions of the judge (seems, seem) questionable.

2.   A hamburger with a double order of french fries (is, are) my usual lunch.

3.   One of my son's worst habits (is, are) leaving an assortment of dirty plates on the kitchen counter every morning.

4.   The rust spots on the back of Emily's car (needs, need) to be cleaned with a special polish.

5.   The collection of medicine bottles in my bathroom (overflows, overflow) the cabinet shelves.

VERB BEFORE SUBJECT

A verb agrees with its subject even when the verb comes *before* the subject. Words that may precede the subject include *there*, *here*, and, in questions, *who*, *which*, *what*, and *where*. These words are *not* the subjects of the sentences.

On Bill's doorstep <u>were</u> two <u>police officers</u>.
There <u>are</u> many pizza <u>places</u> in our town.
Here <u>is</u> your <u>receipt</u>.
Where <u>are</u> <u>they</u> <u>going</u> to sleep?

If you are unsure about the subject, ask *who* or *what* of the verb. With the first example above, you might ask, "*Who* were on the doorstep?" The answer, *police officers*, is the subject.

Activity: Choosing Correct Verb Forms

Write the correct form of the verb in the space provided.

was, were   1. There _____ not enough glasses for all the guests at the party.

is, are   2. Here _____ the tickets for tonight's ball game.

do, does   3. Where _____ you go when you want to be alone?

is, are   4. There _____ too many people in the room for me to feel comfortable.

was, were   5. Stuffed into the mailbox _____ ten pieces of junk mail and three ripped magazines.

COMPOUND SUBJECTS

Subjects joined by *and* generally take a plural verb.

<u>Maple syrup</u> and <u>sweet butter</u> <u>taste</u> delicious on pancakes.
<u>Fear</u> and <u>ignorance</u> <u>have</u> a lot to do with hatred.

When subjects are joined by *either ... or, neither ... nor, not only ... but also*, the verb agrees with the subject closer to the verb.

Either <u>Shania Twain and her band</u> or <u>Randy Travis</u> <u>deserves</u> the award for the best country album of the year.

The nearer subject, *Randy Travis*, is singular, and so the verb is singular.

Activity: Choosing Correct Verb Forms

Write the correct form of the verb in the space provided.

is, are   1. An egg and a banana _____ required for the recipe.

was, were   2. Owning a car and having money in my pocket _____ the chief ambitions of my adolescence.

visits,   3. My aunt and uncle from Ireland _____ us every other
visit   summer.

was, were   4. Before they saw a marriage therapist, Peter and Jenny _____ planning to get divorced.

acts, act   5. Not only the property manager but also her children _____ unfriendly to us.

INDEFINITE PRONOUNS

The following words, known as *indefinite pronouns,** always take *singular verbs:*

(-one words)	*(-body words)*	*(-thing words)*	
one	nobody	nothing	each
anyone	anybody	anything	either
everyone	everybody	everything	neither
someone	somebody	something	

Note: *Both* always takes a *plural verb.*

Activity: Using Verb Forms Appropriately with Indefinite Pronouns

Write the correct form of the verb in the space provided.

pitches,   1. If each of us _____ in, we can finish this job in an hour.
pitch

* *Indefinite pronouns* replace nouns in a "nonspecific" way. They are indefinite because they indicate in a general way negative or unspecified quantities of people or things.

was, were 2. Everybody in the theatre _____ getting up and leaving before the movie ended.

provides, provide 3. Neither of the restaurants _____ facilities for people in wheelchairs.

likes, like 4. No one in our family _____ housecleaning, but we all take a turn at it.

steals, steal 5. Someone in our neighbourhood _____ vegetables from people's gardens.

■ Review Test

Underline the correct verb in parentheses.

1. The lettuce in most of the stores in our area now (costs, cost) almost one dollar a head.

2. Nobody in the class of fifty students (understands, understand) how to solve the equation on the blackboard.

3. The packages in the shopping bag (was, were) a wonderful mystery to the children.

4. My exercise class of five students (meets, meet) every Thursday afternoon.

5. Anyone who (steals, steal) my purse won't find much inside it.

6. Business contacts and financial backing (is, are) all that I need to establish my career as a dress designer.

7. Each of those breakfast cereals (contains, contain) a high proportion of sugar.

8. The serious look in that young girl's eyes (worries, worry) me.

9. All of the cars on my block (has, have) to be moved one day a month for street cleaning.

10. The job is not for people who (stumbles, stumble) over tough decisions.

CONSISTENT VERB TENSE

Introductory Project

Find and underline the two mistakes in verb tense in the following selection.

> Ali's eyes burned and itched all day long. When he looked at them in a mirror, he also discovers there were red blotches on his neck. He spoke to his mother about the symptoms, and she said that maybe he was allergic to something. Then he remembers he had been cuddling the kitten that Ayesha had just bought the day before. "Good grief. I must be allergic to cats," he said to himself.

Answers are on page 552.

KEEPING TENSES CONSISTENT

Do not shift verb tenses unnecessarily. If you begin writing a paper in the present tense, don't shift suddenly to the past. If you begin in the past, don't shift without reason to the present. Notice the inconsistent verb tenses in the following selection:

> The shoplifter *walked* quickly toward the front of the store. When a clerk *shouts* at him, he *started* to run.

The verbs must be consistently *in the present tense*:

> The shoplifter *walks* quickly toward the front of the store. When a clerk *shouts* at him, he *starts* to run.

Or the verbs must be consistently *in the past tense*:

> The shoplifter *walked* quickly toward the front of the store. When a clerk *shouted* at him, he *started* to run.

Activity 1: Using Consistent Verb Tenses

In each selection one verb must be changed so that it agrees in tense with the other verbs. Cross out the incorrect verb and write the correct form in the space provided.

Example _carried_ Ted wanted to be someplace else when the dentist ~~carries~~ in a long needle.

_____ 1. I played my stereo and watched television before I decide to do some homework.

_____ 2. The hitch-hiker stopped me as I walks from the highway washroom and said, "Are you on your way to Red Deer?"

_____ 3. Some students attend all their classes in school. They listen carefully during lectures but they don't take notes. As a result, they often failed tests.

_____ 4. His parents stayed together for his sake; only after he graduates from college were they divorced.

_____ 5. In the movie, artillery shells exploded on the hide of the reptile monster. It just grinned, tosses off the shells, and kept eating people.

_____ 6. Several months a year, monarch butterflies come to live on Point Pelee along the Lake Erie shore. Thousands and thousands of them hang from the trees and fluttered through the air in large groups.

_____ 7. After waking up each morning, Harry stays in bed for a while. First he stretches and yawned loudly, and then he plans his day.

_____ 8. The salespeople at The Bay are very helpful. When people asked for a product the store doesn't carry or is out of, the salesperson recommends another store.

_____ 9. Part-time workers at the company are the first to be laid off. They are also paid less, and they received no union representation.

_____ 10. Smashed cars, ambulances, and police cars blocked traffic on one side of the highway. On the other side, traffic slows down as drivers looked to see what happened.

Activity 2: Using the Past Tense Correctly

In the following selection, change verbs where needed so that they are consistently in the past tense. Cross out each incorrect verb and write the correct form above it, as shown in the example. You will need to make nine corrections.

Late one rainy night, Shawna woke to the sound of steady dripping.

When she got out of bed to investigate, a drop of cold water ~~splashes~~ *splashed* onto

her arm. She looks up just in time to see another drop form on the ceiling,

hang suspended for a moment, and fall to the carpet. Stumbling to the

kitchen, Shawna reaches deep into one of the cabinets and lifts out a large

roasting pan. As she did so, pot lids and baking pans clattered out and

crash onto the counter. Shawna ignored them, stumbled back to the

bedroom, and places the pan on the floor under the drip. But a minute after

sliding her icy feet under the covers, Shawna realized she is in trouble. The

sound of each drop hitting the metal pan echoed like a gunshot in the quiet

room. Shawna feels like crying, but she finally thought of a solution. She

got out of bed and returns a minute later with a thick bath towel. She lined

the pan with the towel and crawls back into bed.

■ Review Test

In the following selection, change verbs where needed so that they are consistently in the past tense. Cross out each incorrect verb and then write the correct form above it. You will need to make ten corrections in all.

Balancing the green plastic bag full of garbage, Craig yanked the front

door open. As he stepped onto the front porch, he notices that a light snow

was already falling. He remembers that when he called to rent the cabin,

he was told that it was not too early to expect snow in this mountain

community. He glances up at the sky and then walks briskly to the end of

the driveway. There he deposited the overflowing bag into one of the large

garbage cans. Shivering from the cold, he turned around and starts back

toward the house, but then he pauses suddenly. At the south-west corner

of the cabin, standing on its hind legs, was an enormous black bear. For a

long terrible second, Craig was positive the bear was staring right at him.

Looking for a promising direction to run, Craig turns around and saw a small bear cub scampering away from behind another garbage can. Before Craig had time to react, the large bear went down on all fours, sprints past the house, and started after the cub. Craig breathed a sigh of relief, races into the cabin, and locks the door behind him.

1. _____   6. _____
2. _____   7. _____
3. _____   8. _____
4. _____   9. _____
5. _____   10. _____

PRONOUN AGREEMENT, REFERENCE, AND POINT OF VIEW

Pronouns are words that take the place of nouns (persons, places, or things). In fact, the word *pronoun* means "for a noun." Pronouns are shortcuts that keep you from unnecessarily repeating words in writing. Here are some examples of pronouns:

Ivana had not finished *her* paper. (*Her* is a pronoun that takes the place of *Ivana's.*)

Tony swung so heavily on the tree branch that *it* snapped. (*It* replaces *branch.*)

When the three little pigs saw the wolf, *they* pulled out cans of pepper spray. (*They* is a pronoun that takes the place of *pigs.*)

This section presents rules that will help you avoid three common mistakes people make with pronouns. The rules are as follows:

1 A pronoun must *agree in number* with the word or words it replaces.

2 A pronoun must *refer clearly to the word it replaces.*

3 Pronouns *should not shift unnecessarily in point of view.*

PRONOUN AGREEMENT

A pronoun must agree in number with the word or words it replaces. If the word a pronoun refers to is singular, the pronoun must be singular; if that word is plural, the pronoun must be plural. (Note that the word a pronoun refers to is also known as the *antecedent. Antecedent* means "going before" in Latin.)

Barbara agreed to lend me (her) Bryan Adams albums.

People walking the trail must watch (their) step because of snakes.

In the first example, the pronoun *her* refers to the singular word *Barbara;* in the second example, the pronoun *their* refers to the plural word *People.*

Activity: Choosing an Appropriate Antecedent Pronoun

Write the appropriate pronoun (*their, they, them, it*) in the blank space in each of the following sentences.

Example   I lifted the pot of hot potatoes carefully, but _____it_____ slipped out of my hand.

1. The value that people receive for _____ dollars these days is rapidly diminishing.

2. Kim never misses his daily workout; he believes _____ keeps him healthy.

3. Sometimes, in marriage, partners expect too much from _____ mates.

4. For some students, college is often their first experience with an unsupervised learning situation, and _____ are not always ready to accept the responsibility.

5. Our new neighbours moved in three months ago, but I have yet to meet

_____.

Indefinite Pronouns

The following words, known as *indefinite pronouns*, are *always singular*.

(*-one* words)	(*-body* words)	
one	nobody	each
anyone	anybody	either
everyone	everybody	neither
someone	somebody	

If a pronoun in a sentence refers to one of these singular words, the pronoun should be singular.

Each father felt that (his) child should have won the contest.

One of the women could not find (her) purse.

Everyone must be in (his) seat before the instructor takes attendance.

In each example, the circled pronoun is singular because it refers to one of the special singular words.

Note: The last example is correct if everyone in the class is a man. If everyone in the class was a woman, the pronoun would be *her*. If the class had both women and men, the pronoun form would be *his or her*:

Everyone must be in his or her seat before the instructor takes attendance.

In the last few years, the use of *their* (the plural form of the possessive pronoun) has come to be acceptable in such phrases as "in their seat." Ask your instructor what his or her preference is.

Some writers follow the traditional practice of using *his* to refer to both women and men. Many now use *his or her* to avoid an implied sexual bias. To avoid using *his* or the somewhat awkward *his or her*, a sentence can often be rewritten in the plural:

Students must be in their seats before the instructor takes attendance.

Activity: Choosing the Correct Pronoun

Underline the correct pronoun.

1. Someone has blocked the parking-lot exit with (his or her, their) car.

2. Everyone in the women's group has volunteered some of (her, their) time for the voting drive.

3. Neither of the men arrested as terrorists would reveal information about (his, their) group.

4. Not one of the women coaches will be returning to (her, their) job next year.

5. Each of the CEO's advisers offered (his or her, their) opinion about the rail strike.

PRONOUN REFERENCE

A sentence may be confusing and unclear if a pronoun appears to refer to more than one word, or if the pronoun does not refer to any specific word. Look at this sentence:

Joe almost dropped out of high school, for he felt *they* emphasized discipline too much.

Who emphasized discipline too much? There is *no specific word* that *they* refers to. Be clear:

Joe almost dropped out of high school, for he felt *the teachers* emphasized discipline too much.

Following are sentences with other kinds of faulty pronoun references. Read the explanations of why they are faulty and look carefully at how they are corrected.

Faulty	*Clear*
Julie told Maria that *she* lacked self-confidence.	Julie told Maria, "You lack self-confidence."
(*Who* lacked self-confidence: Julie or Maria? Be clear.)	(Quotation marks, which can sometimes be used to correct an unclear reference, are explained on pages 353–360.)
Nancy's mother is a hairdresser, but Nancy is not interested in *it*.	Nancy's mother is a hairdresser, but Nancy is not interested in becoming one.
(There is no specific word that *it* refers to. It would not make sense to say, "Nancy is not interested in hairdresser.")	
Ron blamed the police officer for the ticket, *which* was foolish.	Foolishly, Ron blamed the police officer for the ticket.
(Does *which* mean that the officer's giving the ticket was foolish, or that Ron's blaming the officer was foolish? Be clear.)	

Activity: Using Clear Pronoun References

Rewrite each of the following sentences to make clear the vague pronoun reference. Add, change, or omit words as necessary.

Example   Our cat was friends with our hamster until he bit him.

Until the cat bit the hamster, the two were friends.

1. Shelley's mother let her wear her new earrings to school.

_____

2. When I asked why I failed my driver's test, he said I drove too slowly.

_____

3. Dad ordered my brother to paint the garage because he didn't want to do it.

_____

4. Harry dropped his psychology courses because he thought they assigned too much reading.

_____

5. I love Parmesan cheese on veal, but it does not always digest well.

PRONOUN POINT OF VIEW

Pronouns should not shift their point of view unnecessarily. When writing a paper, *be consistent* in your use of first-, second-, or third-person pronouns.

Type of Pronoun	*Singular*	*Plural*
First-person pronouns	I (my, mine, me)	we (our, us)
Second-person pronouns	you (your)	you (your)
Third-person pronouns	he (his, him)	they (their, them)
	she (her)	
	it (its)	

Note: Any person, place, or thing (noun) as well as any indefinite pronoun like *one*, *anyone*, *someone*, and so on (page 297), is a *third-person word*.

For instance, if you start writing in the third person *she*, don't jump suddenly to the second person *you*. Or if you are writing in the first person *I*, don't shift unexpectedly to *one*. Look at the examples.

Inconsistent	*Consistent*
I enjoy movies like *The Return of the Vampire* that frighten *you*. (The most common mistake people make is to let a *you* slip into their writing after they start with another pronoun.)	*I* enjoy movies like *The Return of the Vampire* that frighten *me*.
As soon as a person walks into Helen's apartment, *you* can tell that Helen owns a cat. (Again, the *you* is a shift in point of view.)	As soon as *a person* walks into Helen's apartment, *he or she* can tell that Helen owns a cat. (See also the note about *his or her* references on pages 297–298.)

Activity: Inconsistent Pronoun Use

Cross out inconsistent pronouns in the following sentences, and write the correct form of the pronoun above each crossed-out word.

Example   My dreams are always the kind that haunt ~~you~~ *me* the next day.

1. Whenever we take our children on a trip, you have to remember to bring snacks, tissues, and toys.

2. In our society, we often need a diploma before you are hired for a job.

3. A worker can take a break only after a relief person comes to take your place.

4. If a student organizes time carefully, you can accomplish a great deal of work.

5. Although I know you should watch your cholesterol intake, I can never resist corn on the cob dripping with melted butter.

■ Review Test 1

Cross out the pronoun error in each sentence and write the correction in the space provided at the left. Then circle the letter that correctly describes the type of error that was made.

Examples

his (or her)   Each player took ~~their~~ position on the court.
Mistake in: a. pronoun reference (b.) pronoun agreement

the store   I was angry when ~~they~~ wouldn't give me cash back when I returned the sweater I had bought.
Mistake in: (a.) pronoun reference   b.   pronoun point of view

_I_   I love Jello because ~~you~~ can eat about five bowls of it and still not feel full.
Mistake in: a. pronoun agreement (b.) pronoun point of view

_____   1. Dan asked Mr. Lalonde if he could stay an extra hour at work today.
Mistake in: a. pronoun reference   b.   pronoun agreement

_____   2. Both the front door and the back door of the abandoned house had fallen off its hinges.
Mistake in: a. pronoun agreement   b.   pronoun point of view

_____   3. I hate going to the supermarket because you always have trouble finding a parking space there.
Mistake in: a. pronoun agreement   b.   pronoun point of view

_____   4. Norm was angry when they raised the provincial tax on cigarettes again.
Mistake in: a. pronoun agreement   b.   pronoun reference

_____ 5. Every one of those musicians who played for two hours in the rain truly earned their money last night.
Mistake in: a. pronoun agreement   b. pronoun reference

_____ 6. As I entered the house, you could hear someone giggling in the hallway.
Mistake in: a. pronoun reference   b. pronoun point of view

_____ 7. Each of the contestants is asked a thought-provoking question and then judged on their answer.
Mistake in: a. pronoun agreement   b. pronoun reference

_____ 8. Sometimes I take the alternative route, but it takes you two hours longer.
Mistake in: a. pronoun agreement   b. pronoun point of view

_____ 9. At the dental office, I asked him if it was really necessary to take X-rays of my mouth again.
Mistake in: a. pronoun agreement   b. pronoun reference

_____ 10. My favourite subject is abnormal psychology because the case studies make you seem so normal by comparison.
Mistake in: a. pronoun agreement   b. pronoun point of view

■ Review Test 2

Underline the correct word in parentheses.

1. As we sat in class waiting for the test results, (you, we) could feel the tension.

2. Hoping to be first in line when (they, the ushers) opened the doors, we arrived two hours early for the concert.

3. If a person really wants to appreciate good coffee, (he or she, you, they) should drink it black.

4. I love science fiction because it lets (you, me) escape to other worlds.

5. Lisa often visits the reading centre in school, for she finds that (they, the tutors) give her helpful instruction.

6. Nobody seems to know how to add or subtract without (his or her, their) pocket calculator any more.

7. Cindy is the kind of woman who will always do (their, her) best.

8. Each of my brothers has had (his, their) apartment broken into.

9. If someone is going to write a composition, (he or she, you, they) should pre-pare at least one rough draft.

10. I've been taking cold medicine, and now (it, the cold) is better.

PRONOUN TYPES

This chapter describes some common types of pronouns: subject and object pronouns, possessive pronouns, and demonstrative pronouns.

SUBJECT AND OBJECT PRONOUNS

Pronouns change their form depending on the purpose they serve in a sentence. In the box that follows is a list of subject and object pronouns.

Subject Pronouns	Object Pronouns
I	me
you	you (no change)
he	him
she	her
it	it (no change)
we	us
they	them

Subject Pronouns

Subject pronouns are subjects of verbs.

She is wearing blue nail polish on her toes. (*She* is the subject of the verb *is wearing*.)

They ran up three flights of steps. (*They* is the subject of the verb *ran*.)

We children should have some privacy too. (*We* is the subject of the verb *should have*.)

Rules for using subject pronouns, and several kinds of mistakes people sometimes make with subject pronouns, are explained below.

Rule 1: Use a subject pronoun in spots where you have a *compound* (more than one) *subject*.

Incorrect	**Correct**
Sally and *me* are exactly the same size.	Sally and *I* are exactly the same size.
Her and *me* share our wardrobes with each other.	*She* and *I* share our wardrobes with each other.

Hint: If you are not sure what pronoun to use, *try each pronoun by itself in the sentence*. The correct pronoun will be the one that sounds right. For example, "*Her* shares her wardrobe" does not sound right; "*she* shares her wardrobe" does.

Rule 2: Use a subject pronoun after forms of the verb *to be*. Forms of *to be* include *am, are, is, was, were, has been,* and *have been*.

It was *I* who called you a minute ago and then hung up.

It may be *they* entering the bar.

It was *he* who put the white tablecloth into the washing machine with a red sock.

The sentences above may sound strange and stilted to you because they are seldom used in conversation. When we speak with one another, forms such as "It was me," "It may be them," and "It is her" are widely accepted. In formal writing, however, the grammatically correct forms are still preferred.

Hint: To avoid having to use a subject pronoun form after *to be*, you can simply reword a sentence. Here is how the preceding examples could be reworded:

I was the one who called you a minute ago and then hung up.

They may be the ones entering the diner.

He put the white tablecloth into the washing machine with a red sock.

Rule 3: Use subject pronouns after *than* or *as*. The subject pronoun is used because a verb is understood after the pronoun.

Mark can hold his breath longer than *I* (can). (The verb *can* is understood after *I*.)

Her thirteen-year-old daughter is as tall as *she* (is). (The verb *is* is understood after *she*.)

You drive much better than *he* (drives). (The verb *drives* is understood after *he*.)

Hint: Avoid mistakes by mentally adding the "missing" verb at the end of the sentence.

Object Pronouns

Object pronouns (*me, him, her, us, them*) are the *objects of verbs or prepositions*. (*Prepositions* are connecting words like *for, at, about, to, before, by, with*, and *of*. See also page 234.) An object, in grammatical terms, receives the action of a verb, or completes a prepositional phrase.

Lee pushed *me*. (*Me* is the object of the verb *pushed*.)

We dragged *them* all the way home. (*Them* is the object of the verb *dragged*.)

She wrote all about *us* in her diary. (*Us* is the object of the preposition *about*.)

Vera passed a note to *him* as she walked to the pencil sharpener. (*Him* is the object of the preposition *to*.)

People are sometimes uncertain about what pronoun to use when two objects follow the verb.

Incorrect	*Correct*
I argued with his sister and *he*.	I argued with his sister and *him*.
The cashier cheated Rick and *I*.	The cashier cheated Rick and *me*.

Hint: If you are not sure what pronoun to use, *try each pronoun by itself in the sentence*. The correct pronoun will be the one that sounds right. For example, "I argued with he" does not sound right; "I argued with him" does.

Activity: Choosing Subject or Object Pronouns

Underline the correct subject or object pronoun in each of the following sentences. Then show whether your answer is a subject or an object pronoun by circling the *S* or *O* in the margin. The first one is done for you as an example.

(**S**) **O** 1. Kenny and (<u>she</u>, her) kept dancing even after the band stopped playing.

S **O** 2. The letters Mom writes to Stella and (I, me) are always handwritten in red.

S **O** 3. No one has more nerve than (he, him).

S   *O*   4. Their relay team won because they practised more than (we, us).

S   *O*   5. (We, Us) choir members get to perform for the premier.

S   *O*   6. The rest of (they, them) came to the wedding by train.

S   *O*   7. (She, Her) and Sammy got divorced and then remarried.

S   *O*   8. My sister keeps track of all the favours she does for my brother and (I, me).

S   *O*   9. Steve and (he, him) look a lot alike, but they're not even related.

S   *O*   10. Our neighbours asked Maria and (I, me) to help with their parents' surprise party.

POSSESSIVE PRONOUNS

Possessive pronouns show *ownership or possession*.

Using a small branch, Dave wrote *his* initials in the wet cement.
The furniture is *mine*, but the car is *hers*.

Here is a list of possessive pronouns:

my, mine	our, ours
your, yours	your, yours
his	their, theirs
her, hers	
its	

Note: A possessive pronoun *never* uses an apostrophe. (See also page 348.)

Incorrect	*Correct*
That earring is *hers'*.	That earring is *hers*.
The orange cat is *theirs'*.	The orange cat is *theirs*.

Activity: Choosing Correct Possessive Pronouns

Cross out the incorrect pronoun form in each of the sentences below. Write the correct form in the space at the left.

Example   ____hers____   Those gloves are ~~hers'~~.

_____ 1. A porcupine has no quills on its' belly.

_____ 2. The stereo set is theirs'.

_____ 3. You can easily tell which team is ours' by when we cheer.

_____ 4. The car with the pink car seats is hers'.

_____ 5. Grandma's silverware and dishes will be yours' when you get married.

DEMONSTRATIVE PRONOUNS

Demonstrative pronouns *point to or single out a person or thing*. There are four demonstrative pronouns:

this	these
that	those

Generally speaking, *this* and *these* refer to things close at hand; *that* and *those* refer to things farther away. The four pronouns are commonly used in the role of demonstrative adjectives as well.

The following examples show *adjectival* use of demonstratives:

This milk has gone sour.

My son insists on saving all *these* car magazines.

I almost tripped on *that* roller skate at the bottom of the steps.

Those plants in the corner don't get enough light.

Note: Do not use *them, this here, that there, these here,* or *those there* to point out. Use only *this, that, these,* or *those.*

Activity: Correct Use of Demonstrative Pronouns

Cross out the incorrect form of the demonstrative pronoun and write the correct form in the space provided.

Example   _Those_   ~~Those there~~ tires look worn.

_____ 1. This here child has a high fever.

_____ 2. These here pants I'm wearing are so tight I can hardly breathe.

_____   3. Them kids have been playing in the alley all morning.

_____   4. That there umpire won't stand for any temper tantrums.

_____   5. I save them old baby clothes for my daughter's dolls.

■ **Review Test**

Underline the correct word in the parentheses.

1. If I left dinner up to (he, him), we'd have Weetabix every night.

2. Julie's words may have come from the script, but the smile is all (hers', hers).

3. My boyfriend offered to drive his mother and (I, me) to the mall to shop for his birthday present.

4. (Them, those) little marks on the floor are scratches, not crumbs.

5. I took a picture of my brother and (I, me) looking into the hallway mirror.

6. When Lin and (she, her) drove back from the airport, they talked so much that they missed their exit.

7. (That there, That) orange juice box says "Fresh," but the juice is made from concentrate.

8. Eliot swears that he dreamt about (she, her) and a speeding car the night before Rose was injured in a car accident.

9. The server brought our food to the people at the next table, and gave (theirs, theirs') to us.

10. Since it was so hot out, Crystal and (he, him) felt they had a good excuse to study at the beach.

ADJECTIVES
AND ADVERBS

ADJECTIVES

What Are Adjectives?

Adjectives *describe nouns* (names of persons, places, or things) or pronouns.

Ernie is a *rich* man. (The adjective *rich* describes the noun *man*.)
He is also *generous*. (The adjective *generous* describes the pronoun *he*.)
Our grey cat sleeps a lot. (The adjective *grey* describes the noun *cat*.)
She is *old*. (The adjective *old* describes the pronoun *she*.)

Adjectives usually come before the word they describe (as in *rich man* and *grey cat*). But they also come after forms of the verb *to be* (*is*, *are*, *was*, *were*, and so on). They also *follow "sense" verbs* such as *to look*, *to appear*, *to seem*, *to become*, *to sound*, *to taste*, and *to smell*.

That speaker was *boring*. (The adjective *boring* describes the speaker.)
The Petersons are *homeless*. (The adjective *homeless* describes the Petersons.)
The soup looked *good*. (The adjective *good* describes the soup.)
But it tasted *salty*. (The adjective *salty* describes the pronoun *it*.)

Using Adjectives to Compare

For all one-syllable adjectives and some two-syllable adjectives, add *-er* when comparing two things and *-est* when comparing three or more things.

My sister's handwriting is *neater* than mine, but Mother's is the *neatest*.
Canned juice is sometimes *cheaper* than fresh juice, but frozen juice is often the *cheapest*.

For some two-syllable adjectives and all longer adjectives, add *more* when comparing two things and *most* when comparing three or more things.

> Typing something is *more efficient* than writing it out by hand, but the *most efficient* way to write is on a computer.
>
> Jeans are generally *more comfortable* than slacks, but sweat pants are the *most comfortable* of all.

You can usually tell when to use *more* and *most* by the sound of a word. For example, you can probably tell by its sound that "carefuller" would be too awkward to say and that *more careful* is thus correct. In addition, there are many words for which both *-er* or *-est* and *more* or *most* are equally correct. For instance, either "a more fair rule" or "a fairer rule" is correct.

To form negative comparisons, use *less* and *least*.

> When kids called me "Dum-dum," I tried to look *less* hurt than I felt.
>
> They say men gossip *less* than women do, but I don't believe it.
>
> Suzanne is the most self-centred, *least* thoughtful person I know.

Points to Remember about Comparing

Point 1: Use only one form of comparison at a time. In other words, do not use both an *-er* ending and *more* or both an *-est* ending and *most:*

Incorrect	*Correct*
My Newfoundland accent is always *more stronger* after I visit my family in Bonavista.	My Newfoundland accent is always *stronger* after I visit my family in Bonavista.
My *most luckiest* day was the day I met my wife.	My *luckiest* day was the day I met my wife.

Point 2: Learn the irregular forms of the words shown below.

	Comparative (for Comparing Two Things)	*Superlative (for Comparing Three or More Things)*
bad	worse	worst
good, well	better	best
little (in amount)	less	least
much, many	more	most

Do not use both *more* and an irregular comparative or *most* and an irregular superlative.

Incorrect	*Correct*
It is *more better* to stay healthy than to have to get healthy.	It is *better* to stay healthy than to have to get healthy.
Yesterday I went on the *most best* date of my life—and all we did was go on a picnic.	Yesterday I went on the *best* date of my life—and all we did was go on a picnic.

Activity: Using Comparative and Superlative Adjectives

Add to each sentence the correct form of the word in the margin.

bad   **Examples** The _____worst_____ scare I ever had was when I thought my son was on an airplane that crashed.

wonderful The day of my divorce was even __more wonderful__ than the day of my wedding.

good   1. The _____ way to diet is gradually.

popular 2. Vanilla ice cream is even _____ than chocolate ice cream.

bad   3. One of the _____ things you can do to people is ignore them.

light   4. A kilo of feathers is no _____ than a kilo of stones.

little 5. The _____ expensive way to accumulate a wardrobe is by buying used clothing whenever possible.

ADVERBS

What Are Adverbs?

Adverbs describe verbs, adjectives, or other adverbs. They usually end in *-ly*.

The referee *suddenly* stopped the fight.
(The adverb *suddenly* describes the verb *stopped*.)

Her yellow rosebushes are *absolutely* beautiful.
(The adverb *absolutely* describes the adjective *beautiful*.)

The auctioneer spoke so *terribly* fast that I couldn't understand him.
(The adverb *terribly* describes the adverb *fast*.)

A Common Mistake with Adverbs and Adjectives

People often mistakenly use an adjective instead of an adverb after a verb.

Incorrect	*Correct*
I jog *slow*.	I jog *slowly*.
The nervous witness spoke *quiet*.	The nervous witness spoke *quietly*.
The first night I quit smoking, I wanted a cigarette *bad*.	The first night I quit smoking, I wanted a cigarette *badly*.

Activity: Choosing Adjectives or Adverbs

Underline the adjective or adverb needed. (Remember that adjectives describe nouns, and adverbs describe verbs, adjectives, or other adverbs.)

1. During a quiet moment in class, my stomach rumbled (loud, loudly).

2. I'm a (slow, slowly) reader, so I have to put aside more time to study than some of my friends.

3. Thinking no one was looking, the young man (quick, quickly) emptied his car's ashtray onto the parking lot.

4. The kitchen cockroaches wait (patient, patiently) in the shadows; at night they'll have the place to themselves.

5. I hang up the phone (immediate, immediately) whenever the speaker is a recorded message.

Well and Good

Two words that are often confused are *well* and *good*. *Good* is an adjective; it describes nouns. *Well* is usually an adverb; it describes verbs. *Well* (rather than *good*) is also used when referring to a person's health.

Activity: Choosing an Adjective or an Adverb

Write *well* or *good* in each of the sentences that follow.

1. I could tell by the broad grin on Ginny's face that the news was

   _____.

2. They say he sang so _____ that even the wind stopped to listen.

3. The food at the salad bar must not have been too fresh because I didn't feel
   _____ after dinner.

4. When I want to do a really _____ job of washing the floor, I
   do it on my hands and knees.

5. The best way to get along _____ with our boss is to stay out
   of his way.

■ **Review Test**

Underline the correct word in the parentheses.

1. In Egypt, silver was once (more valued, most valued) than gold.

2. After seeing Mark get sick, I didn't feel too (good, well) myself.

3. The (littler, less) coffee I drink, the better I feel.

4. Light walls make a room look (more large, larger) than dark walls do.

5. One of the (unfortunatest, most unfortunate) women I know is a millionaire.

6. The moths' (continuous, continuously) thumping against the screen got on my
   nerves.

7. Some Mennonite groups manage (good, well) without radios, telephones, or
   television.

8. A purple crocus had burst (silent, silently) through the snow outside our
   window.

9. It is (good, better) to teach people to fish than to give them fish.

10. Today a rocket can reach the moon more (quick, quickly) than it took a stage-
    coach to travel from one end of England to the other.

MISPLACED MODIFIERS

WHAT MISPLACED MODIFIERS ARE
AND HOW TO CORRECT THEM

Modifiers are descriptive words. *Misplaced modifiers* are words that, *because of awkward placement*, do not describe the words the writer intended them to describe. Misplaced modifiers often obscure the meaning of a sentence. To avoid them, *place words as close as possible to what they describe.*

Misplaced Words	*Correctly Placed Words*
Enzo bought an old car from a crooked dealer with a *faulty transmission.* (The dealer had a faulty transmission?)	Enzo bought an old car with a faulty transmission from a crooked dealer. (The words describing the old car are now placed next to *car.*)
I *nearly* earned a hundred dollars last week. (You just missed earning a hundred dollars, but in fact earned nothing?)	I earned nearly a hundred dollars last week. (The meaning—that you earned a little under a hundred dollars—is now clear.)
Bill yelled at the howling dog *in his underwear.* (The *dog* wore underwear?)	Bill, in his underwear, yelled at the howling dog. (The words describing Bill are placed next to him.)

Activity: Correctly Placing Misplaced Modifiers

Underline the misplaced word or words in each sentence. Then rewrite the sentence, placing related words together and thereby making the meaning clear.

Examples   The suburbs <u>nearly</u> had ten centimetres of rain.

The suburbs had nearly ten centimetres of rain.

We could see the football stadium <u>driving across the bridge</u>.

Driving across the bridge, we could see the football stadium.

1. I saw mountains of uncollected garbage walking along the city streets.

_____

2. I almost had a dozen job interviews after I sent out my resume.

_____

3. Bill swatted the wasp that stung him with a newspaper.

_____

4. Joanne decided to live with her grandparents when she attended college to save money.

_____

5. Charlene returned the hamburger to the supermarket that was spoiled.

_____

6. Roger visited the old house still weak with the flu.

_____

7. The phone almost rang fifteen times last night.

_____

8. My uncle saw a kangaroo at the window under the influence of whisky.

_____

9. We decided to send our daughter to college on the day she was born.

_____

10. Fred always opens the bills that arrive in the mailbox with a sigh.

_____

■ Review Test

Write *M* for *misplaced* or *C* for *correct* in front of each sentence.

_____ 1. Rita found it difficult to mount the horse wearing tight jeans.

_____ 2. Rita, wearing tight jeans, found it difficult to mount the horse.

_____ 3. I noticed a crack in the window walking into the delicatessen.

_____ 4. Walking into the delicatessen, I noticed a crack in the window.

_____ 5. A well-worn track shoe was found on the locker bench with holes in it.

_____ 6. A well-worn track shoe with holes in it was found on the locker bench.

_____ 7. I almost caught a hundred fireflies.

_____ 8. I caught almost a hundred fireflies.

_____ 9. In a secondhand store, Willie found a television set that had been stolen from me last month.

_____ 10. Willie found a television set in a secondhand store that had been stolen from me last month.

_____ 11. Willie found, in a secondhand store, a television set that had been stolen from me last month.

_____ 12. There were four cars parked outside the café with Saskatchewan licence plates.

_____ 13. There were four cars with Saskatchewan licence plates parked outside the café.

_____ 14. The Prime Minister was quoted on the *CBC News* as saying that the recession was about to end.

_____ 15. The Prime Minister was quoted as saying that the recession was about to end on the *CBC News*.

DANGLING MODIFIERS

WHAT DANGLING MODIFIERS ARE
AND HOW TO CORRECT THEM

A modifier that opens a sentence must be followed *immediately* by the word it is meant to describe. Otherwise, the modifier is said to be *dangling*, and the sentence takes on an unintended meaning. For example, in the sentence

> While smoking a pipe, my dog sat with me by the crackling fire.

the unintended meaning is that the *dog* was smoking the pipe. What the writer meant, of course, was that *he*, the writer, was smoking the pipe. He should have said,

> While smoking a pipe, *I* sat with my dog by the crackling fire.

The dangling modifier could also be corrected by placing the subject within the opening word group:

> While *I* was smoking my pipe, my dog sat with me by the crackling fire.

Here are other sentences with dangling modifiers. Read the explanations of why they are dangling and look carefully at how they are corrected.

Dangling	*Correct*
Swimming at the lake, a rock cut Sue's foot. (*Who* was swimming at the lake? The answer is not *rock* but *Sue*. The subject *Sue* must be added.)	Swimming at the lake, Sue cut her foot on a rock. *Or:* When Sue was swimming at the lake, she cut her foot on a rock.
While eating my sandwich, five mosquitoes bit me. (*Who* is eating the sandwich? The answer is not *five mosquitoes*, as it unintentionally seems to be, but *I*. The subject *I* must be added.)	While *I* was eating my sandwich, five mosquitoes bit me. *Or:* While eating my sandwich, *I* was bitten by five mosquitoes.
Getting out of bed, the tile floor was so cold that Maria shivered all over. (*Who* got out of bed? The answer is not *tile floor* but *Maria*. The subject *Maria* must be added.)	Getting out of bed, *Maria* found the tile floor so cold that she shivered all over. *Or:* When *Maria* got out of bed, the tile floor was so cold that she shivered all over.

Dangling	*Correct*
To join the team, a C average or better is necessary. (*Who* is to join the team? The answer is not *C average* but *you*. The subject *you* must be added.)	To join the team, *you* must have a C average or better. *Or:* For *you* to join the team, a C average or better is necessary.

The preceding examples make clear the two ways of correcting a dangling modifier. *Decide on a logical subject* and do one of the following:

1 Place the subject *within* the opening word group:

When Sue was swimming at the lake, she cut her foot on a rock.

Note: In some cases an appropriate subordinating word such as *When* must be added, and the verb may have to be changed slightly as well.

2 Place the subject right *after* the opening word group:

Swimming at the lake, Sue cut her foot on a rock.

Activity: Placing the Subject Near the Modifier

Ask *Who?* of the opening words in each sentence. The subject that answers the question should be nearby in the sentence. If it is not, provide the logical subject by using either method of correction described above.

Example   While sleeping at the campsite, a Frisbee hit Bill on the head.

While Bill was sleeping at the campsite, a Frisbee hit him on the head.

or   *While sleeping at the campsite, Bill was hit on the head by a Frisbee.*

1. Watching the horror movie, goose bumps covered my spine.

_____

_____

2. After putting on a corduroy shirt, the room didn't seem as cold.

_____

_____

3. Flunking out of school, my parents demanded that I get a job.

_____

_____

4. Covered with food stains, my mother decided to wash the tablecloth.

_____

_____

5. Joining several college clubs, Mike's social life became more active.

_____

_____

6. While visiting the Jungle Park Safari, a baboon scrambled onto the hood of their car.

_____

_____

7. Under attack by beetles, Charlotte sprayed her roses with insecticide.

_____

_____

8. Standing at the ocean's edge, the wind coated my glasses with a salty film.

_____

_____

9. Braking the car suddenly, my shopping bags tumbled off the seat.

_____

_____

10. Using binoculars, the hawk was clearly seen following its prey.

_____

_____

■ Review Test

Write _D_ for _dangling_ or _C_ for _correct_ in front of each sentence. Remember that _the opening words are a dangling modifier if they have no logical subject to modify._

_____ 1. Advertising in the paper, Frank's car was quickly sold.

_____ 2. By advertising in the paper, Frank quickly sold his car.

_____ 3. After painting the downstairs, the house needed airing to clear out the fumes.

_____ 4. After we painted the downstairs, the house needed airing to clear out the fumes.

_____ 5. Frustrated by piles of homework, Heather was tempted to watch television.

_____ 6. Frustrated by piles of homework, Heather's temptation was to watch television.

_____ 7. After I waited patiently in the bank line, the teller told me I had filled out the wrong form.

_____ 8. After waiting patiently in the bank line, the teller told me I had filled out the wrong form.

_____ 9. When dieting, desserts are especially tempting.

_____ 10. When dieting, I find desserts especially tempting.

_____ 11. Looking through the telescope, I saw a brightly lit object come into view.

_____ 12. As I was looking through the telescope, a brightly lit object came into view.

_____ 13. Looking through the telescope, a brightly lit object came into my view.

_____ 14. Weighing thousands of kilos, no one knows how the enormous stones were brought to Stonehenge.

_____ 15. No one knows how the enormous stones, weighing thousands of kilos, were brought to Stonehenge.

FAULTY PARALLELISM

Introductory Project

Read aloud each pair of sentences below. Put a check mark beside the sentence that reads more smoothly and clearly and sounds more natural.

I made resolutions to study more, to lose weight, and watching less TV. _____

I made resolutions to study more, to lose weight, and to watch less TV. _____

A consumer group rates my car as noisy, expensive, and not having much safety. _____

A consumer group rates my car as noisy, expensive, and unsafe.

_____

Pei-Ti likes wearing soft sweaters, eating exotic foods, and to bathe in scented bath oil. _____

Pei-Ti likes wearing soft sweaters, eating exotic foods, and bathing in scented bath oil. _____

Single life offers more freedom of choice; more security is offered by marriage. _____

Single life offers more freedom of choice; marriage offers more security. _____

Answers are on page 552.

PARALLELISM EXPLAINED

Words in pairs or series should have parallel structure. By *balancing the items in a pair or a series so that they have the same kind of structure*, you will make a sentence clearer and easier to read. Notice how the parallel sentences that follow read more smoothly than the nonparallel ones.

Nonparallel (Not Balanced)	*Parallel (Balanced)*
I made resolutions to lose weight, to study more, and *watching* less TV.	I made resolutions to lose weight, to study more, and to watch less TV. (A balanced series of *to* verbs: *to lose, to study, to watch*)
A consumer group rates my car as noisy, expensive, and *not having much safety*.	A consumer group rates my car as noisy, expensive, and unsafe. (A balanced series of descriptive words: *noisy, expensive, unsafe*)
Pei-Ti likes wearing soft sweaters, eating exotic foods, and *to bathe* in scented bath oil.	Pei-Ti likes wearing soft sweaters, eating exotic foods, and bathing in scented bath oil. (A balanced series of *-ing* words: *wearing, eating, bathing*)
The single life offers more freedom of choice; *more security is offered by marriage*.	The single life offers more freedom of choice; marriage offers more security. (Balanced verbs and word order: *single life offers...; marriage offers...*)

You need not worry about balanced sentences when writing first drafts. But when you rewrite, you should try to put matching words and ideas into matching structures. Such parallelism will improve your writing style.

Activity: Writing Balanced Sentences

The unbalanced part of each of the following sentences is *italicized*. Rewrite the unbalanced part so that it matches the rest of the sentence. The first one is done for you as an example.

1. Jim Carrey's movies are clever, well-acted, and *have a lot of humour*.
   ___humorous___

2. Filling out an income tax return is worse than wrestling a bear or *to walk* on hot coals. _____

3. The study-skills course taught me how to take more effective notes, to read a textbook chapter, and *preparing* for exams. _____

4. Crystal plans to become a model, a lawyer, or *to go into nursing.*

   _____

5. Maria Grimaldi likes *to water* her garden, walking her fox terrier, and arguing with her husband. _____

6. Filled with talent and *ambitious*, Charlie plugged away at his sales job.

   _____

7. When I saw my room-mate with my girlfriend, I felt worried, angry, and *embarrassment* as well. _____

8. Cindy's cat likes sleeping in the dryer, lying in the bathtub, and *to chase* squirrels. _____

9. The bacon was fatty, *grease was on the potatoes*, and the eggs were cold.

   _____

10. People in the lobby munched popcorn, sipped pop, and *were shuffling* their feet impatiently. _____

■ Review Test 1

On separate paper, write five sentences of your own that use parallel structure.

■ Review Test 2

Draw a line under the unbalanced part of each sentence. Then rewrite the unbalanced part so that it matches the other item or items in the sentence. The first one is done for you as an example.

1. Our professor warned us that he would give surprise tests, the assignment of term papers, and allow no makeup exams.
   assign term papers _____

2. Pesky mosquitoes, humidity that is high, and sweltering heat make summer an unpleasant time for me.

   _____

3. I want a job that pays high wages, provides a complete benefits package, and offering opportunities for promotion.

_____

4. My teenage daughter enjoys shopping for new clothes, to try different cosmetics, and reading fashion magazines.

_____

5. My car needed the brakes replaced, the front wheels aligned, and recharging of the battery.

_____

6. I had to correct my paper for fragments, misplaced modifiers, and there were apostrophe mistakes.

_____

7. They did not want a black-and-white TV set, but a colour set could not be afforded.

_____

8. The neighbourhood group asked the town council to repair the potholes and that a traffic light be installed.

_____

9. Having a headache, my stomach being upset, and a bad case of sunburn did not put me in a good mood for the evening.

_____

10. The Gray Panthers is an organization that not only aids older citizens but also providing information for their families.

_____

PAPER FORMAT

When you hand in a paper for any course, it will probably be judged first by its format. It is important, then, to make the paper look attractive, neat, and easy to read. Here is a checklist you should use when preparing a paper for an instructor:

_____ ■ Is the paper full-sized, 21.5 cm × 28 cm ($8\frac{1}{2}$ by 11 inches)?

_____ ■ Are there wide margins, 2.5 cm (1 to $1\frac{1}{2}$ inches) all around the paper? In particular, have you been careful not to crowd the right-hand or bottom margin?

_____ ■ If the paper is word-processed, have you:

Checked whether your instructor prefers full justification or "ragged right" line format?

Double-spaced the text of each paragraph of your paper?

Used any header information your instructor may require?

Removed tear-strips from the edges of printer paper?

_____ ■ If the paper is handwritten, have you:

Used a blue or black pen?

Been careful not to overlap letters or to make decorative loops on letters?

Made all your letters distinct, with special attention to *a*, *e*, *i*, *o*, and *u*—five letters that people sometimes write illegibly?

Kept all your capital letters clearly distinct from small letters?

_____ ■ Have you centred the title of your paper on the first line of page 1? Have you been careful *not* to put quotation marks around the title or to underline it? Have you capitalized all the words in the title except for short connecting words like *of*, *for*, *the*, *and*, *in*, and *to?*

_____ ■ If your paper is handwritten, have you skipped a line between the title and the first line of your paper?

_____ ■ If your paper is word-processed, have you inserted two double lines of space between the title and the opening line of your paper?

_____ ■ Have you indented the first line of each paragraph about five spaces (1.25 cm) from the left-hand margin? If you are word-processing your paper, your instructor may prefer that you do not "tab" or indent a first line of a new paragraph, but leave two lines of space between each separate paragraph.

_____ ■ Have you made commas, periods, and other punctuation marks firm and clear? If typing, have you left a double space after a period?

_____ ■ If you have broken any words at the end of a line, have you been careful to break only between syllables?

_____ ■ Have you put your name, the date, and other information at the end of the paper, on the title page, or wherever your instructor has specified?

Titles and Topic Sentences

Also keep in mind these important points about the *title* and *first sentence* of your paper:

■ The title should simply be several words that tell what the paper is about. It should usually *not* be a complete sentence. For example, if you are writing a paper about one of the most frustrating jobs you have ever had, the title could be just "A Frustrating Job."

■ Do not rely on the title to help explain the first sentence of your paper. The first sentence must be independent of the title. For instance, if the title of your paper is "A Frustrating Job," the first sentence should *not* be "It was working as a baby-sitter." Rather, the first sentence might be "Working as a baby-sitter was the most frustrating job I ever had."

Activity 1: Identifying Errors in Formatting

Identify the mistakes in format in the following lines from a student paragraph. Explain the mistakes in the spaces provided. One mistake is described for you as an example.

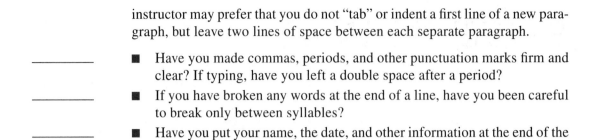

	"an unpleasant dining companion"
	My little brother is often an unpleasant dining companion. Last
	night was typical. For one thing, his appearance was disgusting
	His shoes were not tied, and his shirt was unbuttoned and han-
	ging out of his pants, which he had forgotten to zip up. Traces
	of his afternoon snack of grape juice and chocolate cookies were

1. <u>Hyphenate only between syllables</u>

2. _____

3. _____

4. _____

5. _____

6. _____

Activity 2: Writing Suitable Titles

As already stated, a title should tell in several words (but *not* a complete sentence) what a paper is about. Often a title can be based on the topic sentence—the sentence that expresses the main idea of the paper. Following are five topic sentences from student papers. Write a suitable and specific title for each paper, basing the title on the topic sentence. (Note the example.)

Example   <u>Compromise in a Relationship</u>

Learning how to compromise is essential to a good relationship.

1.   Title: _____

Some houseplants are dangerous to children and pets.

2.   Title: _____

A number of fears haunted me when I was a child.

3.   Title: _____

To insulate a house properly, several important steps should be taken.

4.   Title: _____

My husband is compulsively neat.

5.   Title: _____

There are a number of drawbacks to having a room-mate.

Activity 3: Writing Independent Topic Sentences

As has already been stated, you must *not* rely on the title to help explain your first sentence. In four of the five sentences that follow, the writer has, inappropriately, used the title to help explain the first sentence.

Rewrite the four sentences so that they stand independent of the title. Write *Correct* under the one sentence that is independent of the title.

Example   Title: My Career Plans
First sentence: They have changed in the last six months.
Rewritten: *My career plans have changed in the last six*
months.

1. Title: Contending with Dogs
    First sentence: This is the main problem in my work as a letter carrier.

    Rewritten: _____

    _____

2. Title: Study Skills
    First sentence: They are necessary if a person is to do well in college.

    Rewritten: _____

    _____

3. Title: Summer Vacation
    First sentence: Contrary to popular belief, a summer vacation can be the most miserable experience of the year.

    Rewritten: _____

    _____

4. Title: My Wife and the Sunday Newspaper
    First sentence: My wife has a peculiar way of reading it.

    Rewritten: _____

    _____

5. Title: Overcrowded Highways
    First sentence: They are one of the chief hazards today's driver must confront.

    Rewritten: _____

    _____

■ Review Test

In the space provided on the next page, rewrite the following sentences from a student paper. Correct the mistakes in format.

	"disciplining our children"
	My husband and I are becoming experts in disciplining our child-
	ren. We have certain rules that we insist upon, and if there are
	any violations, we are swift to act. When our son simply doesn't
	do what he is told to do, he must write that particular action
	twenty times. For example, if he doesn't brush his teeth, he
	writes, "I must brush my teeth." If a child gets home after the

CAPITAL LETTERS

Introductory Project

You probably know a good deal about the uses of capital letters. Answering the questions below will help you check your knowledge.

1. Write the full name of a person you know: _____

2. In what city and province or country were you born? _____

3. What is your present street address? _____

4. Name a country where you would like to travel: _____

5. Name a school that you attended: _____

6. Give the name of a store where you buy food: _____

7. Name a company where someone you know works: _____

8. What day of the week gives you the best chance to relax? _____

9. What holiday is your favourite? _____

10. What brand of toothpaste do you use? _____

11. Give the brand name of a candy or gum you like: _____

12. Name a song or a television show you enjoy: _____

13. Give the title of a magazine you read: _____

Items 14–16:   Three capital letters are needed in the lines below. Underline the words that you think should be capitalized. Then write them, capitalized, in the spaces provided.

the caped man started his black car, waved good-bye, and roared out of town. My heart thrilled when i heard someone say, "that was Batman. You don't see his kind much, any more."

14. _____   15. _____   16. _____

Answers are on page 552.

MAIN USES OF CAPITAL LETTERS

Capital letters are used with:

1 First word in a sentence or direct quotation

2 Names of persons and the word *I*

3 Names of particular places

4 Names of days of the week, months, and holidays

5 Names of commercial products

6 Names of organizations such as religious and political groups, associations, companies, unions, and clubs

7 Titles of books, magazines, newspapers, articles, stories, poems, films, television shows, songs, papers that you write, and the like

Each use is illustrated on the pages that follow.

First Word in a Sentence or Direct Quotation

The street person touched me and asked, "Do you have any change?"

(Capitalize the first word in the sentence.)   (Capitalize the first word in the direct quotation.)

"If you want a ride," said Brenda, "get ready now. Otherwise, I'm going alone."

(*If* and *Otherwise* are capitalized because they are the first words of sentences within a direct quotation. But *get* is not capitalized because it is part of the first sentence within the quotation.)

Names of Persons and the Word *I*

Last night I ran into Tony Silva and Sheila Morrison.

Names of Particular Places

Candi graduated from St. Boniface High School in Winnipeg, Manitoba. She then moved with her parents to Red Deer, Alberta, and worked there for a time at Freda's Gift Shop. Eventually she married and moved with her husband to a Canadian Forces Base in Norfolk County, Ontario. She takes courses two nights a week at Fanshawe College. On weekends, she and her family drive to Point Pelee National Park and go bird-watching and swimming in Lake Erie. She does volunteer work at the Simcoe Hospital in connection with Holy

Trinity Church. In addition, she works during the summer as a host at the Convention Centre and the Holiday Inn.

But: Use small letters if the specific name of a place is not given.

Candi sometimes remembers her unhappy days in high school and at the gift shop where she worked after graduation. She did not imagine then that she would one day be going to college and doing volunteer work for a church and a hospital in the community where she and her husband live.

Names of Days of the Week, Months, and Holidays

I was angry at myself for forgetting that Sunday was Mother's Day.

During July and August, Fred's company works a four-day week, and he has Mondays off.

Bill still has a scar on his ankle from a firecracker that exploded near him on Victoria Day and a scar on his arm where he stabbed himself with a fishhook on a Labour Day weekend.

But: Use small letters for the seasons—summer, fall, winter, spring.

Names of Commercial Products

Louis uses Scope mouthwash, Certs mints, and Dentyne gum to drive away the taste of the Export cigarettes and Pantera cigars that he always smokes.

My sister likes to play Monopoly and Sorry; I like chess and poker; my brother likes Scrabble, baseball, and table tennis.

But: Use small letters for the *type* of product (mouthwash, mints, gum, cigarettes, and so on).

Names of Organizations Such as Religious and Political Groups, Associations, Companies, Unions, and Clubs

Tom Wilcox attended the United Church for many years but converted to Catholicism when he married. Both he and his wife, Louise, are members of the Liberal Party. Both belong to the Canadian Automobile Association.

Louise works part-time as a service representative at Eaton's. Tom is an ambulance driver and belongs to the Canadian Union of Public Employees.

Enzo met Carla when he was a Boy Scout and she was a Girl Guide; she claimed he needed some guidance.

Titles of Books, Magazines, Newspapers, Articles, Stories, Poems, Films, Television Shows, Songs, Papers That You Write, and the Like

On Sunday Anna read the first chapter of *Whale Music*, a book required for her writing course. She looked through her parents' copy of *The Globe and Mail*. She then read an article titled "Thinking about a Change in Your Career" and a poem titled "Montreal Migraine" in *Saturday Night* magazine. At the same time, she played an old Stones' CD, *Aftermath*. In the evening, she watched *Forever Knight* on television and a movie, *Black Robe*, about Jesuit explorers and Native Canadians. Then, from 11 p.m. to midnight, she worked on a paper called "Trends in Mall Occupancy in the 1990s" for her retail marketing course.

Activity: Capitalizing

Cross out the words that need capitals in the following sentences. Then write the capitalized forms of the words in the spaces provided. The number of spaces tells you how many corrections to make in each case.

Example   I brush with ~~Crest~~ toothpaste but get cavities all the time. _Crest_

1. A spokesperson for general motors announced that the prices of all chevrolets will rise next year.

   _____   _____   _____

2. Steve graduated from Maplewood high school in june 1988.

   _____   _____   _____

3. The mild-mannered reporter named clark kent said to the Wolfman, "you'd better think twice before you mess with me."

   _____   _____   _____

4. While watching television, Bill drank four pepsis, ate an entire package of half moons, and finished up a bag of oreo cookies.

   _____   _____   _____   _____

5. A voyageur bus almost ran over Tony as he was riding his yamaha to a friend's home in quebec.

   _____   _____   _____

6. Before I lent my polaroid camera to Janet, I warned her, "be sure to return it by friday."

   _____   _____   _____

7. Before Christmas George took his entire paycheque, went to the bay, and bought a twenty-inch zenith colour television.

_____   _____   _____

8. On their first trip to Montreal, Tom and Louise visited the seagram Building and place Ville Marie. They also saw the Montreal canadiens play at the Forum.

_____   _____   _____

9. Rob was listening to The Tragically Hip's recording of "Blow at high Dough," Elaine was reading an article in *Saturday night* titled "till Death Do Us Part," and their son was watching sharon, Lois, and Bram.

_____   _____   _____   _____

10. When a sign for a tim horton's rest stop appeared on the highway, anita said, "let's stop here and stretch our legs for a bit."

_____   _____   _____   _____

OTHER USES OF CAPITAL LETTERS

Capital letters are also used with:

1 Names that show family relationships
2 Titles of persons when used with their names
3 Specific school courses
4 Languages
5 Geographic locations
6 Historical periods and events
7 Races, nations, and nationalities
8 Opening and closing of a letter

Each use is illustrated on the pages that follow.

Names That Show Family Relationships

I got Mother to baby-sit for me.
I went with Grandfather to the church service.
Uncle Carl and Aunt Lucy always enclose five dollars with birthday cards.

But: Do not capitalize words like *mother*, *father*, *grandmother*, *aunt*, and so on, when they are preceded by a possessive word (*my*, *your*, *his*, *her*, *our*, *their*).

I got my mother to baby-sit for me.

I went with my grandfather to the church service.

My uncle and aunt always enclose five dollars with birthday cards.

Titles of Persons When Used with Their Names

I wrote to Senator Laurent and Mayor Jones.

Professor Snorrel sent me to Chair Ruck, who sent me to Dean Rappers.

He drove to Dr. Helen Thompson's office after the cat bit him.

But: Use small letters when titles appear by themselves, without specific names.

I wrote to my senator and mayor.

The professor sent me to the chairperson of the department, who sent me to the dean.

He drove to the doctor's office after the cat bit him.

Specific School Courses

I got an A in both Accounting I and Small Business Management, but I got a C in Human Behaviour.

But: Use small letters for general subject areas.

I enjoyed my business courses but not my psychology or language courses.

Languages

She knows German and Spanish, but she speaks mostly Canadian slang.

Geographic Locations

I grew up in the Maritimes. I worked in the East for a number of years and then moved to the West Coast.

But: Use small letters in directions.

A new high school is being built at the south end of town.

Because I have a compass in my car, I know that I won't be going east or west when I want to go north.

Historical Periods and Events

Hector did well answering an essay question about the Second World War, but he lost points on a question about the Great Depression.

Races, Nations, Nationalities

The research study centred on Native Canadians and Québécois.

They have German knives and Danish glassware in the kitchen, an Indian wood carving in the bedroom, Mexican sculptures in the study, and an Oriental rug in the living room.

Opening and Closing of a Letter

Dear Sir:

Dear Madam:

Sincerely yours,

Truly yours,

Note: Capitalize only the first word in a closing.

Activity: Capitalizing Correctly

Cross out the words that need capitals in the following sentences. Then write the capitalized forms of the words in the spaces provided. The number of spaces tells you how many corrections to make in each case.

1. Although my grandfather spoke german and polish, my mother never learned either language.

   _____   _____

2. The chain letter began, "dear friend—You must mail twenty copies of this letter if you want good luck."

   _____   _____

3. Tomorrow in our history class, dr. connalley will start lecturing on the war of 1812.

   _____   _____   _____   _____

4. aunt Sarah and uncle Hal, who are mennonites, took us to their church services when we visited them on the prairies.

   _____   _____   _____   _____

5. My sister has signed up for a course titled eastern religions; she'll be studying buddhism and hinduism.

   _____   _____   _____   _____

UNNECESSARY USE OF CAPITALS

Many errors in capitalization are caused by using capitals where they are not needed.

Activity: Finding Inappropriate Capitals

Cross out the incorrectly capitalized words in the following sentences. Then write the correct forms of the words in the spaces provided. The number of spaces tells you how many corrections to make in each sentence.

1. Although the Commercials say that Things go better with Coke, I prefer Root Beer.

   _____   _____   _____   _____

2. The old man told the Cabdriver, "I want to go out to the Airport, and don't try to cheat me."

   _____   _____

3. A front-page Newspaper story about the crash of a commercial Jet has made me nervous about my Overseas trip.

   _____   _____   _____

4. During Hurricane Hazel in the 1950s, People's Houses were flooded in Toronto.

   _____   _____

5. I asked the Bank Officer at Royal Bank, "How do I get an identification Card to use the automatic teller machines?"

   _____   _____   _____

■ Review Test 1

Cross out the words that need capitals in the following sentences. Then write the capitalized forms of the words in the spaces provided. The number of spaces tells you how many corrections to make in each sentence.

1. wanda and i agreed to meet on saturday before the football game.

   _____   _____   _____

2. Between the Gaspé peninsula and the gulf of St. Lawrence lies a long, thin island called anticosti island.

_____ _____ _____ _____

3. When I'm in the supermarket check-out line, it seems as if every magazine on display has an article called "how You Can Lose Twenty pounds in two weeks."

_____ _____ _____ _____

4. At the bookstore, each student received a free sample pack of bayer aspirin, arrid deodorant, and prell shampoo.

_____ _____ _____

5. "can't you be quiet?" I pleaded. "do you always have to talk while I'm watching *general hospital* on television?"

_____ _____ _____ _____

6. On father's day, the children drove home and took their parents out to dinner at the ramada inn.

_____ _____ _____ _____

7. I will work at the holly Day School on mondays and fridays for the rest of september.

_____ _____ _____ _____

8. royal trust, where my sister Kathy works, is paying for her night course titled business accounting I.

_____ _____ _____ _____

9. I subscribe to one newspaper, the *daily planet;* and two magazines, *maclean's* and *glamour.*

_____ _____ _____ _____

10. On thanksgiving my brother said, "let's hurry and eat so i can go watch the football game on our new sony TV."

_____ _____ _____ _____

■ Review Test 2

On separate paper,

1. Write seven sentences demonstrating the seven main uses of capital letters.
2. Write eight sentences demonstrating the eight additional uses of capital letters.

NUMBERS AND ABBREVIATIONS

NUMBERS

1   Spell out numbers that can be expressed in one or two words. Otherwise, use numerals—the numbers themselves.

During the past five years, over twenty-five barracuda have been caught in the lake.

The parking fine was ten dollars.

In my grandmother's attic are eighty-four pairs of old shoes.

But

Each year about 250 baby trout are added to the lake.

My costs after contesting a parking fine in court were $135.

Grandmother has 25 old copies of *Eaton's Catalogue* in her attic.

2   *Be consistent* when you use a *series of numbers*. If some numbers in a sentence or paragraph require more than two words, then use numerals throughout the selection:

During his election campaign, Provincial Premier Lou Stanek went to 3 county fairs, 16 parades, 45 cookouts, and 112 club dinners, and delivered the same speech 176 times.

3   Use numerals for dates, times, addresses, percentages, and parts of a book.

The letter was dated April 3, 1872.

My appointment was at 6:15. (*But:* Spell out numbers before *o'clock*. For example: The doctor didn't see me until seven o'clock.)

He lives at 212 West 19th Street.

About 20 per cent of our class has dropped out of school.

Turn to page 179 in Chapter 8 and answer questions 1–10.

Activity: Writing Numbers Correctly

Cross out the mistakes in numbers and write the corrections in the spaces provided.

1. Rich was born on February fifteenth, nineteen seventy.

   _____

   _____

2. When the 2 children failed to return from school, over 50 people volunteered to search for them.

   _____

   _____

3. At 1 o'clock in the afternoon last Thursday, a tornado destroyed at least 20 buildings in Barrie.

   _____

   _____

ABBREVIATIONS

While abbreviations are a helpful time-saver in note-taking, you should avoid most abbreviations in formal writing. Listed below are some of the few abbreviations that can acceptably be used in compositions. Note that a period is used after most abbreviations.

1 Mr., Mrs., Ms., Jr., Sr., Dr. when used with proper names:

Mr. Tibble   Dr. Stein   Ms. O'Reilly

2 Time references:

A.M. or a.m.   P.M. or p.m.   B.C. and A.D., or B.C.E. and C.E.

3 First or middle initial in a signature:

Pierre E. Trudeau   Otis T. Redding   J. Alfred Prufrock

4 Organizations, technical words, and trade names known primarily by their initials:

RCMP   UN   CBC   FM   MTV

Activity: Correcting Abbreviations

Cross out the words that should not be abbreviated and correct them in the spaces provided.

1. On a Sat. morning I will never forget—Dec. 5, 1992, at ten min. after eight— I came downstairs and discovered that I had been robbed.

   _____   _____   _____

2. For six years I lived at First Ave. and Gordon St., right next to Mercy Memorial Hosp., in W. Edm., AB.

   _____ _____ _____ _____ _____

3. Before her biol. and Eng. exams, Linda was so nervous that her doc. gave her a tranq.

   _____   _____   _____   _____

■ Review Test

Cross out the mistakes in numbers and abbreviations and correct them in the spaces provided.

1. At three-fifteen p.m., an angry caller said a bomb was planted in a bus stat. locker.

   _____   _____

2. Page eighty-two is missing from my chem. book.

   _____   _____

3. Martha has over 200 copies of *People* mag.; she thinks they may be worth money someday.

   _____   _____

4. When I was eight yrs. old, I owned three cats, two dogs, and 4 rabbits.

   _____   _____

5. Approx. half the striking workers returned to work on Jan. third, nineteen ninety-four.

   _____ _____ _____ _____

APOSTROPHES

Introductory Project

1. Larry's motorcycle
   my sister's boyfriend
   Grandmother's shotgun
   the men's room
   Celine Dion's new album

   What is the purpose of the *'s* in the examples above?

   _____

2. They didn't mind when their dog bit people, but now they're leashing him because he's eating all their garden vegetables.

   What is the purpose of the apostrophe in *didn't*, *they're*, and *he's?*

   _____

3. I used to believe that vampires lived in the old coal bin of my cellar. The vampire's whole body recoiled when he saw the crucifix.

   Fred ate two baked potatoes.
   One baked potato's centre was still hard.

   In each of the sentence pairs above, why is the *'s* used in the second sentence but not in the first?

   _____

   _____

Answers are on page 552.

The two main uses of the apostrophe are:

1 To show the omission of one or more letters in a contraction
2 To show ownership or possession

Each use is explained on the pages that follow.

APOSTROPHE IN CONTRACTIONS

A contraction is formed when two words are combined to make one word. An apostrophe is used to show where letters are omitted in forming the contraction. Here are two contractions:

have + not = haven't (the *o* in *not* has been omitted)
I + will = I'll (the *wi* in *will* has been omitted)

The following are some other common contractions:

I + am = I'm	it + is = it's
I + have = I've	it + has = it's
I + had = I'd	is + not = isn't
who + is = who's	could + not = couldn't
do + not = don't	I + would = I'd
did + not = didn't	they + are = they're

Note: *Will* + *not* has an unusual contraction: *won't*.

Activity 1: Forming a Contraction

Combine the following words into contractions. One is done for you.

1.   we + are = ___we're___   6.   you + have = _____

2.   are + not = _____   7.   has + not = _____

3.   you + are = _____   8.   who + is = _____

4.   they + have = _____   9.   does + not = _____

5. would + not = _____   10. there + is = _____

Activity 2

Write the contractions for the words in parentheses. One is done for you.

1.   (Are not) ___Aren't___ you coming with us to the concert?

2. (I am) _____ going to take the car if (it is) _____ all right with you.

3. (There is) _____ an extra bed upstairs if (you would) _____ like to stay here for the night.

4. (I will) _____ give you the name of the human resources director, but there (is not) _____ much chance that (he will) _____ speak to you.

5. Linda (should not) _____ complain about the cost of food if (she is)_____ not willing to grow her own by planting a back-yard garden.

Note: Even though contractions are common in everyday speech and in written dialogue, usually it is best to avoid them in formal writing.

APOSTROPHE TO SHOW OWNERSHIP OR POSSESSION

To show ownership or possession, we can use such words as *belongs to*, *possessed by*, *owned by*, or (most commonly) *of*.

the jacket that *belongs to* Tony
the grades *possessed by* James
the gas station *owned by* our cousin
the footprints *of* the animal

But the apostrophe plus *s* (if the word is not a plural ending in *-s*) is often the quickest and easiest way to show possession. Thus we can say:

Tony's jacket
James' grades*
our cousin's gas station
the animal's footprints

* When a name ends with an *s*, or is pluralized with an *s*, possession is shown by an apostrophe after the final *s*.

Points to Remember

1 The *'s* goes with the owner or possessor (in the examples given, *Tony, cousin, the animal*). What follows is the person or thing possessed (in the examples given, *the jacket, gas station, footprints*).

2 When *'s* is handwritten, there should always be a break between the word and the *'s*.

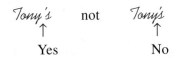

Tony's   not   Tony's

  ↑   ↑

  Yes   No

3 A singular word ending in *-s* (such as *James* on the preceding page) shows possession by adding just an apostrophe (*James'*).

Activity 1: Writing Possessive Forms

Rewrite the italicized part of each of the sentences below, using the *'s* to show possession. Remember that the *'s* goes with the owner or possessor.

Examples   *The toys belonging to the children* filled an entire room.

           The children's toys

1. *The roller skates owned by Pat* have been stolen.

2. *The visit of my cousin* lasted longer than I wanted it to.

3. *The fenders belonging to the car* are badly rusted.

4. *The prescription of a doctor* is needed for the pills.

5. *The jeep owned by Doris* was recalled because of an engine defect.

6. Is this *the hat of somebody*?

7. The broken saddle produced a sore on *the back of the horse*.

8. *The two dogs belonging to my neighbour* ripped open the garbage bags.

_____

9. *The energy level possessed by the little boy* is much higher than hers.

_____

10. *The foundation of the house* is crumbling.

_____

Activity 2: Forming Possessives

Add *'s* to each of the following words to make them the possessors or owners of something. Then write sentences using the words. Your sentences can be serious or playful. One is done for you.

1. dog ____*dog's*____   *That dog's bite is worse than his bark.*

2. instructor _____   _____

_____

3. Crystal _____   _____

_____

4. store _____   _____

_____

5. mother _____   _____

_____

Apostrophe versus Possessive Pronouns

Do not use an apostrophe with possessive pronouns. They already show ownership. Possessive pronouns include *his*, *hers*, *its*, *yours*, *ours*, and *theirs*.

Incorrect	*Correct*
The bookstore lost its' lease.	The bookstore lost its lease.
The racing bikes were theirs'.	The racing bikes were theirs.
The change is yours'.	The change is yours.
His' problems are ours', too.	His problems are ours, too.
His' skin is more sunburned than hers.'	His skin is more sunburned than hers.

Apostrophe versus Simple Plurals

When you want to make most words plural, just add an -*s* or -*es** at the end of the word. Do *not* add an apostrophe. For example, the plural of the word *movie* is *movies*, not *movie's* or *movies'*. Look at this sentence:

Crystal adores Tony's broad shoulders, rippling muscles, and warm eyes.

The words *shoulders, muscles,* and *eyes* are simple plurals, meaning *more than one shoulder, more than one muscle, more than one eye.* The plural is shown by adding -*s* only. On the other hand, the *'s* after *Tony* shows possession—that Tony owns the shoulders, muscles, and eyes.

Activity: Choosing Apostrophes or Plurals

In the space provided under each sentence, add the one apostrophe needed and explain why the other word or words ending in -*s* or -*es* are simple plurals.

Example   Karens tomato plants are almost two metres tall.

Karens: _Karen's, meaning "the plants belonging to Karen"_

plants: _simple plural meaning "more than one plant"_

1. My fathers influence on his brothers has been enormous.

   fathers: _____

   brothers: _____

2. Phils job—slaughtering pigs—was enough to make him a vegetarian.

   Phils: _____

   pigs: _____

3. As Tinas skill at studying increased, her grades improved.

   Tinas: _____

   grades: _____

4. When I walked into my doctors office, there were six people waiting who also had appointments.

   doctors: _____

   appointments: _____

* Plural endings with -*es* include words such as *potatoes*.

5. I asked the record store clerk for several blank cassette tapes and k.d. langs new CD.

    tapes: _____

    langs: _____

6. After six weeks without rain, the nearby streams started drying up, and the lakes water level fell sharply.

    weeks: _____

    streams: _____

    lakes: _____

7. Everyone wanted to enrol in Dr. Lerners class, but all the sections were closed.

    Lerners: _____

    sections: _____

8. When the brakes failed on Phils truck, he narrowly avoided hitting several parked cars and two trees.

    Phils: _____

    cars: _____

    trees: _____

9. My familys favourite breakfast is bacon, eggs, and home-fried potatoes.

    familys: _____

    eggs: _____

    potatoes: _____

10. We like Floridas winters, but we prefer to spend the summers in British Columbia.

    Floridas: _____

    winters: _____

    summers: _____

Apostrophe with Plural Words Ending in *-s*

Plurals that end in *-s* show possession simply by adding the apostrophe, rather than an apostrophe plus *s*.

My *parents'* station wagon is ten years old.

The many *students'* complaints were ignored by the high school principal.
All the *Boy Scouts'* tents were damaged by the hail storm.

Activity: Forming Plural Possessives

In each sentence, cross out the one plural word that needs an apostrophe. Then
write the word correctly, with the apostrophe, in the space provided.

Example _____soldiers'_____ All the ~~soldiers~~ rifles were cleaned for
inspection.

1. My parents car was stolen last night.

    _____

2. The transit workers strike has just ended.

    _____

3. Two of our neighbours homes are up for sale.

    _____

4. The door to the ladies room is locked.

    _____

5. When students gripes about the cafeteria were ignored, many started to bring
    their own lunches.

    _____

■ Review Test 1

In each sentence, cross out the two words that need apostrophes. Then write the
words correctly in the spaces provided.

1. The contestants face fell when she learned she had won a years supply of Vim
    cleanser.

    _____   _____

2. Weve been trying for weeks to see that movie, but theres always a long line.

    _____   _____

3. Freds car wouldnt start until the mechanic replaced its spark plugs and points.

    _____   _____

4. The citys budget director has trouble balancing his own familys books.

    _____   _____

5. Taking Dianes elderly parents to church every week is one example of Toms generous behaviour.

_____   _____

6. Heres a checklist of points to follow when youre writing your class reports.

_____   _____

7. Crystal shops in the mens store for jeans and the childrens department for belts.

_____   _____

8. The cats babies are under my chair again; I cant find a way to keep her from bringing them near me.

_____   _____

9. Because of a family feud, Julie wasnt invited to a barbecue at her cousins house.

_____   _____

10. Phyllis grade was the highest in the class, and Lewis grade was the lowest.

_____   _____

■ Review Test 2

Make the following words possessive and then—on separate paper—use at least five of them in a not-so-serious paragraph that tells a story. In addition, use at least three contractions in the paragraph.

mugger	restaurant	Tony	student
Toronto	sister	children	vampire
duck	Don Cherry	boss	John Candy
customer	bartender	police car	yesterday
instructor	someone	mob	Halifax

QUOTATION MARKS

The two main uses of quotation marks are:

1 To set off the exact words of a speaker or a writer
2 To set off the titles of short works

Each use is explained on the pages that follow.

QUOTATION MARKS TO SET OFF EXACT WORDS OF A SPEAKER OR A WRITER

Use quotation marks when you want to show the exact words of a speaker or a writer.

> "Say something tender to me," whispered Crystal to Tony.
> (Quotation marks set off the exact words that Crystal spoke to Tony.)

> Leonard Cohen once wrote, "I want history to jump on Canada's spine with sharp skates."
> (Quotation marks set off the exact words that Leonard Cohen wrote.)

> "The only dumb question," the instructor said, "is the one you don't ask."
> (Two pairs of quotation marks are used to enclose the instructor's exact words.)

> Sharon complained, "I worked so hard on this paper. I spent two days getting information in the library and two days writing it. Guess what grade I got on it?"
> (Note that the end quotation marks do not come until the end of Sharon's speech. Place quotation marks before the first quoted word of a speech and after the last quoted word. As long as no interruption occurs in the speech, do not use quotation marks for each new sentence.)

Punctuation Hint: In the four examples above, notice that a *comma sets off the quoted part from the rest of the sentence.* Also observe that *commas, periods, and question marks at the end of a quotation always go inside quotation marks.*

Complete the following statements that explain how capital letters, commas, and periods are used in quotations. Refer to the four examples as guides.

1. Every quotation begins with a _____ letter.
2. When a quotation is split (as in the sentence above about dumb questions), the second part does not begin with a capital letter unless it is a _____ sentence.

3. _____ are used to separate the quoted part of a sentence from the rest of the sentence.

4. Commas, question marks, and periods that come at the end of a quotation should go _____ the quotation marks.

The answers are *capital*, *new*, *Commas*, and *inside*.

Activity 1: Placing Quotation Marks Correctly

Place quotation marks around the exact words of a speaker or writer in the sentences that follow.

1. Take some vitamin C for your cold, Crystal told Tony.

2. How are you doing in school? my uncle always asks me.

3. An epitaph on a tombstone in Nova Scotia reads, I told you I was sick!

4. Dave said, Let's walk faster. I think the game has already started.

5. Robertson Davies wrote, Whether you are really right or wrong doesn't matter; it's the belief that counts.

6. Thelma said, My brother is so lazy that, if opportunity knocked, he'd resent the noise.

7. It's extremely dangerous to mix alcohol and pills, Dr. Wilson reminded us. The combination could kill you.

8. Ice-cold drinks! shouted the vendor selling lukewarm drinks.

9. Be careful not to touch the fence, the guard warned. It's electrified.

10. Just because I'm deaf, Lynn said, many people treat me as if I were stupid.

Activity 2: Writing Quotations Correctly

1. Write a sentence in which you quote a favourite expression of someone you know. Identify the relationship of the person to you.

    Example   *One of my father's favourite expressions is, "Don't sweat the small stuff."*

2. Write a quotation that contains the words *Tony asked Crystal*. Write a second quotation that includes the words *Crystal replied*.

_____

_____

_____

_____

3. Copy a sentence or two that interests you from a book or magazine. Identify the title and author of the work.

Example   In <u>Night Shift</u>, Stephen King writes, "I don't like to sleep with one leg sticking out.... If a cool hand ever reached out from under the bed and grasped my ankle, I might scream."

_____

_____

_____

_____

Indirect Quotations

An *indirect quotation* is a *rewording of someone else's comments*, rather than a word-for-word direct quotation. The word *that* often signals an indirect quotation. Quotation marks are *not* used with indirect quotations.

Direct Quotation	**Indirect Quotation**
Fred said, "The distributor cap on my car is cracked."	Fred said that the distributor cap on his car was cracked.
(Fred's exact spoken words are given, so quotation marks are used.)	(We learn Fred's words indirectly, so no quotation marks are used.)
Sally's note to Jay read, "I'll be working late. Don't wait up for me."	Sally left a note for Jay saying she would be working late and he should not wait up for her.
(The exact words that Sally wrote in the note are given, so quotation marks are used.)	(We learn Sally's words indirectly, so no quotation marks are used.)

Activity: Changing Indirect to Direct Quotations

Rewrite the following sentences, changing words as necessary to convert the indirect quotations into direct quotations. The first one is done for you as an example.

1. Fred asked Maria if he could turn on the hockey game.

   Fred asked Maria, "May I turn on the hockey game?"

2. Maria said that he could listen to the game on the radio.

   _____

3. Fred replied he was tired of being told what to do.

   _____

4. Maria said that as long as she was bigger and stronger, she would make the rules.

   _____

5. Fred said that the day would come when the tables would be turned.

   _____

QUOTATION MARKS TO SET OFF TITLES OF SHORT WORKS

Titles of short works are usually set off by quotation marks, while titles of long works are underlined. Use quotation marks to set off the titles of such short works as articles in books, newspapers, or magazines; chapters in a book; short stories; poems; and songs.

On the other hand, you should underline the titles of books, newspapers, magazines, plays, movies, record albums, and television shows.

Quotation Marks	*Underlines*
the article "Yes, There are Canadian Comics"	in the book Canuck Comics
the article "A Day at the Beach"	in the newspaper The Vancouver Sun
the article "Biters Banquet"	in the magazine Canadian Geographic
the chapter "Mila, The Movie"	in the book More Than a Rose
the story "Blossom"	in the book Sans Souci
the poem "Suzanne"	in the book The Spice-Box of Earth
the song "Closing Time"	in the album The Future
	the television show Sliders
	the movie Canadian Bacon

Note: In printed works, titles of books, newspapers, and so on are set off by italics—slanted type that looks *like this*—instead of being underlined.

Activity: Citing Titles Correctly

Use quotation marks or underlines as needed.

1. Spending Smart is the fourth chapter of Dian Cohen's book Money.

2. No advertising is permitted in Consumer Reports, a nonprofit consumer magazine.

3. I cut out an article from Maclean's called Universities 94: The Rankings to use in my sociology report.

4. Tony's favourite television show is Star Trek, and his favourite movie is The Night of the Living Dead.

5. Our instructor gave us a week to buy the textbook titled Personal Finance and to read the first chapter, Work and Income.

6. Every holiday season, our family watches the movie A Christmas Carol on television.

7. Fred bought Homemakers Magazine because he wanted to read the cover article titled Rebel Daughter.

8. Edgar Allan Poe's short story The Murders in the Rue Morgue and his poem The Raven are in a paperback titled Great Tales and Poems of Edgar Allan Poe.

9. When Elaine got her Starweek TV Magazine, she read an article titled Canadian Satire and then thumbed through the listings to see when The Air Farce would be on that week.

10. The night before his exam, he discovered with horror that the chapter Becoming Mature was missing from Childhood and Adolescence, the psychology text that he had bought secondhand.

OTHER USES OF QUOTATION MARKS

1 Quotation marks are used to set off special words or phrases from the rest of a sentence:

Many people spell the words "a lot" as *one* word, "alot," instead of correctly spelling them as two words.

I have trouble telling the difference between "their" and "there."

Note: In printed works, *italics* are often used to set off special words or phrases. That is usually done in this book, for example.

2 Quotation marks are also used to mark off a quotation within a quotation:

The instructor said, "Know the chapter titled 'Status Symbols' in *Adolescent Development* if you expect to pass the test."

Crystal said, "One of my favourite Mae West lines is 'I used to be Snow White, but I drifted.'"

Note: A quotation within a quotation is indicated by *single* quotation marks.

■ Review Test 1

Insert quotation marks where needed in the sentences that follow.

1. Don't you ever wash your car? Crystal asked Tony.

2. When the washer tilted and began to buzz, Zena shouted, Let's get rid of that blasted machine!

3. Take all you want, read the sign above the cafeteria salad bar, but please eat all you take.

4. After scrawling formulas all over the board with lightning speed, my math instructor was fond of asking, Any questions now?

5. Move that heap! the truck driver yelled. I'm trying to make a living here.

6. I did a summary of an article titled Adolescent Anxiety in the latest issue of Canadian Living.

7. Writer's block is something that happens to everyone at times, the instructor explained. You simply have to keep writing to break out of it.

8. A passenger in the car ahead of Steve threw food wrappers and empty cups out the window. That man, said Steve to his son, is a human pig.

9. If you are working during the day, said the counsellor, the best way to start college is with a night course or two.

10. I told the dentist that I wanted Novocaine. Don't be a sissy, he said. A little pain won't hurt you. I told him that a little pain wouldn't bother him, but it would bother me.

■ Review Test 2

Go through the comics section of a newspaper to find a comic strip that amuses you. Be sure to choose a strip where two or more characters are speaking to each other. Write a full description that will enable people who have not read the comic strip to visualize it clearly and appreciate its humour. Describe the setting and action in each panel, and enclose the words of the speakers in quotation marks.

COMMAS

SIX MAIN USES OF THE COMMA

Commas are used mainly as follows:

1 To separate items in a series
2 To set off introductory material
3 Before and after words that interrupt the flow of thought in a sentence
4 Between two complete thoughts connected by *and*, *but*, *for*, *or*, *nor*, *so*, *yet*
5 To set off a direct quotation from the rest of a sentence
6 For certain everyday material

Each use is explained on the pages that follow.

You may find it helpful to remember that the comma often marks a slight pause, or break, in a sentence. Read aloud the sentence examples given for each rule, and listen for the minor pauses, or breaks, that are signalled by commas.

Comma between Items in a Series

Use commas to separate items in a series.

> Do you drink tea with milk, lemon, or honey?
>
> Today the dishwasher stopped working, the garbage bag split, and the refrigerator turned into a freezer.
>
> The television talk shows enraged him so much he did not know whether to laugh, cry, or throw up.
>
> Jan awoke from a restless, nightmare-filled sleep.

Note: A comma is used between two descriptive words in a series only if the word *and* inserted between the words sounds natural. You could say:

> Jan awoke from a restless *and* nightmare-filled sleep.

But notice in the following sentence that the descriptive words do not sound natural when *and* is inserted between them. In such cases, no comma is used.

> Wanda drove a bright blue Saturn. (A bright *and* blue Saturn doesn't sound right, so no comma is used.)

Activity: Placing Commas between Items in a Series

Place commas between items in a series.

1. Godzilla lives for revenge anger and Tokyo's ruin.

2. My father taught me to swim by talking to me calmly holding my hand firmly and throwing me into the pool.

3. Paul added white wine mushrooms salt pepper and oregano to his spaghetti sauce.

4. Baggy threadbare jeans feel more comfortable than pyjamas to me.

5. Mark grabbed a tiny towel bolted out of the bathroom and ran toward the ringing phone.

Comma after Introductory Material

Use a comma to set off introductory material.

> After punching the alarm clock with his fist, Bill turned over and went back to sleep.
>
> Looking up to the sky, I saw a man who was flying faster than a speeding bullet.
>
> Holding a baited trap, Carl cautiously approached the gigantic mousehole. In addition, he held a broom in his hand.
>
> Also, he wore a football helmet in case a creature should leap out at his head.

Notes:

a If the introductory material is brief, the comma is sometimes omitted. In the activities here, you should use the comma.

b A comma is also used to set off extra material at the end of a sentence. Here are two earlier sentences where this comma rule applies:

> A sudden breeze shot through the windows, driving the stuffiness out of the room.
>
> I love to cook and eat Italian food, especially spaghetti and lasagna.

Activity: Placing Commas after Introductory Clauses

Place commas after introductory material.

1. When the prime minister entered the room became hushed.

2. Feeling brave and silly at the same time Tony volunteered to go on stage and help the magician.

3. While I was eating my tuna sandwich the cats circled my chair like hungry sharks.

4. Because my parents died when I was young I have learned to look after myself. Even though I am now independent I still carry a special loneliness within me.

5. At first putting extra hot pepper flakes on the pizza seemed like a good idea. However I felt otherwise when flames seemed about to shoot out of my mouth.

Comma around Words Interrupting the Flow of Thought

Use commas before and after words or phrases that interrupt the flow of thought in a sentence.

My brother, a sports nut, owns over five thousand baseball cards.

That game show, at long last, has been cancelled.

The children used the old Buick, rusted from disuse, as a backyard clubhouse.

Usually you can "hear" words that interrupt the flow of thought in a sentence. However, if you are not sure that certain words are interrupters, remove them from the sentence for a moment. If it still makes sense without the words, you know that the words are interrupters and the information they give is nonessential. *Such nonessential information is set off with commas.* In the sentence

Dody Thompson, who lives next door, won the javelin-throwing competition.

the words *who lives next door* are extra information, not needed to identify the subject of the sentence, *Dody Thompson*. Put commas around such nonessential information. On the other hand, in the sentence

The woman who lives next door won the javelin-throwing competition.

the words *who lives next door* supply essential information—information needed for us to identify the woman being spoken of. If the words were removed from the sentence, we would no longer know who won the competition. Commas are *not* used around such essential information.

Here is another example:

Wilson Hall, which the tornado destroyed, was ninety years old.

Here the words *which the tornado destroyed* are extra information, not needed to identify the subject of the sentence, *Wilson Hall*. Commas go around such nonessential information. On the other hand, in the sentence

The building which the tornado destroyed was ninety years old.

the words *which the tornado destroyed* are needed to identify the building. Commas are *not* used around such essential information.

As noted above, however, most of the time you will be able to "hear" words that interrupt the flow of thought in a sentence, and you will not have to think about whether the words are essential or nonessential.

Activity: Setting Off Interrupting Phrases

Use commas to set off interrupting words.

1. On Friday my day off I went to get a haircut.
2. Dracula who had a way with women is Tony's favourite movie hero. He feels that the Wolfman on the other hand showed no class in handling women.
3. Many people forget that Mackenzie King one of our most effective prime ministers also talked to his dead mother.
4. Mowing the grass especially when it is three centimetres high is my least favourite job.
5. A jar of chicken noodle soup which was all there was in the refrigerator did not make for a very satisfying meal.

Comma between Complete Thoughts

Use a comma between two complete thoughts connected by *and*, *but*, *for*, *or*, *nor*, *so*, *yet*.

> The reception was set for seven o'clock, but the host changed his mind at two.
> We could always tell when our instructor felt disorganized, for his shirt would not be tucked in.
> Rich has to work on Saturday nights, so he tapes the hockey game on his VCR.

Note: Be careful not to use a comma in sentences having *one* subject and a *double* verb. The comma is used only in sentences made up of two complete thoughts (subject/verb and subject/verb). In the following sentence, there is only one subject (*Bill*) with a double verb (*will go* and *forget*). Therefore, no comma is needed:

> Bill will go partying tonight and forget all about tomorrow's exam.

Likewise, the following sentence has only one subject (*Rita*) and a double verb (*was* and *will work*); therefore, no comma is needed:

> Rita was a server at the Holiday Inn last summer and probably will work there this summer.

Activity: Placing Commas between Complete Thoughts

Place a comma before a joining word that connects two complete thoughts (two subjects and two verbs). Remember, do *not* place a comma within sentences that have only one subject and a double verb.

1. The oranges in the refrigerator were covered with blue mould and the potatoes in the cupboard felt like sponges.
2. All the slacks in the shop were on sale but not a single pair was my size.
3. Martha often window-shops in the malls for hours and comes home without buying anything.
4. Tony left the dentist's office with his mouth still numb from the anaesthetic and he talked with a lisp for two hours.
5. I covered the walls with three coats of white paint but the purple colour underneath still showed through.
6. The car squealed down the entrance ramp and sped recklessly out onto the freeway.
7. The dancers in the strip club moved like wound-up Barbie dolls and the men in the audience sat as motionless as stones.
8. The aliens in the science-fiction film visited our planet in peace but we greeted them with violence.
9. I felt like shouting at the gang of boys but didn't dare open my mouth.
10. Lenny claims he wants to succeed in college but he has missed classes all semester.

Comma with Direct Quotations

Use a comma to set off a direct quotation from the rest of a sentence.

His father shouted, "Why don't you go out and get a job?"
"Our modern world has lost a sense of the sacredness of life," the speaker said.
"No," said Celia to Jerry. "I won't go to the bingo hall with you."
"Money," wrote Marshall McLuhan, "is the poor people's credit card."

Note: Commas and periods at the end of a quotation go inside quotation marks. See also page 354.

Activity: Setting Off Direct Quotations

Use commas to set off quotations from the rest of the sentence.

1. The man yelled "Call an ambulance, somebody!"

2. My partner on the dance floor said "Don't be so stiff. You look as if you'd swallowed an umbrella."

3. The question on the anatomy test read "What human organ grows faster than any other, never stops growing, and always remains the same size?"

4. The student behind me whispered "The skin."

5. "My stomach hurts" Bruce said "and I don't know whether it was the hamburger or the math test."

Comma with Everyday Material

Use a comma with certain everyday material.

Persons Spoken To

Tina, go to bed if you're not feeling well.
Cindi, where did you put my shoes?
Are you coming with us, Bob?

Dates

March 4, 1992, is when Martha buried her third husband.

Addresses

Tony's grandparents live at 183 Roxborough Avenue, Toronto, Ontario M4S 1V3.

Note: No comma is used to mark off the postal code (Canada) or zip code (U.S.)

Openings and Closings of Letters

Dear Santa,
Dear Larry,
Sincerely yours,
Truly yours,

Note: In formal letters, a colon is used after the opening: Dear Sir: *or* Dear Madam:

Numbers

The dishonest dealer turned the used car's odometer from 98,170 km to 39,170 km.

Activity: Using Commas Correctly

Place commas where needed.

1. I expected you to set a better example for the others Mike.
2. Janet with your help I passed the test.
3. Canadian movie stars Kitty Katz and Serge Lamour were married on September 12 1991 and moved to 3865 West 7th Avenue Vancouver British Columbia V6K 1Y9 for one month.
4. They received 75000 congratulatory fan letters and were given picture contracts worth $3000000 in the first week of their marriage.
5. Kitty left Serge on October 12 1991 and ran off with their marriage counsellor.

■ Review Test 1

Insert commas where needed. In the space provided below each sentence, summarize briefly the rule that explains the use of the comma or commas.

1. The best features of my new apartment are its large kitchen its bay windows and its low rent.

   _____

2. Because we got in line at dawn we were among the first to get tickets for the concert.

   _____

3. "Why can't a hairdresser" Crystal asked "call you a week before your roots need touching up?"

   _____

4. Without opening his eyes Simon stumbled out of bed and opened the door for the whining dog.

   _____

5. I think David that you had better ask someone else for your $2500 loan.

   _____

6. Hot dogs are the most common cause of choking deaths in children for a bite-size piece can easily plug up a toddler's throat.

   _____

7. Tax forms though shortened and revised every year never seem to get any simpler.

   _____

8. Sandra may decide to go to college full-time or she may enrol in a couple of evening courses.

_____

9. I remember how with the terrible cruelty of children we used to make fun of the cross-eyed boy who lived on our street.

_____

10. Although that old man on the corner looks like a street person he is said to have a Swiss bank account.

_____

■ Review Test 2

Insert commas where needed.

1. My dog who is afraid of the dark sleeps with a night-light.
2. "I wish there were some pill" said Chuck "that would give you the equivalent of eight hours' sleep in four hours."
3. The hot dogs at the ball park tasted delicious but they reacted later like delayed time-bombs.
4. Janice attended class for four hours worked at the hospital for three hours and studied at home for two hours.
5. The old man as he gasped for air tried to assure the hospital clerk that he had his provincial health card somewhere.
6. George and Ida sat down to watch the hockey game with crackers sharp cheese salty pretzels and two frosty bottles of beer.
7. Although I knew exactly what was happening the solar eclipse gave me a strong feeling of anxiety.
8. The company agreed to raise a senior bus driver's salary to $28000 by January 1 1995.
9. Even though King Kong was holding her at the very top of the Empire State Building Fay Wray kept yelling at him "Let me go!"
10. Navel oranges which Margery as a little girl called belly-button oranges are her favourite fruit.

■ Review Test 3

On separate paper, write six sentences, with each sentence demonstrating one of the six main comma rules.

■ Review Test 4

On separate paper, write a brief letter, including full names and the sender's and receiver's full addresses, to a friend. Write about the past week's experiences at college. Be sure to use all commas needed in addresses and salutations, as well as in the body of the letter.

OTHER
PUNCTUATION
MARKS

Introductory Project

Each of the sentences below needs one of the following punctuation marks:

;   —   -   ( )   :

Insert the correct mark in each sentence. Each mark is used once.

1. The following holiday plants are poisonous and should be kept away from children and pets holly, mistletoe, and poinsettias.
2. The freeze dried remains of Annie's canary were in a clear bottle on her bookcase.
3. William Shakespeare 1564–1616 married a woman eight years his senior when he was eighteen.
4. Grooming in space is more difficult than on Earth no matter how much Marc Garneau combs his hair, for instance, it still tends to float loosely around his head.
5. I opened the front door, and our cat walked in proudly with a live bunny hanging from his mouth.

Answers are on page 553.

COLON (:)

Use the colon at the end of a complete statement to introduce a list, a long quotation, or an explanation.

List

The following were my worst jobs: truck loader in an apple plant, assembler in a battery factory, and attendant in a state mental hospital.

Long Quotation

Chief Dan George said: "When the white man came to Canada, we had the land and they had the bibles. Now they have the land and we have the bibles."

Explanation

There are two hockey leagues in our town: Junior A and the bantam league.

Activity

Place colons where needed.

1. Foods that are high in cholesterol include the following eggs, butter, milk, cheese, shrimp, and well-marbled meats.
2. All the signs of the flu were present hot and cold spells, heavy drainage from the sinuses, a bad cough, and an ache through the entire body.
3. In his essay, "The Role of New Media in Social Change," Marshall McLuhan wrote "One of the notable effects of the TV image on those in the primary grades seems to be the development of near-point reading. The average distance from the page of children in the first three grades has recently been measured in Toronto ... The average distance is $6\frac{1}{2}$ inches. The children seem to be striving to do a version of their relation to the TV image."

SEMI-COLON (;)

The main use of the semi-colon is to mark a break between two complete thoughts, as explained on pages 261–262. Another use of the semi-colon is to mark off items in a series when the items themselves contain commas. Here are some examples:

Winning prizes at the national flower show were Roberta Collins, Ontario, azaleas; Sally Hunt, Nova Scotia, roses; and James Weber, Alberta, Shasta daisies.

The following books must be read for the course: *The Handmaid's Tale*, by Margaret Atwood; *The English Patient*, by Michael Ondaatje; and *Man's Search for Meaning*, by Viktor Frankl.

Activity

Place semi-colons where needed.

1. The specials at the restaurant today are eggplant Parmesan, for $3.95 black beans and rice, for $2.95 and chicken pot pie, for $4.95.
2. The top of the hill offered an awesome view of the military cemetery thousands of headstones were ranged in perfect rows.
3. Crystal's favourite old movies are *To Catch a Thief*, starring Cary Grant and Grace Kelly *Animal Crackers*, a Marx Brothers comedy and *The Wizard of Oz*, with Judy Garland.

DASH (—)

A dash signals a degree of pause longer than a comma but not as complete as a period. Use a dash to set off words for dramatic effect:

I didn't go out with him a second time—once was more than enough.

Some of you—I won't mention you by name—cheated on the test.

It was so windy that the van passed him on the highway—overhead.

Notes

a The dash is formed on a typewriter or word processor by striking the hyphen twice (- -). In handwriting, the dash is as long as two letters would be.

b Be careful not to overuse dashes.

Activity

Place dashes where needed.

1. Riding my bike, I get plenty of exercise especially when dogs chase me.
2. I'm advising you in fact, I'm telling you not to bother me again.
3. The package finally arrived badly damaged.

HYPHEN (-)

1   Use a hyphen with two or more words that act as a single unit describing a noun.

The fast-talking salesperson was so good that he went into politics. (*Fast* and *talking* combine to describe the salesperson.)

I both admire and envy her well-rounded personality.

When the dude removed his blue-tinted shades, Lonnell saw the spaced-out look in his eyes.

2   Use a hyphen to divide a word at the end of a line of writing or typing. When you need to divide a word at the end of a line, divide it between syllables. Use your dictionary to be sure of correct syllable divisions (see also page 377). Word processing eliminates the need to divide words.

When Tom lifted up the hood of his Toyota, he realized that one of the radiator hoses had broken.

Notes

a   Do not divide words of one syllable.

b   Do not divide a word if you can avoid doing so.

c   Some Canadian and British spellings hyphenate words like "room-mate" or "semi-colon" which you may see printed elsewhere without hyphens. Check with your instructor, use a Canadian or Oxford dictionary, and *be consistent*.

Activity

Place hyphens where needed.

1. High flying jets and gear grinding trucks are constant sources of noise pollution in our neighbourhood, and consequently we are going to move.

2. When Linda turned on the porch light, ten legged creatures scurried every where over the crumb filled floor.

3. Fred had ninety two dollars in his pocket when he left for the supermarket, and he had twenty two dollars when he got back.

PARENTHESES ( )

Parentheses are used to set off extra or incidental information from the rest of a sentence:

The section of that book on the medical dangers of abortion (pages 35 to 72) is outdated.

Yesterday at Hamburger House (my favourite place to eat), the guy who makes french fries asked me to go out with him.

Note: Do not use parentheses too often in your writing. They minimize and devalue the words placed within them and interrupt the flow of your writing.

Activity

Add parentheses where needed.

1. Certain sections of the novel especially Chapter 5 made my heart race with suspense.
2. Did you hear that George Linda's first husband just got remarried?
3. Sigmund Freud 1856–1939 was the founder of psychoanalysis.

■ Review Test

At the appropriate spot, place the punctuation mark shown in the margin.

; 1. Mary's savings have dwindled to nothing she's been borrowing from me to pay her rent.

— 2. There's the idiot I'd know him anywhere who dumped trash on our front lawn.

- 3. Today's two career couples spend more money on eating out than their parents did.

: 4. H. de Montarville Molson said "My father spoke French with a Bank of Montreal accent."

( ) 5. One-fifth of our textbook pages 401–498 consists of footnotes and a bibliography.

USING THE DICTIONARY

The dictionary is a valuable tool. To take advantage of it, you need to understand the main kinds of information that a dictionary gives about a word. Look at the information provided for the word *murder* in the following entry from *The Oxford Advanced Learner's Dictionary*, fourth edition.*

Spelling and syllabication

Pronunciation

Part of speech

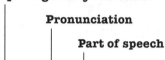

mur•der/ˈmɜdə(r)/ *n* **1** (**a**) [U] unlawful killing of a human being intentionally: *commit murder¡* • *be guilty of murder* • *the murder of a six-year-old child* • [attrib] *Her latest book's a murder mystery.* (**b**) [C] instance of this: *six murders in one week.* Cf HOMICIDE 1, MANSLAUGHTER. **2** [U] (*derog*) sacrifice of large numbers of people (esp in war): *10 000 men died in one battle: it was sheer murder.* **3** [U] (*fig infml*) (**a**) very difficult or frustrating experience: *It's murder trying to find a parking place for the car.* (**b**) ~ (**on sth**) thing that causes great harm or discomfort (to sth): *This hot weather's murder on my feet.* ▷ **mur.der** *v* **1** [Tn, Tn.pr] **sb** (**with sth**) kill (sb) unlawfully and unintentionally: *He murdered his wife with a knife.* **2** [Tn] (*fig infml*) spoil (sth) by lack of skill or knowledge: *murder a piece of music*, ie play it very badly • *murder the English language*, ie speak or write in a way that shows ignorance of correct usage. **mur.der.er** *n*...**mur.der.ess** *n* ←

Meanings and other forms of usage

Other forms of the word

376

SPELLING

The first bit of information, in the boldface (heavy type) entry itself, is the spelling of *murder*. You probably already know the spelling of *murder*, but if you didn't, you could find it by pronouncing the syllables in the word carefully and then looking it up in the dictionary.

Use your dictionary to correct the spelling of the following words:

compatable _____	insite _____
althogh _____	troble _____
aksident _____	untill _____
embelish _____	easyer _____
systimatise _____	prepostrous _____
shedule _____	comotion _____
attenshun _____	Vasaline _____
wierd _____	fatel _____
hurryed _____	busines _____
alright _____	jenocide _____
fony _____	poluted _____
kriterion _____	perpose _____
hetirosexual _____	chalange _____

SYLLABICATION

The second bit of information that the dictionary gives, also in the boldface entry, is the syllabication of *murder*. Note that a dot separates the syllables.

Use your dictionary to mark the syllable divisions in the following words. Also indicate how many syllables are in each word.

j i t t e r   (_____ syllables)

m o t i v a t e   (_____ syllables)

o r a n g u t a n   (_____ syllables)

i n c o n t r o v e r t i b l e   (_____ syllables)

Noting syllable divisions will enable you to *hyphenate* a word: divide it at the end of one line of writing and complete it at the beginning of the next line. You can correctly hyphenate a word only at a syllable division, and you may have to check your dictionary to make sure of a word's syllable divisions.

PRONUNCIATION

The third bit of information in the dictionary entry is the pronunciation of *murder:* (mɜ•də(r)). You already know how to pronounce *murder*, but if you didn't, the information within the parentheses would serve as your guide. Use your dictionary to complete the following exercises that relate to pronunciation.

Vowel Sounds

You will probably use the pronunciation key in your dictionary mainly as a guide to pronouncing different vowel sounds. (Vowels are the letters *a, e, i, o,* and *u.*) Here is part of the pronunciation key in the *Oxford Advanced Learner's Dictionary:*

æ as in **hat** / hæt /	ɪ as in **sit** / sɪt /
ɑ: as in **arm** / ɑ:m /	aɪ as in **five** / faɪv /
eɪ as in **page** / peɪdʒ /	
e as in **ten** / ten /	
i: as in **see** / si: /	

The key tells you, for example, that the sound of the short *a* is pronounced like the *a* in *hat*, the sound of the long *a* is like the *a* in *page*, and the sound of the short *e* is like the *e* in *ten*.

Now look at the pronunciation key in your dictionary. The key is probably located in the front of the dictionary or at the bottom of every page. What common word in the key tells you how to pronounce each of the following sounds?

ɔ _____	ʌ _____
ŏ _____	o͝o _____
ō _____	o͞o _____

(Note that the long vowel always has the sound of its own name.)

The Schwa (ə)

The symbol ə looks like an upside-down *e*. The International Phonetic Alphabet calls this sound a *schwa*, and it stands for the unaccented sound in such words as *ago, item, easily, gallop,* and *circus.* More approximately, it stands for the sound *uh*—like the *uh* that speakers sometimes make when they hesitate. Perhaps it would help to remember that *uh*, as well as ə, could be used to represent the schwa sound.

Here are some of the many words in which the sound appears: *imitation* (*im-uh-tā'shuhn* or *im-ə-tā'shən*); *elevate* (*el'uh-vāt* or *el'ə-vāt*); *horizon* (*huh-ri'zuhn* or *hə-rī'zən*). Open your dictionary to any page, and you will almost surely be able to find words that make use of the schwa in the pronunciation in parentheses after the main entry.

In the spaces below, write three words that make use of the schwa, and their pronunciations.

1. _____   (_____)
2. _____   (_____)
3. _____   (_____)

Accent Marks

Some words contain both a primary accent, shown by a heavy stroke (′) and a secondary accent, shown by a lighter stroke (′). For example, in the word *controversy* (kəntrɒ'vəsɪ), the stress, or accent, goes chiefly on the second syllable (trɒ′).

Use your dictionary to add accent marks to the following words:

preclude (pri klud)*
atrophy (æt rə fɪ)
inveigle (in vā gəl)
ubiquitous (yōō bik wi təs)
prognosticate (prog nos ti kāt)

Full Pronunciation

Now use your dictionary to write the full pronunciation (the information given in parentheses) for each of the following words.

1. inveigh _____

2. diatribe _____

3. raconteur _____

4. panacea _____

*Dictionaries will vary in their notation of vowel sounds. The first two examples show Oxford's system; the final three demonstrate other standard vowel sound notations.

5. esophagus _____

6. Cesarean _____

7. clandestine _____

8. vicarious _____

9. quiescent _____

10. parsimony _____

11. penchant _____

12. antipathy _____

13. capricious _____

14. schizophrenia _____

15. euphemism _____

16. internecine _____

17. amalgamate _____

18. quixotic _____

19. laissez-faire _____

20. antidisestablishmentarianism (This word is probably not in a small-format dictionary, but if you can say *establish* and if you break the rest of the word into individual syllables, you should be able to pronounce it.)

_____

Now practise pronouncing each word. Use the pronunciation key in your dictionary as an aid to sounding out each syllable. Do *not* try to pronounce a word all at once; instead, work on mastering *one syllable at a time*. When you can pronounce each of the syllables in a word successfully, then say them in sequence, add the accent, and pronounce the entire word.

PARTS OF SPEECH

The next bit of information that the dictionary gives about *murder* is *n*. This abbreviation means that the meanings of *murder* as a noun will follow.

Use your dictionary if necessary to fill in the meanings of the following abbreviations:

v. = _____   sing. = _____

adj. = _____   pl. = _____

PRINCIPAL PARTS OF IRREGULAR VERBS

To murder is a regular verb and forms its principal parts by adding *-ed*, *-ed*, and *-ing* to the stem of the verb. When a verb is irregular, the dictionary lists its principal parts. For example, with *give* the present tense comes first (the entry itself, *give*). Next comes the past tense (*gave*), and then the past participle (*given*)—the form of the verb used with such helping words as *have*, *had*, and *was*. Then comes the present participle (*giving*)—the *-ing* form of the verb.

Look up the parts of the following irregular verbs and write them in the spaces provided. The first one is done for you.

Present Tense	Past Tense	Past Participle	Present Participle
tear	tore	torn	tearing
go			
know			
steal			

PLURAL FORMS OF IRREGULAR NOUNS

The dictionary supplies the plural forms of all irregular nouns. (Regular nouns like *murder* form the plural by adding *-s* or *-es*.) Give the plurals of the following nouns. If two forms are shown, write down both.

analysis _____

dictionary _____

criterion _____

activity _____

thesis _____

MEANINGS

When a word has more than one meaning, the meanings are numbered in the dictionary, as with the verb *murder*. In many dictionaries, the most common meanings of a word are presented first. The introductory pages of your dictionary will explain the order in which meanings are presented.

Use the sentence context to try to explain the meaning of the underlined word in each of the following sentences. Write your definition in the space provided. Then look up and record the dictionary meaning of the word. Be sure you pick out the meaning that fits the word as it is used in the sentence.

1. I spend an <u>inordinate</u> amount of time watching television.

   Your definition: _____

   Dictionary definition: _____

2. I appreciated her <u>candid</u> remark that my pants were so baggy they made me look like a clown.

   Your definition: _____

   Dictionary definition: _____

3. The RCMP <u>squelched</u> the intruders' plan to break in on Prime Minister Chrétien.

   Your definition: _____

   Dictionary definition: _____

4. One of the <u>cardinal</u> rules in our house was, "Respect other people's privacy."

   Your definition: _____

   Dictionary definition: _____

5. A special <u>governor</u> prevents the school bus from travelling more than fifty-five miles an hour.

   Your definition: _____

   Dictionary definition: _____

Activity: Using New Words in Sentences

Look again at the list of twenty words on pages 379–380. Choose ten of these words to look up in your dictionary. Write out brief versions of the meanings of each of the ten words *in your own words*. Next, use each of the ten words in a sentence that clearly demonstrate the word's meaning.

ETYMOLOGY

Etymology refers to the origin and historical development of a word. Such information is usually enclosed in brackets and is more likely to be present in a larger-format dictionary than in a pocket-sized one. Good dictionaries include the following:

The Gage Canadian Dictionary
The Oxford Advanced Learner's Dictionary
The Concise Oxford Dictionary
Funk & Wagnalls Canadian College Dictionary

A good large-format dictionary will tell you, for example, that the word *berserk* derives from the name of a tribe of Scandinavian warriors who would work themselves into a frenzy during battle. The word is now a general term to describe someone whose actions are frenzied or crazed.

See if your dictionary says anything about the origins of the following words:

bikini _____

sandwich _____

tantalize _____

breakfast _____

USAGE LABELS

As a general rule, use only standard English words in your writing. If a word is not standard English, your dictionary will probably give it a usage label like one of the following: *informal, nonstandard, slang, vulgar, obsolete, archaic, rare*.

Look up the following words and record how your dictionary labels them. Remember that a recent large-format dictionary will always be the best source of information about usage.

flunk _____

tough (meaning "unfortunate, too bad") _____

creep (meaning "an annoying person") _____

ain't _____

scam _____

SYNONYMS

A *synonym* is a word that is close in meaning to another word. Using synonyms helps you avoid unnecessary repetition of the same word in a paper. A pocket-sized dictionary is not likely to give you synonyms for words, but a good dictionary will. (You might also want to own a *thesaurus*, a book that lists synonyms and antonyms. An *antonym* is a word approximately opposite in meaning to another word.)

Consult a thesaurus or a dictionary that gives synonyms for the following words, and write the synonyms in the spaces provided.

heavy _____

escape _____

necessary _____

run _____

bad _____

louse _____

strong _____

IMPROVING SPELLING

Poor spelling often results from bad habits developed in early school years. With work, such habits can be corrected. If you can write your name without misspelling it, there is no reason you can't do the same with almost any word in the English language. Following are six steps you can take to improve your spelling.

STEP 1: USE THE DICTIONARY

Get into the habit of using the dictionary. When you write a paper, allow yourself time to look up the spelling of all those words you are unsure about. Do not overlook the value of this step just because it is such a simple one. By using the dictionary, you can probably make yourself a 95 per cent better speller.

STEP 2: KEEP A PERSONAL SPELLING LIST

Keep a list of words you misspell and study the words regularly. Use the chart on page 556 as a starter. When you accumulate additional words, put them on the back page of a frequently used notebook or on a separate sheet of paper titled "Personal Spelling List."

To master the words on your list, do the following:

1   Write down any hint that will help you remember the spelling of a word. For example, you might want to note that *occasion* is spelled with two *c*'s, or that *all right* is two words, not one word.

2   Study a word by looking at it, saying it, and spelling it. You may also want to write out the word one or more times, or "air-write" it with your finger in large, exaggerated motions.

3 When you have trouble spelling a long word, try to break the word down into syllables and see whether you can spell the syllables. For example, *inadvertent* can be spelled easily if you can hear and spell in turn its four syllables: *in ad ver tent*. The word *consternation* can be spelled easily if you hear and spell in turn its four syllables: *con ster na tion*. Remember, then: try to see, hear, and spell long words in terms of their syllables.

4 Keep in mind that *review* and *repeated self-testing* are keys to effective learning. When you are learning a series of words, go back after studying each new word and review all the preceding ones.

5 Use a tape recorder. Say each word, then spell it on tape. Replay the tape to help you learn the spellings of each word. Quiz yourself by stopping the tape after you state the word, but before you spell it. Check the spelling by listening to the tape.

STEP 3: MASTER COMMONLY CONFUSED WORDS

Master the meanings and spellings of the commonly confused words on pages 399–406. Your instructor may assign twenty words for you to study at a time and give you a series of quizzes until you have mastered the words.

STEP 4: UNDERSTAND BASIC SPELLING RULES

Explained briefly here are three rules that may improve your spelling. While exceptions sometimes occur, the rules hold true most of the time.

1 *Changing y to* **i.** When a word ends in a consonant plus *y*, change *y* to *i* when you add an ending.

try	+ ed	= tried	easy	+ er	= easier
defy	+ es	= defies	carry	+ ed	= carried
ready	+ ness	= readiness	penny	+ less	= penniless

2 *Final silent* **e.** Drop a final *e* before an ending that starts with a vowel (the vowels are *a*, *e*, *i*, *o*, and *u*).

create	+ ive	= creative	believe	+ able	= believable
nerve	+ ous	= nervous	share	+ ing	= sharing

Keep the final *e* before an ending that starts with a consonant.

extreme + ly = extremely   life + less = lifeless
hope   + ful = hopeful   excite + ment = excitement

3 *Doubling a final consonant.* Double the final consonant of a word when all three of the following are true:*

a The word is one syllable or is accented on the last syllable.

b The word ends in a single consonant preceded by a single vowel.

c The ending you are adding starts with a vowel.

shop + er = shopper   thin   + est = thinnest
equip + ed = equipped   submit + ed = submitted
swim + ing = swimming   drag   + ed = dragged

Activity

Combine the following words and endings by applying the three rules above.

1. worry   + ed   = _____

2. write   + ing = _____

3. marry   + es   = _____

4. run   + ing = _____

5. terrify + ed   = _____

6. dry   + es   = _____

7. forget + ing = _____

8. care   + ful = _____

9. control + ed   = _____

10. debate + able = _____

STEP 5: STUDY A BASIC WORD LIST

Study the spellings of the words in the following list. They are 520 of the words most often used in English. Your instructor may assign twenty-five or fifty words for you to study at a time and give you a series of quizzes until you have mastered the list.

* In addition, Canadian spelling usually doubles the final consonant when adding endings to words. (see "A Note on Canadian Spelling" on pages 392–393.)

Five Hundred and Twenty Basic Words

ability	approve	brake	coffee
absent	argue	breast	collect
accept	around	breath*	college
accident	arrange	breathe*	colour **100**
ache	attempt	brilliant	come
across	attention	brother	comfortable
address	August	building	company
advertise	automobile	bulletin	condition
advice*	autumn	bureau	conservation
advise*	avenue	business	conversation
after	awful	came **75**	copy
again	awkward	can't	daily
against	back	careful	danger
agree	balance	careless	daughter
all right	bargain	cereal	daybreak
almost	beautiful	certain	dear*
a lot	because	chair	death
already	become **50**	change	December
also	been	charity	decide
although	before	cheap*	deed
always	begin	cheat	deer*
amateur	being	cheek	dentist
among	believe	cheep*	deposit
amount	between	chicken	describe
angry **25**	bicycle	chief	did
animal	black	children	died
another	blue	choose	different
answer	board*	church	dinner
anxious	bored*	citizen	direction **125**
appetite	borrow	city	discover
apply	bottle	close	disease
approach	bottom	clothing	distance

* You will find information on *homonyms* (words that sound the same but have different meanings) and on commonly confused words in the chapter titled "Commonly Confused Words" (see page 399).

doctor	forehead	house	listen
does	foreign	however	little
dollar	forty	hundred	loaf
don't	forward	hungry	loneliness
doubt	found	husband	long
down	fourteen	instead	lose
dozen	Friday	intelligence	made
during	friend	interest	making
each	from	interfere	many
early	gallon	interrupt	March
earth	garden **175**	into	marry
easy	general	iron	match
education	get	itself	matter
eight	good	January	may **250**
either	grammar	July	measure
empty	grate*	June	medicine
English	great*	just	men
enough	grocery	kindergarten	middle
entrance	grow	kitchen	might*
evening	guess	knock	million
everything	half	knowledge	minute
examine **150**	hammer	labour	mistake
except	hand	laid	mite*
exercise	handkerchief	language	Monday
exit	happy	last **225**	money
expect	having	laugh	month
fact	head	lead*	more
factory	heard	learn	morning
family	heavy	led*	mother
far	high	left	mountain
February	himself	leisure	mouth
few	hoarse*	length	much
fifteen	holiday	lesson	must
fight	home	letter	nail
flour*	horse*	life	near
flower*	hospital **200**	light	needle

neither	part	quite	sight
never	peace	quiz	since
newspaper **275**	pear*	raise*	sister
nickel	pencil	raze*	sixteenth
niece	penny	read	sleep
night	people	ready **350**	smoke
ninety	perfect	really	soap
noise	period	reason	soldier
none	person	receive	sole*
not	picture	recognize	something
nothing	piece	refer	sometimes
November	pillow	religion	soul*
now	place	remember	soup
number	plain*	repeat	south
ocean	plane*	resource	stamp
o'clock	please	restaurant	state
October	pocket **325**	ribbon	still
offer	police	ridiculous	stockings
often	possible	right	straight*
old	post office	said	strait* **400**
omit	potato	same	street
once	power	sandwich	strong
one	prescription	Saturday	student
only	president	say	studying
operate	pretty	school	such
opinion	probably	scissors	suffer
opportunity	promise	sea*	sugar
optimist **300**	psychology	season	suit
original	public	see*	suite*
ought	pursue	sentence	summer
ounce	put	September **375**	Sunday
overcoat	quart	service	supper
pain*	quarter	seventeen	sure
pane*	quick	several	sweet*
paper	quiet	shoes	take
pare*	quit	should	teach

tear	today	visitor	while
telegram	together	voice	white
telephone	tomorrow	vote	whole
tenant	tongue	wage	who's*
tenth	tonight	wagon	whose*
than	touch	waist	wife **500**
Thanksgiving	toward	wait **475**	window
that	travel **450**	wake	winter
theatre **425**	trouble	walk	without
their*	trousers	warm	woman
them	truly	warning	wonder
there*	twelve	waste	won't
they	uncle	watch	wood*
they're*	under	water	work
thing	understand	wear	world
thirteen	until	weather	worth
this	upon	Wednesday	would*
though	used	week	writing
thousand	usual	weigh	written
thread	valley	welcome	wrong
three	value	well	year
through	variety	went	yesterday
Thursday	vegetable	were	yet
ticket	very	what	young
time	view	whether	your
tired	villain	which	you're

Note: Two spelling mistakes that students often make are to write *a lot* as one word (*alot*) and to write *all right* as one word (*alright*). Do not write either *a lot* or *all right* as one word.

STEP 6: USE ELECTRONIC AIDS

There are three electronic aids that may help your spelling. First, the word-processing program you use with either your computer or the computers at your college undoubtedly has a *spell-checker* as part of its capabilities. Making use of the spell-checker for every document you prepare will enable you to identify incorrectly spelled words and to select from suggested correct spellings. Spell-checking cannot differentiate between unintentional mistakes in word usage, though. "Same sound" words, homonyms like *its* and *it's* or *there*, *their*, and *they're*, spelled correctly but used incorrectly, cannot be corrected by a spell-checker. You may want to highlight these words on your processor screen and double-check your intended meaning and spelling with the dictionary.

Second, *electronic spell-checkers* are pocket-size devices that look much like pocket calculators. They are among the latest examples of how technology can help the learning process. Electronic spellers can be found in the computer and electronics sections of most department, office supplies, or electronics stores. The checker includes a tiny keyboard. You type out the word the way you think it is spelled, and the checker supplies the correct spelling of related words. Some checkers even *pronounce* the word aloud for you. Canadian students will want to ask whether British/Canadian or American spelling systems are programmed into the spell-checker they select, and should find out whether or not instructors permit the use of these devices in classes and exams.

Third, many *electronic typewriters* on the market today will beep automatically when you misspell or mistype a word. They include built-in dictionaries that will then give you the correct spelling.

A NOTE ABOUT CANADIAN SPELLING, AND ABOUT CORRECTNESS

Canadian spelling has become the subject of some contention. You may notice that many Canadian newspapers use what we think of as "American" forms of words such as *neighbor* or *color*. These are choices made by their style guides. Canadian spelling is neither British nor American spelling; it is a hybrid of the two. Student confusion is understandable.

Check with your instructor for his or her preference, but choose *one* spelling system, and *be consistent*. Choose an Oxford dictionary, which this text uses, or a Canadian dictionary, such as *Gage* or *Penguin*. If your word-processing program's spell-check system allows you to choose between British or American spelling, choose British, which is sometimes called "UK Lex."

The main differences between U.S. and Canadian spellings are in *-or/-our* endings (*honour*, *neighbour*, *labour*, *flavour*), *-er/-re* endings (*theatre*, *litre*, *centre*, *fibre*) and *-se/-ce* endings (*defence*, *licence*, *offence*).

Canadian spelling also includes more doubled *l*'s than does U.S. spelling. These double *l*'s appear in nouns such as *tranquillizer* and *counsellor*, and in present and past participle forms of verbs such as *travelling*, *levelled*, *panelled*, *can-*

celled, and *counselled*. Whichever form your dictionary uses, remember that consistent spelling is important.

The importance of spelling correctly will not decline with technological advances in, and changes to, the workplace. The Internet and other international communications systems will be part of your personal and professional future. Clear and understandable communication relies on standardized spelling. Individual illiteracy, bounced off satellites and transmitted through fibre-optic cable, becomes an international liability to employers and private citizens alike.

VOCABULARY DEVELOPMENT

A good vocabulary is a vital part of effective communication. A command of many words will make you a better writer, speaker, listener, and reader. Studies have shown that students with a strong vocabulary, and students who work to improve a limited vocabulary, are more successful in school. *A good vocabulary is a common factor among people enjoying successful careers.* This section will describe three ways of developing your word power: (1) regular reading, (2) vocabulary wordsheets, and (3) vocabulary study books. You should keep in mind from the start, however, that none of the approaches will help unless you truly decide that vocabulary development is an important goal. Only when you have this attitude can you begin doing the sustained work needed to improve your word power.

REGULAR READING

Through reading a good deal, you will learn words by encountering them a number of times in a variety of sentences. Repeated exposure to a word in context will eventually make it a part of your working language.

You should develop the habit of reading a daily newspaper and one or more magazines like *Maclean's*, *Saturday Night*, or even *People*, as well as monthly magazines suited to your interests. In addition, you should try to read some books for pleasure. This may be especially difficult at times when you also have textbook reading to do. Try, however, to redirect a regular half hour to one hour of your recreational time to reading books, rather than watching television, playing computer games, cruising the Internet, or talking on the phone. Doing so, you may eventually reap the rewards of an improved vocabulary *and* the discovery that reading can be truly enjoyable. If you would like some recommendations, ask your instructor for a copy of the "List of Interesting Books" in the Instructor's Manual of *English Skills with Readings*.

VOCABULARY WORDSHEETS

Vocabulary wordsheets are another means of vocabulary development. First, as you read, you should mark off words that you want to learn. Then, after you have accumulated a number of words, sit down with a dictionary and look up basic information about each of them. Put this information on a wordsheet like the one shown below. Be sure also to write down a sentence in which each word appears. A word is always best learned not in a vacuum but in the context of surrounding words.

Study each word as follows.

1. Make sure you can pronounce the word and its derivations correctly. (Pages 378–380 explain the dictionary pronunciation key that will help you pronounce each word properly.)
2. Study the main meanings of the word until you can say them without looking at them.
3. Spend a moment looking at the example of the word in context.

Follow the same process with the second word. Then, after testing yourself on the first and the second words, go on to the third word. Remember to continue to test yourself on all the words you have studied after you learn each new word. Repeated self-testing is a key to effective learning.

Activity

Locate four words in your reading that you would like to master. Enter them in the spaces on the vocabulary wordsheet below and fill in all the needed information. Your instructor may then check your wordsheet and perhaps give you a quick oral quiz on selected words.

You may receive a standing assignment to add at least five words a week to a wordsheet and to study the words. Note that you can create your own wordsheets using loose-leaf paper, or your instructor may give you copies of the wordsheet that appears below.

Vocabulary Wordsheet

1. Word: _____formidable_____ Pronunciation: _____(fôr′ mi də bəl)_____
    Meanings: _____1. feared or dreaded_____
    _____2. extremely difficult_____
    _____

Other forms of the word: _formidably   formidability_ _____

Use of the word in context: _Several formidable obstacles stand between_

Matt and his goal. _____

2. Word: _____ Pronunciation: _____

   Meanings: _____

   _____

   _____

   Other forms of the word: _____

   Use of the word in context: _____

   _____

3. Word: _____ Pronunciation: _____

   Meanings: _____

   _____

   _____

   Other forms of the word: _____

   Use of the word in context: _____

   _____

4. Word: _____ Pronunciation: _____

   Meanings: _____

   _____

   _____

   Other forms of the word: _____

   Use of the word in context: _____

   _____

5. Word: _____ Pronunciation: _____

   Meanings: _____

   _____

   _____

   Other forms of the word: _____

Use of the word in context: _____

_____

VOCABULARY STUDY BOOKS

A third way to increase your word power is to use vocabulary study books. There are books that may be available in the learning-skills centre at your school. These books help you learn a word by asking you to look at the context—or the words around the unfamiliar word—to unlock its meaning. This method is called *using context clues*, or *word clues*.

Many vocabulary books and programs are available. The best are those that present words in one or more contexts and then provide several reinforcement activities for each word. These books will help you increase your vocabulary if you have the determination required to work with them on a regular basis.

COMMONLY
CONFUSED
WORDS

Introductory Project

Circle the five words that are misspelled in the following passage. Then write the correct spellings in the spaces provided.

You're mind and body are not as separate as you might think. Their is a lot of evidence, for instance, that says if you believe that a placebo (a substance with no medicine) will help you, than it will. One man is said too have rapidly recovered from an advanced case of cancer after only one dose of a drug that he believed was highly effective. Its not clear just how placebos work, but they do show how closely the mind and body are related.

1. _____

2. _____

3. _____

4. _____

5. _____

Answers are on page 553.

HOMONYMS

The commonly confused words on the following pages have the same sounds but different meanings and spellings; such words are known as *homonyms*. Complete the activity for each set of words, and check off and study the words that give you trouble.

all ready   completely prepared
already   previously; before

> We were *all ready* to start the play, but the audience was still being seated.
> I have *already* called the police.

Fill in the blanks: I am _____ for the economics examination

because I have _____ studied the chapter three times.

brake   stop; the stopping device in a vehicle
break   come apart

> His car bumper has a sticker reading, "I *brake* for animals."
> "I am going to *break* up with Bill if he keeps seeing other women," said Rita.

Fill in the blanks: When my car's emergency _____ slipped, the car rolled back and demolished my neighbour's rose garden, causing a

_____ in our good relations with each other.

coarse   rough
course   part of a meal; school subject; direction; certainly (as in *of course*)

> By the time the server brought the customers the second *course* of the meal, she was aware of their *coarse* eating habits.

Fill in the blanks: Ted felt that the health instructor's humour was too _____

for his taste and was glad when he finished the _____.

hear   perceive with the ear
here   in this place

> "The salespeople act as though they don't see or *hear* me, even though I've been standing *here* for fifteen minutes," the woman complained.

Fill in the blanks: "Did you _____ about the distinguished visitor

who just came into town and is staying _____ at this very hotel?"

hole   empty spot
whole   entire

"I can't believe I ate the *whole* pizza," moaned Damian. "I think it's going to make a *hole* in my stomach lining."

Fill in the blanks: The _____ time I was at the party I tried to conceal the _____ I had in my trousers.

its   belonging to it
it's   shortened form for *it is* or *it has*

The car blew *its* transmission (the transmission belonging to it, the car).
It's (it has) been raining all week and *it's* (it is) raining now.

Fill in the blanks: _____ hot and unsanitary in the restaurant kitchen I work in, and I don't think the restaurant deserves _____ good reputation.

knew   past form of *know*
new   not old

"I had *new* wallpaper put up," said Sarah.
"I *knew* there was some reason the place looked better," said Bill.

Fill in the blanks: Crystal _____ that getting her hair cut would give her face a _____ look.

know   to understand
no   a negative

"I don't *know* why my dog Fang likes to attack certain people," said Maria.
"There's *no* one thing the people have in common."

Fill in the blanks: I _____ of _____ way of telling whether that politician is honest or not.

pair   set of two
pear   fruit
pare   to peel

"What a great *pair* of legs Tony has," said Crystal to Yvonne. Tony didn't hear her, for he was feeling very sick after munching on a green *pear*, which he'd had to *pare*.

Fill in the blanks: In his lunch box was a ＿＿＿＿＿＿ of ＿＿＿＿＿s.

passed   went by; succeeded in; handed to
past   time before the present; beyond, as in "We worked past closing time."

Someone *passed* him a wine bottle; it was the way he chose to forget his unhappy *past*.

Fill in the blanks: I walked ＿＿＿＿＿＿＿ the instructor's office but was

afraid to ask her whether or not I had ＿＿＿＿＿＿＿ the test.

peace   calm
piece   a part

Nations often risk world *peace* by fighting over a *piece* of land.

Fill in the blanks: Maria did not have any ＿＿＿＿＿＿＿ until she gave

her pet dog a ＿＿＿＿＿＿＿ of her meat loaf.

plain   simple; flat area
plane   aircraft

The *plain*, unassuming young man on the *plane* suddenly jumped up with a grenade in his hand and announced, "We're all going to Tibet."

Fill in the blanks: The game-show contestant opened the small box wrapped in

＿＿＿＿＿＿＿ brown paper and found inside the keys to his own jet

＿＿＿＿＿＿＿.

principal   main; person in charge of a school
principle   law, standard, or rule

Note: It might help to remember that the *e* in *principle* is also in *rule—the meaning of principle.*

Pete's high school *principal* had one *principal* problem: Pete. This was because there were only two *principles* in Pete's life: rest and relaxation.

Fill in the blanks: The ＿＿＿＿＿＿＿ reason she dropped out of school

was that she believed in the ＿＿＿＿＿＿＿ of complete freedom of choice.

right   correct; opposite of *left*
write   what you do in English

If you have the *right* course card, I'll *write* your name on the class list.

Fill in the blanks: Eddie thinks I'm weird since I _____ with both

my _____ and my left hands.

than (thăn)   word used in comparisons
then (thĕn)   at that time

Note: It might help to remember that th*en* is also a tim*e* signal.

When we were kids, my friend Elaine had prettier clothes *than* I did. I really
envied her *then*.

Fill in the blanks: Marge thought she was better _____ the rest

of us, but _____ she got the lowest grade on the history test.

their   belonging to them
there   at that place; neutral word used with verbs like *is, are, was, were, have,*
            and *had*
they're   short form of *they are*

Two people own that van over *there* (at that place). *They're* (they are) going
to move out of *their* apartment (the apartment belonging to them) and into
the van, in order to save money.

Fill in the blanks: _____ not going to invite us to _____

table because _____ is no room for us to sit down.

threw   past form of *throw*
through   from one side to the other; finished

The fans *threw* so much litter on the field that the teams could not go *through*
with the game.

Fill in the blanks: When Mr. Jefferson was _____ screaming about

the violence on television, he _____ the newspaper at his dog.

to   verb part, as in *to smile*; toward, as in "I'm going *to* heaven"
too   overly, as in "The pizza was *too* hot"; also, as in "The coffee was hot, *too.*"
two   the number 2

Tony drove *to* the park *to* be alone with Crystal. (The first *to* means "toward"; the second *to* is a verb part that goes with *be*.)

Tony's shirt is *too* tight; his pants are tight, *too*. (The first *too* means "overly"; the second *too* means "also.")

You need *two* hands (2 hands) to handle a Whopper.

Fill in the blanks: _____ times tonight, you have been _____ ready _____ make assumptions without asking questions first.

wear   to have on
where   in what place

André wanted to *wear* his light pants on the hot day, but he didn't know *where* he had put them.

Fill in the blanks: _____ exactly on my leg should I _____ this elastic bandage?

weather   atmospheric conditions
whether   if it happens that; in case; if

Some people go on vacations *whether* or not the *weather* is good.

Fill in the blanks: I always ask Bill _____ or not we're going to have a storm, for he can feel rainy _____ approaching in his bad knee.

whose   belonging to whom
who's   short form for *who is* and *who has*

Who's the teacher *whose* students are complaining?

Fill in the blanks: _____ the guy _____ car I saw you in?

your   belonging to you
you're short form of *you are*

You're (meaning "you are") not going to the fair unless *your* brother (the brother belonging to you) goes with you.

Fill in the blanks: _____ going to have to put aside individual differences and play together for the sake of _____ team.

OTHER WORDS FREQUENTLY CONFUSED

Following is a list of other words that people frequently confuse. Complete the activities for each set of words, and check off and study the words that give you trouble.

a, an   Both *a* and *an* are used before other words to mean, approximately, "one."

Generally you should use *an* before words starting with a vowel (*a, e, i, o, u*) or a vowel-like sound such as the *h* in *hour* or the *X* in *X-ray:*

an ache   an experiment   an elephant   an idiot   an ox

Generally you should use *a* before words starting with a consonant (all other letters):

a card   a brain   a cheat   a television   a gambler

Fill in the blanks: The girls had _____ argument over _____ former boyfriend.

accept (ăk sĕpt′)   receive; agree to
except (ĕk sĕpt′)   exclude; but

"I would *accept* your loan," said Bill to the bartender, "*except* that I'm not ready to pay 25 per cent interest."

Fill in the blanks: _____ that she can't _____ any criticism, Lori is a good friend.

advice (ăd vīs′)   noun meaning "an opinion"
advise (ăd vīz′)   verb meaning "to counsel, to give advice"

I *advise* you to take the *advice* of your friends and stop working so hard.

Fill in the blanks: I _____ you to listen carefully to any _____ you get from your boss.

affect (uh fĕkt′)   verb meaning "to influence"
effect (ĭ fĕkt′)   verb meaning "to bring about something"; noun meaning "result"

The full *effects* of marijuana and alcohol on the body are only partly known; however, both drugs clearly *affect* the brain in various ways.

Fill in the blanks: The new tax laws go into _____ next month, and they are going to _____ your income tax deductions.

among   implies three or more
between   implies only two

> We had to choose from *among* 125 shades of paint but *between* only 2 fabrics.

Fill in the blanks: The lay-off notices distributed _____ the unhappy workers gave them a choice _____ working for another month at full pay and leaving immediately with two weeks' pay.

beside   along the side of
besides   in addition to

> I was lucky I wasn't standing *beside* the car when it was hit.
> *Besides* being unattractive, these uniforms are impractical.

Fill in the blanks: _____ the alarm system hooked up to the door, our neighbours keep a guard dog _____ their front gate.

desert (dĕz′ərt)   stretch of dry land; (di zûrt′) to abandon one's post or duty
dessert (dĭ zûrt′)   last part of a meal

> Sweltering in the *desert*, I was tormented by the thought of an icy *dessert*.

Fill in the blanks: After their meal, they carried their _____ into the living room so that they would not miss the start of the old _____ movie about Lawrence of Arabia.

fewer   word used with things that can be counted
less   refers to amount, value, or degree

> There were *fewer* than seven people in all my classes today.
> I seem to feel *less* tired when I exercise regularly.

Fill in the blanks: With _____ people driving large cars, we are importing _____ oil than we used to.

loose (loos)   not fastened; not tight-fitting
lose (looz)   misplace; fail to win

> Phil's belt is so *loose* that he always looks ready to *lose* his pants.

Fill in the blanks: At least once a week our neighbours _____ their dog; it's because they let him run _____.

quiet (kwī′ĭt) peaceful
quite (kwīt) entirely; really; rather

After a busy day, the children are now *quiet*, and their parents are *quite* tired.

Fill in the blanks: The _____ halls of the church become _____ lively during square-dance evenings.

though (thō) despite the fact that
thought (thôt) past form of *think*

Even *though* she worked, she *thought* she would have time to go to school.

Fill in the blanks: Susan _____ she would like the job, but even _____ the pay was good, she hated the travelling involved.

■ Review Test 1

Underline the correct word in the parentheses. If necessary, look back at the explanations of the words instead of trying to guess.

1. Please take my (advice, advise) and (where, wear) something warm and practical, rather (than, then) something fashionable and flimsy.

2. Glen felt that if he could (loose, lose) ten kilos, the (affect, effect) on his social life might be dramatic.

3. (Their, There, They're) going to show seven horror films at (their, there, they're) Halloween night festival; I hope you'll be (their, there, they're).

4. (Your, You're) going to have to do (a, an) better job on (your, you're) final exam if you expect to pass the (coarse, course).

5. Those (to, too, two) issues are (to, too, two) hot for any politician (to, too, two) handle.

6. Even (though, thought) the (brakes, breaks) on my car were worn, I did not have (quiet, quite) enough money to get them replaced (right, write) away.

7. (Accept, Except) for the fact that my neighbour receives most of his mail in (plain, plane) brown wrappers, he is (know, no) stranger (than, then) anyone else in this rooming house.

8. Because the Randalls are so neat and fussy, (its, it's) hard (to, too, two) feel comfortable when (your, you're) in (their, there, they're) house.

9. (Whose, Who's) the culprit who left the paint can on the table? The paint has ruined a (knew, new) tablecloth, and (its, it's) soaked (threw, through) the linen and (affected, effected) the varnish stain on the table.

10. I would have been angry at the car that (passed, past) me at 120 kilometres an hour on the highway, (accept, except) that I (knew, new) it would not get (passed, past) the radar trap (to, too, two) miles down the road.

■ Review Test 2

On separate paper, write short sentences using the ten words shown below.

their	principal
its	except
you're	past
too	through
then	who's

EFFECTIVE
WORD CHOICE

Introductory Project

Put a check beside the sentence in each pair that you feel makes more effective use of words.

1. I flipped out when Faye broke our date. _____

   I got very angry when Faye broke our date. _____

2. Doctors as dedicated as Dr. Lalonde are few and far between. _____

   Doctors as dedicated as Dr. Lalonde are rare. _____

3. Yesterday I ascertained that Elena and Julio broke up. _____

   Yesterday I found out that Elena and Julio broke up. _____

4. Judging by the looks of things, it seems to me that it will probably rain very soon. _____

   It looks as though it will rain soon. _____

Now see if you can circle the correct number in each case:

    Pair (1, 2, 3, 4) contains a sentence with slang.
    Pair (1, 2, 3, 4) contains a sentence with a cliché.
    Pair (1, 2, 3, 4) contains a sentence with a pretentious word.
    Pair (1, 2, 3, 4) contains a wordy sentence.

Answers are on page 553.

Choose your words carefully when you write. Always take the time to think about your word choices rather than simply using the first word that comes to mind. You want to develop the habit of selecting words that are *appropriate* and *exact for your purposes*. One way you can show sensitivity to language is by avoiding slang, clichés, pretentious words, and wordiness.

SLANG

We often use slang expressions when we talk because they are so vivid and colourful. However, slang is usually out of place in formal writing. Here are some examples of slang expressions:

> My girlfriend *got straight* with me by saying she wanted to see other men.
> Rick spent all Saturday *messing around* with his lacrosse team.
> My boss keeps *riding* me about coming to work on time.
> The tires on the Porsche make the car look like *something else*.
> The crowd was *psyched up* when the game began.

Slang expressions have a number of drawbacks: they go out of date quickly, they become tiresome if used excessively in writing, and they may communicate clearly to some readers but not to others. Also, the use of slang can be a way of evading the specific details that are often needed to make one's meaning clear in writing. For example, in "The tires on the Porsche make the car look like something else," the writer has not provided the specific details about the tires necessary for us to understand the statement clearly. In general, then, you should avoid slang in your writing. If you are in doubt about whether an expression is slang, it may help to check a recently published dictionary.

Activity: Making Appropriate Word Choices

Rewrite the following sentences, replacing the italicized slang words with more formal ones.

Example   The movie was a *real bomb*, so we *cut out* early.

<u>The movie was terrible, so we left early.</u>

1. My boss *came down on me* for *goofing off* on the job.

_____

_____

2. The car was a *steal* for the money until the owner *jacked up* the price.

_____

_____

3. If the instructor stops *hassling* me, I am going to *get my act together* in the course.

_____

CLICHÉS

A cliché is an expression that has been worn out through constant use. Some typical clichés are listed below:

Clichés

all work and no play	saw the light
at a loss for words	short but sweet
better late than never	sigh of relief
drop in the bucket	singing the blues
easier said than done	taking a big chance
had a hard time of it	time and time again
in the nick of time	too close for comfort
in this day and age	too little, too late
it dawned on me	took a turn for the worse
it goes without saying	under the weather
last but not least	where he (she) is
make ends meet	coming from
on top of the world	word to the wise
sad but true	work like a dog

Clichés are common in speech but make your writing seem tired and stale. Also, clichés—like slang—are often a way of evading the specific details that you must work to provide in your writing. You should, then, avoid clichés and try to express your meaning in fresh, original ways.

Activity: Substituting Specific Words for Clichés

Underline the cliché in each of the following sentences. Then substitute specific, fresh words for the trite expression.

Example   I passed the test <u>by the skin of my teeth</u>.
                I barely passed the test.

1. Anyone turning in a paper late is throwing caution to the winds.

   _____

   _____

2. Judy doesn't make any bones about her ambition.

   _____

   _____

3. I met with my instructor to try to iron out the problems in my paper.

   _____

   _____

PRETENTIOUS WORDS

Some people feel they can improve their writing by using fancy and elevated words rather than simple and natural words. They use artificial and stilted language that more often obscures their meaning than communicates it clearly.

Here are some unnatural-sounding sentences:

I comprehended her statement.
While partaking of our morning meal, we engaged in an animated conversation.
I am a stranger to excessive financial sums.
Law enforcement officers directed traffic when the lights malfunctioned.

The same thoughts can be expressed more clearly and effectively by using plain, natural language, as below:

I understood what she said.
While eating breakfast, we had a lively talk.
I have never had much money.
Police officers directed traffic when the lights stopped working.

Activity: Choosing Clear and Specific Words

Cross out the artificial words in each sentence. Then substitute clear, simple language for the artificial words.

Example   The manager ~~reproached~~ me for my ~~tardiness~~.

                 The manager criticized me for being late.

1. One of Tina's objectives in life is to accomplish a large family.

   _____

   _____

2. Upon entering our residence, we detected smoke in the atmosphere.

   _____

   _____

3. I am not apprehensive about the test, which encompasses five chapters of the book.

   _____

   _____

WORDINESS

Wordiness—using more words than necessary to express a meaning—is often a sign of lazy or careless writing. Your readers may resent the extra time and energy they must spend when you have not done the work needed to make your writing direct and concise.

Here are examples of wordy sentences:

Anne is of the opinion that the death penalty should be allowed.

I would like to say that my subject in this paper will be the kind of generous person that my father was.

Omitting needless words improves the sentences:

Anne supports the death penalty.

My father was a generous person.

In the box on the opposite page is a list of some wordy expressions that could be reduced to single words.

Wordy Form	Short Form
a large number of	many
a period of a week	a week
arrive at an agreement	agree
at an earlier point in time	before
at the present time	now
big in size	big
owing to the fact that	because
during the time that	while
five in number	five
for the reason that	because
good benefit	benefit
in every instance	always
in my own opinion	I think
in the event that	if
in the near future	soon
in this day and age	today
is able to	can
large in size	large
plan ahead for the future	plan
postponed until later	postponed
red in colour	red
return back	return

Activity 1: Eliminating Wordiness

Rewrite the following sentences, omitting needless words.

1. After a lot of careful thinking, I have arrived at the conclusion that drunken drivers should receive jail terms.

    _____

    _____

2. The movie that I went to last night, which was fairly interesting, I must say, was enjoyed by me and my girlfriend.

_____

_____

3. Owing to inclement weather conditions of wind and freezing rain, we have decided not to proceed with the athletic competition about to take place on the soccer field.

_____

_____

4. Without any question, it is laudable that the provincial law makes it a require-ment for parents of young children to buckle the children into car seats for safety.

_____

_____

5. Beyond a doubt, the only two things you can rely or depend on would be the sure facts that death comes to everyone and that the government will tax your yearly income.

_____

_____

Activity 2: Practising Effective Word Choices

Make up five sentences that contain slang, clichés, pretentious words, or exam-ples of wordiness. Exchange sentences with a class-mate. Now rewrite the sen-tences you have received, using more effective language. (Suggestion: Take a famous saying, such as the one in question 5 above, and use a wordy or slang ver-sion of that saying for one of your sentences.)

■ Review Test 1

Certain words are italicized in the following sentences. In the space provided, identify the words as *slang* (*S*), *clichés* (*C*), *pretentious words* (*PW*), or *wordiness* (*W*). Then rewrite the sentences, replacing the words with more effective diction.

_____ 1. We're *psyched* for the Tragically Hip concert, which is going to be *totally awesome*.

_____

_____

_____ 2. *Remaining in a single position in the article of furniture before my desk* for hours at a time *on a day usually known as a day of rest* is very annoying.

_____

_____

_____ 3. Getting good grades in college courses is sometimes *easier said than done.*

_____

_____

_____ 4. I *availed myself of* the chance to *participate in* the computer course.

_____

_____

_____ 5. The victims of the car accident were shaken but *none the worse for wear.*

_____

_____

_____ 6. My room-mate *pulled an all-nighter* and almost *conked out* during the exam.

_____

_____

■ **Review Test 2**

Rewrite the following sentences, omitting needless words.

1. Workers who are on a part-time basis are attractive to a business because they do not have to be paid as much as full-time workers for a business.

_____

_____

2. During the time that I was sick and out of school, I missed a total of three math tests.

_____

_____

3. The game, which was scheduled for later today, has been cancelled by the officials because of the rainy weather.

_____

_____

4. At this point in time, I am quite undecided and unsure about just which classes I will take during this coming semester.

_____

_____

5. An inconsiderate person located in the apartment next to mine keeps her radio on too loud a good deal of the time, with the result being that it is disturbing to everyone in the neighbouring apartments.

_____

_____

SENTENCE VARIETY

One aspect of effective writing is to vary the kinds of sentences you write. If every sentence follows the same pattern, writing may become monotonous to read. This chapter explains four ways you can create variety and interest in your writing style. The first two ways involve *co-ordination* and *subordination*—important techniques for achieving different kinds of emphasis in writing.

The following are four methods you can use to make your sentences more varied and more sophisticated:

1 Add a second complete thought (co-ordination).
2 Add a dependent thought (subordination).
3 Begin with a special opening word or phrase.
4 Place adjectives or verbs in a series.

Each method will be discussed in turn.

ADD A SECOND COMPLETE THOUGHT

When you add a second complete thought to a simple sentence, the result is a *compound (or double) sentence*. The two complete statements in a compound sentence are usually connected by a comma plus a joining, or co-ordinating, word (*and*, *but*, *for*, *or*, *nor*, *so*, *yet*).

A compound sentence is used when you want to give *equal weight to two closely related ideas*. The technique of showing that ideas have equal importance is called *co-ordination*.

Following are some compound sentences. Each contains two ideas that the writer regards as equal in importance.

Bill has stopped smoking cigarettes, but he is now addicted to chewing gum.
I repeatedly failed the math quizzes, so I decided to drop the course.
Stan turned all the lights off, and then he locked the office door.

Activity: Forming Compound Sentences

Combine the following pairs of simple sentences into compound sentences. Use a comma and a logical joining word (*and, but, for, so*) to connect each pair.

Note: If you are not sure what *and, but, for,* and *so* mean, review page 260.

Example ■ The CD kept skipping.
 ■ There was dust on the surface.
 The CD kept skipping, for there was dust on the surface.

1. ■ The line at Tim Horton's was long.
   ■ Jake took a place in line anyway.

   _____

   _____

2. ■ Vandals smashed the car's headlights.
   ■ They slashed the tires as well.

   _____

   _____

3. ■ I married at age seventeen.
   ■ I never got a chance to live on my own.

   _____

   _____

4. ■ Mould grew on my leather boots.
   ■ The closet was warm and humid.

   _____

   _____

5. ■ My father has a high cholesterol count.
   ■ He continues to eat red meat almost every day.

   _____

   _____

ADD A DEPENDENT THOUGHT

When you add a dependent thought to a simple sentence, the result is a *complex sentence*.* A dependent thought begins with a word or phrase like one of the following:

Dependent Words

after	if, even if	when, whenever
although, though	in order that	where, wherever
as	since	whether
because	that, so that	which, whichever
before	unless	while
even though	until	who, whoever
how	what, whatever	whose

A *complex sentence* is used when you want to *emphasize one idea over another* within the sentence. Look at the following complex sentence:

Although I lowered the thermostat, my heating bill remained high.

The idea that the writer wants to emphasize here—*my heating bill remained high*—is expressed as a complete thought. The less important idea—*Although I lowered my thermostat*—is subordinated to this complete thought. The technique of giving one idea less emphasis than another is called *subordination*.

Following are other examples of complex sentences. In each case, *the part starting with the dependent word is the less emphasized part of the sentence.*

Even though I was tired, I stayed up to watch the horror movie.

Before I take a bath, I check for spiders in the tub.

When Ivy feels nervous, she pulls on her earlobe.

---

* The two parts of a complex sentence are sometimes called an *independent clause* and a *dependent clause*. A *clause* is simply a word group that contains a subject and a verb. An independent clause expresses a complete thought and can stand alone. A dependent clause does not express a complete thought in itself and "depends on" the independent clause to complete its meaning. Dependent clauses always begin with a dependent, or subordinating, word.

Activity: Forming Complex Sentences with Subordinating Words

Use logical subordinating words to combine the following pairs of simple sentences into sentences that contain a dependent thought. Place a comma after a dependent statement when it starts the sentence.

Example ■ Our team lost.
■ We were not invited to the tournament.

Because our team lost, we were not invited to the tournament.

1. ■ I receive my degree in June.
   ■ I will begin applying for jobs.

   _____

   _____

2. ■ Crystal doesn't enjoy cooking.
   ■ She often eats at fast-food restaurants.

   _____

   _____

3. ■ I sent several letters of complaint.
   ■ Ontario Hydro never corrected my bill.

   _____

   _____

4. ■ Neil's car went into a skid.
   ■ He took his foot off the gas pedal.

   _____

   _____

5. ■ The final exam covered sixteen chapters.
   ■ The students complained.

   _____

   _____

BEGIN WITH A SPECIAL OPENING WORD OR PHRASE

Among the special openers that can be used to start sentences are *-ed* words, *-ing* words, *-ly* words, *to* word groups, and prepositional phrases. Here are examples of all five kinds of openers:

Verbal Phrases

-ed *word*	Tired from a long day of work, Sharon fell asleep on the sofa.
-ing *word*	Using a thick towel, Eng dried his hair quickly.
-ly *word*	Reluctantly, I agreed to rewrite the paper.
to *word group*	To get to bingo on time, you must leave now.
prepositional phrase	With Fred's help, Maria planted the evergreen shrubs.

Activity: Forming Sentences with Verbal or Prepositional Phrases

Combine the simple sentences into one sentence by using the opener shown in the margin and omitting repeated words. Use a comma to set off the opener from the rest of the sentence.

Example   **-ing** *word*
- The toaster refused to pop up.
- It buzzed like an angry hornet.

Buzzing like an angry hornet, the toaster refused to pop up.

-ed *word*

1.
- Bill was annoyed by the poor TV reception.
- He decided to subscribe to cable service.

_____

_____

-ing *word*

2.
- The star forward skated down the rink.
- She passed the puck like a pro.

_____

_____

-ly *word*

3.
- Food will run short on our crowded planet.
- It is inevitable.

_____

_____

to *word group*

4.
- Bill rented a limousine for the night.
- He wanted to make a good impression.

_____

_____

prepositional 5. ■   Lisa answered the telephone.
phrase   ■   She did this at 4 a.m.

_____

_____

-ed *word*   6. ■   Nathan dreaded the coming holidays.
                 ■   He was depressed by his recent divorce.

_____

_____

-ing *word*   7. ■   The people pressed against the doors of the theatre.
                  ■   They pushed and shoved each other.

_____

_____

-ly *word*   8. ■   I waited in the packed emergency room.
                 ■   I was impatient.

_____

_____

to *word*   9. ■   The little boy likes to annoy his parents.
group   ■   He pretends he can't hear them.

_____

_____

prepositional 10. ■   People must wear white-soled shoes.
phrase   ■   They must do this in the gym.

_____

_____

PLACE ADJECTIVES OR VERBS IN A SERIES

Various parts of a sentence may be placed in a series. Among these parts are adjectives (descriptive words) and verbs. Here are examples of both in a series.

Adjectives   The *black, smeary* newsprint rubbed off on my *new butcher-block* table.

Verbs   The goalie *stopped* the puck, *retrieved* it, and *sighed* with relief.

Activity: Using Adjectives, Verbs, or Phrases in Series

Combine the simple sentences into one sentence by using adjectives or verbs in series and by omitting repeated words. In most cases, use a comma between the adjectives or verbs in a series. (See page 362 for comma use with adjectives.)

Example ■ Before Christmas, I made shortbread cookies.

 ■ I decorated the house.

 ■ I wrapped dozens of toys.

Before Christmas, I made shortbread cookies,

decorated the house, and wrapped dozens of toys.

1. ■ My lumpy mattress was giving me a cramp in my neck.

 ■ It was causing pains in my back.

 ■ It was making me lose sleep.

---

2. ■ Lights appeared through the blizzard.

 ■ The lights were flashing.

 ■ The lights were blue.

 ■ The blizzard was blinding.

 ■ The blizzard was thick.

---

3. ■ Before going to bed, I locked all the doors.

 ■ I activated the burglar alarm.

 ■ I slipped my wallet under my mattress.

---

4. ■ Crystal picked sweater hairs off her coat.

 ■ The hairs were fuzzy.

 ■ The hairs were white.

 ■ The coat was brown.

 ■ The coat was suede.

---

5. ■ The contact lens fell onto the floor.
   ■ The contact lens was thin.
   ■ The contact lens was slippery.
   ■ The floor was dirty.
   ■ The floor was tiled.

_____

_____

■ Review Test 1

On separate paper, use co-ordination or subordination to combine the following groups of simple sentences into one or more longer sentences. Omit repeated words. Since various combinations are possible, you might want to jot down several combinations in each case. Then read them aloud to find the combination that sounds best.

Keep in mind that very often, the relationship among ideas in a sentence will be clearer when subordinating rather than co-ordinating words are used.

Example ■ I don't like to ask for favours.
 ■ I must borrow money from my brother-in-law.
 ■ I know he won't turn me down.
 ■ I still feel guilty about it.

I don't like to ask for favours, but I must borrow money from my brother-in-law. Although I know he won't turn me down, I still feel guilty about it.

Comma Hints

a Use a comma at the end of a word group that starts with a subordinating word (as in "Although I know he won't turn me down,…").

b Use a comma between independent word groups connected by _and, but, for, or, nor, so, yet_ (as in "I don't like to ask for favours, but …").

1. ■ My grandmother is eighty-six.
   ■ She drives to her cottage alone every summer.
   ■ She believes in being self-reliant.

2. ■ His name was called.
   ■ Louis walked into the examining room.

- He was nervous.
- He was determined to ask the doctor for a straight answer.

3.
- They left twenty minutes early for class.
- They were late anyway.
- The car overheated.

4.
- John failed the midterm exam.
- He studied harder for the final.
- He passed it.

5.
- A volcano erupts.
- It sends tons of ash into the air.
- This creates flaming orange sunsets.

6.
- Tony got home from the shopping mall.
- He discovered his rented tuxedo did not fit.
- The jacket sleeves covered his hands.
- The pants cuffs hung over his shoes.

7.
- The boys waited for the bus.
- The wind shook the flimsy shelter.
- They shivered with cold.
- They were wearing thin jackets.

8.
- The engine almost caught.
- Then it died.
- I realized no help would come.
- I was on a lonely road.
- It was very late.

9.
- Marian wanted white wall-to-wall carpeting.
- She knew it was a bad buy.
- It would look beautiful.
- It would be very hard to clean.

10.
- Gary was leaving the store.
- The shoplifting alarm went off.
- He had not stolen anything.
- The clerk had forgotten to remove the magnetic tag.
- The tag was on a shirt Gary had bought.

■ Review Test 2

On separate paper, write two sentences of your own that begin with (1) -*ed* words, (2) -*ing* words, (3) -*ly* words, (4) *to* word groups, and (5) prepositional phrases. Also write two sentences of your own that contain (6) a series of adjectives and (7) a series of verbs.

EDITING
TESTS

EDITING AND PROOFREADING
FOR SENTENCE-SKILLS MISTAKES

The five tests in this section will give you practice in editing and proofreading for sentence-skills mistakes. People often find it hard to edit and proofread a paper carefully. They have put so much work into their writing, or so little, that it's almost painful for them to look at the paper one more time. You may simply have to *force* yourself to edit and proofread. Remember that eliminating sentence-skills mistakes will improve an average paper and help ensure a strong grade on a good paper. Further, as you get into the habit of checking your papers, you will also get into the habit of using sentence skills consistently. They are a basic part of clear and effective writing.

■ Editing Test 1

Identify the five mistakes in paper format in the student paper that follows. From the box below, choose the letters that describe the five mistakes and write those letters in the spaces provided.

---

a. The title should not be underlined.

b. The title should not be set off in quotation marks.

c. There should not be a period at the end of the title.

d. All the major words in the title should be capitalized.

e. The title should be just several words and not a complete sentence.

f. The first line of the paper should stand independent of the title.

g. A line should be skipped between the title and the first line of the paper.

h. The first line of the paper should be indented.

i. The right-hand margin should not be crowded.

j. Hyphenation should occur only between syllables.

"my candy apple adventure"

It was the best event of my day. I loved the sweetness that
filled my mouth as I bit into the sugary coating. With my second
bite, I munched contentedly on the apple underneath. Its
crunchy tartness was the perfect balance to the smooth sweet-
ness of the outside. Then the apple had a magical effect on me.
Suddenly I remembered when I was seven years old, walking
through the exhibition grounds, holding my father's hand. We
stopped at a refreshment stand, and he bought us each a candy
apple. I had never had one before, and I asked him what it
was. "This is a very special fruit," he said. "If you ever feel sad,
all you have to do is eat a candy apple, and it will bring you
sweetness." Now, years later, his words came back to me, and
as I ate my candy apple, I felt the world turn sweet once more.

1. _____   2. _____   3. _____   4. _____   5. _____

■ Editing Test 2

Identify the sentence-skills mistakes at the underlined spots in the selection that follows. From the box below, choose the letter that describes each mistake and write it in the space provided. The same mistake may appear more than once.

a. sentence fragment	d. apostrophe mistake
b. run-on	e. faulty parallelism
c. mistake in subject–verb agreement	

Looking Out for Yourself

It's sad but true that "If you don't look out for yourself, no one else will." For example, some people have a false idea about the power of a college <u>diploma, they</u> think

1

that once they <u>possesses</u> the diploma, the world will be waiting on their doorstep. In fact,

2

nobody is likely to be on their doorstep unless, through advance planning, they <u>has</u>

3

prepared themselves for a career. <u>The kind in which good job opportunities exist.</u> Even

4

after a person has landed a job, however, a healthy amount of self-interest is needed.

People who hide in corners or <u>with hesitation</u> to let others know about their skills <u>doesn't</u>

5 6

get promotions or raises. <u>Its</u> important to take credit for a job well done, whether it

7

involves writing a report, <u>kept up with new technology</u>, or calming down an angry

8

customer. Also, people should feel free to ask the boss for a raise. <u>If they work hard and</u>

9

<u>really deserve it.</u> Those who look out for themselves get the <u>rewards, people</u> who

10

depend on others to help them along get left behind.

1. _____   3. _____   5. _____   7. _____   9. _____

2. _____   4. _____   6. _____   8. _____   10. _____

■ Editing Test 3

Identify the sentence-skills mistakes at the underlined spots in the selection that follows. From the box below, choose the letter that describes each mistake and write it in the space provided. The same mistake may appear more than once.

a. sentence fragment	e. missing commas around an interrupter
b. run-on	
c. mistake in verb tense	f. mistake with quotation marks
d. irregular verb mistake	g. apostrophe mistake

Deceptive Appearances

Appearances can be deceptive. While looking through a library window yesterday, I saw a neatly groomed woman walk by. Her clothes were skilfully <u>tailored her</u> make-
1
up was perfect. <u>Then thinking no one was looking she</u> crumpled a piece of paper in her
2
hand. <u>And tossed it into a nearby hedge.</u> Suddenly she no longer <u>looks</u> attractive to me.
3   4
On another occasion, I started talking to a person in my Canadian literature class named Eric. Eric seemed to be a great person. He always got the class laughing with his <u>jokes,</u>
5
<u>on</u> the days when Eric was absent, I think even the professor missed his lively personality.

Eric asked me <u>"if I wanted to get chips in the cafeteria,"</u> and I felt happy he had <u>chose</u>
6   7
me to be a friend. <u>While we were sitting in the cafeteria.</u> Eric took out an envelope with
8
several kinds of pills inside. "Want one?" he asked. "They're uppers." I didn't want <u>one,</u>
9
I felt disappointed. <u>Erics</u> terrific personality was the product of the pills he took.
10

1. _____ 3. _____ 5. _____ 7. _____ 9. _____

2. _____ 4. _____ 6. _____ 8. _____ 10. _____

■ Editing Test 4

Identify the sentence-skills mistakes at the underlined spots in the selection that follows. From the box below, choose the letter that describes each mistake and write it in the space provided. The same mistake may appear more than once.

a. sentence fragment	e. apostrophe mistake
b. run-on	f. dangling modifier
c. irregular verb mistake	g. missing quotation marks
d. missing comma after introductory words	

A Horrifying Moment

The most horrifying moment in my life occurred in the dark hallway. <u>Which led to</u>
1

<u>my apartment house.</u> Though the hallway light was <u>out I</u> managed to find my apartment
2

door. However, I could not find the keyhole with my door key. I then pulled a book of

matches from my pocket. <u>Trying to strike a match,</u> the entire book of matches <u>bursted</u>
3   4

into flames. I flicked the matches away but not before my coat sleeve <u>catched</u> fire. Within
5

seconds, my arm was like a torch. <u>Struggling to unsnap the buttons of my coat,</u> flames
6

began to sear my skin. I was quickly going into shock. <u>And began screaming in pain.</u> A
7

<u>neighbours</u> door opened and a voice cried out, <u>My God!</u> I was pulled through an
8   9

apartment and put under a bathroom shower, which extinguished the flames. I suffered

third degree burns on my <u>arm, I</u> felt lucky to escape with my life.
10

1. _____   3. _____   5. _____   7. _____   9. _____

2. _____   4. _____   6. _____   8. _____   10. _____

■ Editing Test 5

Identify the sentence-skills mistakes at the underlined spots in the selection that follows. From the box below, choose the letter that describes each mistake and write it in the space provided. The same mistake may appear more than once.

a. sentence fragment	e. faulty parallelism
b. run-on	f. apostrophe mistake
c. missing capital letter	g. missing quotation mark
d. mistake in subject–verb agreement	h. missing comma after introductory words

Why I Didn't Go to Church

I almost never attended church in my boyhood years. There was an unwritten code that the guys in Levack <u>was</u> not to be seen in <u>churches'</u>. Although there <u>was</u> many days
                                         1   2   3
when I wanted to attend a church, I felt I had no choice but to stay away. If the guys had heard I had gone to church, they would have said things like, <u>"hey,</u> angel, when are you
                                                                                                                     4
going to <u>fly?</u> With my group of friends, <u>its</u> amazing that I developed any religious feeling
            5   6
at all. Another reason for not going to church was my father. When he was around the house <u>he</u> told my mother, "Mike's not going to church. No boy of mine is a sissy." My
        7
mother and sister went to <u>church, I</u> sat with my father and read the *Sunday Sun* sports
                                   8
pages or <u>watching television.</u> I did not start going to church until years later. <u>When I no
              9   10
longer hung around with the guys in Levack or let my father have power over me.</u>

1. _____   3. _____   5. _____   7. _____   9. _____

2. _____   4. _____   6. _____   8. _____   10. _____

PART FIVE

FIFTEEN
READING
SELECTIONS

PREVIEW

This book assumes that writing and reading are closely connected skills—so that practising one helps the other, and neglecting one hurts the other. Part Five will enable you to work on becoming a better reader as well as a stronger writer. Following an introductory section that offers a series of tips on effective reading, there are fifteen reading selections. Each selection begins with a preview that supplies background information about the piece. After the selection are ten questions to give you practice in key reading comprehension skills. A set of discussion questions is also provided, both to deepen your understanding of the selection and to point out basic writing techniques used in the essay. Then come several writing assignments, along with guidelines to help you think about the assignments and get started working on them.

INTRODUCTION TO
THE READINGS

The reading selections in Part Five will help you find topics for writing. Some of the selections provide helpful practical information. For example, you'll learn how to study more efficiently, how to write a test, and how to go about deciding on a career. Other selections deal with thought-provoking aspects of contemporary life. One article, for instance, deals with lying, and our attitudes toward this too-human failing; another details how one man seemed to successfully handle virtual illiteracy. Still another selection describes the experiences of Canada's only female professional goalie. Today's difficult economic times, and their consequences for you as a student and for other Canadians, are dealt with in two other selections. Human goals and values are explored in pieces as diverse as an essay about one Native Canadian's efforts to preserve his language and culture, and another article in which a young journalist of Chinese background ponders his lack of mathematical ability. The varied subjects and tones should inspire lively class discussions as well as serious individual thought. The selections are mainly current and many are Canadian. They should also provide a continuing source of high-interest material for a wide range of writing assignments.

The selections serve another purpose as well. They will help develop reading skills with direct benefits to you as a writer. First, through close reading, you will learn how to recognize the main idea or point of a selection and how to identify and evaluate the supporting material that develops the main idea. In your writing, you will aim to achieve the same essential structure: an overall point followed by detailed and valid support for that point. Second, close reading will help you explore a selection and its possibilities thoroughly. The more you understand about what is said in a piece, the more ideas and feelings you may have about writing on an assigned topic or a related topic of your own. A third benefit of close reading is becoming more aware of authors' stylistic devices—for example, their introductions and conclusions, their ways of presenting and developing a point, their use of transitions, their choice of language to achieve a particular tone. Recognizing these devices in other people's writing will help you enlarge your own range of writing techniques.

THE FORMAT OF EACH SELECTION

Each selection begins with a short overview that gives helpful background information. The selection is then followed by two sets of questions.

■ First, there are ten reading comprehension questions to help you measure your understanding of the material. These questions involve several important reading skills: recognizing a subject or topic, determining the thesis or main idea, identifying key supporting points, making inferences, and understanding vocabulary in context. Answering the questions will enable you and your instructor to check quickly your basic understanding of a selection. More significantly, as you move from one selection to the next, you will sharpen your reading skills as well as strengthen your thinking skills—two key factors in making you a better writer.

■ Following the comprehension questions are several discussion questions. In addition to dealing with issues of content, these questions focus on matters of structure, style, and tone as well. *Structure* refers to the ways in which the author has given shape to the work; *style* refers to word choice and the technical skills used by the writer; and *tone* is the "feeling" of a piece of work: whether it is serious, light, or comic.

Finally, several writing assignments accompany each selection. Many of the assignments provide guidelines on how to proceed, including suggestions for prewriting and appropriate methods of development. When writing your responses to the readings, you will have opportunities to apply all the methods of development presented in Part Two of this book.

HOW TO READ WELL: FOUR GENERAL STEPS

Skilful reading is an important part of becoming a skilful writer. Following are four steps that will make you a better reader—both of the selections here and in your reading at large.

1   Concentrate as You Read

To improve your concentration, follow these tips. First, read in a place where you can be quiet and alone. Don't choose a spot where a TV or stereo is on or where friends or family are talking nearby. Next, sit in an upright position when you read. If your body is in a completely relaxed position, sprawled across a bed or nestled in an easy chair, your mind is also going to be completely relaxed. The light muscular tension that comes from sitting in an upright chair promotes concentration and keeps your mind ready to work. Finally, consider using your index finger (or a pen) as a pacer while you read. Lightly underline each line of print with your index finger as you read down a page. Hold your hand slightly above the page and move your finger at a speed that is a little too fast for comfort. This pacing with your index finger, like sitting upright on a chair, creates a slight physical tension that will keep your body and mind focused and alert.

2   Skim Material before You Read It

In skimming, you spend about two minutes rapidly surveying a selection, looking for important points and skipping secondary material. Follow this sequence when skimming:

- Begin by reading the overview that precedes the selection.
- Then study the title of the selection for a few moments. A good title is the shortest possible summary of a selection; it often tells you in several words what a selection is about. For example, the title "Shots on Goal" suggests that you're going to read about a time when someone took some chances and tried for some goal.
- Next, form a basic question (or questions) out of the title. For instance, for the selection titled "Shots on Goal," you might ask, "What exactly was the goal?" "What was someone's reason for taking the shots?" "What was the result of taking the shots?" Forming questions out of the title is often a key to locating a writer's main idea—your next concern in skimming.
- Read the first two or three paragraphs and the last two or three paragraphs in the selection. Very often a writer's main idea, *if* it is directly stated, will appear in one of these paragraphs and will relate to the title. For instance, in "Why Should We Hire You?" the author states in the final paragraph that "you need to work hard in order to find the work you desire. That means knowing the reasons you should be hired and taking the steps needed to prepare a solidly based answer before you are asked The Question."
- Finally, look quickly at the rest of the selection for other clues to important points. Are there any subheadings you can relate in some way to the title? Are there any words the author has decided to emphasize by setting them off in *italic* or **boldface** type? Are there any major lists of items signalled by words such as *first*, *second*, *also*, *another*, and so on?

3   Read the Selection Straight Through with a Pen Nearby

Don't slow down or turn back; just aim to understand as much as you can the first time through. Place a check or star beside answers to basic questions you formed

from the title, and beside other ideas that seem important. Number as *1, 2, 3* ...
lists of important points. Circle words you don't understand. Put question marks
in the margin next to passages that are unclear and that you will want to reread.

4   Work with the Material

Go back and reread passages that were not clear the first time through. Look up
words that block your understanding of ideas and write their meanings in the margin. Also, reread carefully the areas you identified as most important; doing so
will enlarge your understanding of the material. Now that you have a sense of the
whole, prepare a short outline of the selection by answering the following questions on a sheet of paper:

- What is the main idea?
- What key points support the main idea?
- What seem to be other important points in the selection?

By working with the material in this way, you will significantly increase your
understanding of a selection. *Effective reading, just like effective writing, does not
happen all at once.* Rather, it is a *process.* Often you begin with a general impression of what something means, and then, by working at it, you move to a deeper
level of understanding of the material.

HOW TO ANSWER THE COMPREHENSION QUESTIONS: SPECIFIC HINTS

Several important reading skills are involved in the ten reading comprehension
questions that follow each selection. The skills are:

- Summarizing the selection by providing a title for it
- Determining the main idea
- Recognizing key supporting details
- Making inferences
- Understanding vocabulary in context

The following hints will help you apply each of these reading skills:

- ***Subject or title.*** Remember that the title should accurately describe the
  entire selection. It should be neither too broad nor too narrow for the material in the selection. It should answer the question "What is this about?" as
  specifically as possible. Note that you may at times find it easier to do the
  "title" question *after* the "main idea" question.

- **_Main idea._** Choose the statement that you think best expresses the main idea or thesis of the entire selection. Remember that the title will often help you focus on the main idea. Then ask yourself the question, "Does most of the material in the selection support this statement?" If you can answer *Yes* to this question, you have found the thesis.

- **_Key details._** If you were asked to give a two-minute summary of a selection, the major details are the ones you would include in that summary. To determine the key details, ask yourself the question, "What are the major supporting points for the thesis?"

- **_Inferences._** Answer these questions by drawing on the evidence presented in the selection and on your own common sense. Ask yourself, "What reasonable judgements can I make on the basis of the information in the selection?"

- **_Vocabulary in context._** To decide on the meaning of an unfamiliar word, consider its context. Ask yourself, "Are there any clues in the sentence that suggest what this word means?"

On pages 558–559 is a chart on which you can keep track of your performance as you answer the ten questions for each selection. The chart will help you identify reading skills you may need to strengthen.

GOALS AND VALUES

Shots on Goal

Brian Preston

Hockey is Canada's gift to the world of sport, and it's a pretty violent gift at that. Fights, injuries, and flying pucks are prerequisites of a decent game, according to many fans. Well, then, what's one of the "delicate nurturing gender" doing in goal? If you're Manon Rhéaume, you're wearing a lot of kilos of equipment, enduring insults and media hype, and using all your grit and technique to take you toward the NHL. Manon plays a position which involves receiving constant physical attacks. In a traditionally male sport, she is the lone female player. The opposition she faces comes not only from the teams firing shots at her, but also from the press and even some of her team-mates. Brian Preston, writing for *Saturday Night* magazine, offers readers a balanced and close-up view of the challenges and pressures Manon Rhéaume faces just trying to stay in the crease.

Lingering after practice, a handful of hockey players amuse themselves by seeing who 1
can putt a puck closest to the centre face-off dot. It's called Instructor Golf, favoured pastime of summer hockey-school teachers. Two more players good-naturedly bellow at each
other. Player A: "F—— you!" Player B: "F—— me!" Ad nauseam. They don't care if
Manon Rhéaume hears. On this team, she's more or less one of the guys.

That's her handling shots from half a dozen team-mates at the far end. It's the day 2
before Rhéaume's debut regular-season start for the Las Vegas Thunder of the International

Hockey League (IHL). The only other feminine presences in this slick 13,000-seat arena are a bare-shouldered blonde pictured in a strip-club advertisement on the boards—this is Vegas, after all—and Tatania Yashin, whose superstar son, Alexei, is playing for the Thunder during the NHL lock-out. Asked what she thinks of a woman playing net, Madame Yashin, translated by her husband, Valery, says, "Women have equal minds, they understand hockey the same as men. But it's necessary for her to be more clever, because men are more strong." Valery Yashin adds, "Our other son plays Double-A Pee Wee in Ottawa. His goalie is named Elizabeth, and she plays not bad." He watches Rhéaume take a high, hard shot off her chest. She shakes it off and sets herself to face the next shooter. "We don't know the finished results of this experiment," Yashin concludes.

Hard data will be available after tomorrow night's game, which the Thunder are hyp- 3
ing as potentially historic: it could be the first win ever by a woman goalie in IHL history. A reporter from Houston, whose Aeros will be Rhéaume's opponents, tells the small
coterie of practice watchers that his team is licking its chops at the thought of facing her.
"Not because she's a woman," he's quick to clarify. "Just because she weighs a hundred
and twenty pounds." He's about to interview her for the first time, and he's having trouble remembering how to pronounce her name. "Ma-none. Ma-no. Ma-NO? Ma-NO!" It's
his momentary mantra. He wonders aloud, "Is it sexist to ask if she has a boyfriend?"
Yes, but he'll ask anyway. After all, she's the first pro goalie to worry about boyfriends.
At least the first who can safely discuss it in public.

Chris McSorley, the Thunder's assistant coach (and brother of NHLer Marty), says 4
Manon Rhéaume is "a phenomenal athlete, the hardest-working player we have on staff,
bar none. She's where she is today because of her work ethic. She's competent enough
to hold the pipes in this league, and I believe in three or four years she'll have a chance
to play a regular-season game in the National Hockey League."

That eventuality would exceed even Manon Rhéaume's expectations. Still on the ice, 5
leaning on the boards by the players' bench, she takes the Houston writer's first question: "Manon, your goal is to play in the NHL—" She interrupts to say, "I've never said
that. I'm realistic. I just said I'll go as far as I can go." Another reporter, a Vegas local,
butts in to ask, "Manon, will you take on Gamble?" The last time Vegas played Houston
there was a huge brawl, and Thunder goalie Clint Malarchuk laid out Houston netmin-
der Troy Gamble with a single punch. Manon laughs easily and responds, "I'll fight him
if I have to." You can't help but like her. She's twenty-two, and even in a second language
knows how to banter with men.

Her team-mates seem to like her too, but whether or not they take her seriously as a 6
goalie is another matter. The Thunder collectively boast 2,500 games' worth of NHL experience: names like Bob Joyce, Jeff Sharples, Marc Habscheid, Andrew McBain, and Jim
Kyte are familiar to serious hockey fans. At the first team practice these men and others
took turns blasting pucks at Rhéaume's head and were surprised when she didn't flinch.
"She's only added to our chemistry," Chris McSorley claims. "The players cut her no slack.
She takes shots to the head, a howitzer every day. She doesn't bitch." In her autobiogra-
phy *Manon: Alone in Front of the Net*, Rhéaume traces her stoicism to "a stinging remark"
her father made once when she cried during a hockey game as a child: "Manon, macramé
isn't painful. Choose!" She learned to "choke back my tears and return to my crease."

No-one doubts her toughness, but whether she deserves, on merit, to be signed to an ⁊
IHL team is another matter. Some team-mates are sincerely enthused, like Jeff Sharples: "She's a pioneer in our sport and I think that's great." But other players have been heard to say privately that they think it's a joke, that she's in over her head in a league whose best teams are on a par with the weaker NHL squads, that she's less a legitimate player than a publicity stunt orchestrated by the team's owner, Ken Stickney. A local reporter recalls Stickney telling him gleefully, "After Gretzky, we've got the most famous hockey player in the world on our team!" The reporter replied, "Have you heard of someone named Mario Lemieux?" But Vegas hockey fans are neophytes, and a telegenic young woman probably does sell more tickets than Lemieux would.

Rhéaume is naturally offended by talk of publicity stunts. In her private dressing room ε
after practice, she tells me, "You know, since I started people have always said it's just for publicity. I don't face hundred-mile-an-hour shots every day and I don't have bruises everywhere on my body to have publicity. I make so many sacrifices because I love the game and I want to get better. And when people still ask and ask this question, it's hard."

The same question gets asked frequently of the Thunder's other two goalies, ⁥
Malarchuk and Pokey Reddick, both former NHL regulars. Reddick refuses to talk about Rhéaume. Their interaction, while not hostile, is minimal. An odd bit of theatre unfolded one morning before practice as Rhéaume, in sweats and a backward baseball cap, ever so slowly made her way towards the arena players' entrance. Reddick, thirty feet behind her and headed the same way, slowed himself to the same pace to avoid catching up to her. It looked like a turtle race. Reddick also refuses to share the net with her during practice. Rhéaume and Malarchuk split duties in the other net, essentially getting a half-share each of practice time.

At thirty-three, Clint Malarchuk has arranged to play out the twilight years of his 1C
career here in Vegas; he negotiated a guaranteed four-year no-trade deal, he bought a ranch nearby and raises horses and emus. His team-mates say he's been a "first-class guy," sharing his time and a career's worth of knowledge with Rhéaume. Malarchuk speaks highly of her. "I think her skill level and her talent are quite exceptional," he says. "But she's small in stature and she's not as strong as a man." I ask if sharing a net with Rhéaume has distracted him from his own game. Last year he led the league in wins, so far this year he's been struggling, giving up close to five goals each outing. "It interrupts the flow having to share and switch," he admits. "You have to be patient. It gets a little upsetting at times because Pokey won't ever let her in his net. It's just me."

"Do you ever bug him that he should?" 11

"Oh yeah. He went along with it for like a week, but the team [management] was- 12
n't exactly honest about it either. We were told she would come out *after* practice, that we wouldn't be affected in any way. That kind of comes into it a little bit."

The next night Clint Malarchuk sits in the stands as the Thunder's third-string goalie skates 13
onto the ice ("Starting in goal, the First Lady of Hockey, Manon Rhéaume!") to the roar of 10,000-plus, the Thunder's largest weeknight crowd ever. Five guys in seats behind the net are wearing customized T-shirts, each with a giant letter on the front: M-A-N-O-N. The press box is a little more cynical. The Houston reporter predicts two periods, maximum.

Just under three minutes into the game the Aeros get a two-on-one break. Rhéaume 14
stays too far back in her net, playing the pass instead of the shooter. A 120-pound goalie
who doesn't come out and challenge leaves a lot of net to shoot at. The Aeros score on
their first shot. The goal rattles her, but eventually she settles down. Her technical skills
equal those of her male counterparts, but her lack of size and strength is obvious. To
someone watching her, it's clear that a woman could play goal in the NHL. But that
woman will be five foot eight, 160 pounds, minimum.

Watching from the stands tonight is Audrey Bakewell, pro hockey's leading power- 15
skating instructor. She taught Clint Malarchuk when he was still a junior; with goalies she
tends to concentrate on balance and agility. "A lot of my ideas are similar to Glenn Hall's
in terms of stance," she says. "I taught Mike Vernon to work on figures and edges, hitting
the point on the blade. With Mike Richter it was things like spinning on the spot and being
able to stop a shot, taking him to the most extreme equilibrium possible and making him
work at that level." Asked how it feels to be female in an overwhelmingly male preserve,
she says the players have always been more accepting of her than the media, but adds the
familiar refrain of any woman trying to crack a male-dominated profession: "In terms of
organization and presentation, I've always had to be better than any man."

Tonight Manon Rhéaume is definitely not performing better than any man. She allows 16
three goals on twelve shots over two periods, and is replaced for the third by Reddick.
After the game the Thunder's head coach, Bob Strumm, presents the media with a baseball analogy as shaky as Rhéaume's performance: she's like a starting pitcher who gives
six innings of solid work, see, then she got pulled so the relief pitcher could come in and
mop up. Yeah, right. Later, by the exit door where the autograph hounds wait for players
to emerge, the five T-shirted guys have been reduced to three. Now they spell M-A-N.

The next day Manon Rhéaume arrives at practice looking sore and dispirited. Asked 17
if she dreamt about the game, she shakes her head. "I was so tired from the pressure,"
she mutters. "I was too exhausted. The pressure ..." Management has decided to send
her down to an easier level for a month or so, to the new Tallahassee franchise in the East
Coast Hockey League, where she'll get more playing time. Last year in that league she
started six games and went 5-0-1.

Pokey Reddick takes his usual tack when asked for his reaction to rumours of 18
Rhéaume's departure: "I answer no questions about Manon," he insists. "I'm just a goalie.
He does all the talking for us," he says, gesturing towards Malarchuk, who's busy with
another interviewer, trying to explain the decline in his play this season. He cites nag-
ging injuries, a four-game suspension for pounding out Gamble, "plus some other things
I can't comment on." The reporter says, "Those other things may be sent to the East Coast
League soon," and the two of them share a smile that says they feel guilty for even thinking it, but it's true.

■ Reading Comprehension Questions

1. Which of the following would be the best alternative title for the selection?
   a. Manon Muscles In
   b. Lightweight Fighter

   c. Choices, Sacrifices, and Bruises
   d. Girls Just Want to Play Goal

2. Which sentence best expresses the main idea of the selection?
   a. Manon Rhéaume would be back in the IHL, or in the NHL, if she'd only gain forty pounds.
   b. Manon fights hard in an all-male sport, but competing for goal time and lack of size work against her.
   c. Manon is a decent minor-league goalie, but she lacks the technique and aggressive edge to play in the NHL.
   d. Manon Rhéaume's skill is impressive, but her main selling-point is the media interest in the novelty of a female goalie.

3. What common idea do Tatania Yashin and Audrey Bakewell hold about women operating in traditionally male fields?
   a. Women can compete equally if they are physically large enough and strong enough.
   b. Women have to be able to beat men at every aspect of a given area of competition in a field.
   c. Women may eventually succeed in pro hockey and other male fields of activity, but only time will tell.
   d. Women must use and develop more intelligence, skill, and professionalism than their male counterparts in most areas of gender competition.

4. *True or false?* _____ Manon believes that she can achieve regular-season NHL status.

5. The other players on the Las Vegas Thunder team
   a. have opinions about Manon ranging from admiration to open hostility.
   b. all think Manon is tough, a great goalie, and "one of the guys."
   c. all know that she is in goal more for publicity than for any other reason.
   d. feel she causes nothing but dissension and problems for the team.

6. According to the author,
   a. Manon's abilities are motivated primarily by vengeful feelings for her father.
   b. Manon is determined and well-respected, but may never play against the top NHL teams.
   c. Manon's main problem may be the exhaustion she suffers from the number of shots she takes.
   d. team politics will prevent Manon's career from advancing much beyond very minor leagues.

7. The author implies that
   a. Thunder's management are eager to promote Manon as a player.
   b. Team owners see their woman goalie as equivalent to a "supermodel."

    c.   Thunder management are less than honest about their handling of Manon.

    d.   Team managers prefer Clint Malarchuk and Pokey Reddick in goal.

8. *True or false?* _____ In general, hockey players are less sexist in their view of women in the sport than are the media.

9. The word *mantra* in "It's his momentary mantra" (paragraph 3) means

    a.   prayer.

    b.   chant.

    c.   joke.

    d.   phrase.

10. The word *stoicism* in "Rhéaume traces her stoicism to 'a stinging remark' her father made once when she cried during a hockey game as a child" (paragraph 6) means

    a.   endurance.

    b.   meanness.

    c.   athletic ability.

    d.   technique.

■ Discussion Questions

About Content

1. Who are the three "feminine presences[s]" in the Las Vegas arena in the opening of the article? What might each figure represent? Why?

2. Why is the reporter from Houston "licking his chops" at the idea of the Aeros playing the Thunder? Is his response an honest one? Why or why not? Where else in the selection do you find his opinion repeated?

3. Chris McSorley has his reasons for admiring Manon. What are they? Why does her response to the Las Vegas reporter in paragraph 5 get a positive response from the author?

4. According to the author's observations of Manon's performance in goal, what are her current deficiencies as a player?

About Structure

5. Preston uses which method, or combination of methods, in his opening paragraph?

    a.   Broad-to-narrow

    b.   Explaining the importance of the topic

    c.   Anecdote

    d.   Situation that is the opposite of the one to be developed

6. How many paragraphs do you read before the author allows Manon Rhéaume to speak directly? How many reported opinions have you read prior to reading her own voice in print? What is the effect of reading others' thoughts first?

7. "Shots on Goal" is written partly in chronological order—that is, in the time sequence in which the events occurred. Find, in the first sentences of paragraphs, at least three "time marker" transition phrases.

Paragraph _____   Time marker phrase: _____

Paragraph _____   Time marker phrase: _____

Paragraph _____   Time marker phrase: _____

Where in the essay do you find these paragraphs? What is the effect of the author's use of such ordering at this point in his essay?

About Style and Tone

8. Much of Preston's article is made up of dialogue, of quotations from other sources. What does reading all these different viewpoints contribute to your perception of the possible "fairness" of Preston's look at Manon Rhéaume? Where do you find examples of Preston's own attitude toward his subject?

■ Writing Assignments

Assignment 1: Writing a Paragraph

A writing assignment based on this selection appears on pages 205–206.

Assignment 2: Writing a Paragraph

Manon Rhéaume faces challenges and criticism from her team-mates, opposing teams, the media, and undoubtedly from within herself. How do you feel about what she is trying to do?

Write a paragraph in the form of a letter in which you state your feelings about what she is doing and offer her advice or encouragement. Explain each of your points clearly, whether your details are of a personal or professional/sports-based type.

Assignment 3: Writing an Essay

Manon is a forerunner in a male-dominated field. More women enter Law Enforcement and Fire Protection programs every year, as well. There are other women, some of whom Nancy Eng mentions in her essay, such as the astronaut Sally Ride and several Canadian women politicians, who have moved into "men's work." There are also men who work at "female jobs" like nursing, and more men who enter Early Childhood Education programs at colleges.

Choose an example of a cross-over career choice for a man or a woman. What qualities would be needed by any person who entered this career? Are these qualities limited to one gender or the other? List the qualities and aptitudes before beginning to draft your essay, and break them into three categories or classifications. Review the section titled "Dividing and Classifying" in Part Two (pages 172–179) for help in this part of your prewriting.

An example of an outline for such an essay might look like this:

Thesis Statement: More men should go into Early Childhood Education, because they have three qualities which are not exclusive to women: patience, helping instincts, and stamina for dealing with young children. They would give children good male role models.

Paragraph 1: patience—no gender difference
– I helped my father raise my sisters—anyone can learn patience/e.g.
– men can be more patient as "coaches" in some skills/e.g.
– men's work often involves very painstaking, patient attention/e.g.

Paragraph 2: helping instincts—no real difference, just habit
– men already in "helping" careers: emergency-care work, etc.
– single fathers I met at school events/e.g.
– same instincts there in men, just "underdeveloped"/e.g.

Paragraph 3: stamina—men & women the same—depends on individual
– men are used to how annoying three-year-old boys are
– enduring kids is no different than enduring your team-mates
– men *may* be better at certain physical demands of ECE/e.g.

Conclusion: Children need to see positive male role models, and men have many of the same qualities necessary for working with young children as women have. They just haven't realized their potential, or how useful these abilities can be.

What to Do with a Severance

David Estok

The 1990s are difficult economic times for many Canadians. Whether you are a student preparing to enter the workplace for the first time, or someone engaged in postsecondary education after early unsatisfying work experiences, David

Estok's article offers useful financial and career information. Tony Caradonna's experience is an unfortunate, if increasingly common, one in this era of cutbacks and lay-offs, but this selection gives solid clear advice about dealing with unexpected career changes. Compare the factual content and examples in Estok's article with Jim Maloney's advice to students in "Why Should We Hire You?" Preparation is the key to economic survival in the 1990s.

Tony Caradonna never took financial planning seriously until he was unemployed. Last 1
fall, the 40-year-old resident of Markham, Ont., lost his job as a senior product manager with Canadian Home Products, a food manufacturer. Although he received a severance payment equal to six months' salary, Caradonna, for the first time in almost a decade, faced a mortgage, loans and other family obligations without a steady paycheque. "The first thing I did was go on an austerity program," he says. "I didn't buy anything that I absolutely did not need." His next step was to put together a financial plan. "If you're unemployed and you don't have a financial planner, get one fast," he says. "You need someone you can trust."

Caradonna's situation is an increasingly common one in the turbulent 1990s. 2
According to Statistics Canada, 75,000 people have lost jobs in the manufacturing sector alone since 1988. Large-scale lay-offs have hit even many successful companies such as Bell Canada, which plans to shed 10,000 workers by 1997. Governments, too, are slashing payrolls: Ottawa is in the process of eliminating 45,000 jobs and, in Ontario, Premier Mike Harris's Conservative government has pledged to cut 12,000 jobs.

Dick Cappon, a career management consultant and president of Toronto-based 3
Cappon Associates, has been working with laid-off people for the past two decades. He says the most important thing a person in that predicament can do is to develop a monthly budget and a statement of net worth. "Most people don't take time out of their lives to do some real planning," he says. "They just assume everything will continue and that the severance is a bit of a windfall." Cappon advises clients to review their credit card bills, bank statements and other records, carefully tracking down where the money goes. "If you're honest with yourself there will be some obvious areas where you can cut back." He also suggests reviewing how much is spent each month on restaurant meals, casual clothing and automobile use. Eliminating or reducing some of those expenses can have a dramatic impact. As for finding a new job, his advice is to hope for the best but be prepared for the worst: it may take a lot longer than first thought.

Scott Snelgrove, an accountant in London, Ont., who also works with the newly 4
unemployed, says it is important to decide whether to take a severance payment as a lump sum or to ask for salary continuance. In many cases, he says, a lump sum offers more flexibility. Even though severance payments are classified as taxable income, Revenue Canada allows terminated employees to deposit a tax-free "retiring allowance"—$2,000 a year for every year or partial year of employment up to 1995—into a registered retirement savings plan. And people who were not members of company pension plans can shelter an additional $1,500 for each year of service before 1989. At the same time,

Snelgrove often encourages clients to ask their former employers if the lump sum can be paid in several instalments or in different years to defer any tax owing.

Caradonna had a special problem. At the time of his dismissal, he was holding stock options in the company that had to be exercised within 90 days. He needed cash, but his financial adviser, Patrick Lumbers, told him to postpone selling the shares until 1996— a decision that saved him $6,000 in taxes. "If Tony had sold before year-end, all the money would count as income. This way it was deferred to the next year," says Lumbers, who knows of 30 clients who have lost their jobs this year at York University in Toronto, the Ontario government and companies such as Via Rail and Bell Canada.

Today, nine months after losing his job, Caradonna is working again, having lined up a six-month marketing contract. He did make one significant purchase after landing that job: a new bike for his six-year-old son. But after his brush with unemployment, he plans to be a lot more careful in the future about managing his money.

■ Reading Comprehension Questions

1. Which of the following would be the best alternative title for this selection?
   a. Financial Formulas for the 1990s
   b. Sensible Strategies for a Severance Situation
   c. Severance Success Story
   d. Planning to Survive

2. Which sentence best expresses the article's main point?
   a. Temporary unemployment is a fact of life in the 1990s.
   b. Adequate financial and tax planning can help anyone survive a lay-off.
   c. Careful money and career planning are necessities in this decade.
   d. Public and private sector job cuts have only begun, and may increase.

3. After losing his job, Tony Caradonna
   a. budgeted his money carefully and sought strategic financial help.
   b. could barely handle his debt load, mortgage, and other obligations.
   c. decided to learn about financial planning.
   d. was short of cash.

4. Strategies for those out of work, according to Dick Cappon, include
   a. cutting off the use of credit cards and cutting out restaurant meals.
   b. monthly budgets, net worth statements, and preparing for longer job searches.
   c. spending their free time going over their bills.
   d. taking advantage of their severance money to enjoy themselves.

5. *True or false?* _____ One expert says that salary continuances are preferable to lump sum severance payments.

6. The article implies that
   a. there is no hope for steady work in this decade.

    b. jobs are still out there, but they take longer to get, and may be only short-term.

    c. the Canadian economy is drying up, and government debt loads are enormous.

    d. even executives' jobs are not safe these days.

7. We can conclude from Estok's article that
    a. Revenue Canada wants its share of our money, including severance.
    b. tax policies on severance are inflexible; employers must help people.
    c. employers and the government offer some tax-sheltering possibilities.
    d. only experts can spot possible tax breaks on severance pay.

8. The author, and the statistics and authorities he cites, allow us to infer that
    a. dealing with job termination and financial strategies has become an industry on its own.
    b. adequate preparation for uncertain employment can make a lay-off almost enjoyable.
    c. no one, even professors or heads of corporations, may ever hold a long-term job again.
    d. everyone should be employing a full-time financial planner.

9. The word *turbulent* in "Caradonna's situation is an increasingly common one in the turbulent 1990s" (paragraph 2) means
    a. frightening.
    b. unsettled, changeable.
    c. fast-moving.
    d. recessionary.

10. The phrase *net worth* in "the most important thing a person in that predicament can do is to develop a monthly budget and a statement of net worth" (paragraph 3) means
    a. self-esteem.
    b. value of all goods and property owned.
    c. sum remaining after all debts are paid.
    d. total of private and business assets.

■ Discussion Questions

About Content

1. How many people have lost manufacturing jobs in the last nine years, according to Statistics Canada? How do federal job cutbacks compare with those planned by the Province of Ontario? What do such numbers mean to you as a student who will be entering the job market?

2. What does Dick Cappon's career suggest about the length of time over which the current job situation has been developing? Why do you think that these

lay-offs and cutbacks are occurring in private industry? Why are they happening in the public sector?

3. What reasons does Scott Snelgrove give for the desirability of lump sum severance payments? If you suddenly found yourself laid off, would you find these reasons applicable to your life? Why?

4. What is Tony Caradonna's current job situation? What trend in today's job market is indicated by this position? How would you deal with this type of position, if it were offered to you?

About Structure

5. What is the thesis of this selection? Write here the number of the paragraph in which it is stated: _____

6. What method of introduction does Estok use to begin his article?
    a. Broad-to-narrow
    b. Explaining the importance of the topic
    c. Anecdote
    d. Situation opposite to the one to be developed

7. What technique does the author use to create unity in the opening and closing paragraphs of his article? What similar phrases appear in the first and final sentences? How does this technique reinforce the content of the selection?

About Style and Tone

8. Three sections of direct dialogue from sources other than Tony Caradonna form a significant portion of this article. Cite the sources and the paragraphs in which these pieces of direct speech are found.

    _____ (paragraph _____)

    _____ (paragraph _____)

    _____ (paragraph _____)

    Do these inclusions add to the credibility, or the appearance of objectivity, of the article? Why?

9. In what type of publication would you be likely to find this selection?
    a. a college economics textbook
    b. a general-interest news magazine
    c. a financial publication
    d. a human resources textbook

    Why would you expect the article to be in the type of publication you selected?

■ Writing Assignments

Assignment 1: Writing a Paragraph

Everyone, these days, knows someone who has lost a job. Write a paragraph in the form of a letter in which you offer three pieces of advice to such a person. The individual may be a real person with whose situation you are familiar, or may be an imagined correspondent. The details you include will depend on your choice.

Begin your letter by reviewing briefly the situation involved, then follow the format used for process writing. Use transitions such as *first*, *next*, *then*, and *finally*. Think of the advice you offer as "steps" in helping the person to whom you are writing. Look at Estok's article and also at Jim Maloney's essay "Why Should We Hire You?" as possible sources of information for your paragraph.

Assignment 2: Writing a Paragraph

You have a part-time job which you have always performed very well. Your manager has often complimented you; customers return to you, and you manage assigned tasks efficiently. One Saturday morning, you find the following memo attached to your time-card:

TO

FROM *MULTITRONICS* Head Office

We have valued your service as an employee over the past three years, and your records indicate superior performance. Your product knowledge and interpersonal skills should make you an asset to any future employer.

At this time, *MULTITRONICS* is downsizing its staff requirements, and installing electronic stock-management and shipping facilities which will enable us to realize significant savings in operating costs on a national basis.

Your employment is terminated at the end of the next two-week pay period. Your manager may be happy to provide a letter of recommendation.

Write a paragraph which will be the body of a memo to your manager in response to this notice of termination. In the prewriting stage of your paragraph, isolate three reasons, with specific supporting details, why you should be allowed to retain your job. The head office has offered you their version of the *causes* for your being laid off; now, respond with what you believe to be valid *reasons* why you should continue to work for your company. Do you have technical training of which your manager is unaware? Have you received any awards as an employee? Conclude with what you believe to be your strongest point.

Assignment 3: Writing an Essay

Dick Cappon states in this selection, "Most people don't take time out of their lives to do some real planning" (paragraph 3). Although he is talking about financial planning, the same could be said of career planning; as we enter the twenty-first century, careers are changeable things, and we must all prepare for careers and for career changes.

What are your plans for your own career at this stage in your life and education? Write an essay in which you explain your hopes and areas of preparation for your future. As you prepare the outline for your essay, set down in one sentence your clearest vision of your goal, and your feelings about that goal. Now, use one of the prewriting techniques in the second chapter to discover *why* you have this goal, and *what* specifically you are doing to prepare yourself to achieve it. Use definite and clear examples to support your points. Having read Estok's article, and perhaps Jim Maloney's essay, you may also want to consider what "allied careers" your training or education may prepare you for, and how such training may ease you through possible career shifts.

What Good Families
Are Doing Right

Dolores Curran

It isn't easy to be a successful parent these days. Pressured by the conflicting demands of home and workplace, confused by changing moral standards, and drowned out by their offspring's rock music and television, today's parents seem to be facing impossible odds in their struggle to raise healthy families. Yet some parents manage to "do it all"—and even remain on speaking terms with their children. How do they do it? Dolores Curran's survey offers some significant suggestions; her article could serve as a recipe for a successful family.

I have worked with families for fifteen years, conducting hundreds of seminars, work- 1
shops, and classes on parenting, and I meet good families all the time. They're fairly easy to recognize. Good families have a kind of visible strength. They expect problems and

work together to find solutions, applying common sense and trying new methods to meet new needs. And they share a common shortcoming—they can tell me in a minute what's wrong with them, but they aren't sure what's right with them. Many healthy families with whom I work, in fact, protest at being called *healthy*. They don't think they are. The professionals who work with them do.

To prepare the book on which this article is based, I asked respected workers in the 2 fields of education, religion, health, family counseling,* and voluntary organizations to identify a list of possible traits of a healthy family. Together we isolated fifty-six such traits, and I sent this list to five hundred professionals who regularly work with families— teachers, doctors, principals, members of the clergy, scout directors, YMCA leaders, family counselors, social workers—asking them to pick the fifteen qualities they most commonly found in healthy families.

While all of these traits are important, the one most often cited as central to close 3 family life is communication: The healthy family knows how to talk—and how to listen.

"Without communication you don't know one another," wrote one family counselor. 4 "If you don't know one another, you don't care about one another, and that's what the family is all about."

"The most familiar complaint I hear from wives I counsel is 'He won't talk to me' 5 and 'He doesn't listen to me,'" said a pastoral marriage counselor. "And when I share this complaint with their husbands, they don't hear *me*, either."

"We have kids in classes whose families are so robotized by television that they don't 6 know one another," said a fifth-grade teacher.

Professional counselors are not the only ones to recognize the need. The phenome- 7 nal growth of communication groups such as Parent Effectiveness Training, Parent Awareness, Marriage Encounter, Couple Communication, and literally hundreds of others tells us that the need for effective communication—the sharing of deepest feelings— is felt by many.

Healthy families have also recognized this need, and they have, either instinctively 8 or consciously, developed methods of meeting it. They know that conflicts are to be expected, that we all become angry and frustrated and discouraged. And they know how to reveal those feelings—good and bad—to each other. Honest communication isn't always easy. But when it's working well, there are certain recognizable signs or symptoms, what I call the hallmarks of the successfully communicating family.

The Family Exhibits a Strong Relationship between the Parents

According to Dr. Jerry M. Lewis—author of a significant work on families, *No Single* 9 *Thread*—healthy spouses complement, rather than dominate, each other. Either husband or wife could be the leader, depending on the circumstances. In the unhealthy families he studied, the dominant spouse had to hide feelings of weakness while the submissive spouse feared being put down if he or she exposed a weakness.

---

* American spellings (such as "counseling") appear in this article and others in this book which have been reprinted from U.S. sources, or from Canadian sources which use U.S. spellings.

Children in the healthy family have no question about which parent is boss. Both par- 10
ents are. If children are asked who is boss, they're likely to respond, "Sometimes Mom, sometimes Dad." And, in a wonderful statement, Dr. Lewis adds, "if you ask if they're comfortable
with this, they look at you as if you're crazy—as if there's no other way it ought to be."

My survey respondents echo Dr. Lewis. One wrote, "The healthiest families I know 11
are ones in which the mother and father have a strong, loving relationship. This seems
to flow over to the children and even beyond the home. It seems to breed security in the
children and, in turn, fosters the ability to take risks, to reach out to others, to search for
their own answers, become independent and develop a good self-image."

The Family Has Control over Television

Television has been maligned, praised, damned, cherished, and even thrown out. It has 12
more influence on children's values than anything else except their parents. Over and
over, when I'm invited to help families mend their communication ruptures, I hear "But
we have no time for this." These families have literally turned their "family-together"
time over to television. Even those who control the quality of programs watched and set
"homework-first" regulations feel reluctant to intrude upon the individual's right to spend
his or her spare time in front of the set. Many families avoid clashes over program selection by furnishing a set for each family member. One of the women who was most des-
perate to establish a better sense of communication in her family confided to me that they
owned nine sets. Nine sets for seven people!

Whether the breakdown in family communication leads to excessive viewing or 13
whether too much television breaks into family lives, we don't know. But we do know
that we can become out of one another's reach when we're in front of a TV set. The term
television widow is not humorous to thousands whose spouses are absent even when
they're there. One woman remarked, "I can't get worried about whether there's life after
death. I'd be satisfied with life after dinner."

In family-communication workshops, I ask families to make a list of phrases they 14
most commonly hear in their home. One parent was aghast to discover that his family's
most familiar comments were "What's on?" and "Move." In families like this one, communication isn't hostile—it's just missing.

But television doesn't have to be a villain. A 1980 Gallup Poll found that the pub- 15
lic sees great potential for television as a positive force. It can be a tremendous device
for initiating discussion on subjects that may not come up elsewhere, subjects such as
sexuality, corporate ethics, sportsmanship, and marital fidelity.

Even very bad programs offer material for values clarification if family members 16
view them together. My sixteen-year-old son and his father recently watched a program
in which hazardous driving was part of the hero's characterization. At one point, my son
turned to his dad and asked, "Is that possible to do with that kind of truck?"

"I don't know," replied my husband, "but it sure is dumb. If that load shifted ..." With 17
that, they launched into a discussion on the responsibility of drivers that didn't have to
originate as a parental lecture. Furthermore, as the discussion became more engrossing
to them, they turned the sound down so that they could continue their conversation.

Parents frequently report similar experiences; in fact, this use of television was rec- 18
ommended in the widely publicized 1972 Surgeon General's report as the most effective
form of television gatekeeping by parents. Instead of turning off the set, parents should
view programs with their children and make moral judgments and initiate discussion.
Talking about the problems and attitudes of a TV family can be a lively, nonthreatening
way to risk sharing real fears, hopes, and dreams.

The Family Listens and Responds

"My parents say they want me to come to them with problems, but when I do, either 19
they're busy or they only half-listen and keep on doing what they were doing—like shaving or making a grocery list. If a friend of theirs came over to talk, they'd stop, be polite,
and listen," said one of the children quoted in a *Christian Science Monitor* interview by
Ann McCarroll. This child put his finger on the most difficult problem of communicating in families: the inability to listen.

It is usually easier to react than to respond. When we react, we reflect our own experi- 20
ences and feelings; when we respond, we get into the other person's feelings. For example:

> *Tom, age seventeen:* "I don't know if I want to go to college. I don't think I'd do very
> well there."
> *Father:* "Nonsense. Of course you'll do well."

That's reacting. This father is cutting off communication. He's refusing either to hear 21
the boy's fears or to consider his feelings, possibly because he can't accept the idea that
his son might not attend college. Here's another way of handling the same situation:

> *Tom:* "I don't know if I want to go to college. I don't think I'd do very well there."
> *Father:* "Why not?"
> *Tom:* "Because I'm not that smart."
> *Father:* "Yeah, that's scary. I worried about that, too."
> *Tom:* "Did you ever come close to flunking out?"
> *Father:* "No, but I worried a lot before I went because I thought college would be full of brains.
> Once I got there, I found out that most of the kids were just like me."

This father has responded rather than reacted to his son's fears. First, he searched 22
for the reason behind his son's lack of confidence and found it was fear of academic ability (it could have been fear of leaving home, of a new environment, of peer pressure, or
of any of a number of things); second, he accepted the fear as legitimate; third, he
empathized by admitting to having the same fear when he was Tom's age; and, finally,
he explained why his, not Tom's, fears turned out to be groundless. He did all this without denigrating or lecturing.

And that's tough for parents to do. Often we don't want to hear our children's fears, 23
because those fears frighten us; or we don't want to pay attention to their dreams because
their dreams aren't what we have in mind for them. Parents who deny such feelings will
allow only surface conversation. It's fine as long as a child says, "School was okay today,"

but when she says, "I'm scared of boys," the parents are uncomfortable. They don't want her to be afraid of boys, but since they don't quite know what to say, they react with a pleasant "Oh, you'll outgrow it." She probably will, but what she needs at the moment is someone to hear and understand her pain.

In Ann McCarroll's interviews, she talked to one fifteen-year-old boy who said he 24 had "*some* mother. Each morning she sits with me while I eat breakfast. We talk about anything and everything. She isn't refined or elegant or educated. She's a terrible house-keeper. But she's interested in everything I do, and she always listens to me—even if she's busy or tired."

That's the kind of listening found in families that experience real communication. 25 Answers to the routine question, "How was your day?" are heard with the eyes and heart as well as the ears. Nuances are picked up and questions are asked, although problems are not necessarily solved. Members of a family who really listen to one another instinc-tively know that if people listen to you, they are interested in you. And that's enough for most of us.

The Family Recognizes Unspoken Messages

Much of our communication—especially our communication of feelings—is nonverbal. 26 Dr. Lewis defines *empathy* as "someone responding to you in such a way that you feel deeply understood." He says, "There is probably no more important dimension in all of human relationships than the capacity for empathy. And healthy families teach empathy." Its members are allowed to be mad, glad, and sad. There's no crime in being in a bad mood, nor is there betrayal in being happy while someone else is feeling moody. The fam-ily recognizes that bad days and good days attack everyone at different times.

Nonverbal expressions of love, too, are the best way to show children that parents 27 love each other. A spouse reaching for the other's hand, a wink, a squeeze on the shoul-der, a "How's-your-back-this-morning?" a meaningful glance across the room—all these tell children how their parents feel about each other.

The most destructive nonverbal communication in marriage is silence. Silence can 28 mean lack of interest, hostility, denigration, boredom, or outright war. On the part of a teen or preteen, silence usually indicates pain, sometimes very deep pain. The sad irony discovered by so many family therapists is that parents who seek professional help when a teenager becomes silent have often denied the child any other way of communicating. And although they won't permit their children to become angry or to reveal doubts or to share depression, they do worry about the withdrawal that results. Rarely do they see any connection between the two.

Healthy families use signs, symbols, body language, smiles, and other gestures to 29 express caring and love. They deal with silence and withdrawal in a positive, open way. Communication doesn't mean just talking or listening; it includes all the clues to a per-son's feelings—his bearing, her expression, their resignation. Family members don't have to say, "I'm hurting," or, "I'm in need." A quick glance tells that. And they have devel-oped ways of responding that indicate caring and love, whether or not there's an imme-diate solution to the pain.

The Family Encourages Individual Feelings and Independent Thinking

Close families encourage the emergence of individual personalities through open sharing of thoughts and feelings. Unhealthy families tend to be less open, less accepting of
differences among members. The family must be Republican, or Bronco supporters, or
gun-control advocates, and woe to the individual who says, "Yes, but...."

Instead of finding differing opinions threatening, the healthy family finds them exhil-
arating. It is exciting to witness such a family discussing politics, sports, or the world.
Members freely say, "I don't agree with you," without risking ridicule or rebuke. They
say, "I think it's wrong ..." immediately after Dad says, "I think it's right ..."; and Dad
listens and responds.

Give-and-take gives children practice in articulating their thoughts at home so that
eventually they'll feel confident outside the home. What may seem to be verbal rambling
by preteens during a family conversation is a prelude to sorting out their thinking and
putting words to their thoughts.

Rigid families don't understand the dynamics of give-and-take. Some label it disre-
spectful and argumentative; others find it confusing. Dr. John Meeks, medical director
of the Psychiatric Institute of Montgomery County, Maryland, claims that argument is a
way of life with normally developing adolescents. "In early adolescence they'll argue
with parents about anything at all; as they grow older, the quantity of argument decreases
but the quality increases." According to Dr. Meeks, arguing is something adolescents need
to do. If the argument doesn't become too bitter, they have a good chance to test their
own beliefs and feelings. "Incidentally," says Meeks, "parents can expect to 'lose' most
of these arguments, because adolescents are not fettered by logic or even reality." Nor
are they likely to be polite. Learning how to disagree respectfully is a difficult task, but
good families work at it.

Encouraging individual feelings and thoughts, of course, in no way presumes that
parents permit their children to do whatever they want. There's a great difference
between permitting a son to express an opinion on marijuana and allowing him to use it.
That his opinion conflicts with his parents' opinion is OK as long as his parents make
sure he knows their thinking on the subject. Whether he admits it or not, he's likely at
least to consider their ideas if he respects them.

Permitting teenagers to sort out their feelings and thoughts in open discussions at
home gives them valuable experience in dealing with a bewildering array of situations
they may encounter when they leave home. Cutting off discussion of behavior unacceptable to us, on the other hand, makes our young people feel guilty for even thinking
about values contrary to ours and ends up making those values more attractive to them.

The Family Recognizes Turn-Off Words and Put-Down Phrases

Some families deliberately use hurtful language in their daily communication. "What did
you do all day around here?" can be a red flag to a woman who has spent her day on
household tasks that don't show unless they're not done. "If only we had enough money"
can be a rebuke to a husband who is working as hard as he can to provide for the fam-

ily. "Flunk any tests today, John?" only discourages a child who may be having trouble in school.

Close families seem to recognize that a comment made in jest can be insulting. A 37 father in one of my groups confided that he could tease his wife about everything but her skiing. "I don't know why she's so sensitive about that, but I back off on it. I can say anything I want to about her cooking, her appearance, her mothering—whatever. But not her skiing."

One of my favorite exercises with families is to ask them to reflect upon phrases they 38 most like to hear and those they least like to hear. Recently, I invited seventy-five fourth- and fifth-graders to submit the words they most like to hear from their mothers. Here are the five big winners:

> *"I love you."*
> *"Yes."*
> *"Time to eat."*
> *"You can go."*
> *"You can stay up late."*

And on the children's list of what they least like to hear from one another are the 39 following:

> *"I'm telling."*
> *"Mom says!"*
> *"I know something you don't know."*
> *"You think you're so big."*
> *"Just see if I ever let you use my bike again."*

It can be worthwhile for a family to list the phrases members like most and least to 40 hear, and post them. Often parents aren't even aware of the reaction of their children to certain routine comments. Or keep a record of the comments heard most often over a period of a week or two. It can provide good clues to the level of family sensitivity. If the list has a lot of "shut ups" and "stop its," that family needs to pay more attention to its relationships, especially the role that communication plays in them.

The Family Interrupts, but Equally

When Dr. Jerry M. Lewis began to study the healthy family, he and his staff videotaped 41 families in the process of problem solving. The family was given a question, such as, "What's the main thing wrong with your family?" Answers varied, but what was most significant was what the family actually did: who took control, how individuals responded or reacted, what were the put-downs, and whether some members were entitled to speak more than others.

The researchers found that healthy families expected everyone to speak openly about 42 feelings. Nobody was urged to hold back. In addition, these family members interrupted one another repeatedly, but no one person was interrupted more than anyone else.

Manners, particularly polite conversational techniques, are not hallmarks of the com-   4
municating family. This should make many parents feel better about their family's dinner conversation. One father reported to me that at their table people had to take a number
to finish a sentence. Finishing sentences, however, doesn't seem all that important in the
communicating family. Members aren't sensitive to being interrupted, either. The inten-
sity and spontaneity of the exchange are more important than propriety in conversation.

The Family Develops a Pattern of Reconciliation

"We know how to break up," one man said, "but who ever teaches us to make up?" Survey   4
respondents indicated that there is indeed a pattern of reconciliation in healthy families
that is missing in others. "It usually isn't a kiss-and-make-up situation," explained one
family therapist, "but there are certain rituals developed over a long period of time that
indicate it's time to get well again. Between husband and wife, it might be a conces-
sionary phrase to which the other is expected to respond in kind. Within a family, it might
be that the person who stomps off to his or her room voluntarily reenters the family circle, where something is said to make him or her welcome."

When I asked several families how they knew a fight had ended, I got remarkably   4
similar answers from individuals questioned separately. "We all come out of our rooms,"
responded every member of one family. Three members of another family said, "Mom
says, 'Anybody want a Pepsi?'" One five-year-old scratched his head and furrowed his
forehead after I asked him how he knew the family fight was over. Finally, he said, "Well,
Daddy gives a great big yawn and says, 'Well …'" This scene is easy to visualize, as one
parent decides that the unpleasantness needs to end and it's time to end the fighting and
to pull together again as a family.

Why have we neglected the important art of reconciling? "Because we have pre-   4
tended that good families don't fight," says one therapist. "They do. It's essential to fight
for good health in the family. It gets things out into the open. But we need to learn to put
ourselves back together—and many families never learn this."

Close families know how to time divisive and emotional issues that may cause fric-   4
tion. They don't bring up potentially explosive subjects right before they go out, for
example, or before bedtime. They tend to schedule discussions rather than allow a matter to explode, and thus they keep a large measure of control over the atmosphere in which
they will fight and reconcile. Good families know that they need enough time to discuss
issues heatedly, rationally, and completely—and enough time to reconcile. "You've got
to solve it right there," said one father. "Don't let it go on and on. It just causes more problems. Then when it's solved, let it be. No nagging, no remembering."

The Family Fosters Table Time and Conversation

Traditionally, the dinner table has been a symbol of socialization. It's probably the one   4
time each day that parents and children are assured of uninterrupted time with one another.

Therapists frequently call upon a patient's memory of the family table during child-   4
hood in order to determine the degree of communication and interaction there was in the

patient's early life. Some patients recall nothing. Mealtime was either so unpleasant or so unimpressive that they have blocked it out of their memories. Therapists say that there is a relationship between the love in a home and life around the family table. It is to the table that love or discord eventually comes.

But we are spending less table time together. Fast-food dining, even within the home, 50 is becoming a way of life for too many of us. Work schedules, individual organized activities, and television all limit the quantity and quality of mealtime interaction. In an informal study conducted by a church group, 68 percent of the families interviewed in three congregations saw nothing wrong with watching television while eating.

Families who do a good job of communicating tend to make the dinner meal an 51 important part of their day. A number of respondents indicated that adults in the healthiest families refuse dinner business meetings as a matter of principle and discourage their children from sports activities that cut into mealtime hours. "We know which of our swimmers will or won't practice at dinnertime," said a coach, with mixed admiration. "Some parents never allow their children to miss dinners. Some don't care at all." These families pay close attention to the number of times they'll be able to be together in a week, and they rearrange schedules to be sure of spending this time together.

The family that wants to improve communication should look closely at its attitudes 52 toward the family table. Are family table time and conversation important? Is table time open and friendly or warlike and sullen? Is it conducive to sharing more than food—does it encourage the sharing of ideas, feelings, and family intimacies?

We all need to talk to one another. We need to know we're loved and appreciated and 53 respected. We want to share our intimacies, not just physical intimacies but all the intimacies in our lives. Communication is the most important element of family life because it is basic to loving relationships. It is the energy that fuels the caring, giving, sharing, and affirming. Without genuine sharing of ourselves, we cannot know one another's needs and fears. Good communication is what makes all the rest of it work.

■ Reading Comprehension Questions

1. Which of the following would be the best alternative title for this selection?
   a. Successful Communication
   b. How to Solve Family Conflicts
   c. Characteristics of Families
   d. Hallmarks of the Communicating Family

2. Which sentence best expresses the article's main point?
   a. Television can and often does destroy family life.
   b. More North American families are unhappy than ever before.
   c. A number of qualities mark the healthy and communicating family.
   d. Strong families encourage independent thinking.

3. *True or false?* _____ According to the article, healthy families have no use for television.

4. Healthy families
   a.   never find it hard to communicate.
   b.   have no conflicts with each other.
   c.   know how to reveal their feelings.
   d.   permit one of the parents to make all final decisions.

5. The author has found that good families frequently make a point of being together
   a.   in the mornings.
   b.   after school.
   c.   during dinner.
   d.   before bedtime.

6. *True or false?* _____ The article implies that the most troublesome nonverbal signal is silence.

7. The article implies that
   a.   verbal messages are always more accurate than nonverbal ones.
   b.   in strong families, parents practise tolerance of thoughts and feelings.
   c.   parents must avoid arguing with their adolescent children.
   d.   parents should prevent their children from watching television.

8. From the article, we can conclude that
   a.   a weak marital relationship often results in a weak family.
   b.   children should not witness a disagreement between parents.
   c.   children who grow up in healthy families learn not to interrupt other family members.
   d.   parents always find it easier to respond to their children than to react to them.

9. The word *aghast* in "One parent was aghast to discover that his family's most familiar comments were 'What's on?' and 'Move'" (paragraph 14) means
   a.   horrified.
   b.   satisfied.
   c.   curious.
   d.   amused.

10. The word *engrossing* in "as the discussion became more engrossing to them, they turned the sound down so that they could continue their conversation" (paragraph 17) means
    a.   disgusting.
    b.   intellectual.
    c.   foolish.
    d.   interesting.

■ Discussion Questions

About Content

1. What are the nine hallmarks of a successfully communicating family? Which of the nine do you feel are most important?

2. How do good parents control television watching? How do they make television a positive force instead of a negative one?

3. In paragraph 20, the author says, "It is usually easier to react than to respond." What is the difference between the two terms *react* and *respond?* Give an example of each word in use, based on your own experience.

4. Why, according to Curran, is a "pattern of reconciliation" (paragraph 44) crucial to good family life? Besides those patterns mentioned in the essay, can you describe a reconciliation pattern you have developed with friends or family?

About Structure

5. What is the thesis of the selection? Write here the number of the paragraph in which it is stated: _____

6. What purpose is achieved by Curran's introduction (paragraphs 1–2)? Why is a reader likely to feel her article will be reliable and worthwhile?

7. Curran frequently uses dialogue or quotations from unnamed parents or children as the basis for her examples. The conversation related in paragraphs 16–17 is one instance. Find three other dialogues used to illustrate points in the essay and write the numbers below:

   Paragraphs _____ to _____

   Paragraphs _____ to _____

   Paragraphs _____ to _____

About Style and Tone

8. Curran enlivens the essay by using some interesting and humorous remarks from parents, children, and counsellors. One is the witty comment in paragraph 5 from a marriage counsellor: "And when I share this complaint with their husbands, they don't hear *me*, either." Find two other places where the author keeps your interest by using humorous or enjoyable quotations, and write the numbers of the paragraphs here:

   _____ _____

■ Writing Assignments

Assignment 1: Writing a Paragraph

A writing assignment based on this selection is on pages 170–171.

Assignment 2: Writing a Paragraph

Curran tells us five phrases that some children say they most like to hear from their parents (paragraph 38). When you were younger, what statement or action of one of your parents (or another adult) would make you especially happy—or sad? Write a paragraph that begins with a topic sentence like one of the following:

> A passing comment my grandfather once made really devastated me.
>
> When I was growing up, there were several typical ways my mother treated me that always made me sad or happy.
>
> A critical remark by my grade five teacher was the low point of my life.
>
> My mother has always had several lines that make her children feel very pleased.

You may want to write a narrative that describes in detail the particular time and place in which a statement or action occurred. Or you may want to provide three or so examples of statements or actions and their effect upon you.

To get started, make up two long lists of childhood memories involving adults— happy memories and sad memories. Then decide which memory or memories you could most vividly describe in a paragraph. Remember that your goal is to help your readers see for themselves why a particular time was sad or happy for you.

Assignment 3: Writing an Essay

In light of Curran's description of what healthy families do right, examine your own family. Which of Curran's traits of communicative families fit your family? Write an essay pointing out three things that your family is doing right in creating a communicative climate for its members. Or, if you feel your family could work harder at communicating, write the essay about three specific ways your family could improve. In either case, choose three of Curran's nine "hallmarks of the successfully communicating family" and show how they do or do not apply to your family.

In your introductory paragraph, include a thesis statement as well as a plan of development that lists the three traits you will talk about. Then present these traits in turn in three supporting paragraphs. Develop each paragraph by giving specific examples of conversations, arguments, behaviour patterns, and so on, that illustrate how your family communicates. Finally, conclude your essay with a summarizing sentence or two and a final thought about your subject.

Decoys and Denial

Frank Jones

Many students have reading and writing difficulties. A few are actually dyslexic, or have physical challenges which slow or impede their progress in communications skills. Although there is still a statistically noted incidence of various types of illiteracy in Canada today, schools are generally quicker to catch dysfunctional problems now. As you will read in the article below, such was not the case for Steve Lloyd in Ontario thirty years ago. He became a successful businessman and a collector of objects that, as author Frank Jones says, are "a bluff and an illusion." Read the story of Steve's two successes in life, and think about why "Steve's whole life has been a decoy."

Steve Lloyd is the decoy man.   1

At the Sportsmen's Show, at the Toronto Hunting and Outdoor Show, you'll find   2
Steve with some of his vast collection of wooden duck decoys talking all day—until he
generally loses his voice—about his great passion.

People wonder what his angle is. He isn't there to sell decoys or to buy them. In fact,   3
he's there at his own expense simply to convince people that Canada's old decoys are
worth preserving—and keeping here, where they belong.

That's remarkable enough. But if you think of a decoy—a wooden or plastic bird   4
used by hunters to lure ducks or geese down to the water—as a bluff and an illusion, then
Steve's whole life has been a decoy.

He's spent years pretending, hiding from a devastating truth that was only revealed   5
to *him* two years ago. And that he talked about openly for the first time when I spoke to
him last week.

First, the Steve Lloyd people know: 6

The story of how Steve, 37, fell in love with decoys sounds like something from   7
Canada's remote past. Growing up in Scarborough, he remembers, as a small boy, being
responsible for his father's basket of decoys when they went hunting in a small boat on
Frenchman's Bay.

It would be pitch dark when they'd set out. As darkness lifted, guns would pop and   8
sometimes shot would rain down from the sky.

"How careful you had to be not to break the decoys' beaks or tails! And you had to   9
count them constantly to make sure you hadn't lost any," he says.

When Steve was 12, the family moved to Belleville, and there were even more oppor-   10
tunities for hunting with his father and his uncle.

At 21 he got married and his dad said it was time he got his own decoys.   11

"Fall was coming and I saw an ad for decoys in the paper," he says.   12

The elderly man who had placed the ad took him out to his garage. "He had at least 1 300 to 400 on a shelf right around the garage. To him they were just working tools for hunting. He wanted $200 for them," says Steve. "I could not remember ever having $200."

He bought four of them for $2 each. Today, he estimates, the decoys would be worth 1 $1,000 each. But when Steve was later offered $10 each for his four, he thought it was easy money.

Thus began an episode over which Steve feels a good deal of guilt. He started scout- 1 ing the countryside for decoys, which he sold to a Toronto dealer. He helped create the present situation where, he says, most of Canada's priceless heritage of decoys, including models of tiny wading birds once hunted on the Toronto Islands, as well as huge, hollow wooden swans, are in the hands of foreigners, with many today going to Japan.

When he really began to appreciate the art of the decoys, he started putting good ones 1 aside. A collector was born—who would one day tell thousands about the beauty of the birds and even be featured nationwide on a CBC show.

But all his life, as he spoke in public about his great interest and rose to positions 1 of power as national sales manager for a couple of large companies, Steve had a secret.

"When will you learn to spell!" an older secretary would ask him at one of the firms, 1 trying to unravel his confused notes. It was worse than that. "I have never read a book in my life," he admitted to me.

At school he was a dud. Spelling tests were nightmares. He simply couldn't make 1 sense of the textbooks.

"My family almost had a celebration if I had a 50 per cent mark," he says. 2

In hands-on work, he was outstanding. His high school shop teacher passed him 2 when he assembled a running engine, even though he couldn't read the manual.

As his career advanced, he developed coping mechanisms. "I hid behind the phone. 2 But if I had to write a report, I was lost."

He would even quit a job in frustration—before his shortcomings were exposed. 2

With his wife Debbie and their three daughters, he moved to Calgary for three years, 2 but returned to Brockville so the children could be close to their grandparents. For five years he worked in a factory (the only well-paying job available close to home) before deciding, with Debbie's encouragement, that no matter how painful it was, he must return to college to train for a better job.

It was when he was tested at St. Lawrence College that Gail Easton, a special needs 2 counsellor, discovered he had a learning disability that had prevented him from reading and writing properly.

"I denied it at first. How could I have accomplished so much if this was true?" The 2 answer, he found: "I am always pushing myself to run with two legs when I only have one. I didn't know anything was wrong. That's what's scary."

Now he's grateful to Gail. "She found the key that has taken away a mountain of frus- 2 tration. Now I sleep nights."

But knowing is different from curing. "There's no pill for this. You can't put a crutch 2 under your arm," he was told.

Ironically, the new career Steve had set his heart on was as a developmental service 2 worker: helping people with disabilities. Now he realizes he wasn't just helping "them." He was one of "them."

Working on a college placement with a small boy facing the problems he had at   30
school made him realize that maybe he had special insights, special ways of asking questions, that could bring out that bottled-up intelligence.

He knows his strong points: patience, the gift of the gab, and a love of children.   31
Today, he's bringing them all to bear at his new job at the Rideau Centre for the developmentally handicapped at Smiths Falls. The best part: seeing if you can make someone's
day better.

He's found there is, too, a crutch for him. At work, he carries a desktop computer   32
that, with Debbie's help, he has programmed to help him make out his reports. Most of
the people he works with, he says, aren't aware of his disability.

A page of print still looks like a confusing jumble to Steve. (It will take him more   33
than an hour to figure out what this article is about.)

But Wendy, 14, is proud of him. "My dad went back to school—and passed every-   34
thing," he's heard her tell people. Alisa, 9, "reads and spells beautifully," he says. And
Mallory, 6, has caught on to her dad's tricks. "Well that's very interesting," she will say
when he pretends to read her a book, picking up clues from the pictures, "but it's not the
story Mom read."

■ Reading Comprehension Questions

1. Which of the following would be the best alternative title for this selection?
   a. A Collector's Passion
   b. Steve's Story
   c. Secrets, Self-Discovery, and Success
   d. Collecting a Cover Story

2. Which sentence best expresses the main idea of the selection?
   a. People develop amazing compensating skills, but facing and working on
      deficiencies releases us to do our best.
   b. Steve Lloyd's whole life was a sham and an amazing cover-up.
   c. Literacy problems can cripple a person's entire life.
   d. Steve Lloyd's guilt over his decoy collection nearly prevented his early
      success in life.

3. Steve Lloyd currently makes his living
   a. selling highly collectable duck decoys.
   b. teaching children to read.
   c. working with developmentally challenged people.
   d. as a powerful sales executive.

4. According to the author, Lloyd feels guilty because
   a. of all the decoys he bought up, which drove up prices on them.
   b. decoys became so desirable that a Canadian craft ended up as an export.
   c. he knowingly destroyed part of Canada's heritage.
   d. he kept all the finest decoys for himself.

5. Lloyd's major discovery about himself was caused by
   a. the poor pay he received at the only job he could get.
   b. the fact that he works so hard at everything he tries.
   c. his and his wife's decision that he should go back to college.
   d. the fact that he couldn't write a business report.

6. The author implies that
   a. Lloyd could make a living as a spokesperson for Canadian crafts.
   b. Lloyd liked decoys only because he enjoyed hunting so much.
   c. Lloyd collects decoys only to remind himself not to trick people any more.
   d. Lloyd's success kept him from realizing how much he was fooling himself.

7. The author implies that Steve Lloyd's compensating skills
   a. actually made him more persuasive, and more of a success in business.
   b. were strictly a result of his enthusiasm for decoys.
   c. weren't quite enough to prevent growing frustration and career problems.
   d. landed him in a dead-end job ultimately.

8. *True or false?* _____ Steve Lloyd enjoys helping others with learning disabilities because he has overcome his own.

9. The word *devastating* in "He's spent years pretending, hiding from a devastating truth that was only revealed to *him* two years ago" (paragraph 5) means
   a. horrible.
   b. hidden.
   c. shattering.
   d. obvious.

10. The words *developmentally handicapped* in "his new job at the Rideau Centre for the developmentally handicapped at Smiths Falls" (paragraph 31) mean
    a. learning skills impaired.
    b. physically challenged.
    c. motor skills impaired.
    d. mentally challenged.

■ Discussion Questions

About Content

1. Why does the journalist Frank Jones call Lloyd "the decoy man" in his opening sentence?

2. Read paragraphs 1–17 and find at least three qualities in Steve Lloyd which would make him someone worthy of a newspaper columnist's interest.

3. What do you find to be the most amazing fact about Steve Lloyd's school years? Why?

4. Why does Jones describe Steve Lloyd's new career choice as ironic in paragraph 29? Why might it have been an excellent choice?

About Structure

5. Jones opens his article with a simple sentence with multiple meanings, two of which are discussed in the first five paragraphs. Starting with paragraph 6, find three divisions or breaks in Lloyd's story, and indicate the paragraph numbers and "signal words" which begin those paragraphs. What is the subject of each section of the narrative? List the paragraph numbers, the signal words, and a phrase which covers the subject of each section you indicate below:

   Paragraph 6 – _____ Signal word: _____ Subject: _____

   Paragraph _____ – _____ Signal word: _____ Subject: _____

   Paragraph _____ – _____ Signal word: _____ Subject: _____

6. The author lets Steve Lloyd tell his own story in direct speech, and includes dialogue quotations from other people. How do at least three of these pieces of dialogue support the thesis of the selection?

About Style and Tone

7. The author quotes Steve Lloyd as he uses certain figures of speech called *metaphors*. A metaphor is simply the verbal substitution of one idea for another, as in "My friend is a *rock* to lean on when I'm worried." No "like" or "as" is used (such a figure of speech is a *simile*); a metaphor is a *direct* substitution of one idea for another.

   One example of a metaphor is found in paragraph 26, where Lloyd says, "I am always pushing myself to run with two legs when I only have one." What does he mean by this?

   Find two other examples of metaphors used in the dialogue quoted in the article, and explain what is meant by them.

8. Jones concludes his article with quotations from Lloyd's children. How do the first two comments confirm Lloyd's achievements? What does Mallory Lloyd's final observation about her father's story-reading talents suggest about the "decoy man"?

■ Writing Assignments

Assignment 1: Writing a Paragraph

We have all known people who have overcome great obstacles in their lives. Sometimes, we *are* those people. Some develop coping or managing skills, so that their disability or problem is never apparent to others. Sometimes such people can be a source of inspiration, or actual help, to others.

Write a paragraph about someone you know, or about yourself, which describes three ways in which that person has dealt with a major problem or a disability. As you prepare to write, describe the problem precisely, and list the efforts or trials which the person has undergone to try to overcome, or compensate for, their obstacle. Choose the three strongest details from your list as support for your point, and conclude with a statement about the end result of this individual's efforts for him- or herself and for others.

Assignment 2: Writing a Paragraph

How successful are any of us at fooling others? Can you or I maintain a "decoy" personality which hides what we don't wish others to see? To some degree, society and manners dictate that we all must hide some of our feelings and desires to maintain ordinary levels of politeness and social function. But when, if ever, does this habit become a liability? Is the harm in maintaining "multiple personalities" only a matter of "how often" and "for how long?" Or do we sometimes end up hurting ourselves and others by hiding what we feel are vulnerable spots?

Write a paragraph about some "coping mechanisms" of your own, or those of someone you know well. Describe whatever it is that you are trying to hide or compensate for—shyness, lack of mathematical ability, feeling too short or too tall; then describe the actions and evasive manoeuvres you've used to avoid drawing attention to what you feel to be a deficiency. Have your attempts always succeeded? Or have you faced up to your perceived deficiency and dealt with it? Try to analyze where your "decoys" have taken you, and conclude with an evaluation of how you feel now about the way you coped with this aspect of yourself.

Assignment 3: Writing an Essay

How do *you* react to stories like that of Steve Lloyd and those of rich and successful people with little education? Lloyd faced his demon and put his disability to good use. The American magazine *Esquire* published a similar story, "The Man Who Couldn't Read," about a U.S. college teacher and real-estate millionaire, John Corcoran, who is now a literacy advocate. Other people, with great weaknesses in communications skills but high persuasive and mechanical abilities, have simply proceeded to sell the world their success stories while boasting that they never read a newspaper. Apparently, they can live with their "decoy" skills.

Has the advent of high-technology-based business lessened the need for communications skills? Decide how important you feel reading and writing are to your professional future in the twenty-first century. If you could barely read a memo or computer screen, much less make sense of a technical report, could you find ways around those problems?

Choose your response to this statement, made by a student:

> I can live without English, and half the time I fail it anyway, but without accounting and my tech courses, I'll never make a decent salary.

Line up possible point-form responses under the headings "Agree" and "Disagree." Reread Jones' article, especially paragraphs 18–23. Consider your own career hopes or choices, and write a persuasive essay which agrees or disagrees with the student's statement above. Remember that persuading your audience depends on facts and logic, as well as on the force of your feelings. Your three supporting points should be carefully thought out and based as much on experience or your reading as possible.

A possible scratch outline for an "I disagree" essay might look like the following:

Thesis: – disagree/I'm in accounting
    – numbers important, but must report to boss, etc.
    – must also read tax and business reports, audits & understand
    – have to write to clients after entry level & represent firm

Paragraph 1: accuracy & math skills essential to accounting, but have to read memos, write them, give presentations, talk to management

Paragraph 2: already have to read thick books on tax laws & understand annual reports & company audits—will only have to read more in future

Paragraph 3: want to be promoted, to have individual & even corporate clients to succeed/money belongs to *people*—have to write to them about what I do with it & bigger clients want formal reports/write as rep. of company

Truth or Consequences

Laura J. Turner

Have you ever told a lie? Answering no to that question would create an immediate contradiction for all of us. We all lie, bend the truth, give exciting excuses for things undone, and flatter people without many second thoughts.

But how serious is this very human habit? When does it become a problem? When does it seem "necessary"? Laura J. Turner, formerly in public relations and now an English student at the University of Regina, has an interesting view of how we evaluate the relative "sinfulness" of this most common human habit.

When we intentionally make false statements, we lie. Lies are regarded as sins, vices, transgressions, and immoral offences. Lies are not modern phenomena: lies have been around forever. They permeate all cultures and all eras of history; lies are universal. That we should not lie is implied by one of the Ten Commandments. Nevertheless, whether we are pious or not, we generally agree that lies are socially and morally wrong. We despise lies, and more especially, we despise liars. We regard liars as social deviants, reprobates; we rank them near the bottom of the social hierarchy. Still, we all lie.

We are inherently prone to lying, I suppose because we are subject to original sin. To tell a lie is to be intrinsically human. Yet we regard lying as wicked depravity while, at the same time, we continue to lie. Lies come in different shapes and sizes. Though all are lies by definition, some lies are sanctioned by society, some are tolerated and others, of course, frowned upon. How are we able simultaneously to hold these conflicting viewpoints concerning lies? We classify lies as little white lies, half-truths, and barefaced lies and then impose upon them a ranking according to their degree of social acceptance or the severity of their immorality.

We categorize lies so that little white lies are less profane and more socially and morally acceptable than the lies of the opposite end of the scale, barefaced lies; half-truths fall in the middle range. In other words, this hierarchical system of lies we have developed enables us to justify the telling of harmless little white lies, to condone half-truths, and to disapprove of barefaced lies.

We first encounter little white lies at birth; we are cooed at: "My, isn't she beautiful. She looks just like you." This is a lie, albeit a little white lie. Babies are not beautiful; they are red and wrinkly and do not resemble their parents at all. Little white lies are often told by kind, polite persons in an attempt to be socially or politically correct. When we wish to say the right thing, spare someone's feelings, pay a compliment, or make someone feel better, we make selfless statements that bend or stretch the truth, usually to benefit someone else.

If we tell little white lies to be courteous, then we tell half-truths often to benefit or protect ourselves. We neglect to tell the whole truth, opting instead to omit the incriminating half of the story. Other half-truths are merely exaggerations. Many half-truths, like little white lies, are part of ordinary, daily conversation. Half-truths seem less brash and, perhaps, more socially and morally forgivable, but the omitted half can haunt. Yet half-truths have become so hackneyed that many exist as clichés in our society. "I gave at the office," "the cheque is in the mail," "we'll do lunch," and "I'll call you sometime" are everyday jargon; they illustrate the social amnesty granted the telling of half-truths.

Barefaced lies are socially unacceptable. Liars of the barefaced genre are self-centred and self-serving. Barefaced lies are committed in the pursuit of profit, prestige, power, vengeance, or any combination of these moral turpitudes. The barefaced liar has little or no concern for the welfare of others. A barefaced liar might be the accused in a murder trial who, without conscience, declares himself "not guilty" when, in fact, he has killed someone. A barefaced liar may be someone who emphatically declares "I *am* telling you the truth!" or "no, I definitely didn't do that!"—claiming innocence, or deny-ing guilt, when the opposite is true. A moral felon who falls into this area of the lie labyrinth lies consciously and deliberately. Thus, the barefaced lie of the pathological liar is regarded as the most iniquitous of lies.

Regardless of which category one may have lied his or her way into, it is not the com-mitting of the lie, but the lie's potential to cause hurt or damage, that becomes the mea-sure of its sinfulness. Because the majority of lies fall in the little white lie and half-truth categories, and so are less severe than barefaced lies, lying has become commonplace. One of the qualities that distinguishes humans from other creatures is our ability to jus-tify and rationalize our behaviour, especially our deviant behaviour. Toward this end, we have ranked and classified lies so that some, such as little white lies, and half-truths, are tolerable while barefaced lies are regarded as offences. We are more able to accept white lies and half-truths because we can rationalize that the ends justify the means. 7

■ Reading Comprehension Questions

1. Which of the following would be the best alternative title for this selection?
   a. The Least Deadly Sin
   b. Just Lying and Self-Justifying
   c. Little White Lies
   d. Lies Hurt Everyone

2. Which sentence best expresses the essay's main point?
   a. Lying is such an normal activity that we easily break it into categories.
   b. Compliments and conventional lies are socially acceptable.
   c. A lie's acceptability depends on how easily we can justify its harmfulness.
   d. Lying is an unavoidable part of being a sinful person.

3. *True or false?* _____ We tolerate liars simply because we all lie ourselves.

4. The author states that white lies are less offensive than half-truths because
   a. they are told by kind, decent people.
   b. they are for the good of others, rather than for our own benefit.
   c. they are more socially acceptable than half-truths.
   d. they can't come back to haunt us.

5. Turner says that "lying has become commonplace" (paragraph 7) because
   a. it is mortal to lie, and we are all only mortal.
   b. we have given up on trying to justify our behaviour.
   c. most lies fall into the two least harmful classes of lies.
   d. we no longer see most lies as "sinful" or morally wrong.

6. The author implies that
   a. she understands exactly why people tell lies.
   b. she feels that lying can be unintentional and tolerable.
   c. our attitudes toward lying are simple and uncomplicated.
   d. she sees lying as evidence of our contradictory human nature.

7. *True or false?* _____ The essay implies that we have set up an order for "lie classification" because we find our capacity for lying so hard to deal with in ethical terms.

8. From the essay, we can conclude that
   a. the purpose of a lie is often the way we reconcile guilt over having lied.
   b. humans can justify any immoral behaviour in themselves.
   c. since we understand the types of lies, they are no longer problematic.
   d. as long as we don't hurt other people, any lie is acceptable.

9. The word *permeate* in "They permeate all cultures and all eras of history; lies are universal" (paragraph 1) means
   a. dominate.
   b. destroy.
   c. spread through.
   d. distort.

10. The word *turpitudes* in "profit, prestige, power, vengeance, or any combination of these moral turpitudes" (paragraph 6) means
    a. wickednesses.
    b. goals.
    c. horrors.
    d. tendencies.

■ Discussion Questions

About Content

1. What are the five elements of Turner's opening definition of lies? Which is the closest to an "objective dictionary definition?" Why?

2. Why do we have such problems with lying if it's such an ordinary human activity? What are the effects of our dilemma on us?

3. What are the distinctions between a half-truth and a white lie? What are the problems with half-truths?

4. Why is a barefaced lie the least acceptable form of lie? If *all* lies are intentional, why is this last type the worst?

About Structure

5. What is the effect of the short sentence at the end of the first paragraph? How does this sentence affect your understanding of the rest of the paragraph?

6. In which paragraph and in which sentence does the author reveal her categories of lies? In which paragraph does she explain her divisions?

7. How does the structure of the rest of "Truth or Consequences" follow from the transition sentence at the end of the third paragraph? What is the function of each of paragraphs 4, 5, and 6?

About Style and Tone

8. Turner uses samples of direct speech as examples of types of lies. Find and list the pieces of direct speech used.

   _____   _____

   _____   _____

   _____   _____

   _____   _____

   What is the effect on you when you read these phrases? Do they make the author's points more clearly?

■ Writing Assignments

Assignment 1: Writing a Paragraph

An assignment based on this selection appears on pages 150–151.

Assignment 2: Writing a Paragraph

You have undoubtedly experienced some or all of the three types of lies Turner defines. List her three headings and, under each heading, note examples from your own life. Which did you find the most harmful or hurtful? Why? Which have you experienced the most often? Write a paragraph defining *in your own terms* the kind of lie you find the worst, and give clear examples, perhaps using direct speech, which support your definition of "the worst kind of lie."

Assignment 3: Writing an Essay

Turner writes in her final paragraph: "One of the qualities that distinguishes humans from other creatures is our ability to justify and rationalize our behaviour, especially our deviant behaviour" (paragraph 7). Consider some action or behaviour of your own of which you are not particularly proud, such as keeping extra change miscounted by a salesclerk or cheating on a girlfriend or boyfriend. How did you justify your action to yourself? How did you rationalize it? How did you finally settle things with your own conscience? How did you finally settle matters with the person or people involved? If the issue is still unsettled, what might you still do?

Write an essay about one such action in your own life. Begin with an introduction, which defines clearly the nature of the "sin" and gives a brief background for what led to your choice of action. In your prewriting, label your three body paragraphs with headings such as *my mistake*, *my reasons for doing it*, and *the consequences/how I dealt with them*. Conclude your essay with a summarizing sentence or two, and a final thought about human nature and what you may have learned.

EDUCATION AND SELF-IMPROVEMENT

Power Learning

Sheila Akers

> For many students, cramming for tests, staying up late to do assignments, and having an incomplete grasp of information are a natural part of college life. After all, there is so much to do, and almost none of it is easy. If you are one of those students who never seem able to catch up, you may find the following selection a revelation. It might convince you that even though you study hard in school, you may need to learn more about how to study better.

Jill had not been as successful in high school as she would have liked. Since college 1 involved even more work, it was no surprise that she was not doing any better there.

The reason for her so-so performance was not a lack of effort. She attended most of her 2 classes and read her textbooks. And she never missed handing in any assignment, even though it often meant staying up late the night before homework was due. Still, she just got by in her classes. Before long, she came to the conclusion that she just couldn't do any better.

Then one day, one of her instructors said something to make her think otherwise. 3 "You can probably build some sort of house by banging a few boards together," he said. "But if you want a sturdy home, you'll have to use the right techniques and tools. Building carefully takes work, but it gets better results. The same can be said of your education. There are no shortcuts, but there are some proven study skills that can really help. If you don't use them, you may end up with a pretty flimsy education."

Prompted by this advice, Jill signed up for a course in study skills at her school. She 4 then found out a crucial fact—that learning how to learn is the key to success in school. There are certain dependable skills that have made the difference between disappointment and success for generations of students. These techniques won't free you from work, but they will make your work far more productive. They include three important areas: time control, classroom note-taking, and textbook study.

Time Control

Success in college depends on time control. Time control means that you deliberately organize and plan your time, instead of letting it drift by. Planning means that you should never be faced with a night-before-the-test "cram" session or an overdue term paper.

There are three steps involved in time control. The *first step* is to prepare a large monthly calendar. Buy a calendar with a large white block around each date, or make one yourself. At the beginning of the college semester, circle important dates on this calendar. Circle the days on which tests are scheduled; circle the days when papers are due. This calendar can also be used to schedule study plans. You can jot down your plans for each day at the beginning of the week. An alternative method would be to make plans for each day the night before. On Tuesday night, for example, you might write down "Read Chapter 5 in psychology" in the Wednesday block. Be sure to hang this calendar in a place where you will see it every day—your kitchen, your bedroom, even your bathroom!

The *second step* in time control is to have a weekly study schedule for the semester. To prepare this schedule, make up a chart that covers all the days of the week and all the waking hours in each day. Part of one student's schedule is shown opposite. On your schedule, mark in all the fixed hours in each day—hours for meals, classes, job (if any), and travel time. Next, mark in time blocks that you can *realistically* use for study each day. Depending on the number of courses you are taking and the demands of the courses, you may want to block off five, ten, or even twenty or more hours of study time a week. Keep in mind that you should not block off time for study that you do not truly intend to use for study. Otherwise, your schedule will be a meaningless gimmick. Also, remember that you should allow time for rest and relaxation in your schedule. You will be happiest, and able to accomplish the most, when you have time for both work and play.

Time	Monday	Tuesday	Wednesday	Thursday	Friday	Saturday	Sunday
6:00 A.M.							
7:00	B	B	B	B	B		
8:00	Math	STUDY	Math	STUDY	Math		
9:00	STUDY	Biology	STUDY	Biology	STUDY	Job	
10:00	Psychology	↓	Psychology	↓	Psychology		
11:00	STUDY	English		English			
12:00 NOON	L		L	↓	L	↓	

The *third step* in time control is to make a daily or weekly "to do" list. This may be the most valuable time-control method you ever use. On this list, you write down the things you need to do for the following day or the following week. If you choose to write a weekly list, do it on Sunday night. If you choose to write a daily list, do it the night before. You may use a three- by five-inch notepad or a small spiral-bound notebook for this list. Carry the list around with you during the day. Always concentrate on doing first the most important items on your list. Mark high-priority items with an asterisk and give them precedence over low-priority items in order to make the best use of your time. For instance, you may find yourself wondering what to do after dinner on Thursday evening. Among the items on your list are "Clean inside of car" and "Review chapter for math quiz." It is obviously more important for you to review your notes at this point; you can clean the car some other time. As you complete items on your "to do" list, cross them out. Do not worry about unfinished items. They can be rescheduled. You will still be accomplishing a great deal and making more effective use of your time. Part of one student's daily list is shown below.

To Do	Tuesday
*1. Review biology notes before class	
*2. Proof-read English paper due today	
3. See Dick about game on Friday	
*4. Gas for car	
5. Read next chapter of psychology text	

Classroom Note-Taking

One of the most important single things you can do to perform well in a college course 9
is to take effective class notes. The following hints should help you become a better note-taker.

First, attend class faithfully. Your alternatives—reading the text or someone else's 10
notes, or both—cannot substitute for the experience of hearing ideas in person as someone presents them to you. Also, in class lectures and discussions, your instructor typically presents and develops the main ideas and facts of the course—the ones you will be expected to know on exams.

Another valuable hint is to make use of abbreviations while taking notes. Using 11
abbreviations saves time when you are trying to get down a great deal of information. Abbreviate terms that recur frequently in a lecture and put a key to your abbreviations at the top of your notes. For example, in a sociology class, *eth* could stand for *ethnocentrism*; in a psychology class, *STM* could stand for *short-term memory*. (When a lecture is over, you may want to go back and write out the terms you have abbreviated.) In addition, abbreviate words that often recur in any lecture. For instance, use *ex* for *example*, *def* for *definition*, *info* for *information*, + for *and*, and so on. If you use the same abbreviations all the time, you will soon develop a kind of personal shorthand that makes taking notes much easier.

A third hint when taking notes is to be on the lookout for signals of importance. Write 12
down whatever your instructor puts on the board. If he or she takes the time to put mater-

ial on the board, it is probably important, and the chances are good that it will come up later on exams. Always write down definitions and enumerations. Enumerations are lists of items. They are signaled in such ways as: "The four steps in the process are ..."; "There were three reasons for ..."; "The two effects were ..."; "Five characteristics of ..."; and so on. Always number such enumerations in your notes (1, 2, 3, etc.). They will help you understand relationships among ideas and organize the material of the lecture. Watch for emphasis words—words your instructor may use to indicate that something is important. Examples of such words are "This is an important reason ..."; "A point that will keep coming up later ..."; "The chief cause was ..."; "The basic idea here is ..."; and so on. Always write down the important statements announced by these and other emphasis words. Finally, if your instructor repeats a point, you can assume it is important. You might put an R for *repeated* in the margin, so that later you will know that your instructor has stressed it.

Next, be sure to write down the instructor's examples and mark them with an X. The 13 examples help you understand abstract points. If you do not write them down, you are likely to forget them later when they are needed to help make sense of an idea.

Also, be sure to write down the connections between ideas. Too many students 14 merely copy the terms the instructor puts on the board. They forget that, as time passes, the details that serve as connecting bridges between ideas quickly fade. You should, then, write down the relationships and connections in class. That way you'll have them to help tie your notes together later on.

Review your notes as soon as possible after class. You must make them as clear as 15 possible while they are fresh in your mind. A day later may be too late, because forgetting sets in very quickly. Make sure that punctuation is clear, that all words are readable and correctly spelled, and that unfinished sentences are completed (or at least marked off so that you can check your notes with another student's). Add clarifying or connecting comments whenever necessary. Make sure important ideas are clearly marked. Improve the organization if necessary, so that you can see at a glance main points and relationships among them.

Finally, try in general to get down a written record of each class. You must do this 16 because forgetting begins almost immediately. Studies have shown that within two weeks you are likely to have forgotten 80 percent or more of what you have heard. And in four weeks you are lucky if 5 percent remains! This is so crucial that it bears repeating: to guard against the relentlessness of forgetting, it is absolutely essential to write down what you hear in class. Later on you can concentrate on working to understand fully and to remember the ideas that have been presented in class. And the more complete your notes are at the time of study, the more you are likely to learn.

Textbook Study

In many college courses, success means being able to read and study a textbook skill- 17 fully. For many students, unfortunately, textbooks are heavy going. After an hour or two of study, the textbook material is as formless and as hard to understand as ever. But there is a way to attack even the most difficult textbook and make sense of it. Use a sequence in which you preview a chapter, mark it, take notes on it, and then study the notes.

Previewing. Previewing a selection is an important first step to understanding. 18
Taking the time to preview a section or chapter can give you a bird's-eye view of the way
the material is organized. You will have a sense of where you are beginning, what you
will cover, and where you will end.

There are several steps in previewing a selection. First, study the title. The title is 19
the shortest possible summary of a selection and will often tell you the limits of the material you will cover. For example, the title "FDR and the Supreme Court" tells you to
expect a discussion of President Roosevelt's dealings with the Court. You know that you
will probably not encounter any material dealing with FDR's foreign policies or personal
life. Next, read over quickly the first and last paragraphs of the selection; these may contain important introductions to, and summaries of, the main ideas. Then examine briefly
the headings and subheadings in the selection. Together, the headings and subheadings
are a brief outline of what you are reading. Headings are often main ideas or important
concepts in capsule form; subheadings are breakdowns of ideas within main areas.
Finally, read the first sentence of some paragraphs, look for words set off in **boldface** or
italics, and look at pictures or diagrams. After you have previewed a selection in this way,
you should have a good general sense of the material to be read.

Marking. You should mark a textbook selection at the same time that you read it 20
through carefully. Use a felt-tip highlighter to shade material that seems important, or
use a regular ballpoint pen and put symbols in the margin next to the material: stars,
checks, or NBs (for *nota bene*, a Latin phrase meaning "note well"). What to mark is not
as mysterious as some students believe. You should try to find main ideas by looking for
the following clues: definitions and examples, enumerations, and emphasis words.

1   *Definitions and examples:* Definitions are often among the most important ideas in 21
    a selection. They are particularly significant in introductory courses in almost any
    subject area, where much of your learning involves mastering the specialized vocab-
    ulary of that subject. In a sense, you are learning the "language" of psychology or
    business or whatever the subject might be.

    Most definitions are abstract, and so they usually are followed by one or more 22
    examples to help clarify their meaning. Always mark off definitions and at least one
    example that makes a definition clear to you. In a psychology text, for example, we
    are told that "rationalization is an attempt to reduce anxiety by deciding that you have
    not really been frustrated." Several examples follow, among them: "A young man,
    frustrated because he was rejected when he asked for a date, convinces himself that
    the woman is not very attractive and is much less interesting than he had supposed."

2   *Enumerations:* Enumerations are lists of items (causes, reasons, types, and so on) 23
    that are numbered 1, 2, 3, … or that could easily be numbered in an outline. They
    are often signaled by addition words. Many of the paragraphs in a textbook use words
    like *first of all*, *another*, *in addition*, and *finally* to signal items in a series. This is a
    very common and effective organizational method.

3   *Emphasis words:* Emphasis words tell you that an idea is important. Common 24
    emphasis words include phrases such as *a major event*, *a key feature*, *the chief fac-*

tor, *important to note*, *above all*, and *most of all*. Here is an example: "The most significant contemporary use of marketing is its application to non-business areas, such as political parties."

Note-Taking. Next, you should take notes. Go through the chapter a second time, 2 rereading the most important parts. Try to write down the main ideas in a simple outline form. For example, in taking notes on a psychology selection, you might write down the heading "Kinds of Defense Mechanisms." Below the heading you would number and describe each kind and give an example of each.

Defense Mechanisms

a.   *Definition: Unconscious attempts to reduce anxiety*
b.   *Kinds:*

   (1) *Rationalization: Attempt to reduce anxiety by deciding that you have not really been frustrated*
       Example: Man turned down for a date decides that the woman was not worth going out with anyway

   (2) *Projection: Attributing to other people motives or thoughts of one's own*
       Example: Wife who wants to have an affair accuses her husband of having one

Studying Notes. To study your notes, use the method of repeated self-testing. For 2 example, look at the heading "Kinds of Defense Mechanisms" and say to yourself, "What are the kinds of defense mechanisms?" When you can recite them, then say to yourself, "What is rationalization?" "What is an example of rationalization?" Then ask yourself, "What is projection?" "What is an example of projection?" After you learn each section, review it, and then go on to the next section.

Do not simply read your notes; keep looking away and seeing if you can recite them 2 to yourself. This self-testing is the key to effective learning.

In summary, remember this sequence in order to deal with a textbook: previewing, mark- 2 ing, taking notes, studying the notes. Approaching a textbook in this methodical way will give you very positive results. You will no longer feel bogged down in a swamp of words, unable to figure out what you are supposed to know. Instead, you will understand exactly what you have to do and how to go about doing it.

■

Take a minute now to evaluate your own study habits. Do you practise many of the above 2 skills in order to control your time, take effective classroom notes, and learn from your textbooks? If not, perhaps you should. The skills are not magic, but they are too valuable to ignore. Use them carefully and consistently, and they will make academic success possible for you. Try them, and you won't need convincing.

■ Reading Comprehension Questions

1. Which of the following would be the best alternative title for this selection?
   a. The Importance of Note-Taking
   b. Good Study Skills: The Key to Success
   c. Easy Ways to Learn More
   d. How to Evaluate Your Study Habits

2. Which sentence best expresses the main idea of the selection?
   a. Good study skills can increase academic success.
   b. Note-taking is the best way to study difficult subjects.
   c. More and more schools are offering courses on study skills.
   d. Certain study techniques make college work easy for everyone.

3. Which of these is *not* a good way to organize your time?
   a. Make a monthly calendar.
   b. Keep a weekly study schedule.
   c. Prepare a "to do" list.
   d. Always use extra time for studying.

4. Which is the correct sequence of steps in studying from a textbook?
   a. Preview, self-test, take notes.
   b. Take notes, preview, mark, self-test.
   c. Take notes, mark, preview, self-test.
   d. Preview, mark, take notes, self-test.

5. When marking the textbook for main ideas, do *not*
   a. mark it while you are previewing.
   b. highlight definitions and examples.
   c. include lists of items.
   d. look for "emphasis" words.

6. *True or false?* _____ The author implies that it is better to write too much rather than too little when taking classroom notes.

7. The author implies that one value of class attendance is that you
   a. need to get the next assignment.
   b. will please the instructor, which can lead to better grades.
   c. can begin to improve your short-term memory.
   d. increase your understanding by hearing ideas in person.

8. *True or false?* _____ The author implies that studying does not require any memorization.

9. The word *abstract* in "The examples help you understand abstract points" (paragraph 13) means
   a. simple.
   b. difficult.

    c. ordinary.

    d. correct.

10. The word *capsule* in "Headings are often main ideas or important concepts in capsule form" (paragraph 19) means

    a. adjustable.

    b. larger.

    c. complicated.

    d. abbreviated.

■ Discussion Questions

About Content

1. Evaluate Jill's college course work. What was she doing right? What was she probably doing wrong?

2. When taking notes in class, how can we tell what information is important enough to write down?

3. What are the three steps in time control? Which do you think would be most helpful to you?

4. What are some of the ways you can spot main ideas when marking a textbook chapter?

About Structure

5. Does Akers use time order or emphatic order in presenting the three study skills?

6. Write down seven different transitional words and phrases used in "Classroom Note-Taking":

  _____

  _____

  _____

  _____

7. Akers tells us that emphasis words (paragraphs 12 and 24) are keys to important ideas. What are three emphasis words or phrases that she herself uses at different places in the article?

  _____ (paragraph _____)

  _____ (paragraph _____)

  _____ (paragraph _____)

About Style and Tone

8. Why has Akers chosen to present most of her essay in the second person—"you"? Why didn't she continue to use Jill, or another student, as an example?

■ Writing Assignments

Assignment 1: Writing a Paragraph

A writing assignment based on this selection is on page 141.

Assignment 2: Writing a Paragraph

Akers says, "A third hint on taking notes is to be on the lookout for signals of importance." Pay close attention to these signals in your classes over the next few days. Watch for use of the board, for definitions, for enumerations, and for other ways your instructors might stress information. On a special sheet of paper, keep track of these signals as they occur. Then use your notes to write a paragraph on ways that your instructors signal that certain ideas are important. Be sure to provide specific examples of what your instructors say and do. Possible topic sentences for this paragraph might be: "My psychology instructor has several ways of signalling important points in her lectures" or "My instructors use several signals in common to let students know that ideas are important."

Assignment 3: Writing an Essay

For many students, the challenge of college is not just to learn good study skills. It is also to overcome the various temptations that interfere with study time. What pulls you away from success at school? Time with friends or family? Card games? Extracurricular activities? Cable TV? Time spent daydreaming or listening to music? An unneeded part-time job?

Make a list of all the temptations that distract you from study time. Then decide on the three that interfere most with your studying time. Use these three as the basis for an essay, "Temptations in College Life."

Here is one student's outline for an essay:

Thesis statement: The local coffee shop, television, and my girlfriend often tempt me away from what I should be doing in school.

Topic sentence 1: The time I spend at the coffee shop interferes with school in three ways.
a. Skipping classes
b. Going right after class, instead of checking notes
c. Long lunches with friends, instead of studying

<u>Topic sentence 2:</u> I also find that the time I spend watching television interferes with school.

a. Time away from study because of sports and other shows
b. Getting to sleep too late because of late-night TV

<u>Topic sentence 3:</u> Finally, I am often with my girlfriend, who is not a student and does not need to study.

a. Time spent together on nonschool activities
b. Studying poorly when she is around

In your final paragraph, include one or two sentences of summary and, perhaps, comment on any changes you plan to make to improve your study time.

As an alternative, you may want to write generally (rather than personally) about "Temptations Faced by College Students." In such a paper, you will use a third-person point of view rather than the first person ("I"), and you will provide examples based on your observations of others.

How to Write a Test

Eileen A. Brett

Writing tests never seems as trying for some students as it does for others. A few are calm, plan their attack, and finish on time. Many, however, perspire on their exam books, chew their pens, and never complete a test. If you, like the Canadian editor of this text, belong to the latter group, Eileen A. Brett has some sensible down-to-earth advice about approaching and managing test-taking. Ms. Brett, a student at the University of British Columbia, writes with a light touch about a subject of serious concern. Both her recommendations and her information are concrete, specific, and, it is hoped, valuable and interesting to you.

It is the day of the final exam or perhaps it is just a unit quiz. (Of course, in today's aca- 1
demic courses, when entire grades are sometimes comprised of quiz marks, there is no such thing as a mere quiz.) Whether quiz, test, or examination, does the very suggestion of being tested induce fear and panic? Rest assured; writing tests need not be a frightening experience. If you sit in a place without distractions, bring the right tools, relax, think positively, and organize yourself, you will survive the experience. You may even surprise yourself by doing well on the test.

As you enter the classroom the day of the test, your first priority should be to choose 2 where to sit. The important point here is not to find the most comfortable seat but to avoid windows. When a task of importance is unpleasant, eyes tend to wander toward windows and scenes of interest outside. When this happens, inevitably, concentration is relaxed. Equally distracting can be a seat at the back of the room where the back view of any number of attractive blondes or rugged athletes will be in your direct line of vision. Always choose a seat in the front row.

To be prepared you will have brought with you at least two pens and one pencil 3 accompanied by a bottle of correction fluid, an eraser, and a watch. Often I have forgotten this last item and suffered tremendously from judging incorrectly how much time remained. These are the essential tools of any test. The pencil may be used substantially more than the pen, for reasons that will be discussed later. One pencil is sufficient, since the walk to the pencil sharpener provides a practical excuse to exercise leg muscles. I stress, however, that this is not an opportunity to cheat. The walk over to the pencil sharpener is not only a form of physical release, it is also a "brain break." However short this walk may be, the brain welcomes the chance to escape deep mental concentration for the non-strenuous act of sharpening a pencil.

Many students spend the remaining few minutes before the test cramming crucial 4 bits of information into their heads. This effort is wasteful since, in my experience, last minute cramming serves to confuse and is not actually remembered anyway. Why not, instead, spend those moments in mental relaxation and deep breathing? At the same time, analyze the mood in the room. If absolutely everyone else, not having read these helpful hints, is deeply engrossed in last minute preparation, this is a fairly positive indication that the exam will be a difficult one. In this case, it is best that you breathe deeply rather than analyze. If, on the other hand, the majority is calm, cool, and collected, either the test is going to be easy or you have got the date wrong. In both cases, you have nothing to worry about.

The interval between the time the test is placed in front of you and the time you are 5 told you may begin is the time to take the Attitude Adjustment Approach, which concerns the mindset in which you will commence writing the exam. During this time, students who want only to scrape by will decide to put minimum effort into the exam. In contrast, students who want a good, if not exceptional, grade will use this time to prepare mentally for the challenge ahead.

As the examination begins, take a moment to glance through the test. The decision 6 as to where to start is yours. However, a word to the wise: multiple choice questions should be attacked first for two reasons. First, tidbits of information can often be gleaned from them and then reworked to fit nicely (and inconspicuously) into sentence answers or essays. Second, since the answer is right in front of you, multiple choice questions are the least painful way of easing into the task ahead.

In examinations, an organized student has the advantage over a disorganized student. 7 An organized system for writing tests involves using a pen or pencil, depending on how confident you are with the material. Those answers of which you are fairly certain should be answered in pen. Otherwise, pencils are ideal for answering tests because answers can be changed easily. However, since numerous studies have found that, particularly with multiple choice, the first answer chosen is most often the correct one, be 110 percent sure before you change an answer. Should time permit double-checking, it will be necessary to review only those answers in pencil as answers in pen are likely to be correct. If an answer is elusive, make a mark beside the question so you will be able to quickly identify those questions to which you did not know the answers. Then move on and go back to them later.

A few techniques have been developed for writing essays. Of course, understanding exactly what the question is asking is essential. If, for example, there is more than one essay question, ideas may flow more freely if you switch back and forth among them. When I begin to get frustrated for lack of ideas, often new thoughts will surface as I answer another question and I will quickly jot them down. Still, other people find staying with one essay until it is completed more beneficial. If all else fails, use the technique of free-writing: write on anything that is even remotely connected with the essay topic until you feel inspired. But perhaps you should take a brain break.

The technique you choose is of less importance, though, than the interest level of your essays. Not many teachers enjoy perusing forty essay exams on "The Effect of Green Pesticides on Small Herbivores." If you want a good mark, you will strive to keep the professor not only awake but also excited at your discussion of genetic differences in field mice. Imagination is a wonderful asset, but if it is not one of yours, description or examples are also effective. Easy reading is also enhanced by grammatically correct writing.

Before you finish the exam, remember to finish those multiple choice questions that 1 you had found impossible to answer. If the process of elimination does not yield an answer that is satisfactory, depending on the amount of time remaining, one of two options is open: count up how many *A* answers you have, how many *B*, etc., and choose the letter that has the least number of answers; or take a reasonable guess. If all else fails, write your professor a note telling him or her of the immense satisfaction and enjoyment you derived from doing the exam, and extend holiday greetings. Then, with hope, you wait for the results and you trust that:

(a) Without your knowledge, your teacher has sent in several of your essays from the examination to Mensa, which extends the honour of membership to you.
(b) The test was for the government, which does not care anyway.
(c) The teacher appreciated your note.

■ Reading Comprehension Questions

1. Which of the following would be the best alternative title for the selection?
   a. Seven Steps to Success
   b. Fool-Proof Ways to Pass
   c. Tested Techniques for Taking Tests
   d. Easy Ways to Ace Exams
2. Which sentence best expresses the main idea of the selection?
   a. Mental and physical strategies and organization help you to better handle tests.
   b. Bringing the right equipment to an exam is half the battle.

    c. Writing entertaining essay answers and using a clever system for multiple-choice answers guarantee exam success.

    d. A positive mental attitude and last-minute extra studying can ensure a passing grade.

3. Which of these is *not* a good idea when you enter the exam room?
    a. Finding a chair or desk that feels comfortable
    b. Sitting away from the window
    c. Taking a seat at the front of the room
    d. Bringing enough pens

4. Brett suggests that cramming just before a test is pointless
    a. because you can't analyze the mood in the exam room.
    b. because it adds to your mental clutter and you won't remember those facts.
    c. because you can overprepare and go to the wrong location in your confusion.
    d. because you can't meditate and practise deep-breathing as you cram.

5. The most important steps in approaching a test are
    a. choosing a good seat, bringing lots of equipment, and having the right attitude.
    b. arriving on time, at the right location, and handling multiple-choice questions correctly.
    c. choosing the right location and materials, being calm enough to write in an organized way, and knowing how to write a good essay answer.
    d. remembering your watch, keeping your pencils sharp, and using the information from multiple-choice questions in your essays.

6. The author implies that
    a. intense total concentration is the best mental state for dealing with a test.
    b. test results may benefit from brief pauses in concentration.
    c. large muscle exercise is necessary to do well on tests.
    d. several short strolls through the exam room are advisable.

7. *True or false?* _____ Brett implies that final marks are partly the result of decisions made by the student as he or she first looks at the exam.

8. You may conclude that
    a. a good essay answer depends on your ability to amuse the professor.
    b. a good essay answer may result from the use of correct grammar and spelling.
    c. a good essay answer results from an innovative approach, solid content, and attention to language usage.
    d. a good essay answer will result from exciting new discoveries you make in your subject area.

9. The word *gleaned* in "tidbits of information can often be gleaned from them and then reworked to fit nicely (and inconspicuously) into sentence answers or essays" (paragraph 6) means
   a. stolen.
   b. sneaked.
   c. rewritten.
   d. picked up.

10. The word *herbivores* in "The Effect of Green Pesticides on Small Herbivores" (paragraph 9) means
   a. fieldmice.
   b. plant-eating animals.
   c. houseflies.
   d. rodents.

■ Discussion Questions

About Content

1. What are Eileen A. Brett's five recommendations for writing better tests? Which of the five have you tried? Have any that you practise worked for you? Why?

2. Why should you bring only one pencil? Are you going to use the pencil more or less often than your pen? Why?

3. What is the "Attitude Adjustment Approach"? Why is this important?

4. What is the point of doing any multiple-choice questions first? Why bother to use two different writing implements?

About Structure

5. What method of ordering, common to all process writing, is used for this essay? In the opening paragraph, which elements recommended by this text for the first paragraphs of process writing do you find?

6. How many paragraphs does the author devote to each of the five steps she lists as parts of the process? List the stages or steps and the numbers of the paragraphs in which they are discussed.

   Step 1 _____ (paragraph _____)

   Step 2 _____ (paragraph _____)

   Step 3 _____ (paragraph _____)

   Step 4 _____ (paragraph _____)

   Step 5 _____ (paragraph _____)

   Which of the steps receives the most attention from the author? Why?

7. How does the writer link the stages in her process? Does she use transition words, "time marker" words and phrases, and/or repetition of important ideas? Which of these devices do you find in which paragraphs? Where are the transition devices placed?

About Style and Tone

8. The author uses some humorous phrases and a tone that is upbeat and lively. What is the effect on you as a reader of the mixture of a light tone with serious subject matter?

9. Where do you find examples of Brett's sense of humour? Some techniques to look for include (1) exaggeration, (2) unlikely combinations of ideas, and (3) unexpected ideas or turns of phrase.

    List an example of each of these below:

    1. _____

    2. _____

    3. _____

■ Writing Assignments

Assignment 1: Writing a Paragraph

Brett notes that the result of not knowing how to take tests is panic. She suggests that such tension may be the result of many factors, such as disorganization, last-minute cramming, mental attitude, and lack of understanding of test design and marking.

Write a paragraph about one memorable exam or test experience of your own. Decide while you are prewriting whether you have more bad or good experiences to list. Your point of view or attitude expressed will result from the list which is longer and contains clearer details or memories. Your paragraph may reflect details and suggestions from Brett's essay. A good exam experience of your own may or may not be the result of having followed some of the author's suggestions, while suffering through a particularly terrible test may bring back some very vivid details. Such strong memories may produce a good paragraph.

Your paragraph should isolate the *causes* of such a good or bad test-writing experience. The end result will be a topic sentence such as "The worst exam I ever wrote was the result of three problems: _____."

Assignment 2: Writing a Paragraph

Should such techniques as note-taking, test-writing, time-management, and study skills in general be part of your college's course offerings? Many students arrive at postsecondary education without much knowledge of such skills. Do you believe that a half-semester course covering these areas would be of use to you?

Write a paragraph which argues for or against such a course, covering *three* skills areas you believe would help you most. Be sure to choose three skills you would most like to acquire, and for each of these, list the reasons you feel these should or should not be part of college curricula. If you wish to dispute the value of such a course, you may find justification in the availability of articles such as Eileen A. Brett's, or Sheila Akers' "Power Learning," or other personal experiences which have helped your study skills.

Assignment 3: Writing an Essay

Taking tests and exams is only one of life's challenges. We all face situations and personal trials where a bit of advice, or someone else's experience and techniques, could prove useful. "How to" books are among the best-selling titles in any bookstore.

Here is a list of ordinary social situations with which you may have some experience. What these situations have in common is the often unspoken set of rules governing what to do. Select one of these topics and begin to draft an outline, listing your own set of steps for a process essay which tells someone how to handle just such an event or problem.

1. Attending the funeral of someone to whom you are not closely attached
2. Giving a speech at a wedding reception
3. Looking after someone else's child for a day
4. Saying thank you for a gift you disliked
5. Saying no to a particularly forceful salesperson
6. Refusing a date or invitation from someone you like, but are not that fond of
7. Getting out of attending a family dinner or major family celebration
8. Being best man or maid/matron of honour at a friend's wedding

You may want to refer back to the chapter on process writing (pages 134–141) for a review of how to construct a process essay. In your outline, be sure to include in the opening paragraph the final result of the process, and whatever benefits you think will result from following your procedures. Indicate also roughly how many steps will be involved, any anticipated difficulties, as well as any equipment or materials needed to complete the process.

Divide your list of steps or stages into three sections, and give precise details concerning how to complete each step successfully. Try not to omit any necessary steps, or leave room for mistakes caused by omitting complete instructions. Be sure to make good use of transitions to help your reader through the process.

Finish your essay with a summary of what the reader has now accomplished, and a parting thought on the value of such an achievement. You may certainly treat your subject with humour, if you are comfortable doing so.

Why Should We Hire You?

Jim Maloney

The workplace of the 1990s is a new place: perhaps a not-so-pleasant prospect for the college student, and a place of decreasing possibilities for the already-employed individual. Neither "a job for a lifetime" nor the chance of steady advancement in a field of personal expertise can be expected, much less taken for granted by anyone. A diploma, a degree, and a snappy resume are no guarantees of a lifetime's steady employment. Instead, a sense of direction, steady and careful academic preparation, and active job research during the college years are needed to face the realities of the twenty-first-century job market. Jim Maloney, professor of English at Seneca College and long-time expert in career-based areas of writing, poses student readers "The Question"— a question he faced, and a question most companies' Human Resources personnel will ask any student reading this essay: "Why should we hire you?"

I

"Why should we hire you for this position?" 1

I remember the first time I was asked that question. I remember it the same way I 2 remember the first time a police officer asked to see my driver's licence and registration. I was no more prepared to be caught speeding than I was prepared to explain why I should be permanently employed teaching English at a community college. In both cases, I experienced a sinking feeling in my stomach, and a quickening of my pulse: the sensations that come with being caught.

I got a speeding ticket, but I didn't get the job. 3

Looking back at the difficulty I had with that basic question, I can't believe that I 4 approached the interview so badly prepared. If I had been as prepared for the job interview as I was for doing the job, I would have felt no surprise. I had had a number of previous jobs where I was hired only for my ability to perform physical tasks, so the interviews for these jobs were far less crucial than was the simple ability to do the work. However, just as exceeding the speed limit will, when traffic police are performing properly, lead to a speeding ticket, so being interviewed for an attractive career-entry position will, when the interviewer knows what to look for, lead directly or indirectly to the question "Why should we hire you?"

The question is a significant one, not just because you will encounter it, in some form, as part of a job interview, along with other "open-ended" queries designed to uncover your understanding of the position and of the suitability of your qualifications. The question is also important to consider in preparing your resume and application letter—documents crucial to creating possible interviews. Moreover, the question is relevant to you, who haven't yet finished your postsecondary career preparation and, therefore, won't be immediately facing interviews for positions in your chosen field. For you at this stage, the question "Why should we hire you?" may seem pointless, premature, or irrelevant. Try turning the question around: "Why should *I* be hired?" Now the question may have more meaning to you. Indeed, considered in this form, the question can guide you towards preparing for a career. So, thinking about how you will answer such a question will help you not only to understand the significance of the question but also to back up your answers with the right credentials, skills, and experiences.

II

Too frequently, students seem to take for granted their right, or even their access, to interviews and to jobs needed to begin their careers. Such optimism can no longer be justified. Ten years ago, graduating students were warned that continued employment in one field for one company for one's entire working life was increasingly becoming a thing of the past. Students could expect three or four career shifts. Today, many college or university graduates will never have the chance even to begin careers in their chosen fields. Others may find only part-time or contract work. The last decade has produced enormous changes in the way business and industry operate in North America, and in the ways in which people are employed.

Corporate downsizing—reductions in the workforce needed by a company for operating purposes—has been a fact in business life for some time now. Global competition is usually given as the reason for smaller workforce requirements, while, it is claimed, technological developments, especially computerization, have led to massive employee lay-offs with no loss to productivity. Of course, there is an alternative view of downsizing: that remaining employees are expected to be more productive—to work longer and harder—to pick up the slack. A consequence of downsizing and technological change is a reduced full-time workforce, many of whom either handle more tasks or perform more specialized technological activities. In some companies, another consequence of a smaller workforce is the replacement of permanent full-time employees who receive higher salaries and significant benefit packages with part-time or contract workers who are offered lower salaries and few, if any, benefits. Some companies have virtually nothing to offer but these limited, rather unpromising positions.

These changes are not limited to the private sector. Recently, the governments of Alberta and Ontario initiated large-scale downsizing projects in their civil services. Many job lay-offs in health care, education, and local governments have resulted from such funding cuts. For someone wishing to begin a new career, the prospects are starting to look nasty and brutish, and the immediate picture is distinctly short of jobs, hours, and rewards for new employees. Quite simply, there may not be jobs for college and university graduates who don't know how they fit into this brave new workworld.

Consequently, it is now more important than ever for you to consider and act on The   9 Question while there is still time for you to learn the needs of employers and to make yourself capable of meeting those needs.

III

There are numerous reasons why students may not be seriously addressing The Question. 10 Many students place so much trust in the educational system that they fail to look onward to life beyond graduation. Often, the very fact that students are attending college or university may be the reason they don't take advantage of their school years to prepare themselves effectively for the next step. Some students make the error of seeing an employment ad's requirement of a postsecondary diploma or degree as a guarantee of entry into that career. These students may be so impressed by their status as college or university students that they are complacent about their futures. Unfortunately, being a student is not a career and, with few exceptions, is not very profitable. Other students may find their academic work difficult and demanding enough without adding the headache of anticipating yet more demands. Still others may trust their chosen vocationally based academic program to put them on the correct job track. The problem is that they may not actually know where it is that they are going. I am amazed every semester by the number of students in specialized programs who are utterly unaware of jobs that may be available to them, of skills needed and of the actual nature of duties they may be expected to perform. Clueless in an academic fool's paradise, all of these students are caught in wishful rather than realistic thinking.

But what *actual* difference will it make to familiarize yourself with job specifica- 11 tions and employment prospects during your education instead of when you graduate? Preparing yourself to be desirable to prospective employers can have clear advantages during your college or university years. Even if there were no other consequences, a sense of the ultimate purpose of your studies should make your efforts more significant, less abstract—less academic. Being aware of the competition you face in your chosen field could certainly make the pursuit of good grades more meaningful. If you are in a program with a variety of optional courses, your knowledge of the job market's demands will help you to make more informed decisions. Should you be registered in a more rigidly structured program, knowing that the real requirements of the job you want differ from your program's offerings could indicate that you should supplement your education with additional courses beyond your curriculum. Reading job descriptions during your school years will teach you that certain types of work experience are desired, even for entry-level positions. Therefore, choosing summer or part-time work in an area related to your chosen career, even if the pay is less attractive, may ultimately be more rewarding. Most career-advice agencies now recommend volunteer work, and many students volunteer their time to organizations connected to their career paths. In the cases of both occasional and volunteer work, the contacts made and the experience gained can be very valuable. Finally, you may never need a total personality make-over, but you should think about personal characteristics of successful people in your chosen field.

IV

With all these advantages to be gained from planning ahead for employment, how do you 12 go about finding out what employers want?

One place to start is within your school. Many vocationally based programs have a 13 faculty member responsible for student employment. Some of your instructors may be actively involved in their fields; others may have informal but vital contacts with employers or former students in business and technology. You may discover that it is quite easy to gain insight into your field of interest just by sounding out your teachers. Yet another source of information is your school's student employment office. As well as placing graduating students, this facility usually offers a range of services including personality testing, career counselling, information resources on companies, and job profiles. Graduation is too late to find out what your school has to offer.

Don't feel limited to these paths as you try to discover a career direction. Find out 14 requirements for actual jobs in order to become the candidate you want to be. Even though you are not applying for a permanent position now, make a habit of following not only jobs listed in your school's employment office but also those advertised in newspapers, professional journals, or occupational periodicals. Best of all, visit human resources offices of major employers in your field; check job requirements for current or future positions; meet personnel officers, and read any information available about their companies. The time spent will pay off in your career.

At this point, you may be ready to get in touch with someone already working in your 15 chosen field to gain first-hand knowledge of positions you would like. You don't need to know personally someone who fits this description; one of your teachers or friends may know someone you can contact. Alternatively, speaking with or writing to an employer in your field may help you to find a person suitably placed to answer your questions about qualifications, duties, and responsibilities. You would be surprised by how easy it is to get information, even from a stranger. If you try some of these approaches, you are on your way to a personal network.

Today, you need to work hard to find the work you desire. That means knowing the 16 reasons you should be hired and taking the steps needed to prepare a solidly based answer before you are asked The Question.

■ Reading Comprehension Questions

1. Which of the following would be the best alternative title for this selection?
   a. Diplomas and Dim Prospects
   b. Prepare to Work to Find Work
   c. Career Confusion
   d. The Best Degree Is No Guarantee

2. Which sentence best expresses the main idea of the selection?
   a. Intelligent choices of the right courses give students fair chances of getting work on graduation.
   b. The workplace is a crowded "buyer's market," and students must work to prepare themselves to be the "right product."
   c. Today's students must expect several changes in career paths, and several different employers in their professional futures.
   d. Technological developments have eliminated many traditional job opportunities.

3. Maloney believes that
   a. students should concentrate on the employer's viewpoint as they acquire education, skills, and experience.
   b. concentrating on writing good resumes and cover letters will ensure job interviews.
   c. students can focus on career goals from the beginning of their college experience.
   d. due to changes in business and industry, finding a job in the next few years is a hopeless task.

4. Corporate downsizing has led to
   a. a need for more highly trained technological workers.
   b. a mixture of highly versatile and very specialized workers.
   c. companies consisting only of part-time workers.
   d. changes only in the private sector.

5. *True or false?* _____ Maloney believes that choice of a diploma program in a developing area of industry and careful attention to course work can maximize chances for full-time future employment.

6. The author implies that
   a. looking toward the employment market involves looking at all aspects of oneself.
   b. looking forward to job interviews is pointless and terrifying.
   c. it is never too early to start preparing a good resume and cover letter.
   d. looking for work in the public sector is a waste of time.

7. The essay suggests that
   a. being in focused vocational training is a demanding occupation and gives students enough of an advantage in the job search.
   b. a sense of future job needs may motivate students toward better performance, better course choices, and the acquisition of suitable experience.
   c. knowing which skills will be needed and what jobs may be available will lead to success.
   d. becoming "the ideal lab technician" or "the perfect accountant" while in college is the only way to ensure job interviews.

8. *True or false?* _____ Professional contacts, college student employment offices, "go-see" interviews, and daily reading of employment ads are enough to guarantee a shot at the ideal job.

9. The word *crucial* in "documents crucial to creating possible interviews" (paragraph 5) means
   a. special.
   b. justifiable.
   c. reasonable.
   d. important.

10. The word *anticipating* in "without adding the headache of anticipating yet more demands" (paragraph 10) means
   a. awaiting.
   b. worrying about.
   c. denying.
   d. considering.

■ Discussion Questions

About Content

1. Why does Professor Maloney recall so vividly the first time he heard the question "Why should we hire you?"

2. The essay's proposed strategy for early focusing on future work is opposed to some traditional thinking which saw college years as a time for discovering yourself and your goals. Do you agree with Maloney's suggestions? What do you think of such "one-track" end-directed approaches to your college experience?

3. What are the early advantages the author sees for the student who is aware of future job needs and possibilities?

4. What resources are available to students within their own colleges?

About Structure

5. The thesis of many essays is found near the beginning or the end. Locate the thesis statement of "Why Should We Hire You?" and write it here.

_____

6. Which method(s) of introduction does the author use in this selection?
   a. Broad-to-narrow
   b. Explaining the importance of the topic
   c. Anecdote
   d. Situation opposite to the one developed

7. What methods of achieving transitions between paragraphs does Maloney use more than once in this selection?
   a. Repetition of key words
   b. Transitional phrases
   c. Questions followed by explanations

   Find examples of at least three of these, and note them below, with the appropriate paragraph numbers.

   _____ (paragraph _____)

   _____ (paragraph _____)

   _____ (paragraph _____)

About Style and Tone

8. Maloney begins his essay with a highly personal and directly voiced confession containing a comparison between two apparently dissimilar events.

   How does the tone of the opening three paragraphs compare with that of the rest of the essay? What do you learn about the author, and how does what you discover affect your connection with him as writer? Does it make the information in the essay more or less credible? Why?

9. After the introductory paragraphs, the essay is divided into three sections. How would you subtitle each of these sections?

   1. _____

   2. _____

   3. _____

   What general method of organization do your subtitles seem to suggest?

■ Writing Assignments

Assignment 1: Writing a Paragraph

A writing assignment based on this selection is on page 179.

Assignment 2: Writing a Paragraph

Put yourself in Jim Maloney's position as he begins his essay. Imagine you have successfully graduated from your current program, have your resume in hand, and are sitting in a job interview. Now answer "The Question" posed by the essay's title. Start with a specific job you may have in mind, or may have read about in the paper. Now, list what you think the employer may be looking for in terms of skills, academic training, and part-time experience. Your paragraph should answer

"The Question." You may want to begin with a topic sentence like "Fire Protection has been a life-long goal of mine, and I've done a lot of academic and practical preparation to get ready to enter the field." Make use of the groups of details you've listed under the headings above to build up your paragraph.

Assignment 3: Writing an Essay

You are an employer in the 1990s. *You* ask "The Question." You're a human resources officer in a company, and *you* must write the job description to be read by all those eager college graduates.

Write an essay which follows the format of a job description for a position for which your diploma is preparing you. To see examples of these, go to your Student Services office, or look at some periodicals special to your area of study for employers' advertisements. Your mission is to find and persuade that "ideal candidate" that this job is what that person is after. Be as specific in your details as possible. You can't offer "the world on a string"; you have limited salary and promotion possibilities in this uncertain economy. But you're going to be facing hundreds of applicants.

Make an outline similar to the following:

<u>Thesis/Introduction:</u> Omnitech Incorporated is looking for an energetic and ambitious entry-level _____. The successful candidate will have three main qualifications: _____, _____, and especially _____. (The introduction should include a brief company description and approximate salary range, as well as any special requirements, such as a willingness to travel.)

<u>Topic Sentence 1:</u> Your background and education will include

a. _____

b. _____

c. _____

<u>Topic Sentence 2:</u> The skills we're looking for are

a. _____

b. _____

c. _____

<u>Topic Sentence 3:</u> The types of experience we prefer are

a. _____

b. _____

c. _____

Conclude by summarizing your needs, and by emphasizing that the successful applicant will come close to or exceed all the requirements listed, and by stating that only resumes received within a certain time frame will be considered.

The True Meaning of Literacy

Mary Curran

Students in colleges today hear a lot of discussion about their literacy levels and the literacy skills they will need in business and industry. Many students feel inadequate about their own achievements in reading and even less certain about their abilities in writing. John Langan, earlier in this book, speaks directly to such students; he assures them that writing and its inseparable companion, reading, are *learnable skills* which improve with practice. Nonetheless, persistent memories of reading difficulties and bad marks on writing assignments haunt many students enough to make assigned college tasks daunting and difficult. Writing is, as Langan states on page 13, "plain hard work" for almost everyone. Practice, journal-writing, and learning the process of writing itself may help dispel the unhappy combination of early experiences and of deadly definitions of "literacy" derived from Oxford or Mount Olympus. Mary Curran is a high school teacher in Scarborough, a suburb of Toronto; she takes a compassionate look backward at her brother's writing experiences, then casts a discerning eye on her current classroom. She finds that a sense of self-worth is a vital element for self-expression.

I own a cardboard box filled with old letters collected over the years from family, friends and acquaintances. And I attach more than mere sentiment to these writings. 1

Some time ago, I added a letter with a Hong Kong postmark to that box. It was from my brother who works in India. Separated by continents from his family and friends, he wrote in transit and, since he usually phones across the oceans, I was surprised by his writing. 2

He spoke happily on paper of work, family, memories of school Latin and of his new-found urge to write lengthy letters to special people in his life. Amidst the humor, he mentioned gently his recent ill-health. Something dangerous, contained, he said. No need to worry. But the dark news seeped through the friendly words recorded effortlessly on the page. 3

Thirty years on, the eloquence of that letter confounded my parents' grim despair at his high school English marks and his teacher's laconic comments beside his D average. I remembered this one day while watching my own students write earnest essays at my command.

I also noticed (as September merged into fall and those same students relaxed in their own company) a quiet flurry of handwriting in agenda books, followed by discreet exchanges and furtive readings when they were officially at work on formal essays. Curious about this letter writing, I joined them.

Dear Mario, I wrote, why were you late this morning? Dear Patsy, tell me why you distracted us today? In the written conversations that developed, I read about four hockey games in a week and early morning family quarrels.

Fascinated by the dialogue, I invited the class to write weekly letters. I heard about pet goldfish, infatuations born in the cafeteria and much loved, lost and grieved for grandparents and relatives. The humor and pathos of life, similar to my brother's, appeared before me in my classroom.

About the same time the results of the most recent of ministry of education writing and reading tests for Grade 9 students arrived, prompting me to wonder why we fail to see beyond the obvious in our fastidious literacy watch over our youth.

How easy to reward 14-year-olds who write confidently about events in their lives and ideas in their heads; to feel impatient with the hesitant who hunch over pages with Liquid Paper in hand and caution in their hearts; and to despair for those who pen only a few barren lines with the plaintive refrain "Nothing happens in my life."

How logical to respond to such writing by narrowing the search for literacy with a heavy emphasis on its practical, economic benefits and a fearful obsession with its measurement.

How myopic, too, when we ignore a problem more profound than bad grammar or poor spelling. Students who believe their lives and their thoughts are of little consequence, who cannot imagine a world where others are interested in them or their ideas, stutter on the written page and fall silent before us, to be graded with a D grade (like my brother) or worse.

Today, my brother's faded pencil notes are still visible inside an ancient poetry book which sits on my bookshelf. How he writes has changed little. His handwriting looks much the same now but there are differences in what he writes and who reads his words. The commands and evaluation that muzzled his teenage written speech are gone.

That old book shares a shelf with copies of the literary giants, and my cardboard collection of handwritten mementoes (including my brother's letter). I keep these together to remind me that literacy is never just about money and measurement. It is also about that first moment when each of us realizes that those thoughts on the page are our own proud creation, not someone else's.

Then literacy stands affirmed, not denied.

■ Reading Comprehension Questions

1. Which of the following would be the best alternative title for this selection?
   a. Literacy Past and Present
   b. Pride and Prejudgements

    c. The Benefits of Literacy

    d. Ourselves and Our Words

2. Which sentence best expresses the main idea of the selection?

    a. Having students keep journals and write letters is enough to encourage literacy.

    b. People will never value the writing of those who don't have an early mastery of grammar and spelling.

    c. Literate writing is valuable for careers, but it is the product of valuing and taking pride in expressing our own lives.

    d. Literacy is mainly a matter of measuring how well students meet certain "benchmark" criteria, and rewarding the student appropriately.

3. Curran was surprised by her brother's letter because

    a. he was extremely ill, and hadn't written more about this.

    b. he lived so far away and they'd lost contact.

    c. he'd been such an excellent English student.

    d. he normally phoned, and had discovered a new desire to write.

4. The writer noticed that her own students

    a. hated writing and avoided it whenever possible.

    b. hadn't much to say on paper when they did write.

    c. wrote uninteresting journals and responses unrelated to anything.

    d. wrote and read all the time informally when assigned formal writing.

5. Curran implies that recent provincial education testing

    a. overlooks the fact that writing begins with our sense of ourselves.

    b. shows that the "real world" benefits of writing should be stressed.

    c. demonstrates that Ontario students' literacy lags behind that of other provinces.

    d. uncovers the inadequacy of our testing and measurement standards.

6. The author implies that

    a. only her brother's illness unlocked his innate writing ability.

    b. valuing his life and growing beyond early judgements made her brother's writing enjoyable to read.

    c. students do their best only when they are not being judged by academic standards.

    d. most people write well only when they are writing about personal matters.

7. *True or false?* _____ We can conclude that the author feels that most students' writing problems stem from similar causes.

8. The article suggests that

    a. discipline and clear goals are the best incentives to developing literacy.

    b. literacy can develop naturally with maturity and experience.

    c. self-confidence is the only requirement for the development of literacy.

    d. literacy is a process originating in our taking pride in what we write.

9. The word *laconic* in "his teachers' laconic comments beside his D average" (paragraph 4) means

    a. sour.

    b. mean.

    c. brief.

    d. vicious.

10. The word *fastidious* in "to wonder why we fail to see beyond the obvious in our fastidious literacy watch over our youth" (paragraph 8) means

    a. painstaking.

    b. obsessive.

    c. bad-natured.

    d. academic.

■ Discussion Questions

About Content

1. What were the subjects of Mary Curran's brother's letter to her? Which was of the greatest concern to her? What else surprised her about the way this subject appeared in his letter? Why?

2. Which two aspects of her brother's school years contrast with "the eloquence of that letter" (paragraph 2)? How do these ideas connect the author to her current situation? How does she connect her life-experience to her teaching and to her students?

3. Is it "logical" to respond to students who have difficulty writing about personal matters by emphasizing the need for writing in business and industry? Will this approach make their problems easier to deal with? Why, or why not?

About Structure

4. Which method of introduction does the author use to begin her article?

    a. Broad-to-narrow

    b. Explaining the importance of the topic

    c. Situation opposite to the one to be developed

    d. Anecdote

5. The thesis of this article is found in one of the two positions usually selected to best draw the readers' attention. What are these two possible locations?

    1. _____

    2. _____

Find the thesis statement, and write it here:

_____

_____

6. Curran opens a box of memories, then writes about the present, and concludes
    with a synthesis, or mixture of past and present. What transitional phrases
    does she use at the beginnings of her paragraphs to indicate her ordering
    method for content?

    _____   (paragraph _____)

    _____   (paragraph _____)

    _____   (paragraph _____)

    _____   (paragraph _____)

About Style and Tone

7. The author's tone in general is straightforward and direct. There are two pas-
    sages in the article where the tone shifts; the first occurs in Curran's entries
    on letter writing to her students. In which paragraphs do you find this change
    of tone?

    Paragraph _____

    Paragraph _____

    How does her change of tone affect your perception of her as a teacher? What
    do you learn from these paragraphs? What did she learn?
        The second shift in tone is toward a more formal type of address. This
    change is signalled by a formal rhetorical device, but a very simple one: that
    of repetition. What grammatical structure is repeated, and in which para-
    graphs does this repetition occur?

    Paragraph _____

    Paragraph _____

    Paragraph _____

        What is the effect on you as a reader of these repetitions? How is their
    use related to the subject matter of these paragraphs? Is your sense of the
    author's point of view and identity changed by her shift in tone? How?

8. Curran uses some dramatic and vivid phrases to describe students who suf-
    fer difficulties in putting thoughts on paper. Find the paragraph which best
    pictures these students, and list the phrases you find most touching. How does
    her accuracy of detail help you to "see" and "feel for" these students?

■ Writing Assignments

Assignment 1: Writing a Paragraph

A writing assignment based on this selection is on page 133.

Assignment 2: Writing a Paragraph

Imagine you are in Mary Curran's class. You receive a note like the following:

> Dear _____,
>
> You seem very quiet lately. Normally, I can count on you to chatter away in class, answer questions, and write pages of journal entries. The last few days you've seemed far away, and rather distracted. I miss your interesting and thought-provoking journal entries. If there's something you'd feel comfortable writing about, would you like to do so? As always, your journals are completely confidential, strictly between you and me.

Write a paragraph which consists of a letter responding to Ms. Curran's inquiry. You may write about events from your own life which have kept you from communicating easily at one time or another, or you may create a fictional situation based on a friend's experiences. Explain why you have been having difficulties lately, and why this is affecting your writing. Possible causes for your or your friend's problem may be poor marks in this or other subjects, family attitudes, or outside activities. Prewrite by making a list of such likely distractions; these would be your *causes*, or reasons for the *effect*, which is not writing.

You may want to conclude with a summation of how all these matters have led to your current situation, and a final thought.

Assignment 3: Writing an Essay

Curran feels very strongly that "literacy is never just about money and measurement. It is also about that first moment when each of us realizes that those thoughts on the page are our own proud creation" (paragraph 13). She writes that Ontario's schools have done English students a disservice by neglecting and de-emphasizing the personal roots of expression. Punishing a student who finds writing difficult with unexplained bad marks and threats of future failure can hardly result in anything but even shorter sentences and more blank pages. Write an essay which explains the origins of three of your major problems with writing. Have you been a hesitant writer? Was it never made clear to you why writing would be important to you? Was no writing occasion ever enjoyable? Were you intimidated by a teacher's comments, or lack thereof? Did grammar seem unfathomable? Were you taught how to correct your areas of difficulty? Do you read for pleasure?

You may want to write a sentence outline for your essay. Look at the student paper on page 31, about that student's reasons for disliking English. If that paragraph were to be expanded to an essay, an outline would look like this:

Thesis statement: There were three main reasons why I disliked English.

Topic sentence 1: I grew up in a blue-collar family and environment where no emphasis was put on English skills.
a. My father and everyone we knew worked at technical and manual jobs in a steel mill.
b. Daily conversations centred on factory concerns and machinery.
c. No one considered writing important.

Topic sentence 2: Public school and high school years reinforced my attitudes and experiences, and added the concept that "writing/English" was "not for boys."
a. Public school emphasized math skills for boys, and trades were seen as the only vocational goals for boys.
b. Writing was barely even taught in public school.
c. High school English teachers had a grim attitude toward the value of English; it seemed "unmanly."

Topic sentence 3: In college, I had to face the fact that my English skills were well below acceptable standards.
a. I failed my first essay assignment miserably.
b. My old expectations and attitudes were things of the past, and could harm my future.
c. I had to take remedial writing courses just to catch up with other first-year students.

To complete your essay, you may wish to summarize your main points, and express some concluding thoughts that are relevant to your current college career and to your current writing experiences.

Memoirs of a Book-Molesting Childhood

Adele Wiseman

Adele Wiseman was an accomplished writer and artist with a life-long addiction—to reading. In the selection that follows, she looks back with humour and affection at her "book-molesting childhood" in Winnipeg. For many students today, her devotion to stories and books may be more understandable if they relate it to our addiction to screens: TV screens, video-game screens, and our home computer screens with all those riotous floating CD images. For Wiseman, reading was a private, secret pleasure, at odds with school requirements. Like Basil Johnston in the selection "Spiritual Storyteller," Adele Wiseman was entranced by the power of stories. How many of us are not enchanted by stories—those on CD or tape, or even those of our favourite soap operas? But will there ever be a book titled *Memoirs of an Internet-Molesting Childhood?*

I can't remember exactly when I learned to read. There are plenty of stories about how **1** gorgeous I was, and about my precocity as a flaming nuisance, but I've never managed to persuade anyone to tell of my having taught myself to read before the age of six months, and gone on to a career as a Renaissance toddler. I can recall, however, when I first realized that there was such a phenomenon as reading, and that I was left out.

I sit at the kitchen table, eyeing my big sister and big brother. They sit across from and **2** *beside me, but ignore me completely. Each is totally absorbed in what Mama calls A BOOK. What is this inactivity called READING which can capture them so utterly that sitting here with me at the table they are completely out of reach? I resent this exclusive absorption of theirs, suspect it is somehow spurious. Showing off. Mama asks them to set aside their books and eat. Hah!*

We're sitting at the table again. I'm big too, now, and we are all three reading. Was there **3** *ever a time when I wasn't? Mama is pleading with us to put aside our books and eat. I work my book onto my lap and scrunch down so low I can smell the oilcloth under the dishes.*

Mama is still pleading, and now my little brother has joined the pleaders. **4**

Mama has prevailed. We know that even when Daddy isn't home we are not supposed to **5** *read at table. Mealtimes are asquabble with our determination to prevent each other from doing so.*

There was always someone trying to interfere with your reading. At school, where **6** it all began, it was as though they'd showed you you had a magic wand but then grudged you the use of it. They even tried to stop you from reading ahead of the class in the textbooks. And they spoiled the textbooks by insisting you had to LEARN from them. What distrust of school-learning I learned from those countless short-term memory hurdles over the unmemorable and now unremembered. As for real books, there was hardly anything to read in the schools I went to. At most you might have a few volumes on a shelf in a classroom. I remember the anxious fervour with which I dreamed of "passing" to a classroom that actually contained such a "library," how I worried I wouldn't be considered "smart enough" according to the mysterious standards of teachers, to whom my sloppiness and poor penmanship and general unruliness clearly represented a serious failure of intelligence. And when I did get there I found the books surrounded by rules about when you could or could not get to look at them.

In order not to waste those long hours wondering what happened next, I usually 7 brought my reading matter along with me to school. It was always open and ready, in the mess of my desk, to be slipped out onto my lap, or tucked between the pages of the text or scribbler in which I was supposedly absorbed. Luckily, I could usually get my assigned work done quickly enough, and if I hadn't got myself into some other trouble along the way, I would be able to find a little time, even in school, in which to be happy. How much more thrilling were the exploits of Robin Hood and his merry men, when the very act of reading about them seemed to partake of their daring effrontery. The tricky moments were, of course, when the teacher was TEACHING, and you hadn't noticed, and she lit on you suddenly with a question that jerked you from your book without the faintest notion of what she was talking about.... I was a good reader for my age, so the teacherly mind figured I didn't need any practice, whereas my penmanship was lousy. But half a century later, my handwriting is still irrelevantly lousy, and I am still learning to read.

I fell in love with stories even before I knew that stories were to be written, when I 8 was a tot and could hardly wait for Daddy to come home from work and tell us tales at bedtime. Indeed my first memorable success as a story-teller, a triumph I still gloat over, occurred when I managed to keep my kid brother Morris in a state of helpless laughter for an astonishingly long time in a story I made up all by myself. A lot of eggs got dropped, broken, sat on, smashed, slipped over, thrown, crushed-in-mouth, swallowed whole, regurgitated, totalled on colliding runaway wagons, and in a variety of other bizarrely farcical and obscurely satisfying ways in the process, and I have never forgotten the joy and the power and the wonder of my words being able to keep the chubby little guy chortling and rolling on the bed with mirth.

For real books the St John's Public Library in Winnipeg's north end was our Fort 9 Knox, and sometimes seemed as hard to crack. Librarians in those days were something like teachers. They loved absolute quiet and goody-goodies and were not inclined to recognize legitimate book lust in the scruffier, sloppier, cheekier, and clearly foreign among the young. As for me, I was a politically conscious child, as most of us were at that time in North Winnipeg. I knew the library had been endowed by a rich American capitalist. I was puzzled by several fine points re the question of conscience money, but I knew that it should certainly not be allowed to go to waste. So I tried to play the game. I tried not to rush madly from title to title, piling up armloads. I tried to look delicate and smiley and good, tried to keep my trap shut, only whispered sometimes, tried to handle the books carefully, tried to manage what I suppose was at best an uncouth decorum. I was no more successful with this, I'm afraid, than I was with my yearly September vow before the school term began, that this year I would try harder not to get into trouble and make the teachers hate me. In spite of the eternal hopefulness in my eyes, I could tell by the way they vibrated when they saw me that the librarians were convinced that this one was nothing but another congenitally sinful book molester.

Not only books; once the reading habit set in no figured word was safe from the youthful printingester. When I was prevented from sneaking a book into our single bathroom, much in demand by a family of six plus a variable population of boarders, I sat and pored over the labels of the bottle of yellow cod-liver oil, the brown bottle of iodine, the fine print on the little blue Ex-Lax tin. Then I tried to decipher the disappearing imprint on the bar of crisply aromatic Lux soap that my mom preferred to the musky green Palmolive I always found at my aunt's. I subjected each crackly square of faded red, green, or white tissue paper that had originally wrapped an orange, lemon, pear, or apple, but which my uncle Abie the peddler had saved for us, to pensive scrutiny anew, before bestowing it its final Sunkist kiss. I even read the toilet bowl, a habit that has brought some unexpected discoveries in later years. I don't remember which deathless example of dramatic art I was seeing in a West-End London theatre when, at intermission, I discovered my first Crapper, but I certainly remember that moment of linguistic revelation.

It seems pretty clear to me now that just as important as the specific books which affected me at particular times were the experiential impurities of the reading process, the mutual contamination of the lived life and the lived reading. I have never been able to separate the act of reading from the acts of living. Reading is experience. I remember how it felt at different times, why I read what I read, what the reading meant to me, and what the books seemed to mean in relation to each other and to life. I remember the circumstances, how I used the very act of reading, in different ways, as part of the inner politics of the conduct of my existence. I avidly wanted to know, but I seldom read simply for intellectual information. I had to feel what I was reading, know what I was feeling, feel my knowing. I was never able to divorce myself from the emotional content of the words and word combinations, the suggestion, the overtones, the balances, the ambiguities, the implications, the contradictions, as well as the direct, naked thrusts of meaning that drew blood in infinite varieties of comprehending protest, pain, and pleasure.

Reading accompanied, and sometimes usurped, nearly every vital function. In this I was surely not alone, though perhaps I may have gone further than some. Who in those days had not sneaked a flashlight into bed in order to read under the covers after mom had finally and definitively come in herself and turned out the lights? Failing flashlight, sometimes there was a good moon by which to test the keenness of youthful sight, and some star splash, enhanced, with luck, by the bright reflecting dazzle of snow. Only galactic pre-television could upstage the secret nighttime read. The northern lights alone, aurora borealis, throbbing and thrumming across the prairie sky, could draw the child's mind into another read entirely, with a plot she never tired of trying to grasp.

Books were a route into life and reality and simultaneously an escape from life and reality, from the searing quality of every moment of the raw-nerved child's encounters with existence. They carved a path through the life into which I was locked, showed possible ways through the jungle of experience to the yearned-for civilization of the happy ending.

■ Reading Comprehension Questions

1. Which of the following would be the best alternative title for this selection?
   a. A Reading Prodigy
   b. Reading and Living
   c. Stolen Pleasures Are Sweetest
   d. The Winnipeg Wonderchild

2. Which sentence best expresses the main idea of the selection?
   a. For Wiseman, the experience of reading is vital to the experience of living.
   b. Reading took over Adele Wiseman's childhood life to an unhealthy extent.
   c. Reading represented an escape from a childhood in which the author felt maladjusted.
   d. Reading was mainly part of Adele Wiseman's search for intellectual stimulation.

3. Wiseman learned to read
   a. because she was such a precocious child.
   b. because everyone around her was caught up in reading.
   c. because people tried to stop her from doing so.
   d. because she was encouraged to read at school.

4. The author's anxiety about reading the books at school was increased by
   a. her teachers' disapproval of her writing and personal habits, and the regulations for using those books.
   b. her worry about passing to a high enough grade where there would be books in the classroom.
   c. her lack of intelligence represented by her poor handwriting skills and behavioural problems.
   d. fear of the teacher discovering the mess on her desk.

5. *True or false?* _____ Wiseman learned the value and joy of stories only after she learned to read.

6. The author implies
   a. that her primary school teachers didn't know what they were doing.
   b. that Winnipeg schools had an unfair policy about books and reading.
   c. that her teacher, aware of Adele's abilities, tried to interest her in the rest of the curriculum.
   d. that she was unable to do her in-class work, and thus her reading did not impress her teacher.

7. Paragraph 9 implies that the author
   a. continued to be a rebellious and scheming child outside of school.
   b. felt she was discriminated against because of her "foreign" appearance.

   c. resented the American funding which had endowed the library.

   d. knew she might never "adapt" or "fit in" enough to satisfy her desire to read.

8. We can conclude from the selection that

   a. reading represented a kind of paradox, or contradiction, to the author.

   b. reading overtook Wiseman's life to the exclusion of all else.

   c. reading showed the author that happy endings were possible in life.

   d. reading appealed primarily to the author's mind, rather than her feelings.

9. The word *Renaissance* in "gone on to a career as a Renaissance toddler" (paragraph 1) means

   a. Middle Ages, mediaeval: old-fashioned person.

   b. remarkable, extraordinary.

   c. period of revival of belief in human abilities: multi-talented person.

   d. newly born, ready for anything.

10. The word *effrontery* in "the very act of reading about them seemed to partake of their daring effrontery" (paragraph 7) means

   a. bravery.

   b. dishonesty.

   c. cruelty.

   d. boldness.

■ Discussion Questions

About Content

1. Who were the first people to interfere with the author's desire to read? What were their reasons for doing so? How might this interference have affected Wiseman's attitude toward reading? How would it affect your obsession with a habit you loved?

2. What does Adele Wiseman remember as her three major signs of lack of intelligence in primary school?

3. Why does Wiseman see her sneaking a read in school as comparable to the exploits of Robin Hood?

4. What was so special about fruit wrappers for the young author? What is suggested about the family's economic circumstances by this fact? What other detail in the selection might confirm your judgement?

About Structure

5. In which paragraph do you find the author's thesis statement? _____

Now, rewrite her thesis in your own words in the space below.

_____

_____

_____

Which one of the two traditional points of emphatic positioning has she chosen for her thesis? Why?

6. What type of order has Wiseman chosen for her selection? Which paragraph does not conform to her general ordering format? _____ How does this paragraph actually help to create the unified effect of the piece on the reader?

About Style and Tone

7. Wiseman loves stories, she tells us. What specific elements of the selection give this piece such a "narrative" feeling?

 a. informal direct address to the reader _____

 b. varied levels of vocabulary and diction _____

 c. direct dramatic inclusions _____

 In the blanks provided, note the paragraphs in which these elements appear.

8. Many elements of good description are also present in this selection:

 a. precise physical details _____

 b. lively use of action verbs _____

 c. metaphors and similes _____

 Note the paragraphs in which you find these elements in the spaces provided. Choose _one_ of these elements of description and list three examples below:

_____

_____

_____

9. From the title onward, there are many humorous moments in this piece. Find two phrases or ideas which you find amusing, and discuss why you find humour in them.

■ Writing Assignments

Assignment 1: Writing a Paragraph

Write a memoir of _your_ childhood. You have only one paragraph, so choose, as Adele Wiseman did, one particular aspect of your early years that you remember especially well—perhaps some activity that got you into trouble, or some habit that puzzled your family or teachers. As you work on your prewriting, try to think of this one activity, habit, or whatever, and of the *dominant impression* that it left with you; in other words, how you feel about it. Work on stating this dominant impression in one sentence, your topic sentence. Now brainstorm for, or list, three examples or experiences which back up this dominant impression. Try to use vivid and precise words to describe the people, places, and things involved. Use direct dialogue, if you are comfortable with it.

Assignment 2: Writing a Paragraph

Wiseman humorously termed her reading "book-molesting." Apparently, teachers and librarians saw it as a bad habit. Choose a bad habit of your own, and use the division and classification format to break it into three categories according to *one* principle of classification.

You might choose something like "procrastination" and use *people this annoys* as your categorizing group. A plan for such a paragraph might look like the following:

Bad Habit: procrastination

How do I feel about it? I live with it; I lie sometimes, and it makes me feel sneaky and uncomfortable.

People my habit annoys:
1. my family: – I'm never ready on time
                  – I'm slow with chores
                  – they think I'll never do things
2. my teachers: – my papers are always late
                  – I'm full of excuses; it bothers me, too
                  – I'm never prepared for classes
3. my girlfriend: – I'm always late picking her up from college
                  – I even gave her her birthday gift a week late
                  – I arrived at her parents' house for dinner two hours late

Assignment 3: Writing an Essay

Adele Wiseman loved to read. Not everyone does, especially these days. In spite of the growth of visually based technology, reading will not decrease in importance; in fact, more information will appear on more screens and print-outs, and in more formats, than we may be able to imagine. We will have to be able to read well and accurately to make a living and perhaps even to survive in the twenty-first century.

Wiseman describes her early exposure to her family reading as having been a stimulus to read. Was this true for you? Why do some people take such pleasure in reading, and others find it an agony?

Write an essay which describes and accounts for your own feelings about reading. You are, in this essay, explaining and justifying your personal experiences and feelings, so make sure that your three major points are clear and distinct from each other. Use specific details from your life to back up the three points which support the basis of your argument or your thesis. If you hated reading because you didn't like Dr. Seuss, and your early teachers belittled you, and you fell behind two grades because you couldn't manage your textbooks, then form an argument, with your ideas placed in emphatic order, which states this. Conclude with a summarizing statement and a final thought about your current attitude toward reading.

HUMAN GROUPS AND SOCIETY

Have You Seen My Missing Math Gene?

Tony Wong

One of Canada's favourite stereotypes is that of the Asian math and computer whiz. As high school and college students, we automatically assume that the Asian student next to us will get an *A* in Accounting and can probably program our PC to do everything but cook dinner. All nations and peoples are prone to stereotyping; it's one of the ways in which our brains learn to classify and sort information. However, when we apply these categorizing principles to people, the results can range from silly social mistakes to deep-seated and harmful prejudices such as neo-Nazism and apartheid. Tony Wong, a reporter for *The Toronto Star*, takes a light-hearted look at the Canadian perception of the typical Asian: its origins in economic necessity, and its effects on him and his nontypical brother and cousin.

It seems every year I am asked to speak to Asian kids about alternate careers.

An alternate career for an Asian child being defined as anything but a doctor, dentist, pharmacist, accountant or any vocation requiring addition.

I am uniquely qualified to give these seminars, it seems, because I must be one of the few Asians, according to programs like *60 Minutes* (which once did a segment on why so many Asians are taking over the medical schools of America), who cannot add. Or subtract or multiply.

I also stink at chess and have trouble turning on my computer. 4

To this day I have not figured out how to properly program my VCR, although I have 5
cleverly got rid of the flashing 12 o'clock sign by pasting electrical tape over it. So you
see, I am not bereft of resources.

If there is a math gene for Chinese folk, I have somehow missed out. 6

Philippe Rushton would have a field day with me, and I have not even got into the 7
issue of Asian versus Black versus Caucasian penis size, which has been—for goodness
sake—the topic of the good professor's latest research. I already have enough of a complex, thank you.

But do not despair for me, for I have been living a fulfilling life despite my handi- 8
cap, although my job has been made more difficult with China's win this summer at, what
else, the International Math Olympiad, where, to top things off, Canada's top-gun was
Chinese Canadian.

This leaves folks like me in a precarious situation, burdened with trying to lead Asian 9
youth out of their computer and slide rule-induced stupor.

I remember one year where Metro Councillor Olivia Chow and I were dragged out as 10
mathematically challenged role models for a workshop on alternate career skills for teens.

Olivia, who can actually add but faked it for my benefit, seemed doubly qualified 11
for this job as she started life as an artist before becoming a high-powered politician.

For the occasion, I wrote a skit to demonstrate the pressures faced by Asian kids at 12
home. Olivia kindly agreed to play my mom, while I played a bratty kid who wants to
be an artist. I gave Olivia all the good lines.

Olivia: "Jimmy Li got into pharmacy. His mother said he got scholarship, too." 13

Me: "That's nice, Mom. I think I'll continue practising my Spider-Man doodle. You 14
never know when Marvel will call."

Actually my own segue into the writing life wasn't so difficult. My brother Victor 15
inadvertently paved the way when he decided to be an artist.

When my mother got a look at his work, which included the influences of Matisse 16
and Rubens with a little *Playboy* thrown in, she was not amused.

She seemed relieved when I told her I just wanted to be a starving writer. 17

She changed her tune, though, after a visit to the Barnes exhibition at the Art Gallery 18
of Ontario.

"That looks like something your brother would draw," she would exclaim seeing 19
Matisse's dance of life which consists of a bunch of fat nudes frolicking. It was then she
figured that my poor brother had not been "marketed" properly, especially after seeing
that a bunch of naked people dancing in a park by a dead guy could fetch so much money.
Moreover, my brother is alive to boot.

It reminded me of the time my cousin Walter, a photographer who had shot covers for 20
all the top international fashion magazines, including *Vogue, Elle* and *Cosmopolitan*, was
told by his mother that he shouldn't have a studio upstairs where no one could see him.

After all, suppose someone wanted to get a passport picture? He would lose busi- 21
ness. It was the ever-pragmatic Asian philosophy at work. Don't forget the walk-by traffic. At that time, national media profiles pegged his daily fee at $50,000. But, as my aunt
would say, you never know when another $9.95 might come in handy.

So you see, there can be life after math. Diversity is the name of the game. And ̶ stereotypes, like bad clichés, just won't hold any water—at least if you don't subscribe to them.

■ Reading Comprehension Questions

1. Which of the following would be the best alternative title for this article?
   a. Adding Up Those Accurate Asians
   b. A Writer of a Different Colour
   c. Asians and the Arts
   d. Sticky Stereotypes and Tricky Truisms

2. Which sentence best expresses the main idea of the selection?
   a. Asian students are driven by their families into science-based careers.
   b. Tony Wong comes from an artistically gifted family.
   c. People of any racial group are prone to vary in their gifts and abilities.
   d. Asians are basically practical in their view of valuable life-skills.

3. The stereotype of Asians as gifted only in areas of technical expertise
   a. is part of our social fabric, and further exploited by media and academics.
   b. is probably true because of Chinese students' abilities in math and medicine.
   c. is a product of the Western drive for economic success.
   d. makes life almost impossible for Chinese young people gifted in other areas.

4. The author found that starting a career as a writer was less difficult because
   a. he was mathematically challenged anyway.
   b. his brother had already become an artist.
   c. his mother thought it was better than being a cartoonist.
   d. there wasn't much Asian competition in the field.

5. Wong's aunt believed that his cousin should have a street-level office
   a. because her own view of economics suggested that he might miss out on daily customers.
   b. because she wanted him to take passport pictures.
   c. because she didn't know what he really did for a living.
   d. because upstairs offices are bad for business.

6. The author implies that
   a. he feels threatened by Chinese abilities in technical fields.
   b. Asian students are perhaps not encouraged toward less practical careers.
   c. he is so inept that he had to become a writer to explain himself.
   d. a sense of humour is not appreciated in Asian cultures.

7. *True or false?* _____ Wong's mother's main objection to Victor Wong's career as an artist was that he painted mostly naked women.

8. Paragraphs 19–21 imply that Tony Wong
   a. finds the Asian culture too money-conscious.
   b. thinks his mother's values are out of touch with reality.
   c. respects the survival instinct in his culture, but sees the irony in it.
   d. envies those more successful than he is.

9. The word *precarious* in "This leaves folks like me in a precarious position, burdened with trying to lead Asian youth out of their computer and slide rule-induced stupor" (paragraph 9) means
   a. uncertain.
   b. scary.
   c. impossible.
   d. overworked.

10. The word *pragmatic* in "It was the ever-pragmatic Asian philosophy at work" (paragraph 21) means
    a. changing.
    b. working.
    c. stubborn.
    d. realistic.

■ Discussion Questions

About Content

1. What careers does Tony Wong give as those expected of Asian students? Why?

2. What reasons does the author offer for being "uniquely qualified" to give seminars on "alternate careers" for Asian students? How serious is he, do you think? Why?

3. What made Wong's mother decide that his brother's choice of career was not so stupid? What did she decide was the problem with his being an artist?

About Structure

4. Wong's article divides itself into three sections, with an introductory and a concluding paragraph. What subtitles would you give these sections? Fill in the spaces below with appropriate subtitles.

   Paragraphs 2–? _____

   Paragraphs ?–14 _____

   Paragraphs 15–? _____

   Why have you chosen your subtitles? What is the subject of each of these sections? How does each section advance Wong's main idea?

5. In which paragraph do you find the author's thesis? _____
   Why do you think he has chosen this position for his thesis?

6. What do you believe to be the key word in the author's thesis statement? What examples in the essay support this key word? Which examples seem to contradict the idea implied by this word?

About Style and Tone

7. Tony Wong is evidently a writer with a sense of humour. Some techniques natural to the comic writer or comedian include the following: exaggeration, understatement or deflation, unlikely comparisons, shifts in vocabulary levels, and the use of surprising "punch lines."

   Find examples of four of these comic techniques in the article, and list the phrases after the paragraph number in which you find the example required.

   Exaggeration _____ (paragraph _____)

   Understatement _____ (paragraph _____)

   Shift in vocabulary level _____ (paragraph _____)

   Unexpected "punch line" _____ (paragraph _____)

8. After reading this selection, what type of publication would you expect to find it in: a weekly magazine or daily newspaper, a scholarly journal on sociology, or a text on race relations in Canada?

   What do the word choices, subject matter, and tone suggest about the audience Wong is writing for?

■ Writing Assignments

Assignment 1: Writing a Paragraph

A writing assignment based on this selection is on page 189.

Assignment 2: Writing a Paragraph

People often surprise us because they don't always conform to our stereotypes or judgements about them based on appearances. Either their behaviour or their reasons for their actions do not follow our preconceived notions. Tony Wong's mother and his aunt are examples of apparent adherence to the Asian stereotype of practicality, but both manage to adapt to their offspring's radical career choices. Wong himself, his brother, his cousin Victor, and Toronto civic official Olivia Chow are contradictions to the stereotypical Asian.

Write a paragraph about a person whose appearance completely misled you (or someone else) at first. Describe the person's appearance and characteristics in some detail and contrast this with what you found to be the person's underlying character. Be sure to be precise in your choice of details and to contrast them with details which relate to your first impressions, so that the reader will follow your discovery of the difference between appearance and reality.

You might want to begin with a topic sentence like the following, which gives your remembered first or dominant impression of your subject, based solely on what you first observed about him or her:

> Jim's three earrings, Metallica T-shirt, ripped black jeans, and shaved head had him marked as one mean punk in my mind, and the silver skull on his belt buckle did nothing to change my opinion.

Conclude your paragraph with a summary of what you learned and a statement of your current feelings about this person.

Assignment 3: Writing an Essay

Tony Wong mentions in his fifth paragraph a controversial professor from an Ontario university, Philippe Rushton. Rushton studies racial and genetic patterns in human beings. His findings, where human intelligence is concerned, have prompted criticism of his supposed racist views. When carried to an extreme, or when misapplied, judgements or findings based on race are always questionable, and have led to horrendous social problems, persecution, and such atrocities as Nazism and the recent events in Bosnia.

Although stereotyping or classifying is indeed a standard part of the learning process, wherein humans learn to distinguish one thing from another and to group similar ideas, it is very dangerous when applied to people. Most Canadian students attend colleges and universities where diversity in the classroom is the rule, not the exception. Moreover, our laws and college charters guarantee the rights of all Canadians. A fast glance at any major Canadian city's newspaper will, unfortunately, disabuse us of the notion that we have created the "perfect egalitarian society"; various racial groups continue to labour under stereotypes, and factions continue to form which support racist views.

Write an essay which tackles an experience of your own with stereotyping, whether on your part, or as applied to you by someone else. Make use of the cause and effect format for your essay. What caused you or someone else to make a premature judgement, and what were the consequences? You may choose a light-hearted approach, as Tony Wong has, or you may treat the subject seriously.

Some options for opening sentences in your thesis statement paragraphs could be as follows:

Because I am a female student of Italian descent, people sometimes assume I must be a good cook, interested in babies, and intensely religious. Are they in for some surprises.

When I registered in my first course in chemical engineering, and answered to the name "Littlefeather, Jim" on the attendance list, the student in the next chair raised his hand to me and said, "How." I said, "I don't know; do you?"

Arriving from Beijing was difficult enough, but registering in a new school system, dealing with an unfamiliar language, and trying to understand the other students' behaviour all seemed just too much.

Spiritual Storyteller

Daniel Smith

Basil Johnston is an amazing Canadian character. The author of several books, and a former teacher, he is an unpretentious and learned Native Canadian who wears his knowledge lightly and in a most charming fashion. The Canadian editor of this text was fortunate enough to have had Mr. Johnston as a high school history teacher, and can still remember his dry wit and his ability to make the dustiest patches of European politics seem interesting. Basil Johnston is a storyteller with a mission: to keep alive the language and beliefs of his Ojibway culture, and to do so by making these things relevant to our lives today.

Two precocious kids figure strongly in Basil Johnston's quest to celebrate a rich if imperiled touchstone of Canada's soul. 1

The first kid is Johnston himself, age 6. It's 60 years ago, and his entire family has just moved from the Ojibway reserve on Port Parry Island to the Cape Croker reserve on the Bruce Peninsula. 2

Johnston's mom, Mary, is determined none of the new arrivals would tumble off the Niagara Escarpment running behind his grandmother's house. So she warns them of the full assortment of perils lurking in the bush. 3

"Don't you know there are *maemaegawaehnssiwuk* (little people) out there? *Weendigoes?* (Cannibals.) And the Iroquois down there? And the white people over there?" 4

Now Basil, as is the way of the young, doesn't put much stock in these warnings until one day—after some still unrevealed misdeed involving another local kid—he hears the alien sound of a popping motorcycle engine. 5

"I thought, 'Oh, they're coming for me!'" Johnston recalls. "I ran down and hid to take my chances with the Iroquois. It turned out the motorcycle belonged to a magazine salesman. I got a damned good licking anyway. 6

"So that was my introduction to the *manitous*." 7

Johnston met a second pivotal kid some decades later in a Grade 5 classroom in North York. Johnston, now a high school teacher in Willowdale, is visiting a class that is wrapping up a five-week study of Indians. 8

Except the students hadn't pondered Indians as people, as human beings. They studied what Johnston describes as things—totem poles and lodges. Nothing about values and spiritualism and a world view so different from our own dominant Western modes of thinking. 9

"Is this all there is?" asks one downcast boy. "Of course not," replies Johnston, knowing full well he has no books, no material to direct the boy to. 10

"So that made me realize what needed to be done," Johnston concludes. 11

All his stories work out that way. They amble out, cross a bridge or two, maybe get their boots muddy, but then they always circle back to the point. "So that's how ..." 12

Johnston sees story-telling as the base of all good writing and good teaching. It's the focus of his ever-broadening campaign to revive the rich folktales of the Anishinaubae—the Ojibway, Ontario's dominant Indian tribe. 13

As one of the few people around who still speaks and writes the Ojibway language, plus his experience as a teacher and later as a Royal Ontario Museum lecturer, Johnston is ideally placed to shoulder such a burden. 14

Not that he sees his calling that way. Johnston does not see himself as carrying the responsibility for the survival of a threatened culture. He's just a guy whose upbringing, language, and teaching skills have come together at a time when they are needed—just as the heroes in the Anishnaubae tales arrive by seeming happenstances in the nick of time. 15

Not for him the endless round of political meetings and lobby efforts which bedevil the lives of so many Indian activists. He's been there, in the '60s, including a stint with the old Indian-Eskimo Association and other forerunners to today's more polished native organizations. 16

And he has already told the dark side of the old Indian schools, like the Spanish Indian Residential School he wrote about in *Indian School Days*,[1] before going on to become one of the first Indian post-secondary degree holders in Ontario. 17

Instead, from either his Richmond Hill semi or the log house he completed at Cape Croker in 1967, Johnston, at 66, avoids the political limelight to concentrate on a body of work which has brought him renown and honors across North America. 18

His 11th and 12th books came out this fall. *The Bear-Walker*, published by the ROM, is another collection of previously-gathered tales, some of his own and some from such story-telling pals as Sam Ozawamik and Alex McKay, who he credits for always reminding him to ask, "What does it mean?" 19

---

[1] *Indian School Days* is listed in the Instructor's Manual for this text. Your teacher may recommend some of Johnston's other fiction and nonfiction titles to you.

But the book that featured the kind of multi-city book tour few native authors have received is *The Manitous—The Spiritual World of the Ojibway*.

In *The Manitous*, Johnston finally attempts to pull together the rich pantheon of Ojibway folk heroes into a comprehensive whole, one that doubles as a one-stop peek at the Anishinaubae world view.

Many people by now have heard of Nana'b'oozoo, the half-human, half-manitou figure whose bumbling efforts to do what pops into his head so often end up doing good, despite chaos on the way. But few know of Nana'b'oozoo's brothers—Maudjee-kawiss, Pukawiss and Cheeby-aub-oozoo—and the very different gifts they brought the human beings.

The brothers and all the other manitous—from the little *maemaegawaehnssiwuk* with their special interest in children to the more celebrated *weendigoes* and their devouring habits—aren't presented as curios from the past. Johnston argues the strengths and weaknesses of what's still known about the manitous reflect the values and lessons that form the ancient Ojibway notions of what's important for humans in the world—respect for all living things, for individual rights and responsibilities, and so on.

So the manitous aren't dead; just harder to see. Except for the weendigoes—they have become the giant lumber companies clear-cutting the vast tracts of forest, the bankers, and so on—all the agents of greed and folly which have so much impact on all our lives.

As always, Johnston has a bunch of other projects on the go. There's a children's book and another set of humor stories, in the vein of his Leacock Award-nominee *Moose Meat and Wild Rice*. And he's finishing his latest version of an Ojibway language lexicon, no small challenge for a tongue which has few of its complex grammatical niceties codified anywhere.

"It's all context and prefixes," explains Johnston. "The idea of the manitou covers everything from the creatures themselves to manitou-like feelings or places, depending on context.

"And the grammar! Take the word *inaendumcowin*, which means the operation of the mind. It takes more than 200 different prefixes. You end up with a dictionary of some 200,000 words, and it only works if you know how it all comes together and your ear is fine enough to distinguish those prefixes."

Johnston bristles at the oft-repeated description of his work as preserving a dying language and folklore.

"Sure, I want to draft the hardware for the teachers and for the kids who want to learn about themselves, then go on to enrich it," he says firmly. "But I'm not an adder-to, not a historian. I want these stories to grow, not become stale. That's why you've got to put some modern interpretations on them, to allow them to become accessible."

Of the more than 50 aboriginal languages in full flower in Canada 500 years ago, only Ojibway—along with Cree and Inuktitut, the language of the Inuit—are seen as having any chance of surviving another generation or two. For all the efforts being made by Indian traditionalists, schools and cultural activists like Johnston, the English of the television set and the bigger cities is winning the battle.

Even on the more remote Anishinaubae reserves, few people under 40 can speak their own language. Even Johnston's three adult kids, for all the childhood grilling in those prefixes they endured from their dad, would need "a good six months' immersion" to recover what they've lost.

"Native kids aren't flocking to night schools to recapture their language," says 32
Johnston. "They're accepting the benefits of being native without accepting the responsibility to live their culture."

The chapter on Nana'b'oozoo in *The Manitous*, for example, ends after his depar- 33
ture from the Ojibway on this discomforting note:

> Because of the present generation's indifference to its language, traditions and 34
> heritage, the Nana'b'oozoo is unlikely to return to inspire storytellers to add to the
> national Anishinaubae legacy and the value of the bequest as it is meant to be
> enriched. And there are few who mourn the loss of the Anishinaubae nation.

Such a loss would, of course, leave Canada a poorer place as well. It's sobering to 35
realize how few people like Basil Johnston are left, struggling against all our modern corporate manitous to keep alive the very powers which kept the manitous of old at bay.

■ Reading Comprehension Questions

1. Which of the following would be the best alternative title for this selection?
   a. The Manitou and the Magician
   b. An Ojibway Hero
   c. Aboriginal Stories for Today's World
   d. Lost Languages and Lost Lives

2. Which sentence best expresses the main idea of the selection?
   a. Basil Johnston wants to revive Native Canadian culture through story-telling.
   b. Johnston believes profoundly in the power of Ojibway mythology.
   c. Johnston blames ecological/corporate disasters on the continuing presence of Ojibway evil spirits.
   d. Canada is at risk of losing part of its cultural identity without the work of people like Basil Johnston.

3. Six-year-old Basil Johnston believed
   a. his mother's warnings were not very important.
   b. that the motorcycle's engine was either evil spirits or the Iroquois.
   c. that he wouldn't fall off the escarpment.
   d. that the white people were the most frightening possibility.

4. The grade five students, in five weeks, had learned
   a. all about Indian living styles and culture.
   b. only Indian myths and legends.
   c. the facts about Indian homes and artifacts, but nothing about their values.
   d. the differences between Western and Native Canadian lives.

5. *True or false?* _____ Johnston wants the Ojibway language and mythology preserved as part of history.

6. The selection implies that
   a. to Johnston, the concept of manitous is valuable as a historical idea.
   b. the manitous demonstrate important universal moral and ethical values.
   c. the manitous are no longer evident in modern industrial society.
   d. manitous belong mainly in Johnston's dictionary of the Ojibway language.

7. The author implies that aboriginal languages are dying out because
   a. they are too difficult to learn, with all their complex grammar.
   b. they are not taught in schools on the reserves.
   c. English is the language of business and media, and of "the good life."
   d. they deal only with concepts and ways of living that are now in the past.

8. We can conclude from the selection that
   a. language often holds the spirit and heritage of a culture.
   b. the Ojibway won't regret the loss of their stories and language.
   c. modern and ancient myths are at war with each other.
   d. even Johnston's children are indifferent to their heritage.

9. The word *imperiled* in "Two precocious kids figure strongly in Basil Johnston's quest to celebrate a rich if imperiled touchstone of Canada's soul" (paragraph 1) means
   a. dangerous.
   b. lost.
   c. unknown.
   d. endangered.

10. The word *bequest* in "to add to the national Anishinaubae legacy and the value of the bequest as it is meant to be enriched" (paragraph 34) means
   a. history.
   b. inquiry.
   c. inherited gift.
   d. tradition.

■ **Discussion Questions**

About Content

1. What is ironic about the noise Johnston hears as he is playing near his grandmother's house? How does this little story relate to Johnston's ideas about the continuing presence of Ojibway culture?

2. Why is the student in the second anecdote described as "downcast" at the end of his five-week course in Indian culture? Why would both this child and Johnston be called "precocious" by author Smith?

3. Why does Johnston not participate in political activities for aboriginal rights, according to the selection? What does he see as his mission?

4. How many native languages have survived from the time of Canada's "discovery" by Cartier and other explorers? What does the size of this loss suggest to you?

About Structure

5. In which paragraph do you find the best expression of the author's thesis? How would you state this idea in your own words? Do you agree with Johnston?
6. What method of introduction does Daniel Smith use in this article?
   a. Explaining the importance of the topic
   b. Anecdote
   c. Broad-to-narrow
   d. Situation opposite to the one to be developed

   Why is Smith's choice of introduction particularly suitable to his subject and to the content of the article?
7. How many change-of-direction transition words do you find in this selection? List the paragraphs beginning with such words.

   _____   _____   _____   _____   _____

About Style and Tone

8. Daniel Smith uses a figure of speech in paragraph 12 to describe Basil Johnston's way of relating information. When we give a nonhuman thing human qualities, the use of this figure of speech is called *personification*. What is personified in this paragraph? Why would such a usage be appropriate to Johnston, given what is told about him in the selection?
9. How do the Ojibway words and Johnston's explanations of the complexity of his language in the article affect you as a reader? How does it affect your perception of Native North American languages and culture?

■ Writing Assignments

Assignment 1: Writing a Paragraph

Each of us knows at least one person who has been a sort of "story-teller" character for us. This person might be a relative who has kept alive family stories and history, or might be a friend or acquaintance who can turn the simplest explanation into a "tall tale." Perhaps you have had a teacher, who, like Basil Johnston, used stories to teach and to entertain. Write a paragraph which is a portrait of your story-teller.

Begin by thinking of what best characterizes this person's stories and/or their story-telling style. Jot down a series of the descriptive words that come to mind under their name. Think of one or two of their best stories, and note a few phrases to remind you of the details you want to remember.

Now try to answer the question, "Why was (or is) _____ such a great (or important) story-teller to me?" Put your answer in one sentence, such as, "My best friend Lena can turn the dullest trip to the mall into an entertaining story with her funny observations about people, her bizarre chats with salespeople, and her ability to find the most disgusting washrooms in the universe." Be sure to use specific details to back up each point you make about the story-teller, their stories, or their style of telling their tales.

Assignment 2: Writing a Paragraph

Most cultures are kept alive by story-telling, what is sometimes called "the oral narrative tradition." From tiny moments in our lives, like that in Basil Johnston's grade five class when the little boy asked "Is that all there is?" come stories and memories that may become important to us. Even if we feel that our background is perhaps bland and typical of many people, there are still unique aspects to each of our lives. Your subject could be as "ordinary" as your grandmother's butter tarts, or as distinctive as the way your family celebrates a particular holiday. Write a paragraph which describes some thing or some tradition or habit which is unique to you, your family, or your cultural heritage. Explain how you came to experience this event or thing, and why it has significance to you.

Assignment 3: Writing an Essay

Is Canada the cultural mosaic it claims to be? Will the media make English the dominant language of the next century? Will our increasing dependence on technology and information media destroy the diverse cultural identities of various groups of people? In the case of Native Canadians, a loss of 47 languages seems to indicate a lack of tolerance, if not outright insensitivity, on the part of dominant cultures over the course of several centuries. As one Native rock group's lyric goes, "When Columbus came, the question was, Who discovered who?"

What about other cultural groups? English is a necessity for professional communication in most of Canada's provinces, but are we all like the young Native Canadians Johnston accuses of "accepting the benefits of being [Canadian] without accepting the responsibility to live [our] culture"? Within one generation a language can be forgotten; is a culture forgotten with it?

Write an essay which argues for or against people's retaining their own original languages in twenty-first-century Canada. You may wish to address the issue of Native Canadians, or perhaps that of another national group from which your family comes, or that of francophone Canadians. Is there a need for people to retain a knowledge of another language important to their background culture?

Here is one student's essay outline:

<u>Thesis statement:</u> My family is from the Ukraine, and my father tried to teach us the language, and sent us to all the cultural festivals ... but I just found them funny, and never wanted to speak Ukrainian.
– we wanted to be like our friends (all "Canadians")
– the language was too hard to learn, and we had French at school, too
– except for odd cable shows we hated, TV & radio & books were in English

<u>Topic sentence 1:</u> We came here to be Canadian, and no one at school, even the students whose parents came from Germany and Poland, knew more than a few words of their families' languages, so I didn't want to feel "different" or "foreign."
– our special holidays and church festivals were different enough for me
– we always felt dragged to the Ukrainian cultural events—would rather have been with our friends
– it was hard to relate to family pride in history—school didn't mention it

<u>Topic sentence 2:</u> Learning another language at home, on top of school work, was too difficult
– when would I use Ukrainian, outside the family?
– it's too different from English or French
– languages are not my strong point, academically

<u>Topic sentence 3:</u> All the TV we watch, the radio and music we listen to, and my favourite books are in English—can't imagine "Slavic Rock" ...
– only very occasional cable shows, which don't interest me at all, are in Ukrainian
– TV, music, and movies are my favourite entertainment—in English
– Stephen King and R. L. Stine write in English, and at least I enjoy reading them

The Joy of Being Fat Free

Sharon Doyle Driedger

Alanis Morissette sings, "Isn't it ironic?" Well, here is an article which is certainly an ironic commentary on where humanity chooses to place its values. Despite feminists' attempts to help women to re-evaluate their self-esteem, despite a growing demand for larger-figured, more normal-looking models, and despite the inherent risks of surgery, liposuction (literally *fat-sucking*, from the Latin) has become a million-dollar industry, appealing mainly to women. Apparently, North Americans and Europeans, the best-fed and least-exercised people in the world's history, have chosen surgery in response to the demands of fashion and vanity. If you think only movie stars and talk-show hosts would have their fat vacuumed out, read on, and think about what people are willing to risk, and the uses to which we put medical science.

Yvette Oberg hated her "enormous" hips and the "flabby fat" around her tummy. But no matter how much she jogged, skied and dieted, she could not shed the bulges. "I worked out for an hour and a half a day," recalls the 42-year-old Oberg, who owns a shoe store in Kelowna, B.C. "I could do sit-ups until the cows come home—but I could not get the fat off." Last October, a Vancouver plastic surgeon removed the excess weight from her stomach with liposuction—a procedure that vacuums fat cells out of the body. "I now have an incredibly flat stomach," says Oberg. "I was so thrilled that I went back and had my hips and my bum done last February." The surgeon removed more than three and a half litres of fat from Oberg's body. In a few hours, she went from a size 32 to size 28 jeans. "When I go to the gym now, I wear these cute little outfits and I don't feel at all embarrassed working out with 20-year-olds," says Oberg. "I can get into a bikini—isn't that amazing?"   1

Pioneered in Europe in the 1960s, liposuction came to North America in 1982. At first, plastic surgeons used the procedure exclusively on thighs, buttocks and torso. Now, refined techniques allow for the removal of tiny fat deposits, even in the face. "You can practically go from head to toe," says Dr. Gérald Rheault of Montreal, who uses liposuction to eliminate small pads of fat from the cheeks and neck, reduce large "saddlebags" or trim an ankle. Liposuction is expensive—from $1,000 to $5,000, depending on the number of sites treated. Still, it has become North America's most popular cosmetic operation. In the United States, surgeons earned $465 million in 1994 from liposuction. Rheault notes that 90 per cent of his clients are women, many aged 30 to 50. "But there are some men," he adds, "especially for the spare tire."   2

One appeal of liposuction is that it not only eliminates fat—it appears to keep it off. "In liposuction, you remove the cells in which fat can be deposited," says Rheault. It is possible to gain weight afterward, but doctors believe it does not accumulate in the treated area. Says Rheault: "In general, fat removed in this fashion is removed permanently."   3

The procedure, which usually lasts from one to two hours, is straightforward if crude. The surgeon makes a small incision in the skin, then inserts a fine blunt-tipped metal tube into the layers of fat. He moves the tube back and forth, loosening fat cells that are then sucked up through the tube into a container. "It requires a fair amount of strength," says Rheault, as well as skill and good judgment. The surgeon must contour the remaining fat, leaving enough to provide a smooth, even surface. Many doctors perform so-called tumescent liposuction, injecting fluid into the treated area—a less painful technique that decreases blood loss. Some are experimenting with ultrasound to break up fat cells before   4 they are suctioned out. And a few surgeons save the fat and freeze it for use as a filler for wrinkles.

While liposuction may be a boon to some, it cannot cure obesity. "It is not a way of   5
losing weight," says Rheault, explaining that only small amounts of fat can safely be removed at one time. "Liposuction is useful for specific fatty deposits in a patient with normal weight," he emphasizes. The procedure will not remove stretch marks or cellulite—skin with a lumpy appearance. Nor will it tighten saggy, wrinkled flesh. In fact, liposuction works best on taut toned skin, with enough resiliency to shrink into place after fat is removed.

Like any surgery, liposuction carries some risk. "Some people think it is like having   6
their hair done," says Dr. Richard Warren, a Vancouver plastic surgeon. Complications— although rare—include temporary numbness of skin, excessive bleeding and infection. Skin texture may be damaged, resulting in scarring or bagginess. To date, there has been one death attributed to liposuction in Canada. In 1991, a 44-year-old Toronto real estate broker died after liposuction when a massive blood clot blocked an artery.

Gloria, a 32-year-old Edmonton property manager, understood the risks when she   7
underwent liposuction to remove "pronounced saddlebags" a year ago. "It's not a science," says Gloria, who needed a second operation to smooth out one thigh. "It's the doctor's ability—he uses his eye to judge the results." Her convalescence—normal, considering the large area that was treated—was painful. "I had black bruising," says Gloria. "I sat on pillows for quite a few weeks." And, like many patients, she had to wear a girdle-like garment for more than a month, to help her skin compress and to minimize swelling. "I hated it," recalls Gloria. "It's extremely binding, but necessary if you want good results." Gloria did not achieve perfection. "I have very tiny scars," she says. "And it doesn't get rid of cellulite." Still, she insists that "it was well worth it." The payoff, says Gloria, is her gratifyingly smooth silhouette.

■ Reading Comprehension Questions

1. Which of the following would be the best alternative title for this selection?
   a. Vanity and the Vacuum
   b. Losing Your Lipids and Loving It
   c. Pain, Pleasure, and the Pursuit of Happiness
   d. Liposuction: Risks and Rewards
2. Which sentence best expresses the main idea of the selection?
   a. For those who can afford it and are not obese, liposuction offers a cosmetic advantage and some risk.
   b. Liposuction removes fat cells permanently and offers the hope of a perfect body shape.
   c. Liposuction is a simple and straightforward surgical procedure with relatively few dangers.
   d. Liposuction offers the perfect solution to those who have tried dieting, exercise, and other alternatives to achieving weight loss.

3. For Yvette Oberg, the main appeal of liposuction was that
   a. she could now get into a bikini and feel twenty years younger.
   b. she lost fat deposits which exercise had not altered.
   c. she was relieved of litres of fat, which could be saved for re-use.
   d. her body type changed.

4. Liposuction, as a type of surgery, is
   a. now refined, simple, and not demanding for the surgeon.
   b. still dangerous and as messy as other types of cosmetic surgery.
   c. a crude procedure, requiring a surgeon's brute strength and intuition.
   d. able to achieve major improvements in skin tone and body contour.

5. The most undesirable aspects of liposuction are
   a. loss of skin sensation, risks of bleeding and infection, bruising, swelling, and its cost.
   b. massive scars and sagging stretches of unused skin.
   c. its inability to remove cellulite and wrinkles.
   d. the length of the operation and the risk of fat being redeposited on the body.

6. The article implies that
   a. liposuction is sometimes performed for the sake of the patient's health.
   b. liposuction is strictly a procedure performed for the sake of vanity.
   c. liposuction can result in amazing changes to the patient's body-type.
   d. liposuction is a good way of recycling human fat.

7. Paragraph 4 implies that
   a. most liposuction is nonspecific in its fat-cell removal, quite painful, and involves considerable blood loss.
   b. liposuction is as primitive in its methods as early Egyptian embalming methods.
   c. liposuction has now been perfected, and no further experimental procedures are being tried.
   d. liposuction always leaves a smooth, taut, youthful skin surface.

8. We can conclude from the selection that
   a. liposuction is the twenty-first century's answer to obesity problems.
   b. liposuction's risks outweigh its value as a surgical procedure.
   c. liposuction involves a lengthy recovery period, if not permanent damage.
   d. liposuction offers at least temporary pleasure to those for whom it works.

9. The word *torso* in "At first, plastic surgeons used the procedure exclusively on thighs, buttocks and torso" (paragraph 2) means
   a. abdomen.
   b. trunk of the body.
   c. stomach.
   d. thorax.

10. The word *tumescent* in "Many doctors perform so-called tumescent liposuction, injecting fluid into the treated area" (paragraph 4) means
    a. swollen.
    b. liquid.
    c. experimental.
    d. cushioned.

■ Discussion Questions

About Content

1. What motivated Yvette Oberg's decision to undergo a second liposuction operation? What do you think of her reasons for doing so, as demonstrated in her own statements?

2. If liposuction has overtaken rhinoplasty ("nose jobs") and bleroplasty ("eyebag jobs") as "North America's most popular cosmetic operation" (paragraph 2), what does this fact say about our society, about the way we see ourselves, and about our value systems?

3. Dr. Gérald Rheault says in the fifth paragraph of the article that liposuction "is not a way of losing weight" and that it "is useful for specific fatty deposits in a patient with normal weight." If this is so, then what are the need for and the function of this operation, which did remove nearly a gallon of fat from Ms. Oberg?

4. What unpleasant after-effects did Gloria, the woman from Edmonton, experience as results of her surgery?

About Structure

5. List the transition words, and their paragraph numbers, which you find at the beginning of three of the paragraphs in the body of the article.

   Transition word _____ (paragraph _____)

   Transition word _____ (paragraph _____)

   Transition word _____ (paragraph _____)

   What is the function of each of these transitions, as they relate to the content of the paragraph which they begin?

6. Sharon Doyle Driedger achieves overall unity in her article with the use of an "echo effect." What has she done to create this effect? Which paragraphs create this unified result? How?

7. The central five paragraphs of the selection differ somewhat in content and tone from the opening and closing paragraphs. How do these body paragraphs

differ from the introduction and conclusion? What is the effect of this difference on the article's meaning to you?

About Style and Tone

8. Paragraphs 4, 5, and 6 contain vivid and carefully worded descriptions of medical matters. How do these passages contrast with the wording and vocabulary of the paragraphs where the patients themselves speak directly? What is the end result of reading such direct, casual speech after examining the technical passages? How is your view of the subject affected by this contrast in tones, styles, and content?

■ Writing Assignments

Assignment 1: Writing a Paragraph

Imagine that a friend of yours feels that he or she is suffering socially and emotionally because of some physical defect, such as the shape of his or her nose or the size of his or her stomach. Write a paragraph in the form of a letter to this friend, giving them reasons they should or should not consider plastic surgery. Avoid generalizations such as "your real friends don't care what you look like"; no one is persuaded by such statements, and you will not be addressing the real causes or effects of your friend's unhappiness. In your prewriting, list what you imagine or know to be possible reasons for low self-esteem resulting from physical differences. Now list the possible effects these could have on someone. Choose "pro-surgery" or "con-surgery." Use your three strongest reasons for the side you choose, and try to persuade your friend.

Assignment 2: Writing a Paragraph

Write a paragraph which contrasts the risks of cosmetic surgery with possible benefits to be derived from it. Reread the selection for specific details, and make use of an outline for one of the two formats recommended in the text's chapter titled "Comparing or Contrasting" (pages 152–164). Your conclusion should result naturally from the details you list in your outline.

Assignment 3: Writing an Essay

What has our well-fed and healthy society come to? Where are our values? Finally, other than for purposes of necessary reconstructive surgery, why is medical expertise, time, and research money spent on cosmetic procedures? Could we be finding cures for cancer, AIDS, and deadly new viruses instead of vacuuming away flab?

Write a persuasive essay which takes one side or the other of the following argument:

Elective cosmetic surgery, in this period of hospital cutbacks, decreased medical funding, and increasing deaths from STDs, cancer, and new viruses, should not be available in our province.

Write a clear outline, and do some outside reading, if necessary, to find solid supporting facts and details for each of the three major points you use to defend your argument.

Adolescent Confusion

Maya Angelou

In this selection from her highly praised autobiographical work, *I Know Why the Caged Bird Sings*, Maya Angelou writes with honesty, humour, and sensitivity about her sexual encounter with a neighbourhood boy. Angelou captures some of the confused feelings about sex we all experience when we are growing up; she is frightened but curious, outwardly aggressive yet inwardly shy; calculating and innocent at the same time. Angelou's outrageous plan for finding out what it is like to be a "real woman" may seem shocking. But her candour makes us respond to her account with understanding and delight.

A classmate of mine, whose mother had rooms for herself and her daughter in a ladies' 1 residence, had stayed out beyond closing time. She telephoned me to ask if she could sleep at my house. Mother gave her permission, providing my friend telephoned her mother from our house.

When she arrived, I got out of bed and we went to the upstairs kitchen to make hot 2 chocolate. In my room we shared mean gossip about our friends, giggled over boys, and whined about school and the tedium of life. The unusualness of having someone sleep in my bed (I'd never slept with anyone except my grandmothers) and the frivolous laughter in the middle of the night made me forget simple courtesies. My friend had to remind me that she had nothing to sleep in. I gave her one of my gowns, and without curiosity or interest I watched her pull off her clothes. At none of the early stages of undressing was I in the least conscious of her body. And then suddenly, for the briefest eye span, I saw her breasts. I was stunned.

They were shaped like light-brown falsies in the five-and-ten-cent store, but they were real. They made all the nude paintings I had seen in museums come to life. In a word, they were beautiful. A universe divided what she had from what I had. She was a woman.

My gown was too snug for her and much too long, and when she wanted to laugh at her ridiculous image I found that humor had left me without a promise to return.

Had I been older I might have thought that I was moved by both an esthetic sense of beauty and the pure emotion of envy. But those possibilities did not occur to me when I needed them. All I knew was that I had been moved by looking at a woman's breasts. So all the calm and casual words of Mother's explanation a few weeks earlier and the clinical terms of Noah Webster did not alter the fact that in a fundamental way there was something queer about me.

I somersaulted deeper into my snuggery of misery. After a thorough self-examination, in the light of all I had read and heard about dykes and bulldaggers, I reasoned that I had none of the obvious traits—I didn't wear trousers, or have big shoulders or go in for sports, or walk like a man or even want to touch a woman. I wanted to be a woman, but that seemed to me to be a world to which I was to be eternally refused entrance.

What I needed was a boyfriend. A boyfriend would clarify my position to the world and, even more important, to myself. A boyfriend's acceptance of me would guide me into that strange and exotic land of frills and femininity.

Among my associates, there were no takers. Understandably the boys of my age and social group were captivated by the yellow- or light-brown-skinned girls, with hairy legs and smooth little lips, whose hair "hung down like horses' manes." And even those sought-after girls were asked to "give it up or tell where it is." They were reminded in a popular song of the times, "If you can't smile and say yes, please don't cry and say no." If the pretties were expected to make the supreme sacrifice in order to "belong," what could the unattractive female do? She who had been skimming along on life's turning but never-changing periphery had to be ready to be a "buddy" by day and maybe by night. She was called upon to be generous only if the pretty girls were unavailable.

I believe most plain girls are virtuous because of the scarcity of opportunity to be otherwise. They shield themselves with an aura of unavailableness (for which after a time they begin to take credit) largely as a defense tactic.

In my particular case, I could not hide behind the curtain of voluntary goodness. I was being crushed by two unrelenting forces: the uneasy suspicion that I might not be a normal female and my newly awakening sexual appetite.

I decided to take matters into my own hands. (An unfortunate but apt phrase.)

Up the hill from our house, and on the same side of the street, lived two handsome brothers. They were easily the most eligible young men in the neighborhood. If I was going to venture into sex, I saw no reason why I shouldn't make my experiment with the best of the lot. I didn't really expect to capture either brother on a permanent basis, but I thought if I could hook one temporarily I might be able to work the relationship into something more lasting.

I planned a chart for seduction with surprise as my opening ploy. One evening as I   13
walked up the hill suffering from youth's vague malaise (there was simply nothing to do),
the brother I had chosen came walking directly into my trap.

"Hello, Marguerite." He nearly passed me.   14

I put the plan into action. "Hey." I plunged, "Would you like to have a sexual inter-   15
course with me?" Things were going according to the chart. His mouth hung open like
a garden gate. I had the advantage and so I pressed it.

"Take me somewhere."   16

His response lacked dignity, but in fairness to him I admit that I had left him little   17
chance to be suave.

He asked, "You mean, you're going to give me some trim?"   18

I assured him that that was exactly what I was about to give him. Even as the scene   19
was being enacted, I realized the imbalance in his values. He thought I was giving him
something, and the fact of the matter was that it was my intention to take something from
him. His good looks and popularity had made him so inordinately conceited that they
blinded him to that possibility.

We went to a furnished room occupied by one of his friends, who understood the sit-   20
uation immediately and got his coat and left us alone. The seductee quickly turned off
the lights. I would have preferred them left on, but didn't want to appear more aggressive than I had been already—if that was possible.

I was excited rather than nervous, and hopeful instead of frightened. I had not con-   21
sidered how physical an act of seduction would be. I had anticipated long soulful
tongued kisses and gentle caresses. But there was no romance in the knee which forced
my legs, nor in the rub of hairy skin on my chest.

Unredeemed by shared tenderness, the time was spent in laborious gropings,   22
pullings, yankings, and jerkings.

Not one word was spoken.   23

My partner showed that our experience had reached its climax by getting up   24
abruptly, and my main concern was how to get home quickly. He may have sensed that
he had been used, or his lack of interest may have been an indication that I was less than
gratifying. Neither possibility bothered me.

Outside on the street we left each other with little more than "OK, see you around."   25

Thanks to Mr. Freeman nine years before, I had had no pain of entry to endure, and   26
because of the absence of romantic involvement neither of us felt much had happened.

At home I reviewed the failure and tried to evaluate my new position. I had had a   27
man. I had been had. Not only didn't I enjoy it, but my normality was still a question.

What happened to the moonlight-on-the-prairie feeling? Was there something so wrong   28
with me that I couldn't share a sensation that made poets gush out rhyme after rhyme, that
made Richard Arlen brave the Arctic wastes and Veronica Lake betray the entire free world?

There seemed to be no explanation for my private infirmity, but being a product (is   29
"victim" a better word?) of the Southern Negro upbringing, I decided that I "would understand it all better by and by." I went to sleep.

Three weeks later, having thought very little of the strange and strangely empty night,   30
I found myself pregnant.

■ Reading Comprehension Questions

1. Which of the following would be the best alternative title for this selection?
   a. A Wasted Life
   b. The Story of a Teenage Pregnancy
   c. The Pain and Confusion of Growing Up
   d. A Handsome Young Man

2. Which sentence best expresses the main idea of the selection?
   a. Teenage girls feel more insecure about sex than teenage boys do.
   b. A sexual experience is the first step toward adulthood.
   c. Maya Angelou's innocence led her to a joyless experience with sex and an unplanned pregnancy.
   d. Women who are sexually aggressive often become pregnant.

3. In the days following her sexual experience, the author
   a. talked to her mother about her feelings.
   b. wrote about the incident.
   c. asked her class-mates for advice.
   d. virtually ignored what had happened.

4. The author chose the boy she did to experiment with because
   a. he had shown some interest in her.
   b. she wanted to start with one of the two most eligible boys in the neighbourhood.
   c. she knew he would be kind to her.
   d. she had a crush on him.

5. The author expected that
   a. having a boyfriend would help her become a woman.
   b. she would feel guilty about her actions.
   c. she would no longer be plain.
   d. she would probably get pregnant.

6. The author implies that
   a. she would become a homosexual.
   b. she had little sense of right and wrong.
   c. she had little idea of what love, sex, or femininity really mean.
   d. none of the girls she knew had had a sexual experience.

7. *True or false?* _____ The author implies that she had discussed the facts of womanhood with her mother.

8. The author implies that
   a. she wanted the boy to marry her.
   b. she was raped as a child.

    c. the boy's lack of tenderness was expected.

    d. the movies had taught her the facts of life.

9. The word *inordinately* in "His good looks and popularity had made him so inordinately conceited" (paragraph 19) means

    a. timidly.

    b. excessively.

    c. unexpectedly.

    d. unknowingly.

10. The word *malaise* in "I walked up the hill suffering from youth's vague malaise" (paragraph 13) means

    a. patience.

    b. pleasure.

    c. ambition.

    d. uneasiness.

■ Discussion Questions

About Content

1. For what reasons did Angelou decide she needed a boyfriend?

2. In what ways did Angelou's actual experience differ from what she expected it to be? Find passages in the selection that describe (a) Angelou's expectations and (b) the reality of the experience.

3. What was the young man's reaction to Angelou's seduction? What does his reaction reveal about him?

About Structure

4. A narrative selection most often focuses on a single event. But this selection is developed through two narratives. What are the two narratives? Why does Angelou include both?

5. Within her narratives, Angelou uses contrast to develop her paragraphs. For example, she contrasts her body and her class-mate's body, and the "pretties" and "unattractive females." Find two other areas of contrast and write them below:

_____

_____

6. Paragraph 23 consists of just one sentence: "Not one word was spoken." What effect does Angelou achieve by making this paragraph so short?

About Style and Tone

7.   Angelou enlivens her narrative with humour. Find two places where she touches on the humorous side of her experience and write the paragraph numbers here:

_____   _____

8.   Find two other places where the tone is quite serious.

_____   _____

■ Writing Assignments

Assignment 1: Writing a Paragraph

A writing assignment based on this selection is on page 197.

Assignment 2: Writing a Paragraph

Because of her confusion and insecurity, Angelou acted without consulting any-one else about her problem. Pretend that the young Maya has come to you with her doubts and her plan to seduce a boy. What advice would you give her? In a paragraph written in the form of a letter to Maya, explain what you would say to her.

Assignment 3: Writing an Essay

Do we all need to prove ourselves on the field of romance? Why is seduction nec-essary? In matters of the heart, does anything ever change? Write an essay which outlines and explains an ideal first experience. Do not concentrate on graphic phys-ical details; Angelou, and most people, suffer more from the emotional and psy-chological effects of unsatisfactory romantic or sexual initiations. Find the three elements which would make a good first experience for *both* partners, and define these elements clearly as you begin each of your essay's three body paragraphs.

The Importance of Cooking Dinner

Nancy Eng

Do you remember the first time you tried to cook a meal? Cooking is never as easy as recipes or relatives make it seem. Food, its preparation, and the rituals of the table are important parts of our daily social and family lives. In the

1990s, it seems that everyone is interested in food, if not in cooking. But despite the advances of feminist advice, statistics show that most cooking is still done by women, and is regarded (other than in the elevated realm of the great chefs) as part of essential female knowledge and skills. Nancy Eng, an English student at the University of British Columbia, takes issue with the idea that the honourable womanly place in the kitchen is somehow genetically inherited.

This was not to be just any dinner. This meal was to be a part of my rites of passage, 1 another step into womanhood. Like the first pair of pantyhose, the first teetering steps on high heels, and the first taste of lipstick, an entire dinner prepared on one's own has always been an initiation into the adult female ranks. Despite all the advances women have made in this male-dominated world, despite the inspiration of the Sandra Day O'Connors, the Pat Carneys, and the Sally Rides, woman continues to carry certain limiting connotations. When one thinks of women, terms like *gentle*, *maternal*, and *domestic* still spring even to some of the most liberal minds. No matter how capable a woman is in the work world, it is still difficult to shake the time-honoured tradition of Mom baking cookies for her family, or Grandma fixing turkey for the clan. So, as I entered the kitchen that fateful day of my fifteenth year, armed with *The Joy of Cooking* and enshrouded in a "Kiss the Cook" apron, I was ready to tackle green salad, roast chicken, and chocolate mousse. I rolled up my sleeves, took a deep breath, and went to work.

The salad was easy enough. For that, I didn't even need to consult the cooking bible. 2 I managed to wash and tear up a quantity of lettuce, and I threw in a variety of appropriately coloured vegetables so that my bowl more or less resembled green salad. This accomplished, I moved on with an air of confidence to the next course.

The chicken sat in all its slimy glory on a roasting pan, awaiting an expert touch. 3 Cold and slippery in my hands, it was placid and cooperative as I dangled it awkwardly from one of its slick little limbs, trying to decide which end was up. I viewed my fowl friend from several angles, puzzled as to where exactly its head had been during its previous life. The directions called for stuffing the animal, so I located my box of Stouffer's Stovetop and contemplated where it belonged. Flipping the chicken around a few more times, I finally discovered an opening. I peered into its damp darkness, feeling slightly perverse about my actions, and hoping the chicken didn't mind this kind of intrusion. I couldn't see how I was going to hold that small hole open wide enough to fill the creature up, until I spied a funnel hanging invitingly from its hook in the cupboard. Inserting the funnel's tip into the bird, I poured in the contents of the box of stuffing, not realizing the dry, crumbly mess I was forcing in was meant to be cooked first. The chicken soon bulged slightly with uncooked stuffing and the innards, which I had not bothered to remove. Pleased with its bumpy plumpness, I went on to basting.

"Butter outer chicken generously," the book directed. I partially unwrapped a cold 4 block of margarine, hoping such a substitution wouldn't offend anyone too much, and proceeded to rub the block over the surface of the equally cold, nubbly chicken skin with as much generosity as I could muster toward raw poultry. Large clots of yellow stuck here and there on the uneven epidermis, along with some bits of gold foil from the margarine wrapper. Good enough, I thought as I flicked off some of the larger, more conspicuous pieces of foil, time for seasoning. Nothing warms the heart of an inexperienced cook more than a spice rack chock full of multicoloured substances that one can sprinkle and toss with a certain chef-like finesse. I sprinkled and tossed to my heart's content until, inspecting my masterpiece, I discovered that I had liberally covered my poor chicken with cinnamon, garlic powder, and sugar. Quickly, I snapped out of my Julia Child act and remedied my mistake by attempting to wipe off my wrongs with a paper towel. Shreds of tissue now decorated the main course, alongside the already present foil. As dinnertime was nearing, I tried to hurry myself along and ended up dusting the bird with allspice, something that sounded like a good general spice to me, but which I later discovered to be the chief flavouring for gingerbread and apple and pumpkin pies. Being behind schedule, I didn't bother with any more fancy stuff; I popped the chicken into the oven and cranked the temperature up to 500° to speed up the cooking time.

Finally, it was time to prepare the dessert. A cinch, I said: no problem. Setting a large pot on the burner, I began to throw in haphazardly whatever the recipe called for: squares of semisweet chocolate, cream, butter, three separated eggs. Separated from what? I wondered; from their shells, I guess. Happy with my conclusion, I continued, smashing the eggs along the rim of the pot, and watching the bright yellow yolks float on top of the chocolate with only a few bits of shell mixing in with them. I stirred the concoction vigorously, but it failed to resemble the light, fluffy delicacy from the glossy picture in the cookbook. Since the recipe said that this dessert was supposed to set awhile before serving, I left it on the stove, assuming it would magically take on the appearance of the cookbook picture by the time I spooned it out. Satisfied with my efforts, I left my dinner roasting and setting while I wandered off to watch *Donahue*.

In the middle of "Bisexual Men and Voodoo Priestesses—Compatible Marriages?" a crescendo of domestic noise swelled in my ears. The smoke alarm wailed, the oven bell clanged, and the stove crackled and sputtered. Something had gone terribly wrong. Sprinting into the kitchen, I leaped up toward the smoke alarm, waving my arms frantically in an attempt to clear the smoke and shut off the ear-piercing screech. A sharp rap with a broom handle finally silenced that contraption and allowed me to attend to what was left of dinner. The chicken was charred beyond recognition, with the bits of paper towel burning brightly and the foil glinting mockingly at me. The mousse had not transformed itself into a dessert delight that would elicit praise from my family; instead, it had melded itself to the bottom of the pot, hardening to the point where it had become an immovable part of the metal. Even my previously trouble-free salad had succumbed to the disaster surrounding it. Left sitting on the stove, the lettuce had wilted and turned an unsightly brown around its edges. As I stood in the midst of this catastrophe, in came my mother, two aunts, and my grandmother. They shook their heads sadly, and I think I actually saw tears welling up in the eyes of my grandmother. I had failed the initiation; I would never be a traditional female. No one would savour my cookies or ask for second helpings at supper. Somehow, I'd proven myself incomplete.

Suddenly, in the midst of this horrible, laughable affair, it dawned on me that I didn't really mind. I didn't care. This was not the be-all and end-all; I would be a woman yet.

Culinary skills or not, I would amount to something. I would be one of the new breed of women who throw aside tradition to be themselves. My heart lightened. I threw off my baking mitts, untied the apron, tossed them to my grandmother, and yelled, "Call Pizza Pizza."

■ Reading Comprehension Questions

1. Which of the following would be the best alternative title for the selection?
   a. Dinner, Denial, and Disaster
   b. Chicken à la Nancy
   c. The Importance of Poisoning Your Family
   d. Cooking Means Caring

2. Which sentence best expresses the main idea of the selection?
   a. Cooking, like caring and cleaning, is seemingly inseparable from the idea of womanhood.
   b. Cooking dinner for the family is a time-honoured coming-of-age ritual for all women.
   c. With the right cookbook, equipment, and ingredients, anyone can prepare a dinner.
   d. Failing at cooking dinner for the author meant failure in the traditional arts of womanhood.

3. The concept of womanhood, according to Nancy Eng,
   a. has changed radically because of a female astronaut and female politicians.
   b. is still narrowed by expectations of nurturing, gentleness, and domesticity.
   c. carries a double burden: workplace success and kitchen miracles.
   d. necessitates the wearing of high heels, lipstick, and an apron.

4. *True or false?* _____ The author messed up the initial preparation of every course in her meal.

5. Ms. Eng's main problem with preparing the chicken was
   a. not knowing which end to stuff.
   b. not removing the heart, liver, and gizzards prior to stuffing the bird.
   c. leaving foil and paper towel on its skin.
   d. all of the above, and more.

6. The author implies that
   a. she had at least read the recipes before trying to cook dinner.
   b. she had watched female relatives cook enough to know the basics.
   c. she had looked at the cookbook and examined her materials in advance.
   d. she mistook dressing for the event and grabbing a book for cooking.

7. Ms. Eng implies that she believed
   a. that the rules and techniques for cooking weren't that important.
   b. that all good women take time for a TV break during meal preparation.

    c.   she would never be a real woman.

    d.   dinner would somehow be edible, if not praiseworthy.

8. *True or false?* _____ The author implies that this has been a real life-crisis, as well as a rite of passage (paragraph 1) for her.

9. The word *enshrouded* in "So, as I entered the kitchen that fateful day of my fifteenth year, armed with *The Joy of Cooking* and enshrouded in 'Kiss the Cook' apron" (paragraph 1) means

    a.   dressed.

    b.   disguised.

    c.   wrapped up.

    d.   trapped.

10. The word *crescendo* in "a crescendo of domestic noise swelled in my ears" (paragraph 6) means

    a.   rumblings.

    b.   build-up.

    c.   shriek.

    d.   cacophony.

■ Discussion Questions

About Content

1. What characteristics of womanhood does Eng list as persisting into the 1990s? Do you agree with her? Are these innate aspects of all women?

2. Why does the author feel "slightly perverse" (paragraph 3) about what she was doing with the stuffing mix?

3. Do you agree with Nancy Eng that "nothing warms the heart of an inexperienced cook more than a spice rack chock full of multicoloured substances" (paragraph 4)? Why do people feel this way? What's the problem with this feeling?

4. What had happened to each of the author's dishes? Why, in each case?

About Structure

5. How does the author link her title with the content of her essay in the opening paragraph? Which sentences support and expand on the meaning of the title? List the number of the sentence, note the appropriate phrase, and briefly explain how each connects to the title.

    Sentence _____   Phrase _____

    Sentence _____   Phrase _____

    Sentence _____   Phrase _____

6. This is a comic version of a process essay. Generally, such essays contain transitional words and phrases to direct and assist the reader in following the process. Do you think that Nancy Eng wants you to follow her process?

   There are, in fact, *two* types of process essays: prescriptive ("how-to"), and descriptive (telling how by describing). Which type of process essay is "The Importance of Cooking Dinner"? Why?

7. The transitions in this essay are unusually placed. They are more like "time marker" phrases, which indicate the progress of an event or process.

   Where do you find such phrases in paragraphs 2–5? What are the phrases, and what do they have in common?

About Style and Tone

8. The chicken is clearly an object for the author to contend with. Which of the rhetorical comic devices listed below does Ms. Eng use to make her description in paragraph 3 of her struggles with the bird so funny?

   a. Personification (giving an object human qualities) _____

   b. Alliteration (beginning closely placed words with the same letter) _____

   c. Exaggeration _____

   d. Puns or word-play _____

   List examples of any of these comic devices which you find, and suggest why they are amusing in the context of the essay.

9. For what type of publication (and its reading audience) would such an article be likely to be written? Why?
   a. a feminist magazine
   b. a cookbook or cooking magazine
   c. a general-interest monthly magazine
   d. a sociology text

■ Writing Assignments

Assignment 1: Writing a Paragraph

There are "rites of passage" for every person: special (although sometimes quite mundane) activities, which, when first performed, have time-marking significance for all of us. These actions or events signal some change or turning-point in our lives. Some are gender-specific, such as shaving the face (as opposed to shaving the legs, which would be a female "rite of passage"), and some transcend gender boundaries, such as learning to drive.

Write a paragraph about "The Importance of...." Describe a particular "first" coming-of-age ritual which you experienced. Why was it important to you? What was its importance to that stage in your life? Consider the first time you played a game of pool, your first date, the first time you changed the oil or a tire, or some such turning point.

As Eng does, begin with some background information about yourself and the importance of the event. Then describe the stages in the process you went through in your personal "rite of passage." Be sure to use very specific details so that readers may re-experience the event along with you. Conclude with a statement of the significance, or lack thereof, which this "rite" had for you.

Assignment 2: Writing a Paragraph

We have all tried to cook something. Our first attempts may not have been as disastrous as was Nancy Eng's; in fact, some of us are natural cooks, and those first scrambled eggs may have been quite edible. Write a paragraph in which you describe your first try at cooking for other people. If your first meal was suitable only for a decent burial, give the causes for the awful results; on the other hand, if you succeeded in not poisoning your family or guests, make sure your paragraph tells clearly *why* you managed to cook reasonably well.

Follow the cause-and-effect format on pages 144–145 as you structure your paragraph. Begin with what you achieved, then explain the reasons for the meal which resulted, whether it was good or bad.

Assignment 3: Writing an Essay

Will you, like Nancy Eng, be among the "new breed" of men or women who have left behind the expectations and stereotypes of previous generations? Is this possible, or are certain characteristics innate within each gender? Do we want to disturb all fundamental male and female qualities as we know them?

Write a prescriptive ("how to") process essay about *your* views on "the new man" or "the new woman." Does each really exist? Do you know any examples of either? What elements would make up such creatures? Would there be changes in personality, in behaviour, in appearance? How much do we really want men and women to change, and why?

Here is your chance to play Dr. Frankenstein: Construct a new being. Tell your readers how to become "The New Man" or "The New Woman" in the traditional "three easy steps." Because this is a direct-advice process essay, address your reader directly as "you." If there are things you would rather not change about the gender in question, say so, but tell the reader how and why he or she should retain an existing quality you value.

Before beginning your outline, review the chapter on process writing (pages 134–141). Decide on your viewpoint first of all. You may take a reverse or comic view, and give instructions on how to become "a traditional gentleman" (which may in fact be a new creature) or "a real lady" (perhaps equally mythic). Consider what ingredients may be needed. In either case, list your steps, then group them into logical stages which become your three body paragraphs, and flesh out your instructions with careful details about becoming the "gender-perfect creature." Watch out for potential pitfalls or problems in your stages, and give lots of transitional help. Remember, you may be creating a new being.

ACKNOWLEDGMENTS

Sheila Akers, "Power Learning." Copyright © 1986. Reprinted by permission of the author.

Maya Angelou, "Adolescent Confusion" (editor's title), from *I Know Why the Caged Bird Sings*. Copyright © 1969 by Maya Angelou. Reprinted by permission of Random House, Inc.

Eileen A. Brett, "How to Write a Test," from *Contest: Essays by Canadian Students*, 2nd edition, by Robert Hookey and Joan Pilz. Copyright © 1994 Harcourt Brace & Company, Canada, Inc. All rights reserved. Reprinted by permission of Harcourt Brace & Company Canada, Limited.

Dolores Curran, "What Good Families Are Doing Right," from *McCall's* (March 1983). Reprinted by permission of Dolores Curran.

Mary Curran, "The True Meaning of Literacy," from *The Toronto Star* (January 6, 1996). Reprinted by permission of Mary Curran.

Sharon Doyle Driedger, "The Joy of Being Fat Free," from *Maclean's* (July 8, 1996). Reprinted by permission of *Maclean's*.

Nancy Eng, "The Importance of Cooking Dinner," from *Contest: Essays by Canadian Students*, 2nd edition, by Robert Hookey and Joan Pilz. Copyright © 1994 Harcourt Brace & Company, Canada, Inc. All rights reserved. Reprinted by permission of Harcourt Brace & Company Canada, Limited.

David Estok, "What to Do with a Severance," from *Maclean's* (July 8, 1996). Reprinted by permission of *Maclean's*.

Frank Jones, "Decoys and Denial," from "Hunting for Decoys is Collector's Passion," *The Toronto Star* (September 25, 1993). Reprinted by permission of The Toronto Star Syndicate.

Jim Maloney, "Why Should We Hire You?" Reprinted by permission of Jim Maloney.

Brian Preston, "Shots on Goal," from *Saturday Night* (February 1995). Reprinted by permission of Brian Preston.

Daniel Smith, "Spiritual Storyteller," from *The Toronto Star* (December 31, 1995). Reprinted by permission of The Toronto Star Syndicate.

Laura J. Turner, "Truth or Consequences," from *Contest: Essays by Canadian Students*, 2nd edition, by Robert Hookey and Joan Pilz. Copyright © 1994 Harcourt Brace & Company, Canada, Inc. All rights reserved. Reprinted by permission of Harcourt Brace & Company Canada, Limited.

Adele Wiseman, "Memoirs of a Book-Molesting Childhood," edited from *Memoirs of a Book-Molesting Childhood and Other Essays* by Adele Wiseman. Copyright © 1987 Oxford University Press. Reprinted by permission of Tamara Stone.

Tony Wong, "Have You Seen My Missing Math Gene?" from *The Toronto Star* (January 2, 1996). Reprinted by permission of Tony Wong.

APPENDIX

ANSWERS
AND
CHARTS

PREVIEW

This Appendix provides answers for the Introductory Projects in Part Four. It also provides four useful charts: an assignment chart, a spelling list to be filled in by the student, a general form for planning a paragraph, and a reading comprehension chart.

ANSWERS TO INTRODUCTORY PROJECTS

Sentence Fragments (page 239)

1. verb
2. subject
3. subject ... verb
4. express a complete thought

Run-On Sentences (page 255)

1. period
2. *but*
3. semi-colon
4. *When*

Standard English Verbs (page 269)

enjoyed ... enjoys; started ... starts; cooked ... cooks
1. past ... *-ed*
2. present ... *-s*

Irregular Verbs (page 278)

1. crawled, crawled (regular)
2. brought, brought (irregular)
3. used, used (regular)
4. did, done (irregular)
5. gave, given (irregular)
6. laughed, laughed (regular)
7. went, gone (irregular)
8. scared, scared (regular)
9. dressed, dressed (regular)
10. saw, seen (irregular)

Subject–Verb Agreement (page 286)

The second sentence in each pair is correct.

Consistent Verb Tense (page 291)

discovered … remembered

Pronoun Agreement, Reference, and Point of View (page 295)

The second sentence in each pair is correct.

Misplaced Modifiers (page 314)

1. Intended: A young man with references is wanted to open oysters.
   Unintended: The oysters have references.
2. Intended: On their wedding day, Carlo and Charlotte decided they would have two children.
   Unintended: Carlo and Charlotte decided to have two children who would magically appear on the day of their wedding.
3. Intended: The students who failed the test no longer like the math instructor.
   Unintended: The math instructor failed the test.

Dangling Modifiers (page 318)

1. Intended: My dog sat with me as I smoked a pipe.
   Unintended: My dog smoked a pipe.
2. Intended: He looked at a traffic accident.
   Unintended: His sports car looked at a traffic accident.
3. Intended: A beef pie baked for several hours.
   Unintended: Grandmother baked for several hours.

Faulty Parallelism (page 323)

The second sentence in each pair reads more smoothly and clearly.

Capital Letters (page 332)

All the answers to questions 1 to 13 should be in capital letters.

14. The   15. I   16. "That …"

Apostrophes (page 344)

1. The purpose of the *'s* is to show possession (that Larry owned the motorcycle, the boyfriend belonged to the sister, Grandmother owned the shotgun, and so on).
2. The purpose of the apostrophe is to show the omission of one or more letters in the contractions—two words shortened to form one word.
3. The *'s* shows possession in each of the second sentences: the body of the vampire; the centre of the baked potato. In each first sentence, the *s* is used to form simple plurals: more than one vampire; more than one potato.

Quotation Marks (page 353)

1. The purpose of quotation marks is to set off the exact words of a speaker. (The words that the young man actually spoke aloud are set off with quotation marks, as are the words that the old woman spoke aloud.)
2. Commas and periods go inside quotation marks.

Commas (page 361)

1. a. Fred's interests are Maria, television, and sports.
   b. My mother put her feet up, sipped some iced tea, and opened the newspaper.
2. a. Although the Lone Ranger used lots of silver bullets, he never ran out of ammunition.
   b. To open the cap of the aspirin bottle, you must first press down on it.
3. a. Kitty Katz and Serge Lamour, Canada's leading romantic stars, have made several movies together.
   b. Sarah, who is my next-door neighbour, just entered the hospital with an intestinal infection.
4. a. The wedding was scheduled for four o'clock, but the bride changed her mind at two.
   b. Francesca took three coffee breaks before lunch, and then she went on a two-hour lunch break.
5. a. Crystal's mother asked her, "What time do you expect to get home?"
   b. "Don't bend over to pat the dog," I warned, "or he'll bite you."
6. a. Roy ate seventeen hamburgers on July 29, 1992, and lived to tell about it.
   b. Roy lives at 817 Ouellette Street, Windsor, Ontario.

Other Punctuation Marks (page 371)

1. pets: holly
2. freeze-dried
3. Shakespeare (1564–1616)
4. Earth; no
5. proudly—with

Commonly Confused Words (page 398)

Your mind and body.... *There* is a lot of evidence....
then it will ... said *to* have ... *It's* not clear

Effective Word Choice (page 408)

1. *Flipped out* is slang.
2. *Few and far between* is a cliché.
3. *Ascertained* is a pretentious word.
4. The first sentence here is wordy.

CHARTS

ASSIGNMENT CHART

Use this chart to record daily or weekly assignments in your composition class. You might want to print writing assignments and their due dates in capital letters so that they stand out clearly.

Date Given	Assignment	Date Due

Date Given	Assignment	Date Due

SPELLING LIST

Enter here the words that you misspelled in your papers (note the examples). If you add to and study this list regularly, you will not repeat the same mistakes in your writing.

Incorrect Spelling	Correct Spelling	Points to Remember
alright	all right	two words
ocasion	occasion	two "c"s

FORM FOR PLANNING A PARAGRAPH

To write an effective paragraph, first prepare an outline. Often (though not always) you may be able to use a form like the one below.

Topic sentence: _____

_____

_____

Support (1): _____

_____

Details:

Support (2): _____

_____

Details:

Support (3): _____

_____

Details:

READING COMPREHENSION CHART

Mark an *X* through the numbers of any questions you missed while answering the comprehension questions for each of the fifteen reading selections in Part Five. Then write in your comprehension score. (To calculate your score for each reading, give yourself 10 points for each item that is *not* *X*'d out.) The chart will make clear any skill question you get wrong repeatedly, so that you can pay special attention to that skill in the future.

Selection	Subject or Title	Thesis or Main Idea	Key Details	Inferences	Vocabulary in Context	Comprehension Score
Preston	1	2	3 4 5	6 7 8	9 10	%
Estok	1	2	3 4 5	6 7 8	9 10	%
D. Curran	1	2	3 4 5	6 7 8	9 10	%
Jones	1	2	3 4 5	6 7 8	9 10	%
Turner	1	2	3 4 5	6 7 8	9 10	%
Akers	1	2	3 4 5	6 7 8	9 10	%
Brett	1	2	3 4 5	6 7 8	9 10	%
Maloney	1	2	3 4 5	6 7 8	9 10	%
M. Curran	1	2	3 4 5	6 7 8	9 10	%
Wiseman	1	2	3 4 5	6 7 8	9 10	%
Wong	1	2	3 4 5	6 7 8	9 10	%

Selection	Subject or Title	Thesis or Main Idea	Key Details	Inferences	Vocabulary in Context	Comprehension Score
Smith	1	2	3 4 5	6 7 8	9 10	%
Doyle Driedger	1	2	3 4 5	6 7 8	9 10	%
Angelou	1	2	3 4 5	6 7 8	9 10	%
Eng	1	2	3 4 5	6 7 8	9 10	%

INDEX

STUDENT REPLY CARD

In order to improve future editions, we are seeking your comments on

ENGLISH SKILLS WITH READINGS, First Canadian Edition

After you have read this text, please answer the following questions and return this form via Business Reply Mail. *Your opinions matter. Thank you in advance for your feedback!*

Name of your college or university: _____

Major program of study: _____

Course title: _____

Were you required to buy this book?   yes _____   no _____

Did you buy this book new or used?   new _____   used _____ ($_____)

Do you plan to keep or sell this book?   keep _____   sell _____

Is the order of topic coverage consistent with what was taught in your course?

Are there chapters or sections of this text that were not assigned for your course? Please specify:

Were there topics covered in your course that are not included in this text? Please specify:

What did you like most about this text?

What did you like least?

If you would like to say more, we'd love to hear from you. Please write to us at the address shown on the reverse of this card.

- - - - - - - - - - - - - - - - - *cut here* - - - - - - - - - - - - - - - ┐

- - - - - - - - - - - - - - - - - *fold here* - - - - - - - - - - - - - - -

cut here

Postage will be paid by

MAIL POSTE

Canada Post Corporation / Société canadienne des postes

Postage paid
If mailed in Canada

Port payé
si posté au Canada

Business Reply

Réponse d'affaires

0183560299   01

0183560299-L1N9B6-BR01

Attn.: Sponsoring Editor
College Division

MCGRAW-HILL RYERSON LIMITED
300 WATER ST
WHITBY ON   L1N 9Z9